Food, Farms & Solidarity

NEW ECOLOGIES FOR THE
TWENTY-FIRST CENTURY

· ·

Series Editors: Arturo Escobar,
University of North Carolina, Chapel Hill
Dianne Rocheleau, Clark University

FOOD, FARMS
& SOLIDARITY

French Farmers Challenge Industrial Agriculture
and Genetically Modified Crops

CHAIA HELLER

DUKE UNIVERSITY PRESS
Durham & London 2013

© 2013 Duke University Press
All rights reserved

Printed in the United States of America
on acid-free paper ∞
Designed by Jennifer Hill
Typeset in Fournier by
Tseng Information Systems, Inc.

Library of Congress
Cataloging-in-Publication Data appear on
the last printed page of this book.

Dedicated to Alan Goodman
& Ruby Heller-Goodman

CONTENTS

This series addresses two trends: critical conversations in academic fields about nature, sustainability, globalization, and culture, including constructive engagements between researchers within the natural, social, and human sciences; and intellectual and political conversations among those in social movements and other nonacademic knowledge producers about alternative practices and socionatural worlds. The objective of the series is to establish a synergy between these theoretical and political developments in both academic and nonacademic arenas. This synergy is a sine qua non for new thinking about the real promise of emergent ecologies. The series includes works that envision more lasting and just ways of being-in-place and being-in-networks with a diversity of humans and other living and nonliving beings.

New Ecologies for the Twenty-First Century aims to promote a dialogue between those who are transforming the understanding of the relationship between nature and culture. The series revisits existing fields such as environmental history, historical ecology, environmental anthropology, ecological economics, and cultural and political ecology. It addresses emerging tendencies, such as the use of complexity theory to rethink a range of questions on the nature-culture axis. It also deals with epistemological and ontological concerns, in order to build bridges between the various forms of knowing and ways of being that are embedded in the multiplicity of practices of social actors, worldwide. This series hopes to foster convergences among differently located actors and to provide a forum for authors and readers to widen the fields of theoretical inquiry, professional practice, and social struggles that characterize the current environmental arena.

ACKNOWLEDGMENTS

I especially want to thank members of the Confédération Paysanne for opening their meeting rooms and barn doors to me during the first years of researching this book. The generosity of spirit I experienced there will forever be unparalleled. I want to thank Bruno Latour and Michele Callon for allowing me to play *thesard* as a research fellow at their Centre de Société de l'Innovation at L'École des Mines. The intellectual rigor and my affiliation with this uniquely French prestigious institution provided me the golden key to the city and throughout *outre* Paris (anyplace in France that's not Paris) as well. I also express gratitude to Claire Marris and Les Levidow for keen insight and encouragement. I thank the National Science Foundation and the University of Massachusetts for making the research a financial possibility. Jackie Urla and Rich Fantasia, members of my dissertation committee, you are shining stars. I will always be indebted to the vision, mentorship, and friendship of the father of "green ecology," the political theorist Murray Bookchin. May his soul rest in the utopian light he emanated while alive. Back in the 1980s, he helped me understand the collision course between capital, nature, and culture that is so palpable in this story.

This book would not be possible if it weren't for the rigorous guidance and support of Arturo Escobar. My gratitude is boundless, transcending words. What a rare and eager mind. Who else could bring poststructuralism, postcolonial theory, political economy, political ecology, and anthropology together with such creative and political conviction?

My adoration to Lynn and Jim Morgan for being family friends and warm welcomers as I've tiptoed gingerly through the gates of academia. I thank Donal O'Shea at Mount Holyoke College for having the generosity and dedication to help keep me around. So many thanks to colleagues and students at Mount Holyoke College who continue to make my head spin in a good direction. I thank Eleanor Townsely for her dizzying intellectual embrace. I thank Mary Renda for her patience as I found my feet again in gender studies after my long sojourn into anthropology land. Thanks to Deborah Heath, with that warm wily smile and that passion for sts, food theory, and cool ideas generally.

This project is scented with the utopian aroma of the Institute for Social Ecology (ise). Some people say that one simply writes the same book over and over. And I guess I am guilty of writing variations on a theme: looking for sparkling chips of what is utopian and solidarity based within a neoliberal world. My friends and colleagues at the ise have kept my eyes on the dazzling mirrored ball of hope for a different world. How can I thank you all? Dan and Betsy Chodorkoff, Brian Tokar, Brooke Lehman, Ben Grosscup, Beverly Naidus, Bob Spivey, Ben Paul, Eric Toensmeir, and Michael Dorsey: each of you, in your own way, have kept the rug from completely slipping out from under our collective hopeful feet. What a commendable burden and display of good sense.

On the family front, this project has been touched, held, read, and reread by so many wonderful people. How to count them? My parents, Audrey and Bill Heller, forever stand at the sidelines of book road, cheering me on, hoping my labors might eventually bear fruit. I suppose I won't make it to Carnegie Hall, and I won't ever write, as my father laments, "the great American novel," but this is the best I can do for now. I thank my sisters, Carol and Laura; Sandra and Dick Smith; and Allen and Judy Kronick for being the kind of family one would not just acquire, but would actively choose without hesitation.

Acknowledgments

Too many friends to list, but I will try! Some friends worked directly on pieces of this book, others floated ideas, yet others crossed their fingers: Lizzie Donahue, Jessie Weiner, Ilana and Neil Markowitz. Newer folks in my life since I became a mom: Deb and Kris Thomson-Bercuvitz, Sarah Swersey and Jeff Waggenheim, Caitlin Healey, Eleanor Finley, Owen James, Sarah and Peter Acker, Pam Lewis, Joy Ladin. Older friends to whom I am so indebted: Sally Bellerose, Deborah Cohen, Jaime and Mellissa Campbell-Morton. So many old friends flew the coop from this fabulous valley, but I remember and thank you all for being part of this journey.

I want to thank all of the people at Duke University Press for determining that this story should and would indeed be told. Valerie Millholland and her wonderful staff have been hard at work to bring this book out into the world.

Finally, my heart is a pomegranate, brimming with jeweled seeds, when I think of Alan Goodman and Ruby Heller-Goodman. Alan, you have helped me truly understand the meaning of a biocultural synthesis. To Ruby, as one of the more palpable products of that synthesis, I thank you for putting up with such a busy mama who loves you even when drowsing bleary-eyed before the screen. And Alan, how can one complete such an endeavor without the ongoing support, encouragement, and intellectual prodding of a true soul mate? Thankfully, I will never know that answer because, Alan, you have come through in resplendent colors. You are my best friend and the smartest guy in the room. What a blessing.

It all started with the milk. We heard Vermont farmers—*paysans*—were fighting against genetically modified milk. They'd heard about it, heard it was going to be approved soon, and were fighting it. It's a growth hormone, genetically modified, that makes cows produce more. All *paysans* know that more milk means the end. And so somewhere in 1993, some of us traveled to Vermont to talk to *paysans* there. When we came back, we decided to take up the issue of milk here and oh, did we make a ruckus [*bordel*]. Within just a few months, we had the milk banned Europe wide.
—MARCEL BONITAIRE (personal communication, February 4, 1999)

1

Introduction

Creating a New
Rationality of Agriculture in
a Postindustrial World

And so it all began with overproduced, spilled milk. In the early 1990s, small dairy farmers in France were dumping milk and protesting price drops linked to overproduction. At the same time, talk about genetically modified organisms (GMOs) skittered through the international dairy world.[1] A new GMO was destined for the dairy industry. A genetically modified hormone would be injected into cows worldwide, increasing production and benefiting large-scale farmers operating industrial dairies. News of the new milk poured through the union of self-identified *paysans* (peasants) from the Confédération Paysanne, France's second-largest agricultural union, composed mainly of smallholders. Many had read about GMOs from agricultural newsletters that reported on farmers in Vermont and ecology groups trying to comprehend a new form of agricultural science, agricultural biotechnology. The paysans had even received a few e-mail messages via the union's newly installed Internet connection at its national headquarters just outside Paris.

In 1993 three members of the Confédération Paysanne left their villages (most never having left the country) to fly to central Vermont to do their homework. In return, local Vermont dairy farmers cheerily received the union members. The farmers offered information and warning about the economic pitfalls of the newly approved genetically modified milk. This milk, they explained, is produced by cows injected with recombinant bovine growth hormone, called r-BGH. The idea of GM milk presented a dismaying prospect to dairy farmers already struggling to survive in an era of overproduction.[2] Fortified with facts and figures, the small contingency of the Confédération Paysanne returned to France. Months after their return, they fought for and won an EU-wide ban on genetically modified milk that remains in place today. Not long after, they won the fight to label all GMO products in Europe.

Like the Confédération Paysanne, Vermont dairy farmers and activists led a campaign against GMOs. While their ultimate goal was to ban genetically modified milk, their initial, more modest objective was to request that the product be labeled. After a two-year struggle during 1994 and 1995, the Vermont Supreme Court ruled in favor of the high-powered dairy lobby. According to the courts, labeling requirements represented an infringement on corporations' freedom of speech (Tokar 1999). While the U.S. Food and Drug Administration approved the milk in 1993, the Vermont Supreme Court set the stage for a de facto no-labeling policy for all GMO products, and it remains in place to this day — uniquely in the United States.[3]

A Producer-Led, Anti-GMO Movement:
Rediscovering the Confédération Paysanne

I traveled to France to study the movement against GMOs in early 1997. My original goal was to understand why France (unlike other European countries such as Austria, Germany, or the United Kingdom) lacked an ecology movement strong enough to drive a successful mobilization. I was aware that Greenpeace France did organize a small direct action in which activists blocked cargo ships carrying genetically modified foodstuffs before they arrived in Normandy. However, this action garnered little publicity or popular support. I had yet to imagine that French small-scale farmers, or smallholders, might share much in common (on a strategic and cultural level) with those in the Global South. Outside the Global North, producers such as peasant farmers (rather than consumers and ecologists) primarily spearhead movements against GMOs.[4] As I would soon learn, the same would be true in France. I had failed to remember the French farmers who traveled to Vermont just a few years before—and who, within months, had enjoyed such success in the European policymaking world.

I was unaware that France, like the Global South, was home to a movement of peasant-identified farmers. Peasants, I thought, no longer existed in Europe. I knew that peasants in Britain were driven to near extinction as early as the fifteenth century because of the enclosures of the commons (Neesen 1993). I assumed incorrectly that French peasants had shared the same fate. While bucolic ideas of French peasants still abound in French marketing, film, and tourism, I thought that for centuries they primarily occupied the world of the French imaginary. Upon my first chance encounter with the Confédération Paysanne, I soon learned that the notion of the French peasant—although changed dramatically over time—was still very much alive. Beginning in the 1970s, a set of new paysan movements emerged in France, resisting the industrialization of agriculture that had gotten under way following World War II.

Members of the Confédération Paysanne who traveled to Vermont in 1993 were at that time already plugged into an international network of farmers and indigenous peoples in nongovernmental organizations (NGOs), many located in the Global South. These southern organizations, associated with biologist-activists such as Vandana Shiva and Devaru Nanjundaswamy of the Karnataka State Farmer's union in India, had been discussing the GMO question since the 1980s. They voiced concerns regarding the impending dominance of GMOs in the international agricultural market. Word had it that companies planned to create patented GMOs in the form of seeds for a variety of commodity foodstuffs, beginning with milk. After targeting global staple crops, such as cotton, corn, canola, and soy, biotechnology companies would move on to create genetically modified versions of wheat and rice, perhaps the most crucial staple crops of all. The predictions of southern organizations proved true. In the 1980s, U.S. multinationals (e.g., Monsanto and Novartis) bought small start-up companies developing genetically modified varieties of staple crops and prepared to commercialize these products within the next decade (Rabinow 1996). If all went well, by 1996 several staple crops would appear globally in the form of genetically modified seed and GMOs processed into foodstuffs (Shiva 1993a).

Biotechnology companies won the right to patent genetically modified seeds in 1981, subsequently preventing farmers from saving or sharing seeds purchased from these corporations (Shiva 1988). Farmers purchasing GM seeds from companies such as Monsanto are obliged to sign one-time use agreements that legally forbid them from saving or trading seed issued from GM plants. One-time use agreements break a centuries-old tradition in which farmers save, select, and share seeds gleaned from plants during harvest time. Seed saving is not just central to improving seeds and plants suitable for particular microclimates; it is also a crucial form of solidarity practiced among farmers who have collaborated, since the beginning of agriculture, to create site-specific crops for local communities in a spirit of mutualism, rather than private ownership.

With the advent of one-time use agreements, many smallholders and ecologists pondered the global implications of multinationals inserting themselves into so many nodes of the agriculture production line—from milk, seeds, and inputs to trees, fish, and animals. Could agricultural biotechnology render all farmers, both big and small, dependent on the decisions, practices, and monopolizing tactics of multinational corporations? Biotechnology companies such as Monsanto and Novartis pledged that GMOs would increase production. Targeting large-scale industrial farmers as their primary market, biotechnology companies also promised that their products would lower farmers' costs for herbicide and pesticide. This news fell on the dejected ears of international organizations of smallholders. They were already struggling to survive in an age of overproduction and price drops as peasant communities disappeared across the globe.

The Confédération Paysanne offers a distinctive response to this postindustrial condition. At this historical juncture, industrial agriculture forced smallholders to devise novel strategies to maintain economic means and the meaning of their rural and agricultural ways of life. Instead of simply promoting alternative agricultural practices, such as organic or sustainable agriculture (associated with movements in other countries), the Confédération Paysanne promotes a distinct rationality of agriculture that it calls Paysan Agriculture (*agriculteur paysanne*).

Postindustrial Agriculture: A Useful Heuristic?

The term *postindustrial agriculture* points to that which flows out of, but is distinct from, industrial agriculture. Postindustrial agriculture is both a consequence and an accompanying condition of industrial agriculture. Even

4

though it occupies the same temporal space, postindustrial agriculture is marked by its own distinct features. When most people think about a postindustrial condition, they conjure images of abandoned factory-neighborhoods left behind in cities such as Chicago or Detroit after industry pulled up its roots and moved to the Global South (Raymond 1998; Raymond and Bailey 1997). Or they might envision workers in Malaysia laboring long hours for low pay in electronics factories in free-trade zones with few, if any, services or benefits. Few think "farmer" when they think "postindustrial." But just as postindustrialization drives factory workers into a state of economic and cultural chaos, postindustrial agriculture also represents a set of challenges for farmers. Smallholders live in an era when industrial agriculture attempts to render their services obsolete. The mere existence of smallholders (and their requests for subsidies in the Global North) is considered a nuisance to farm-policy makers fostering the industrial model.

It is useful to offer a brief, working definition of industrial agriculture. While the book cannot present a comprehensive picture of the industrial model, I offer a broad ten-point set of conditions of industrial agriculture. A useful caveat: single components of the ten-point set are not necessarily integral to an industrial system. Rather, it is the grouping of the ten conditions of industrial agriculture—the ways in which they form a systemic gestalt—that endows industrial agriculture with its distinct function and effects.

TEN CONDITIONS OF
INDUSTRIAL AGRICULTURE

1 Intensive farming methods: The concentration of many agricultural products (plant or animal) on a given area of land.

2 Extensive farming methods: The production of agricultural products across large plots of land, often up to thousands of acres.

3 Chemicalization of farming methods for increasing production: The use of synthetic and petroleum products for controlling weeds, pests, soil productivity (fertilizer), fungi, and so on. Since the 1960s, this model also promotes hybrid and genetic-breeding approaches to create "high-yield" seed varieties to be paired with chemical inputs. In the Global South hybrid seed and chemical packages are central to Green Revolution technologies which were introduced between 1940 and 1970 by UN and other international agencies to enhance agricultural production.

4 Motorized and electronic technologies to increase the speed, productivity, and circulation of agricultural products: The intensive reliance on motorized and electronic machines in plowing, harvesting, spraying, transporting, and so on.

5 Monocropping: Replacing a previously diverse model of agricultural production with a model that favors the production of fewer cultivars across vast land areas.

6 Subsidies and loans: Granted by government farm policies and private banks, most often to farmers who embrace the industrial features listed above.

7 Production of "modern foods" (fast foods, pre-prepared foods, frozen foods, and processed foods): Often seen by many consumers as affordable, convenient, and safe.

8 Modern ideal of bigger farms with fewer farmers in rural areas: Often perceived by state bodies and corporations as cost-effective and efficient, relying on fewer workers to pay.

9 Modern agricultural discourse promotes industrial model as universally beneficial and inherently progressive: Focus on food productivity and food security in a world in which overpopulation is a rationalizing force behind industrial productivism.

10 An instrumental rationality informs practices related to industrial agriculture: In general, a logic of efficiency, profitability, and productivity pervades discourses and practices related to the industrial model.

Industrial agriculture has implications for the kind of agricultural product it yields, the amount of land an individual farmer will use, and the environmental and health effects of farming and food production. It also promotes a reliance on a petroleum-based economy for producing and circulating agricultural goods while reducing the genetic biodiversity of cultivars. State and private bodies promote the industrial model through subsidies and loaning practices. Industrial agriculture subsequently reduces the number of farmers eligible to earn a living wage. The system is normalized by an ongoing appeal to an instrumental rationality that promotes the model as modern, progressive, and inevitable. The industrial model is primarily designed to enhance productivity while lowering production costs. Large-scale farms produce high yields (of fewer crops) by using chemicalized, motorized, and electronic farming methods. Farmers who are able to follow this model receive far more farm subsidies and bank loans than smallholders who either cannot or will not do so.

Postindustrial agriculture is a set of social, cultural, and economic conditions that flows out of industrial agriculture — these conditions are neither preindustrial nor industrial. To speak of a postindustrial agricultural condition highlights the historical and cultural specificity of the experiences of smallholders worldwide in both contesting and accommodating the industrial model. It also highlights the practices of industrial corporations in creating their own postindustrial strategies, which include agricultural biotechnology, while also appropriating and dominating markets of organic and so-called natural foods.

TEN CONDITIONS OF
POSTINDUSTRIAL AGRICULTURE

1 Production of agricultural surpluses in staple crops (such as wheat and corn): The result of a subsidized, chemicalized, intensive, and Fordist method of industrial agricultural production. The production of surpluses is facilitated by UN-driven agricultural policies that concentrated the world grain trade in the Global North, leaving peripheral nations in the Global South to engage in low-profit export-oriented cash cropping (Kasaba and Tabak 1995).

2 "Dumping" of surpluses onto the agricultural economies of southern nations: Food materials not destined for the agro-foods industry and retail are sent to the Global South in the form of aid and cheap commodity grains. After just a few dumps, a local agricultural economy in a village in the Global South can be destroyed indefinitely (Wise 2004). This creates a condition of postindustriality for smallholders struggling to survive in southern nations.

3 Deregulation of prewar trade policies for increasing profits: Allows powerful institutions such as the United Nations and the World Trade Organization (WTO) to increasingly determine aid, trade, tariff, and import policies worldwide, eroding small-scale agriculture, particularly in the Global South.

4 Agricultural biotechnology: Inserted into the industrial chemicalized, motorized, and monocrop model.

5 A reduction of biodiversity due to monocropping and the replacement of regional cultivars around the world by multinational corporate seed

varieties: Local knowledges about the value and preparation of local varieties diminish along with a diverse local food supply.

6 Government farm policies and loaning agencies edge smallholders out of farming markets: Rural zones become home to unemployed or underemployed rural dwellers who often relocate to cities.

7 The industrial model creates foods often perceived by consumers as low quality, unsafe, and departing too far from so-called traditional farm products: Increased appetite for artisanal, organic, and traditional haute cuisine foods—particularly in wealthy nations; co-optation of alternate, organic, or local agriculture food discourses and practices by big industrial producers.

8 Fewer farmers leads to neglected rural zones: "Multifunctionality discourse" becomes a way for government agencies to discuss solutions to degraded rural zones regarded as hazardous to local economies, environments, and agro-tourism.

9 Alter-globalization discourses: Promote grassroots organizations composed of peasants, women, the landless, indigenous peoples, the unemployed, and youth. The focus is on food sovereignty, rather than food security. Rather than frame the problem of landlessness and hunger in terms of overpopulation, alter-globalization groups emphasize problems of political underrepresentation in nondemocratic state and private bodies.

10 A solidarity-based rationality informs many aspects of postindustrial agriculture: The rise of international NGOs and grassroots movements composed of smallholders and indigenous peoples signals a collective fight for "people over profit," community self-determination, and a value of cultural fabrics over productivity and efficiency.

At first glance, many of the postindustrial agricultural conditions appear to be integral to the industrial model. However, many represent the intended consequences of industrial agriculture. Supporters in the United States of the industrial model, for instance, hope for surpluses to emerge from industrialized systems. These surpluses are needed to feed the agro-food industry that use agricultural materials necessary for the production of processed, pre-packaged, frozen, and fast foods. Surpluses are also needed for aid-based organizations seeking to dump relatively inexpensive subsidized foods into the agricultural economies of poor southern nations (Vorley 2004;

McCullough, Pingali, and Stamoulis 2005). Of interest here is the synergism between agricultural surpluses, export agriculture, subsidy policies, and deregulated trade practices. Together, these conditions of postindustrial agriculture work together to complement and support the industrial model while disenfranchising smallholders around the world (Van den Ban 1999).

In the Global North—and increasingly in the Global South—smallholders find it difficult to earn a livable wage by feeding a local or regional population. Instead, large-scale farmers around the world dominate the agricultural domain, working to feed the agro-foods complex and cash-cropping export industries (Pollan 2006, 93). Some large-scale farmers achieve degrees of wealth. Most, however, farm intensively and extensively as possible, hoping to maintain a middle-class lifestyle. Those few who head up agro-foods industries, major food distributors, and agrochemical companies make the biggest profits.

Postindustrial agriculture is a global condition. It affects smallholders in both the Global North and South, albeit in different ways. In the Global North, smallholders such as those in the Confédération Paysanne navigate their way around the industrial system, trying to devise strategies to rationalize their own existence. Southern smallholders face a far more dramatic scenario. For decades they have endured the long-lasting effects of land practices associated with UN-generated development schemes, including the Green Revolution. As a result, southern smallholders struggle with problems such as lack of access to tillable lands and waterways for subsistence farming (Kasaba and Tabak 1995). Those fortunate enough to have access to land for small market-oriented ventures face soil erosion and resistant weeds and pests. The problems are often the result of decades of Green Revolution technologies.

Despite these difficulties, powerful institutions often appear disinterested in the plight of smallholders enduring the effects of industrial agriculture. Organizations such as the World Bank and the Gates Foundation still actively promote the Millennium Development Goals. These goals were established by all UN member-states in 2000 with the aim of eradicating extreme poverty and hunger, establishing sustainable agriculture, and attending to the educational and health needs of peoples living in poor countries. Their central strategy has been to reduce the number of farmers engaged in food production. Southern smallholders are thus increasingly headed for landlessness, hunger, and unemployment (Menzel and D'Aluisio 2006). The lucky few who find wage-earning employment are often obliged to toil in urban industrial manufacturing sectors owned by multinationals. In these contexts, peasants are proletarianized, transformed into workers in an industrial sector that is often dehumanizing, dangerous, and exploitative. Postindustriality thus hits smallholders unevenly. While those in the Global North may receive limited subsidies and degrees of social welfare, southern peasants often face chronic poverty, landlessness, and starvation.

Strikingly, northern smallholders in countries such as France stand in solidarity with southern farmers, attempting to build a movement that can create a viable postindustrial condition for smallholders everywhere. Movements to transcend the industrial model represent an effort to level the global agricultural playing field so that everyone gets a chance to farm, eat, and enjoy a dignified way of life.

Postindustriality and the Appropriation of Industrial Alternatives

The ubiquity of mass-produced factory-made food catalyzes a popular and romantic desire for niche markets in haute cuisine and artisanal, local, and organic foods. It also generates a desire for nonedible agricultural products such as "natural" cleaning products and clothing made of organic cotton or hemp. Many in this postindustrial desert wander hungrily through any quaint farmers' market or natural grocery store, searching for an oasis that Michael Pollan calls "Supermarket Pastoral" (2006, 137). Between the 1960s and 1990s, many people disenfranchised by industrial society in the Global North turned to back-to-the land movements. Many became smallholders who produced organic goods for local markets. The entry of these neosmallholders, however, did little to reverse the trend toward the reduction of the number of smallholders generally. There is no balance of power between large and small producers: disempowered organic smallholders still stand on the bottom rung of the economic food chain. Ironically, the idealistic organic smallholder of the 1960s to 1990s prepared a popular appetite for organic foods that is currently satisfied more cheaply by big corporations. Two mega corporations sell most of the fresh organic produce from California today (the state with the largest organic output) (Pollan 2006, 162).

The story of organics in the United States is one of organics gone industrial. From 1998 to 2002, the U.S. Department of Agriculture put in place the National Organic Rule, which set standards for production methods associated with organic foods.[5] While some organic growers today fear that these standards will be lowered over time, others fear that raising government standards will render smallholders unable to afford the techniques and methods required for state certification. And yet other small organic growers eschew organic certification all together for economic and political reasons. Resisting government discipline, they forged terms such as *postorganic* and *beyond organic*, discursively establishing the legitimacy of their own non-certified organic foods.

Meanwhile, nodes in the agro-foods complex (including supermarkets such as Whole Foods Market, Safeway, and Small Planet Foods) sell organic products issued by corporations such as Dole, Cascadian Farm, Greenways Organic, and Earthbound Farm. Produce generated by large-scale organic companies is often incorporated into pre-prepared and processed foods for time-conscious consumers. Earthbound, for example, sells precut carrots packaged with single-serve containers of ranch dip dressing. Cascadian Farm (now a subsidiary of General Mills) produces organic frozen TV dinners. Other value-added organic foods include H. J. Heinz's organic ketchup and PepsiCo's Frito-Lay's organic Tostitos and Sun Chips (Ganis 2002).

One might think that organic smallholders might benefit dramatically from big business's interest in organics. Yet while some small-scale producers do manage to stay afloat through direct sales at farmers' markets, farm stands, and restaurant venues, most are barely able to make a viable living as farmers. Most agro-foods corporations and supermarkets buy produce from industrial-scale organics growers because their monocropping and extensive systems produce more of the same product in a shorter amount of time, which is necessary for freezing, processing, and shipping across wide distances. In addition to posing a threat to organic smallholders who are unable to compete in the swelling organics market, industrial organics perpetuates existing environmental and health problems. Industrial organics means that fewer acres and bodies will be exposed to toxic chemicals, but these benefits cannot be offset by the fossil fuels, packaging, and resource-intensive operations required to produce a limited variety of organic crops. In turn, these crops must be distributed by trucks across highways that span vast distances (Ganis 2002). Organics is one of the fastest-growing sectors in the agricultural world. Large-scale organics increasingly edges into the turf of organic smallholders. Organic farmers working on family farms, or in community-supported agriculture programs, continue to struggle to earn a living wage.

Meanwhile, as the popular craving for organic food is on the rise, cultural notions of food quality spur interest in haute cuisine and fine potables. While haute cuisine certainly predates industrial agriculture, there is a growing synergism between mass-produced industrial food and its perceived opposite, the haute cuisine dish produced by the artisan chef. Ironically, the prevalence of the former feeds consumer desire for the latter. Increasingly, worlds of organic food and haute cuisine collide at upscale restaurants where menus tout dishes containing organic or "local" ingredients. Those who built the organic movement in the 1960s could hardly have envisioned a food culture in which organic produce would be offered in venues other than vegetarian low-culture restaurants. Until the 1990s, organic food was largely associated with counterculture hippies occupying a separate epicurean universe from those engaged in upscale food enterprises.

Yet another postindustrial irony: the same corporations that sell fast-flipped burgers in franchised outlets also offer beef bourguignon in their strings of five-star restaurants (Fantasia 2004). Corporations dominate both ends of a class-based food chain. While the wealthy dine on artisanal beef, the masses consume factory-farmed burgers. As the wealthy drown their culinary sorrows in a fine bottle of Côtes du Rhône, big business devours the food market generally.

Postindustrial Multifunctionality: Accommodating and Contesting the System

In recent decades, postindustrial smallholders in Europe have gone multifunctional. This means that many have adopted a plurality of coping strategies in the attempt to establish themselves as necessary entities in the rural world (Brouwer 2004). Many smallholders promote the popularity of farm-made, local, or organic foodstuffs using a sensibility associated with pre-industrial wholesomeness—while reifying so-called traditional agricultural practices and lifestyles. Again, only a fraction of these well-intentioned smallholders will earn a livable wage by signing on to multifunctionality schemes.

Agro-tourism is another coping strategy adopted by smallholders throughout the Global North. Many smallholders now offer services ranging from wholesome-looking ice cream stands to petting zoos to country inns on the farm. Such agro-tourism strategies signal smallholders' attempts to establish a niche for themselves in the postindustrial agricultural landscape. In addition, European smallholders often receive subsidies for being environmental stewards in rural zones. Many engage in rural public works, including restoring heirloom rural roads, fences, fields, and buildings. Beautifying depopulated rural areas increases the visual appeal of otherwise degraded rural zones for the tourist industry. Smallholders in service to government-subsidized tourist industries thus become quaint symbols of an increasingly romanticized, Disney-fied, and culturally diminished rural world.

Another condition of postindustrial agriculture constitutes what Foucault (1976) calls an explosion of discourses, a proliferation of popular narratives that represent a potent critique of industrial agriculture. These narratives represent the cultural effects of the industrial model. In this way, popular chatter about the quality of various food supplies is in itself a cultural product of the industrial agricultural system. For Anthony Giddens, this chatter could be called an example of reflexive modernity, a moment in which sets of societal actors stand back and gaze up at the industrialized movie screen of their modern lives, considering what they see (1981). Contemporary discourses about food safety or quality are instances of reflexive modernity. In the case of critical food discourse, actors driving and challenging the industrial model benefit from this moment of societal reflexivity. For example, government agents deploy critical food discourse about food safety and quality to bolster claims about the industrial model (Heller 2001a). To guarantee success, they promise to protect the safety and quality of industrial foods, creating and publicizing studies designed to reassure consumers of the viability of their food sources. When government agents make claims about food safety and quality, they tend to emphasize rigorous standards for ensuring that foodstuffs are free of potentially harmful contaminants such as bacteria.

Disenfranchised smallholders also invoke discourses on food quality and safety. Yet, unlike government agents, they do not tend to highlight questions of food contaminants. Instead they attempt to identify themselves with notions of traditional farming methods. In asserting themselves as authentic food experts, smallholders producing organic or local foods challenge the authority of corporations who make similar paternalistic claims about protecting the food base. In this way terms such as *safety* and *quality* become flexible tools to wield in opposing directions to achieve disparate objectives.

Popular discussions about obesity are another opportunity for actors on both sides of the food debate to make claims about preserving food safety and quality. Smallholders and state bodies invoke discourses on diabetic, insulin-dependent, and sedentary bodies to support their claims about various food-production models. While powerful institutions appeal to biomedical discourses related to diet, they also assert strategies for disciplining the civic body through diet and exercise. Critics of the industrial model deploy discourses on alternative health practices while emphasizing the inherent wholesomeness of nonindustrial foods to strengthen claims against the industrial model. In the United States and in Europe, too few actually make links between obesity and the U.S. farm bill or the European Common Agricultural Policy. In my research, I have been unable to find popular articles in national newspapers or magazines that speak about how government agricultural policies shore up an agro-foods industry that churns out foodstuffs containing high contents of fat, salt, a range of food additives, and high-fructose corn syrup. In turn, few media outlets publicly discuss the fact that since the agro-foods industry began to gain power, the price of fresh produce or nonprocessed foods in general has risen dramatically. A farm bill that supports commodity corn growers ends up producing a lot of cheap corn that is incorporated into relatively inexpensive processed and fast food. Instead of pointing to state food policy, the popular media focuses on individual consumers who are blamed for eating too much and exercising too little. In addition to discourses on food quality and safety, another key illustration of postindustrial agriculture is agricultural biotechnology. Agricultural biotechnology is a method of producing seeds, plants, and animal injections that have been genetically engineered to possess particular traits deemed valuable by various producers. While this technology builds upon the industrial model, it departs from it as well. Agricultural biotechnology creates an agricultural product whose objective is related to, yet independent from, narratives about agricultural productivity. There is no data to suggest that GMOs increase production generally. There is evidence—despite many corporations' claims—that increased food production does not necessarily lead to an abatement of global hunger. Scientific consensus maintains that agricultural biotechnology allows large-scale farmers to save money on herbicides, pesticides, and antifungal or antidisease inputs. Global hunger is well understood to result from wars and food policies associated with national governments and supranational trade bodies (Menzel and D'Aluisio 2006).

Agricultural biotechnology is designed to increase profits of agro-chemical companies. Biotechnology companies sell their patented packages of genetically modified seed only when paired with their own chemical inputs. These seed and chemical kits oblige farmers to purchase the same brand of inputs such as herbicides, pesticides, and fungicides each year from the very companies that provide their patented genetically modified seed (Shiva 1993b). U.S. agricultural biotechnology companies establish agro-chemicals and patented seeds as key sites for capital accumulation. In so doing, they join other entrepreneurial efforts to fill the economic crater in the United States associated with deindustrialization. The logic embedded in seed patents extends throughout the postindustrial food chain. The privatization of public water sources, for example, by multinationals is actively reshaping the agricultural landscape (Shiva 2002). Increasingly, potable water sources are bought and sold by private corporations. Rivers are diverted to provide services for relatively distant urban dwellers and consumers who can afford bottled water. Meanwhile, subsistence smallholders struggle to provide irrigation for their own crops.

As Foucault suggests, where there is domination, there is resistance. Integral to the postindustrial agricultural condition is the emergence of new alliances between heterogeneous sets of actors challenging industrial agriculture and the social and ecological effects of the postindustrial condition. Since the 1970s we have seen a rise of both international and local grassroots organizations resisting GMOs, free trade, and a neoliberal system that exploits land, food, and natural resources as commodities. These groups do more than reject a system deemed damaging: they also promote a new kind of society. Groups like the Confédération Paysanne call for a new world built out of a different logic — one that is neither preindustrial nor industrial. During the past decade, many groups have rejected the term *antiglobalization*. Activists may see the term as too often associated with xenophobic and nationalist right-wing critics of globalization. Activists also dismiss the term because it suggests a mere rejection of globalization, rather than prompting a discussion of alternative modalities to the neoliberal model of global economic and political systems. In its stead, many seeking to build a new kind of world use the term *alter-globalization*. It implies the idea of substantive alternatives to neoliberal globalization that could help restore ecological and social justice to the world. This book seeks to understand these movements, examining actors' understandings of the problems and solutions associated with the postindustrial condition.

The Relationship between Industrial and Postindustrial Agriculture

In addressing the temporal dimension of postindustriality, we must recall that even though postindustrial agriculture chronologically follows the industrial approach, it neither fully negates nor replaces industrial agriculture. The industrial plantation model is enjoying robust success in both the Global North and South. Peppered throughout the global industrial model are sets of postindustrial smallholders, each attempting to establish a rationality and means for their own existence. In turn, postindustriality is often a contemporary complement to industriality, sometimes even giving a boost to industrial agriculture. As mentioned earlier, industrial agriculture is currently capturing and profiting from the alternative strategies of postindustrial smallholders. For instance, retailers in the United States such as Whole Foods Market, Safeway, and Stop and Shop often highlight a few baskets containing foods promoted as local, organic, or artisanal. In so doing, they give consumers the impression that foods with low-petroleum global footprints constitute a significant component of the industrial organics enterprise.

There is no single postindustrial agricultural condition. As Akhil Gupta (1998) points out, in the case of the postcolonial condition, there is no monolithic condition of postindustriality. The postindustrial condition is also actively reconfigured, appropriated, and resisted by sets of actors in site-specific cultural settings. For instance, in some cultural contexts, smallholders choose to discontinue farming, selling off or ceasing to rent small tracts of lands. Larger industrialized producers subsequently buy up these lands in order to become even more extensive. In other cases, smallholders continue farming despite the hardships. Each smallholder has his or her own way of enduring stress, poverty, and overwork in a degraded and depopulated rural sphere. Still others farm while simultaneously resisting the system. These actors join unions or farmers' organizations that support their attempt to create a new rationality of agriculture that legitimizes and revitalizes new roles and practices of the smallholder. In turn, powerful institutions have varying responses to postindustriality. Some agro-chemical corporations turn to agricultural biotechnology as a way to increase profits drawn from food-production systems. Other corporations appropriate alternatives produced by smallholders who are critical of the industrial model. And some firms move into what I refer to as the public perception industry, making profits by hiring social scientists to monitor and shape consumer behavior related to discourses of so-called high-risk, safe, local, or quality foods.

To speak of a postindustrial condition is to point to a milieu in which the industrial and that which flows from it meet. The dynamic matrix formed by this juncture engenders a terrain composed of heterogeneous sets of powerful and disempowered actors, institutions, food-related discourses, landscapes, foodstuffs, and bodies. To speak of a postindustrial agricultural condition is to articulate the overlapping cultures constituting a world in which actors promote, contest, appropriate, and accommodate both industrial and postindustrial agricultural conditions.

Postindustrial Agriculture: The Confédération Paysanne

Refusing to completely capitulate to the discipline of states, corporations, and supranational agencies such as the WTO, the Confédération Paysanne's strategy represents instances of both adaptation and refusal. Many individuals within the union accommodate the dominant system in an attempt to survive economically. Some union members are willing to adopt a multifunctional role in the rural world, receiving humble subsidies to improve the aesthetic value of rural zones. Others directly confront the neoliberal farm policy that flourishes under late capitalism, asserting their right to produce food. What is particularly striking about the members of the Confédération Paysanne is that few adopt one narrow strategy. Most members simultaneously accommodate and challenge the system of industrial agriculture that tyrannizes them. Equally remarkable is how the union questions the rationality underlying industrial capitalism itself (Wallerstein 1984). I use the union's campaign against GMOs as a lens through which to analyze the complex strategies the Confédération Paysanne deploys in order to achieve its goals.

While consumer-driven movements tend to propel food controversies in the Global North, in France, producers take the lead. For instance, in the United Kingdom, Australia, the United States, Japan, and Northern Europe, ecology and consumer groups primarily direct controversies over food safety against mad cow disease, *E. coli*, and pesticide use. Many smallholders in the United States and Europe actively resist the industrial model. Yet they rarely possess the cultural clout to inform policymaking bodies. France is perhaps the only country in the Global North where the fight is successfully led by producers rather than nonfarming citizens.

French farmers historically constitute a politically conservative sector marked by an insular and parochial sensibility (Hervieu 1993). But due to an eclectic collision in the 1970s of antimilitarism, Gandhian philosophy, anarcho-syndicalism, and Catholic Marxism, the Confédération Paysanne grew from a series of new paysan movements that break with this conservative tendency. Members of the new paysan movements forged a new empowering identity by redefining the pejorative term *paysan* — a term historically associated with ideas of ignorance and backwardness. The new paysan movements redefined the paysan as a worker-identified smallholder standing in solidarity with other laborers around the world struggling to protect their livelihoods. For those active in these movements, agriculture was more than an economic activity. It was a culturally meaningful way of life. According to the new paysans, this life is threatened by industrial agriculture, which is perceived as a destructive set of practices embedded in a logic of instrumentalism rather than *solidarité* (solidarity).

The Confédération Paysanne was born out of a fusion of groups that comprised the new paysan movements. Since its inception in 1987, the Confédération Paysanne has indeed proven that there is no monolithic postindustrial condition. The Confédération Paysanne offers a distinctive instance of postindustrial agriculture. In the last decade, the Confédération Paysanne has developed a vision of agriculture that is central to a broader discourse on alter-globalization.[6] Alter-globalization represents an alternate rationality of industrial capital, based on a fusion of Gandhian philosophy and values of solidarity, internationalism, and quality of life for the world's peoples, partly inspired by the peasant farmers in the Zapatista movement in Chiapas, Mexico. The Confédération Paysanne adopted the phrase coined by the Zapatistas, *Another world is possible*. As the phrase suggests, its proponents promote alternatives to the dominant industrial neoliberal capitalist system. Alter-globalization activists reject neoliberal globalization based on a rationality of private accumulation, self-interest, and global capitalism.

The Confédération Paysanne's story can best be understood within the context of contemporary social movements actively displacing categories of modernity, progress, and development (Alvarez 2000; Escobar 2005, 344; Smith et al. 1997). The Confédération Paysanne, as well as its supporters and allies, represent new sets of actors, identities, and discourses currently re-shaping how social scientists interpret the forces driving social and political resistance today.

The Early Phase of the French Anti-GMO Movement:
A Debate about Risk

When I arrived in France way back in March 1997, I found to my surprise that the anti-GMO debate had begun to gain a bit of momentum—being driven initially by French ecology and consumer groups that, despite their efforts, still failed to gain significant popular support. During this time, the controversy was framed in scientific terms, focusing primarily on the risks and benefits associated with the technology. The French debate about genetically modified foods did not yet include a discussion of what I called at the time "social issues," such as farmers' critiques of corporate control of agriculture.

The first big story about this new discursive entity, now called GMOs, was published the November before my arrival in an issue of *Libération* (France's second-largest newspaper). On the cover was a photograph of an innocuous pile of soybeans sprawled under the caption "Alert au soja fou" (Watch out for mad soy) (*Libération*, November 27, 1996). During the next few months, newsstands in Paris were increasingly filled with articles covering the GMO controversy. Of the many that I collected, one still stands out. The article appeared in a March edition of the popular science magazine *Eureka* (1997). On the cover was the double image of a pig with a yellow spiral swirling from the top of its head, suggesting a dizzy or crazed animal. The cover title read, "Agriculture: Has It Gone Mad? The Great Fear of Genetically Modified Food" (1997). Most articles I collected during this period delivered the same discourse: GMOs were either scientifically risky or misinterpreted as risky by an irrational public. While the pendulum swung from risky to not risky, all articles highlighted narratives about GMO-related risk. Such discussions were in turn linked to recent food scares, such as mad cow, which had peaked in France in 1994. As promised, the GMOs arriving in France (and throughout Europe) in the fall of 1996 were genetically modified versions of staple crops such as corn, soy, and canola. These crops constituted what the industry called the "first generation" of GMOs, which offered two main types of resistant varieties that were primarily developed by U.S.-based corporations during the 1980s and early 1990s. Bt crops, the first variety, are genetically modified to resist a particular beetle (a common agricultural pest).[7] The other, known as the Round-Up Ready variety, is engineered to resist, or tolerate, heavy doses of Monsanto's popular herbicide Round-Up. Two issues were the focus of this popular controversy. First, GMOs provided benefits to farmers, rather than consumers. Second, a range of actors claimed that Bt and Round-Up Ready GMOs presented a series of understudied environmental and health risks.

During this period, many science and industry agents with whom I spoke openly lamented the fact that the first generation of GMOs had not appeared before the second. According to these actors, once French consumers understood the clear benefits of GMOs, they would accept the new foods without hesitation. In order to divert attention from the risks associated with the first generation, French industry officials and scientists tried to generate excitement about the immanent release of the second. According to these actors, this yet-to-emerge generation of GMOs would provide benefits to consumers, pleasing them with impressive results. It has been many years since 1997, and the second generation has yet to materialize. To date, there are no GMOs on the market that offer improved taste or enhanced nutritional, pharmacological, or aesthetic value. Nor does it appear that a second generation will appear at any time on the biotechnology horizon.

But early in the French debate, the second generation remained in the minds of science and industry officials as an immanent inevitability. Consequently, many political and scientific leaders attributed public concern over GMOs to problems associated with a set of foods aimed at pleasing farmers rather than consumers. Many also linked popular concern regarding GMOs to the media. For many science, industry, and political officials, it was the media that had overreported news about politicians' concerns over GMOs. In so doing, the media had unduly confused the masses. Indeed, the French government had made a series of contradictory decisions — widely publicized — in regard to the risks associated with three varieties of genetically modified Novartis corn (Heller 2002, 2004). The government's confusion regarding these three varieties suggested a general ambivalence regarding GMOs. Should France join the biotechnology race so as not to be surpassed by the United States? Or were GMOs just a trend? If the latter was true, why should the government unnecessarily upset various public constituencies, such as consumers' groups?

Here's how the government's ambivalence played itself out: First, Swiss-

based Novartis had enlisted a French science body, the Committée de Génie Biomoleculaire (Committee on Biomolecular Genetics), to test the Bt
corn. At stake was the scientific risk associated with one particular strain of
Novartis corn that contained antibiotic resistance markers (used in producing the Bt corn). The antibiotic resistance markers in turn raised public concern: if humans ate corn containing the antibiotic resistance markers, would
they become resistant to antibiotics? Novartis had chosen the Committée
de Génie Biomoleculaire due to France's previous supportive stance in regard to the technology. As expected, the committee at once recommended
the corn for approval. Next, Prime Minister Alain Juppé surprised everyone. In March of 1997, he rejected the committee's approval. What is more,
he banned all three varieties for cultivation on French soil, stating that they
presented potential environmental risks. Finally, incoming Prime Minister
Lionel Jospin spun the whole thing around again. He shocked everyone by
overturning Juppé's decision. Jospin's move was all the more baffling because
his Socialist Party had won the election partly due to its alliance with the
French Green Party, which was purportedly against GMOs. This display of
governmental inconsistency created considerable commotion among those
in ecology, farmers,' and consumers' organizations. Increasingly, they were
growing critical of the technology.

For me, all of this proved ethnographically fascinating. Actors on both
sides of the controversy (activists, the media, and public officials) invoked
narratives about scientific risk to bolster their particular claims about GMOs.
They focused on issues of antibiotic resistance, food allergenicity, and other
risks such as gene flow or increased weed and pest resistance. While proponents downplayed risks, critics emphasized them. What they shared was a
common language of risk. Risk discourse played (and continues to play) a
potent role in the GMO debate in France. The potency of scientific risk—a
form of science hegemony—and the later power of counterhegemonic discourses that surface in this story are central to this book (Gramsci and Hoare
1971; Laclau and Mouffe 1985). Risk discourse also plays a key role in GMO
debates around the world. As Raymond Williams suggests, language does
not just reflect historical processes. Linguistic narratives also produce various social realities as actors invent new terms and transfer old terms into new
domains (1976, 12). Williams's notion of "keywords" is particularly useful
in tracing the emergence of terms such as *risk* that emerge within specific
historical junctures. Keywords such as *risk* function in semantic clusters

of interrelated words that emerge at particular times and in places through "networks of usage," relying on each other to create new sets of meanings (Williams 1976, 9). In the case of the GMO debate in France, *risk* emerges as such a keyword, clustered together with other terms such as *expert public*, *benefits*, and *progress*. In my attempt to understand *risk* and other related keywords, I examine them in the context of networks of usage, and how particular keywords reinforce and support others.

Beyond Riskocentrism:
The Confédération Paysanne Politicizes the Debate

The Confédération Paysanne is one of the few organizations in the Global North to present a producer-oriented discourse on GMOs. In addition, they are unique in advancing a position that is critical of GMOs from the start. From the beginning of their anti-GMO campaign, the union went beyond a "riskocentric" perspective by discussing social, political, and, economic problems associated with the technology. Since I first learned about the Confédération Paysanne in Vermont when teaching environmental philosophy and politics at the Institute for Social Ecology, I wanted to discover more about this union of radical self-identified paysans. Due to a happy accident, I bumped into the Confédération Paysanne in March 1997 at the Salon de l'Agriculture—just days after my arrival in France. Despite overwhelming jet lag, I ambled over to the Salon de l'Agriculture, a rare and fascinating event not to be missed. The salon is France's version of a world's fair of agriculture held annually for almost twenty years, just at the edge of Paris. Over four days the Salon de l'Agriculture celebrates the latest techniques, wares, and products of French agriculture. In addition, the salon offers up-to-date scientific displays of agro-technologies and endless booths staffed by various political, industrial, agricultural, ecology, and consumer organizations. Thousands of French citizens from all over the country—farmers and non-farmers—make their annual pilgrimage to the salon. Some wear suits and high heels to dine in makeshift cafés, sampling new wines, cheeses, and pâtés from various parts of the country. Others dress in jeans and pullover sweaters, leaning over the rails of prefab fences to dreamily gaze at the best of French livestock. All of this takes place inside an ultra-modern facility spanning more than twenty buildings.

That year, the salon's central theme was GMOs. In addition to a series of conferences and workshops on the subject, a number of organizations distributed pamphlets with their positions on the technology. I spent several days at the salon, gliding from booth to booth, collecting various organizations' GMO literature and chatting with organizational representatives. After only a few hours of data collecting, it was clear to me that the GMO narratives of various organizations focused on risk. For instance, the largest agricultural union of industrial farmers in France, the Fédération National des Syndicats Exploitants Agriculteurs (National Federation of Agricultural Holders Unions), featured a discussion of the risks and benefits of the technology. Organizations such as consumer or environmental tended to emphasize only the risks (not benefits) associated with the technology. These organizations mainly discussed GMO-related problems of food security or potential environmental hazards.

Then I arrived at the Confédération Paysanne's booth. Gazing upward at the union's bright yellow banner dangling over the stall, I wondered whether this was the union I'd heard about in Vermont. Mary Agnes Fouchet, a national representative for Confédération Paysanne working the union's booth that day, welcomed me, handing me a leaflet discussing the union's GMO policy. While the leaflet featured the usual list of GMO-related risks, it also located GMOs within the broader context of industrial agriculture, discussing the potential social and economic impacts of GMOs on smallholders around the world. The tone of the writing was at once humanistic and *solidaire* (a truly untranslatable term akin to the English terms *solidarity*, *solidarity based*, and *cooperative*). Fouchet seemed more like a political activist than a union representative. Other union representatives, like those of the Fédération National des Syndicats Exploitants Agriculteurs (FNSEA), were dressed in pressed suits and skirts, while Fouchet wore jeans and a simple button-down plaid blouse. Within minutes of talking to Fouchet, I was thrilled to determine that the Confédération Paysanne was indeed the union that had traveled to the United States just three years earlier to learn about genetically modified milk.

A few weeks after the Salon de l'Agriculture, I took the train to Etampes (seventy kilometers outside Paris) to spend the day with Fouchet, dining together in her friend's delectable restaurant and touring the small farm she inherited from her father where she grew sugar beets, sunflowers, and canola. As is the case with most interviews in this book, my discussions with Fouchet were conducted in French. The words of the people I speak with are my own translation from French. Fouchet was the only adult child in her family (she has one younger brother and three younger sisters) who had chosen to take up the farming life. "If I hadn't taken over my father's and uncle's fields, we would have had to sell them to a bigger farm," she explained. "I just couldn't do that. I'd feel defeated" (personal communication, April 12, 1997). As is often the case, adult children of French small farmers are increasingly unable to assume financial responsibility for maintaining the farms of retired relatives, and they have to sell lands to large-scale producers, thus contributing to the overall disappearance of smallholders.

When I asked her when she first heard about GMOs, Fouchet explained that she had attended a meeting in 1995 at her local chamber of agriculture. In France, the national chamber of agriculture has representative and administrative functions on the regional level. In France, agricultural policy is translated into practice on the local level through the country's many chambers of agriculture. It is common, for instance, for new agricultural policies or techniques to be introduced to farmers by their local chambers. Dominated by the FNSEA (which to this day occupies the majority of the chamber's seats), the chamber of agriculture has for decades been oriented toward the promotion of industrial agriculture, or large-scale agri-business. It is in this context that Fouchet understood the potential implications of GMOs:

> I knew right away at this meeting that GMOs were not for paysans. They were just for the [FNSEA]. They were trying to get us all excited about GMOs, saying that they'd help us save on chemical inputs, use less pesticide, for example. They said we'd save money. But no one was asking what the paysans really wanted. We were more concerned about problems of drought. . . . When there's little rainfall, like this year, the large-scale farmers can afford to just dig down deeper and take all the water for themselves, which just worsens the water shortage. The large-scale farmers care only about themselves. GMOs are for the large-scale farmers; they are just more of the same mentality. (Personal communication, April 12, 1997)

For Fouchet, GMOs belonged to a "mentality" of large-scale agribusiness, an instrumental and individualistic way of thinking that focuses on reducing production costs and allegedly solving such problems as water shortage by promoting costly and consequently economically exclusive farming practices. According to Fouchet, this mentality was based on a principle of self-interest for large-scale farmers who "cared only about themselves," rather than holding a principle of *solidarité*. After encountering Fouchet, I became even more interested in this union of paysan farmers that was to become the primary player in the debate to consistently promote a politicized rationality of GMOS.

Instrumental versus Solidarity-Based Rationalities of GMOS

Throughout my attempt to understand this story, I have negotiated boundaries between *emic* and *etic*, attempting to describe two contrasting rationalities that surface in actors' narratives.[8] My goal has been to maintain both theoretical clarity and degrees of authenticity regarding the perceived realities of actors on the ground. I point to a tension between two (often overlapping) worldviews: those presented by actors in the Confédération Paysanne (and other alter-globalization organizations) and those proposed by actors in powerful institutions, such as multinational corporations, science bodies, government agencies, and supranational agencies (e.g., the International Monetary Fund, the World Bank, and the World Trade Organization). Such agencies tend to advance an instrumental logic of efficiency, profitability, risk, and hierarchy. In contrast, groups such as the Confédération Paysanne often advance an alternate solidarity-based rationality linked to their concept of alter-globalization.

The idea of risk—rather than notions of general harm or danger—has a special history in the West. The concept of risk first emerged as merchant capitalists determined whether or not to gamble on financing oceanic voyages of cargo ships. Eventually merchant capitalists appealed to statistics to calculate the chance of disaster (and ensuing financial loss) and began selling the first forms of insurance to shipmasters (Ewald 1991). Industrial capitalists further developed notions and practices of statistics-based insurance-driven risk. Their objective was to calculate the chance that workers would lose limbs or die in industrial accidents. Thus the notion of gambling, chance, and statistical calculation form the foundation for the first insurance policies based on a worldview that measures human lives in terms of dollars. Over time, notions of potential or acceptable risk have become taken for granted. How many of us accept—without thinking—the assumption that life in contemporary society is inevitably rife with sets of capital-driven dangers? We normalize these profit-driven dangers by calling them risks, seeing them as integral to the development of technology or economic progress. Whether it's the risk of dying in an automobile accident (in a flimsily built but afford-able car) or falling ill due to an industrial-driven pollutant, we tend to see these risks as unstoppable and necessary features of everyday life.

It is not that various sectors of the public are unaware that corporations could dramatically improve safety and lessen the chances of harm to citizens (driving cars or breathing air, for example). The reality is that many accept the fact that most corporations choose not to improve safety in order to lower the cost of production. Many inhabitants of industrial societies perceive corporations to be unchangeable and thus become docile and passive when facing those that place public health and environments in jeopardy. When citizens do take overt action against corporations, by demanding improved safety standards and so on, it is more the exception than the rule. The Confédération Paysanne's alter-globalization discourse represents a diversion to this docile and passive trend to accept the instrumental logic that values profits over the well-being of peoples and natures. The union throws a wrench into the instrumental logic of risk discourse, refusing dehumanizing notions of acceptable risk associated with GMOs. Moreover, the Confédération Paysanne rejects the calculative and rationalizing logic that normalizes this way of viewing both human and nonhuman life. The Confédération Paysanne is attempting to redefine, reconfigure, and resist values and practices associated not only with industrial-productivist agriculture but with instrumentalism itself.

In searching for terminology to describe these two contrasting rationalities, I found epistemological insight in the work of Murray Bookchin — insights that are in turn traceable to Max Weber's concerns with the rationalization of life, work, and religion. Even though he was a later theorist of modernity, Bookchin was an environmental and political philosopher concerned with forms of reason that have risen to prominence under late capitalism. Bookchin's work draws from Frankfurt School theorists such as Max Horkheimer (1947) to develop a theory of the individualizing and calculative rationality driving the culture of late capitalism. For Horkheimer there exists within the late-modern period a tension between subjective and objective reason (1947, 16). While the former addresses an individualistic, relativistic, and instrumental rationality concerned with market-based efficiency, the latter considers questions of ethical versus unethical, or just versus unjust. Elaborating on Horkheimer, Bookchin uses the terms *instrumental* and *ethical reason* to depict these two contrasting rationalities.

Drawing in turn from Bookchin and other theorists of modernity (Sayer 1991), I use the term *instrumental rationality* to describe the market-driven calculative approach to agriculture that surfaced in actors' agriculture-related narratives in the French debate. I have chosen, however, not to use Bookchin's term *ethical reason* to distinguish between what is instrumental and what is social-ethical in content. Instead, I deploy the term *rationality of solidarity* to linguistically approximate the French meaning of solidarité, a concept that implies an untranslatable and unquantifiable humanistic concern with maintaining the integrity of social fabrics. By invoking rationalities of solidarity, I attempt to parse out the cooperative dimension of ethical concerns found in actors' narratives in science policymaking forums (Levidow and Carr 1997, 2009; Wynne 1992). As sociologist Brian Wynne suggests, science policymaking forums often instrumentalize and individualize questions of solidarity-based ethics, emptying the concept of political and humanistic content.

For example, in bioethics panels on GMOs in the United States and Europe, the term *ethical* is often used to point to individuals' particular religious concerns related to GMOs. GMOs that might contain genes from pigs (or other animals) that violate kosher or halal criteria are often considered ethical issues. Other ethical considerations taken up by bioethics bodies are religious concerns that GMOs represent man's attempt to play God with nature. Yet other ethical questions focus on the right of individual consumers to know and choose what they are eating. Other experts in bioethics, such as James Dargie of the Food and Agriculture Organization of the United Nations, frame ethics in productive terms, asserting that world hunger represents an ethical mandate to produce GMOs. Such claims are undermined as Dargie (2001) himself admits there is no reliable data to assert that agricultural biotechnology generally enhances productivity — or that world hunger is caused by an overall problem of productivity.

The term *solidarity-based rationalities* blurs the fabricated distinction between economic and ethical issues in policymaking circles. The solidarity-based dimension of economic issues related to GMOs often slips between the epistemological cracks of science and government bodies seeking to establish legitimate categories for evaluating GMOs. In my research of the French case, I found that actors' economic narratives often included solidarity-based ethical judgments regarding the economic implications of GMOs for peoples globally. For instance, while policymakers may categorize monetary impacts of GMOs on farmers in the Global South as economic issues (thus segregating them out of ethical discussions), I will define such economic concerns as solidarity-based issues, implying a humanist-ethical dimension surrounding the fates of peasants and indigenous actors in the Global South.

Overlap and Contradiction: Instrumental and Solidaire Rationalities

Instrumental and solidarity-based rationalities are useful heuristics for pointing to the identifiable and contrasting styles of thinking that surface in the French GMO debate. However, it is worth noting that these rationalities are not mutually exclusive, and they do not correspond to neat economic categories such as "capitalist" and "noncapitalist." The two rationalities share areas of overlap. For instance, there is often a dimension of solidarity in discussions of GMO-related risk, despite the instrumental origins of risk discourse historically. Although risk discourse tends to reduce the GMO question to instrumental and calculative concerns, such as protecting corporate assets and images, actors' discussions of GMO-related risk often reflect humanitarian concerns regarding public health and environmental well-being. And just as there is often a solidarity side to instrumental rationalities of risk, there is an instrumental dimension to solidarity-based rationalities. For instance, the Confédération Paysanne appeals to solidarity-based notions when invoking the "precaution principle" (an international environmental principle that has become central to discourses on global risk management). In turn, actors in the Confédération Paysanne often adopt instrumentalized notions of agricultural quality that reduce food quality to technical terms to promote a solidarity-based model of agriculture.

A key question about the relationship between these rationalities and capitalism by way of analogy: is an instrumental rationality to capitalism as a solidarity-based rationality is to a moral economy? In other words, is instrumentalism an inherent feature of the capitalist system and of no other area of social life? And is solidarity a mark of an economic modality that lies outside profit-driven capitalist markets? The answer is that it is not that simple. To begin, most capitalist activity is indeed marked by a logic of instrumentalism. Many theorists of capitalism recognize the ways in which capitalism reduces peoples, natures, and things to commodities, emphasizing means over ends (Bookchin 1971; Wallerstein 1984; Sayer 1991). Capitalism entails the rationalization of human beings, subsuming all things under a calculus of exchange value. However, while all capitalism is instrumental, not all instrumental activity occurs within capitalist frameworks. An instrumental rationality marked the human time line, allowing our species to use principles of efficiency and regularization to guide a range of technological endeavors. Such principles are perfectly suitable to projects such as architecture and agriculture and to the design of instruments that could be of great use within capitalist or noncapitalist societies. A cultural problem arises when a logic meant for bridge building, for instance, is extended to qualitative realms of everyday life, displacing a logic of sociality.

Those familiar with anticapitalist revolutions that brought us societies such as the former Soviet Union, China, and Cuba are all too aware of how an instrumental rationality can be highly compatible with anticapitalist pursuits. The atrocities of Stalin, for instance, which reduced people to things to be eliminated via massacre, is a harrowing instance of anticapitalism gone terribly instrumental. In so many cases, we can see how the means-ends thinking of any communist or socialist dictator of purportedly mutualistic societies can go terribly awry, using instrumental tactics to "efficiently" govern, punish, and enforce social control. Just as instrumentality can thrive among the most anticapitalist, capitalist enterprises often exploit principles of human solidarity. Many megacorporations throughout the world invoke metaphors of sports teams and families to enhance genuine sentiments of belonging and company loyalty among employees (Ong 1987). On Walmart's website, under a subject heading titled "Diversity," the site's copy reads: "At Walmart, we believe that business wins when *everyone matters*, and that the true strength of diversity is unleashed when *each associate is encouraged to reach their full potential*. Diversity then becomes the foundation for an *inclusive, sustainable* business that embraces and *respects differences*, develops our associates, serves our customers, *partners with our communities* and builds upon an inclusive supplier base" (emphasis mine). The narrative becomes striking when one takes note that Walmart has generated decades-long scandals related to their union prevention, workplace sexism, and generally low salaries and poor working conditions. By clustering together keywords such as *everyone matters, full potential, inclusive, sustainable, respect, partners,* and *communities,* marketing agents mimic a rationality of solidarity they know people in local communities favor.

As seen in the Walmart case, solidarity-based narratives can be quite compatible with a procapitalist stance. While some members of progressive or-

ganizations do put forth an explicitly anticapitalist vision, many others do
not identify as anticapitalist. While critiquing neoliberal forms of capitalism, groups such as the Confédération Paysanne often promote capitalistic
social democracies as part of their alter-globalization vision. Their objective
is to re-empower individual states against supranational institutions, reorga-
nizing the capitalist system in such a way that it more equitably meets the
needs of citizens and environment (Gibson-Graham 2006). Of interest in
this book is the encroachment of an instrumental market logic into cultural
realms such as agriculture. Of note too is the way in which this logic eclipses
a solidarity-based approach to food production. The prominence of instrumental logics of investment and efficiency in communal and even familial
contexts speaks of a broader cultural condition in which actors increasingly
see themselves in market-driven terms. At stake here is the question of how
an instrumental approach is ferried into nearly all realms of social and cultural life.

When a Solidarity-Based Rationality of Agriculture Goes Public

There is a dynamic tension between instrumental and solidarity-based rationalities that circulates through the GMO debate in France. I trace the cultural forces that bring actors in the Confédération Paysanne to mute their
solidarity-based rationalities of GMOs from public forums (particularly in the
first phase of the debate). I am also interested in exploring how and why —
at particular times — actors publicly and successfully promote solidarity-
based rationality of GMOs and of agriculture generally. In 1999 Confédération Paysanne's solidarity-based rationality of GMOs indeed went national.
In 1997 the union's fledgling anti-GMO campaign relied heavily on risk, invoking the expertise of scientists to support claims against the technology.
Subsequently, a series of events in August 1999 brought about a shift in
the style and public receptivity of the Confédération Paysanne's GMO discourse. During the summer of 1999, José Bové had spearheaded a series of
direct actions known as crop pulls. During such an event, a group of farmers
and other activists enter a field containing GM plants. Sometimes, activists
trounce through the fields, breaking plant stems as they go. At other crop
pulls, activists collect garbage bags of GM plants, later dumping the bags
deemed contaminants before the local police station.

After a summer of crop pulls, the local judge of Bové's district was fed up.

And this is why Bové and other members of the union got an unusually high sentence for participating in an anti-McDonald's action that August. In this action Bové and three hundred activists symbolically dismantled a McDonald's construction site in his town of Millau in southern France. While national and international media depicted Bové as "destroying the building" (*New York Times*, xxx xx, 1999), the farmers themselves describe their actions in modest terms, admitting to prying off several tiles from the building's roof in addition to toppling a McDonald's construction sign. The majority of the day featured family-style picnics on the grounds of the building site while Bové and other farmers were interviewed by local press about the rather low-profile action.

In addition to anti-GMO activism, anti-McDonald's actions constituted Bové's second passion. This particular McDonald's action was in retaliation against President Clinton and the WTO. In an attempt to punish Europe for refusing imported U.S. hormone-treated beef, the United States placed a heavy surtax on such French exports as Roquefort cheese. As a producer of ewe's milk (used in creating Roquefort), Bové and the other farmers decided to take symbolic action against Clinton and the WTO, which had legitimized and administrated Clinton's sanctions. After being arrested for the McDonald's action and refusing bail, Bové remained in jail for three weeks, being catapulted to national and international stardom for taking a public stance against McDonald's and ultimately against neoliberal forms of globalization. Suddenly renowned for the McDonald's rather than the GMO issue, Bové seized the opportunity to advance both causes. Through Bové's discourse, GMOs became a symbol, like McDonald's, of neoliberalism, a homogenized global culture, and the commodification of life and culture.

In particular, GMOs became a symbol of *la malbouffe*, a slang term Bové uses that has been translated imperfectly into English as "junk food." In his book that became a national best-seller in France, Bové describes la malbouffe as pointing to a food-related problem of culture and health. The text, *Le monde n'est pas une marchandise: Des paysans contre la malbouffe* (The world isn't merchandise: Peasants against junk food) was translated into twenty-seven languages (the English title is *The World Is Not for Sale: Farmers against Junk Food*) and launched a publishing career for Bové that continues today. For Bové, GMOs were yet another instance of the rationalization of food, along with McDonald's, hormones, and pesticides residues. As an instance of la malbouffe, GMOs represent the reduction of food to a culturally standardized and technically dangerous entity. In popularizing the term *la malbouffe*, Bové expressed the solidarity-based, as well as technical or instrumental, dimensions of GMOS as a scientific entity. GMOS no longer stood for a lofty product of science to be evaluated exclusively by scientists. They now symbolized food, agriculture, and culture, thus falling within the jurisdiction of paysan expertise. In bringing together issues of culture, health, quality, and safety, Bové synthesized an instrumental and solidarity-based rationality of food, agriculture, and science.

After 1999, Bové's alter-globalization discourse became quite palpable in the media. Bové's overlapping identities — anti-GMO and alter-globalization activist — allowed notions of globalization and GMOS to be linked together in public consciousness. The broadening of the GMO debate beyond a problem of calculable risk to include wider issues of neoliberal globalization signaled a shift in the loci of expertise. For the first time in the debate, paysan farmers, as well as scientists, could speak with cultural authority about GMOS. I trace the cultural forces that facilitated the public radicalization of the French GMO debate. I examine the conditions through which actors began to speak publicly about GMOS from a solidarity-based, rather than exclusively instrumental, perspective. In pointing to the transformation of the debate in France, I refer to it as a broadening rather than as a complete shift. Confédération Paysanne's articles on GMOS after the events in 1999 still rely heavily on risk narratives. What is significant is the extent to which public discussion began to also include an alter-globalization perspective. The Confédération Paysanne did not put an end to risk discourse. Rather, it disrupted its primacy, destabilizing the discursive center of gravity that risk had exclusively enjoyed.

It is also important to note the implicitness of the Confédération Paysanne's discursive challenge. Throughout my research, I was continually struck by an absence among actors of what could be called discursive self-consciousness. Science hegemony induces degrees of conformity to particular dominant discursive orders. Actors in the Confédération Paysanne were often unaware of both their reliance on risk discourses and the extent to which their solidarity-based rationalities of GMOS displaced risk's primacy in the public sphere. Nevertheless, actors' discursive maneuvers, particularly those of Bové and the Confédération Paysanne, broadened understandings of what may count as expertise for technoscience practice and policymaking in debates about science in the future.

Introduction

In recent decades, those engaged in the anthropology of modernity have reconfigured the ethnographic site. Researchers have been conducting research in multiple locations, and among heterogeneous communities, with varying degrees of power. In such contexts, anthropologists have found that they must negotiate relationships in complex fields of power. Historically, anthropologists have studied down, which means examining the cultural practices of peoples who have less power than they. But since the 1980s, anthropologists are increasingly studying up, exploring the cultural practices of peoples working within powerful institutions. Studying up allows anthropologists to convey the complexities of power as it circulates through regional, national, and international institutions (e.g., corporations, scientific laboratories, governmental agencies) as well as expert scientific institutions (Nader 1969). For ethnographers interested in contemporary local changes in culture and society, single-sited research can no longer be easily located in a world-system perspective (Marcus 1995; Tsing 2005).

Anthropologists conducting dynamic multisited ethnographies, such as Aihwa Ong (1987), Rayna Rapp (1999), and Emily Martin (1994), have redefined what counts as a field of research. Drawing from their works, I aim for a panoramic and simultaneous view of the French GMO debate. In this spirit, I also draw from Donna Haraway, whose notion of situated knowledges acknowledges that in order to know a thing, one must understand its history. For Haraway, objects of study are always embedded in particular locations within existing fields of power (Haraway 1991). I try to render transparent the heterogeneous networks of peoples, places, and things through which GMOs circulate. GMOs are never insular or universal scientific entities; they represent cultural objects, discourses, and practices that are always contextualized within specific social and political domains. Haraway's insights about situated knowledge are tightly linked to discourses about the need for multisited ethnographies in world systems. To contextualize objects of inquiry that are inherently emergent, circuitous, and mercurial, one must follow objects as they move in and across various societal arenas. The most richly situated knowledges arise from studies of the multiple contexts inhabited by those objects we seek to understand.

During my first phase of research in 1997, I created a preliminary map of the GMO controversy, identifying six sets of key actors playing a central role in shaping the debate, including scientists, farmers, consumer groups, environmental groups, industry officials, and government agents. Over time, the same usual suspects began to reappear with increasing frequency at public conferences, television shows, and newspaper articles, making Paris seem like a relatively small town. There was indeed an identifiable yet small network of key actors and organizations, almost exclusively based in Paris, that gradually came into view as I made my way from forum to forum, quickly trying to follow a debate in the making. As I came to learn, it is indeed often a small number of highly active individuals (and institutions), rather than hoards or masses, that drive public debates or controversies.

In my attempt to conceptualize the broader networks in which these individuals worked and functioned, I have drawn from the actor-network theory (ANT) developed by Bruno Latour (1983, 1988a, 1998), Michel Callon (1986b), and John Law (1987). For these theorists, heterogeneous association of actors (human and nonhuman) constitute the institutions, information flows, and tools that together form the sociopolitical field. Even though I invoke these theorists, this ethnography is not a formal actor-network study. I draw from actor-network theory primarily to convey the webs of relationships that exist among the many actors, institutions, GMOs, and other nonhuman entities that animated the French debate.

Over time, I came to understand GMOs not as an isolatable scientific or commercial entity. Instead, I saw GMOs as an uneven and heterogeneous network of all of the people, organisms, tools, and policies that produced them in laboratories, marketed them throughout the world, forged policy about them in government buildings, and contested them in fields and streets. The network concept unbinds the ethnographic site, revealing it as a truly amorphous, continually shifting, and borderless entity. For me, the idea of a network lifted the burden I would have carried had I actually thought I could convey the totality of a public debate. The more I studied the controversy, the more I understood that I would only be able to capture a small piece of a boundless entity. I knew that I was merely squinting out at a great jigsaw puzzle, one whose myriad shining pieces were continually repositioning themselves into increasingly baffling yet meaningful configurations. While the number of individuals actively constituting this jigsaw puzzle was relatively small, the number and scale of associated institutions proved to be quite overwhelming ethnographically. Instead of scattering myself too thin, I decided to focus primarily on two sets of actors in the broader GMO network: farmers from the Confédération Paysanne and scientists from the Institute National de Recherche Agricole (French National Institute of Agricultural Research). In addition, I focused my attention on key individual actors within consumer, environmental, industrial, and governmental settings. For the purposes of this book, however, I focus mainly on the Confédération Paysanne. Its story is rich, dynamic, and exceptional, so it stands out as a key narrative within the French GMO network.

During this period of French (and international agricultural policymaking), articulations among agriculture, global capital, and farm policy have come under tremendous public scrutiny. Recent agricultural scandals, such as mad cow disease, along with growing concerns among the French public regarding pesticide use, hormone-treated meat, and pollution, have created a climate in which the French public has begun raising questions about agriculture and food quality generally (Heller 2006). The Confédération Paysanne has been actively addressing these questions in an interesting way.

PRIMARY SITE: THE CONFÉDÉRATION PAYSANNE

The Confédération Paysanne headquarters are in Bagnolet, a suburb minutes from Paris. At the headquarters, I conducted many formal interviews with *salariers* (staff members who are not paysans) and paysan representatives. I also attended organizational meetings, with a focus on following the working group compiling a report on GMOs for the French Conseil Économique et Social (French Economic and Social Council). This latter project brought me into contact with a range of actors from industrial, governmental, and scientific bodies that were interviewed by the Confédération Paysanne working group composing the report. At the French Conseil Économique et Social I was able to observe some of the dynamics and tensions between Confédération Paysanne and the FNSEA farmers who serve on the council.

I also attended many public conferences within Paris and villages outside the city, where Confédération Paysanne actors spoke publicly about GMOs. In these forums I observed and compared the public discourse of Confédération Paysanne with narratives attained through more private conversations with Confédération Paysanne actors. In addition, I spent many weekends visiting the farms and families of Confédération Paysanne farmers throughout the country who generously welcomed me into their homes, providing me with the opportunity to develop an appreciation for the concrete realities of small farmers, the multiple stressors and commitments they bear in trying to maintain a paysan way of life. In rain, frost, and shine, I marched with the Confédération Paysanne during demonstrations in Paris that, in addition to addressing GMOs, took on issues ranging from Europe's Politique Agricole Commune (Common Agricultural Policy) to the privatization of Third World water by the French-based multinational Vivendi. Attended by paysans from across the country, these demonstrations gave me insight into the different concerns and perspectives of actors in different geographical and agricultural zones.

In the fall of 1999, Bové invited me to join a delegation of Confédération Paysanne activists on a ten-day excursion that went first to Washington, D.C., to meet with farmers from the National Family Farm Coalition and then to the WTO meetings in Seattle. This journey allowed me to witness Bové and Confédération Paysanne spokesperson François Dufour as they began to develop and negotiate a new and central position and discourse within an emerging alter-globalization movement.

Conclusion

The French case is more than a story of a group of activists challenging the primacy of science hegemony. It is also a story about how a solidarity-based rationality of agriculture—and of the world—gained ascendancy, shifting the discursive terrain to make it more conducive to actors' articulating in public a broader and more complex appreciation of GMOs. While the French case demystifies scientific expertise, it also celebrates emergent forms of knowledge, such as paysan savoir faire. In so doing, actors in this story are broadening understandings of what counts for expertise in debates about science, agriculture, and the global economy in years to come.

PART I

*Toward a New Rationality
of Agriculture*

The New Paysan Movements

*French Industrialized
Agriculture and the Rise of the
Postindustrial Paysan*

Not long after France adopted the industrial model, the nation faced overwhelming problems of agricultural overproduction. Increasingly, French and European agricultural policy disciplined smallholders into becoming what Foucault would call "docile bodies." Paradoxically, just as France became a major agricultural power, the second-largest exporter in the world, it ceased to constitute a truly agrarian society (Hervieu 1996b). For the first time in French history, farmers became a professional minority. In response to this technique of postindustrial governance, a series of new paysan movements emerged that attempted to reorder France's agricultural system according to nonproductivist logic (Atkins and Bowler 2001). Culminating in the formation of the Confédération Paysanne, these new paysan movements represent the collective attempt of smallholders to address the reduction of the paysan as an expendable entity in the rural world. By establishing the paysan as a distinct cultural and political identity, the new paysan movements built a cultural podium from which to articulate a vital and creative critique of the industrial agricultural model.

The First Transition: The Peasantification of France

In France there is a tendency to regard the country's agrarian past in monolithic terms, casting it as a timeless realm of peasants, pastures, morality, and natural order (Hervieu 1996a). This romantic view emerged, paradoxically, during the first major agricultural transition of the late nineteenth century, when France "peasantified" its rural world, emptying it of individuals not directly involved in the agricultural enterprise. During this period the rural world shifted from a richly varied domain with a continuous integration of agricultural, industrial, and artisanal zones to a primarily agricultural domain (Lizet and Ravignant 1987). Unlike Britain, which divided its agricultural and industrial zones as early as the seventeenth century and moved industry to urban centers, France chose a different model of rural development. As late as 1870, 80 percent of France's national product was still produced in rural areas (Grantham 1980). The peasantification of France emerged out of a series of sociopolitical transformations that led France's minister of the interior, Leon Gambetta, to restructure France's rural areas. Political events gave rise to new political instabilities (*Economie Rurale* 1998).

Economic disruptions occurred as Napoléon III introduced into France goods from an international market. This maneuver brought an influx of wool and textiles from Great Britain and the New World. On the agricultural front, a widespread locust infestation destroyed much of the grape harvest in the Midi region, devastating the wine economy for decades (Hervieu 1993, 6). Attempting to stabilize the French economy, Gambetta created France's first ministry of agriculture in 1881, initiating a process of technical modernization and commercial protectionism. In addition, he established an internal ministry of the peasantry, modeling it after the French ministry of colonial affairs. Gambetta hoped that the ministry of the peasantry would manage both territory and markets while also garnering the peasant vote in a teetering republic (Weber 1976). For Gambetta, the landowning peasantry represented a rural bourgeoisie that was instrumental for consolidating support for the republic against monarchists. By forming this group into a class of proprietors, Gambetta sought to turn them into loyal republicans (Blanc 1977). At the same time that he galvanized the support of landowning peasants, Gambetta set in motion a rural exodus of landless peasantry. Along with landless peoples vanished a cultural realm forged by artisanal craftsmen working in domains of metallurgy and textiles. As thousands fled rural areas in search of work in industrial centers, France underwent a dramatic transformation in which rural zones were to be occupied primarily by landowning peasants directly involved in agriculture — as well as a sector of poor peasants who would remain to cultivate land rented from rich landowners.

For the next fifty years, France's agricultural world became what Gambetta had hoped for: a domain dominated by a rich land-owning class of grain producers constituting a politically and religiously conservative lobby. A population of smallholders did remain in rural zones, but only some of these largely poor farmers could afford to own even small plots of land for smallholder cultivation. The majority of smallholders rented farmlands from wealthy landowners. From this time forward, France's rural world morphed into a bifurcated agricultural class structure. Smallholders were dominated by wealthy landowners as the French paysans and countryside were reimagined as idealistic and romantic fixtures in the national consciousness. Today, these ideas are still associated in France with notions of exalted, timeless, and rural "peasant virtues" (Hervieu 1993, 5). The notion of a static French peasantry first instituted by Gambetta still enjoys a central place in the contemporary national imagination. Ideas of the *bon paysan* are still associated with feelings of national responsibility for the relatively recent, and even more dramatic, disappearance of smallholders.

The Second Transition and Les Trentes Glorieuses

During the second transition of French agriculture, a series of events destabilized and reconfigured the image and structure of the rural world in France. The postwar demand for augmented agricultural production, the rise of mechanization, and the rise of a modernist agrarian youth movement came together to once again transform France's agricultural and cultural landscape. The second major transition occurred during *les trentes glorieuses* (the glorious thirty). The period that spanned from 1945 to 1975 represents a period of accelerated modernization that followed the end of World War II. Michel Débatisse (1963) refers to this transition as the *révolution silencieuse* (silent revolution), a set of technical, economic, social, and cultural transformations that accompanied the reorganization of French agricultural policy.

According to Débatisse, the révolution silencieuse was tied to the construction of Europe as well as to a European agricultural policy that strongly supported large-scale industrial agribusiness. This shift in France must be placed in an international context associated with postwar policies such as the Marshall Plan. Developed by the United States after World War II, the Marshall Plan sought to rebuild a Western Europe that would be capable of fending off internal communism. Part of this plan was to design a European industrialized agricultural sector ready to overproduce, export, and dominate agricultural economies in the Global South (McMichael 1995, xiii; Van den Ban 1999). While satisfying its citizens and preventing unrest, the Marshall Plan's agricultural policies sought to deter the spread of communism in the Southern Hemisphere by creating and supporting capitalist food economies there.

France was tightly integrated into a world system that embraced what Immanuel Wallerstein calls "developmentalism" (1991). For Wallerstein, developmentalism is a process through which states were integrated into the Bretton Woods institutional complex (1991: 89). Countries throughout the Global North and South were encouraged to industrialize, modernize, and rationalize all forms of production, including agriculture. Theories extolling the virtues of the modernization process tended to downplay the transformations that were occurring in agricultural and rural life (McMichael 1994; Buttel 2003). What is more, recent studies of late modernity increasingly understand the rural sphere as inevitably embedded in a global-industrial capitalist system. By failing to anticipate future impacts of modernization and industrialization on the rural sphere, powerful policymaking bodies paved the way for the rise of a rural resistance in years to come.

During this transition toward modernization, powerful bodies such as the French ministry of agriculture and the media exercised a crucial discursive maneuver central to the ongoing disciplining of the French farmer (McMichael 2000b). The idea of the romantic (and yet often pejorative) paysan is discursively displaced by a new identity: the modern professionalized *agriculteur* (farmer-entrepreneur), also referred to as *le chef de l'entreprise* (the chief of the enterprise). While the paysan worked within a village collectivity based on local domestic production and consumption, the modern farmer is portrayed as an individual who directs farm activity toward an increasingly international market (Mendras 1984). Whereas the paysan used traditional nonindustrial farming techniques, the industrial farmer incorporates machines, chemicals, and equipment, many of which arrived from the United States. Through new linguistic, technical, and agri-policy practices, the French government discursively remodeled the ideal French farmer into a savvy, technologically oriented entrepreneur who would operate within a larger national and international agricultural economy. Coercing French farmers to adopt modern farming practices and identities, however, was not an easy task. Once again, the older lobby of large-scale grain producers tended to be culturally parochial when it came to viewing their profession as farmers. Even many moderate landowners and smallholders were wedded to an agricultural and rural system that tended to be religiously, politically, and technologically conservative (Pochon 1997, 28).

During the glorious thirty a cultural response to modernization took place not only in rural zones but also throughout the country. This reaction assumes the form of a collective imaginary of the bon paysan that in turn drove a collective longing for what this loss represented — a romanticized world of work and order in tune with the cycles of nature. Rural dwellers and urbanites alike internalized this notion, regarding the French agrarian world as a separate and pure domain. Many believed this domain should remain distinct in custom and habit from the rest of the country (Hervieu 1993, 7).

In the 1970s events such as the circulation of the Club of Rome's *The Limits of Growth: A Report on the Predicament of Mankind* (1972) and the energy crisis in 1973 led Europeans to engage in a collective reappraisal of the industrialized West. Many writers, filmmakers, and cultural critics began to challenge Europe's frenetic postwar drive for modernization (Boissevain 1994). A renewed interest in French history, traditional sites and rituals, folk museums, and foods caused a commoditization of nostalgia, which culminated in an explosion of a veritable "heritage industry" (Hewison 1987). A vibrant wing of this heritage industry is France's popular cinematic endeavors that celebrate an idealized French rural past. In 1962, during the period leading up to the glorious thirty, French author Marcel Pagnol created the classic *Jean de Florette*. This wildly popular novel presents a rural France frozen in time, saturated with imagery of idealized village life and traditional rural values. It was the basis for two films, *Jean de Florette* and *Manon des sources* (Manon of the Spring), both made in 1986 by Claude Berri. The second film again took up this romantic thread, invoking the innocence and wholesomeness of French countryside, personified by the character Manon.

This character symbolizes the idealized traditional French virgin from a time gone by. The popularity of more contemporary films by Yves Robert, such as *My Father's Glory* and *My Mother's Castle* (1990), speaks to the ongoing commodification of French nostalgia that gained momentum during this third transition. A great irony of contemporary French romanticism is that at the precise moment that French (and international) publics celebrate an idealized agrarian past, French agricultural policy takes decisive action to dramatically transform France's rural world. Within a matter of years, France dispossesses itself of most of its smallholders.

The JAC: Politicizing Farm Youths

Crucial to transforming the paysan into the agriculteur was the emergence of another form of governance, the rise of a Catholic popular youth movement. This movement encouraged rural youths to pressure those of the older generation to adopt new farming and business methods. A group of Jesuit priests formed the Jeunnesse Agricole Chrétienne (JAC) in 1929. This dynamic alliance between politically progressive religious clergy, agrarian youths, and Marxist intellectuals constituted both a formal member-based organization and a broader movement. While some youths were intensely engaged with running and participating in the organization for several years, others moved informally in and through the milieu created by the organization, experiencing the alliance as more of a social movement. The organization sought to provide rural youths with a new set of expectations for their own agricultural identities and practices. This distinctive organization blended religious and modernist ideologies to promote an industrial model of agricultural development among rural youths — the children of both wealthy and poorer farmers. This movement was the result of collaboration between Jesuit priests and the state-run École Supérieure d'Agriculture d'Angers (Agricultural School of Angers) in central France (Chavagne 1988). What made the organization special in French history was its emergence outside traditional religious, union, or political forums. Even though it was autonomous from the Catholic Church, this youth-based organization appealed to traditional religious and familial values by promoting its modernist rural agenda. The group did break with the church's traditional missionary style, but it still relied heavily on discourses of traditional Catholicism in its attempt to modernize agricultural and rural life.

The JAC gave rise to a set of discourses that is intriguingly Janus-faced: while promoting an instrumental rationality of agriculture that valued productivism and entrepreneurship, it also promoted a solidaire rationality of agriculture. In the case of the latter, the group appealed to notions of humanism, mutualism, and internationalism, drawn both from Marxist discourse and from more traditional Catholic values of brotherhood and collectivity. From within the seed of these two rationalities, two political tendencies sprang forth. While one leaned toward a more instrumental form of agricultural productivism, the another strived for a solidaire antiproductivist approach to agriculture that led in turn to the formation of the new paysan movements and the Confédération Paysanne.

The JAC: Promoting a Solidaire Rationality

The JAC thus blended Catholic and Marxist discourses to promote ideas of technological progress, human equality, and internationalism. By encouraging modern technology to be a vehicle through which to do "God's work," the leaders of this movement framed human labor as supporting the elevation of humanity itself. Even as they regarded many French rural traditions and values as parochial, JAC members promoted farming as a modern profession. Youths began to challenge stereotypes of farmers as paysans, a romanticized and often pejorative term that had become synonymous with the idea of a *plouc*, roughly synonymous with *country bumpkin*, the stigmatizing term in the United States. Drawing from a missionary idiom, agrarian youths began to reframe the farmer as a righteous provider, feeding and uplifting his brethren while working the land (Launey 1983). The organization promoted a literal reading of the biblical Genesis that established the farmer as an extension of God's arm. Key leaders (many of whom were priests) also advanced a solidaire rationality of agriculture by appealing to Marxist notions regarding the relationship among technology, progress, and social justice.

Bernard Lambert was a member of the movement in his youth, later going on to cofound a new paysan movement. According to Lambert, modernizing the family farm constituted a moral obligation that was linked to social justice. The idea of modern progress represented the chance for humanity to escape unnecessary toil and physical suffering (Chavagne 1988, 34). In addition to providing a new identity for young people in rural areas, the JAC also provided new travel opportunities for agricultural youth. Whereas journeying beyond one's village or region was rare for many farm families, youth missionaries from the organization promoted the slogan "Voir, juger, agir" (See, judge, act), encouraging the idea of visiting other lands. Organization leaders presented travel as a modern virtue. Seeing other towns and villages was a way to compare and understand different worlds beyond one's own rural vista. For the first time, young people of sixteen or seventeen ventured beyond their villages to attend organization gatherings and meet youths in other villages or even relatively far-off regions of the country (Duby and Wallon 1977, 26).

By engaging with movement literature, these youths became familiar with a confrontational political sensibility, one that emphasized notions of human equality and social revolution. Notions of a dynamic and changing social movement flew in the face of traditional French discourse about rural peoples. Such discourses emphasized the idea of an unchangeable and eternal agrarian order and peasantry — notions that were popularized during the Third Republic. Through the JAC rural youths were exposed to humanist thinkers such as Simone Weil, Jacques Maritain, and Emmanuel Mounier. In addition, they encountered the writings of Marx and other Leftist theorists traditionally associated in France with the urban world (Hervieu 1993). The JAC encouraged youths to see themselves as agents of social change. The organization also provided forums in which they could speak for themselves, independent of clerical or scholarly intermediaries. Young people gradually challenged the static view of rural life, proposing the idea of a dynamic modern rural world that is open to society. For many, the old rural world represented a domain closed in on itself, separate from the rest of society. The organization's central goal (echoed later by the Confédération Paysanne) was to establish farmers as a sector continuous with the rest of society. Young people in the movement sought to be considered as full citizens, complete social and political members of society (Duby and Wallon 1977, 28).

Following World War II, France industrialized its agricultural system, bringing into being a new set of practices that included investment in farm machinery and chemicalized agriculture. Taking the government's lead, the JAC encouraged rural youths to regard themselves as entrepreneurs in a capitalist system integrated into an industrial economy. They increasingly promoted calculative cost-benefits logic. Organization leaders supported youths in studying business at local universities or by taking correspondence courses at public agricultural colleges. Such practices often engendered conflict between youths and an older agrarian generation unfamiliar with a modern business mentality.

This shift to a more entrepreneurial mentality among these new rural youths was accompanied by a discursive shift as well. Rejecting the old-fashioned paysan, young people identified with the government's agenda to see themselves as chef de l'entreprise. These terms, associated with professionalism and investment capital, express a collective attempt to redefine the farmer as a part of a modern capitalist sector who is integrated into other entrepreneurial and professional domains (Parodi 1981).

POSTWAR AGRICULTURAL UNIONIZING

While the second transition ushered in the JAC, it also marked the beginning of a new era of agricultural unionizing. Increasingly, farmers' unions began to play a major role in informing French agricultural policy. After 1944, the minister of agriculture, François Tanguy-Prigent, restructured France's agricultural unions. First, he dissolved La Corporation Paysanne (The Peasant Corporation), a farmers' union that was a vestige of the Vichy regime — the French political body that collaborated with Nazi powers during the German occupation. In addition to being associated with the stigmatized Vichy regime, La Corporation Paysanne was also dominated by the conservative lobby of grain producers driven by the agricultural Right. Wanting to distance himself and the face of French agriculture from La Corporation Paysanne, Tanguy-Prigent welcomed the foundation of the Fédération Nationale des Syndicats Exploitants Agriculteurs (FNSEA; National Federation of Agricultural Unions). The FNSEA was seen by the French public as an exemplary agricultural union created by farmers active in wartime resistance movements (Baron 1997, 5). Soon, the FNSEA was able to discredit La Corporation Paysanne by highlighting its shameful association with the Vichy regime. In so doing, the FNSEA subsequently became the sole recognized majoritarian farmers' union in France. It was the only union recognized by major farming cooperatives and lending institutions such as the Crédit Agricole (Agricultural Credit) and Mutualité Agricole (Mutual of Agriculture) (Parodi 1981). Today the FNSEA still remains the majoritarian and most powerful agricultural union in France, representing the primary opponent of the Confédération Paysanne. In 1957, the FNSEA created a youth wing of the union for farmers thirty-five and younger called the Confédération National des Jeunes Agriculteurs (CNJA; National Confederation of Young Farmers).

Founded by members of the JAC, the CNJA became the youth podium within the FNSEA. It is in the CNJA that young farmers throughout France begin to promote their modernist and Leftist-progressive agenda.

During the second transition, yet another form of governmentality emerged: the introduction of the first Lois D'Orientation Agricole (Agricultural Orientation Laws). In 1960 and 1962, French statesman and president Charles de Gaulle, along with the minister of agriculture, Edgar Pisani, implemented the Agricultural Orientation Laws to further fortify techniques of rural governance. As instances of what Foucault would call "knowledge power" (1976), these laws were linguistic interventions that built on the trend of disciplining and disenfranchizing the French smallholder. Promoting discourses of improving the efficiency and productivity of industrialized French agriculture, the Agricultural Orientation Laws reduced the number of agricultural workers, explicitly asserting the inferiority of small farms in terms of productivity. The Agricultural Orientation Laws provided heftier subsidies for large-scale growers while also encouraging greater specialization in farm products and methods. France increased its production of raw materials tailored for its burgeoning agro-foods industry. As the size of farms grew, the numbers of farmers dropped dramatically. During the early 1960s, unemployed agricultural workers began to leave rural areas for cities, such as Marseille and Paris, to find work in burgeoning automobile and electronics industries (Parodi 1981).

The creation of the Agricultural Orientation Laws also marks the beginning of a French agricultural era dominated by the FNSEA and the union that served as its youth wing (the CNJA). From this time forward, these unions would be recognized as key stakeholders in designing and implementing French agricultural policy. In just a few years, these unions greatly informed policies made by the ministry of agriculture and played a key role in determining the educational and technical orientation of national agricultural universities. Through the support of these dominant industrial agricultural unions, French agricultural policy generally began to assume a productivist or industrial orientation.

On the European level, agricultural governance had tremendous implications for French agriculture, which furthered the near eradication of smallholders. In 1957 several European countries signed the Treaty of Rome, which established the Common Agricultural Policy (Politique Agricole Commune), whose primary purpose is to facilitate the circulation of agricultural products throughout member-states and determine farm subsidy policy. Like the U.S. farm bill, the Common Agricultural Policy has the power to contour not only farm size and farm methods but also the very crops that will be grown on European soil. By the 1960s the Common Agricultural Policy had reconfigured French agriculture. As large-scale farmers began to receive larger subsidies and lower-interest loans, smallholders diminished to an increasingly vulnerable minority in the agricultural landscape, unable to compete on the European market.

The Rise of the New Paysan Movements

The third transition began in the 1970s, a time when many internal contradictions associated with the glorious thirty surfaced. In particular, there was a growing contradiction between production and overproduction associated with postindustrial agriculture. The modernist ideal of agricultural development was once synonymous solely with notions of increased production. Now the modernist objective is to manage overproduction associated with increased productivity in the postwar decades.

It is worth noting that at this time the FNSEA contained members who were both general small farmers and members of the JAC. Individuals within these groups struggled to make sense of their places within the larger productivist FNSEA. In particular, they sought to untangle contradictions associated with the Common Agricultural Policy, which promoted productivist large-scale farming. Out of these contradictions emerged the new paysan-identified movements. Above all, the third transition is characterized yet again by a dramatic drop in the number of remaining farmers. At the beginning of the twentieth century, half of the French population worked in agriculture. By the close of World War II, a third of the population was engaged in farming. Just ten years later, in 1955, only a quarter of the French population occupied the agriculture sector, and in 1962, it was just a fifth. Over the next thirty years, between 1962 and 1992, the number of farmers plummeted to a mere 5 percent of the population. Today the number currently hovers around 2 percent of the population (Hervieu 1996a, 9).

This latter period also sees an increasingly aging agricultural population. For every young person entering the profession each year, four farmers retire. Over one-third of all French farmers are older than fifty-five. And only half of French farmers today earn a wage that allows them to farm full time.

These remaining farmers are obliged to work part time in the industrial, retail, or service sectors. The productivity of French farms has also changed dramatically. In 1993, there were eight hundred thousand farms in France—an impressive number. But of those farms, only 20 percent produced two-thirds of the overall national production. In other words, a small number of large-scale farms produce most of France's agricultural materials.

In 1993, 5 percent of French farms (totaling more than 130 hectares) cultivated more than one-fourth of France's Surface Agricole Utile (Utilized Agricultural Area) (Hervieu 1996a, 9). In France, since the 1960s, small-holders stimulate public debate about how the nation's "surface agricole"—or agricultural areas—should be utilized. According to many small-scale farmers, French farmland should be distributed according to a logic of solidarity rather than profit-driven productivity. Within a logic of solidarity, many small farms would democratize the "surface agricole." As farms became larger and fewer, agriculture's primary objective shifted. For the entirety of France's agricultural history, the goal of farming was to produce foods for domestic consumption. But in a postindustrial agricultural condition, farmers are called upon to supply food surpluses that serve as materials for the French agro-foods industry. In addition, postindustrial farmers (mainly smallholders) engage in multifunctional activities such as caretaking the countryside and protecting spaces deemed natural and cultural (e.g., country roads, streams, or centuries-old churches or walls) (Bodiguel 1975).

All of these changes in agricultural scale, production methods, and subsidy and loan practices led to sets of internal contradictions within the FNSEA. By the 1970s, many smallholders who had come of age in the JAC movement no longer felt a sense of unity with large-scale producers in the FNSEA. Increasingly, former JAC members such as a future key Confédération Paysanne leader Guy Le Fur began to challenge union policies that they perceived as ignoring disparities of wealth between small- and large-scale farmers (Guy Le Fur, personal communication, October 27, 1999). The JAC promised that the modernization of French agriculture would benefit all farmers. While some in the organization went on to establish large and viable modern farming enterprises, many smallholders were unable to follow this trajectory. Instead these farmers found themselves struggling to keep their small farms alive in the face of increasing debt to national lending agencies, and they were forced to sell off lands that had been in their families for centuries (Guy Le Fur, personal communication, April 9, 1999).

It was in this third transition that many smallholders began to interrogate the révolution silencieuse that reconfigured the French agricultural landscape into one dominated by productivist ideology. Smallholders began to question modernist discourses of the large-scale agriculteur as well as French and European agricultural policy. When looking back on their years in the JAC, many Confédération Paysanne members today often describe both positive and negative feelings. While some say that the organization opened young people to new people and experiences, others describe it as a propaganda machine that pushed rural youths toward modern farming approaches, encouraging them to pressure their parents and grandparents to do so as well (Guy Le Fur, personal communication, April 11, 1999). The farmers who went on to found the Confédération Paysanne were smallholders within the FNSEA who were increasingly disenchanted by an industrial-modernist discourse on agriculture generally. They came to reject an agro-foods industry they perceived as imposing a new reorganization of labor and increasing debt. Consequently, they began to look elsewhere for a new analysis of and vision for agricultural life (Confédération Paysanne 1998, 3).

BERNARD LAMBERT: THE RISE OF THE PEASANT WORKER

During this period of interrogation, a former member of the JAC, Bernard Lambert, began to articulate an antiproductivist discourse by criticizing the FNSEA for failing to address disparities of government subsidies, bank loans, and land distribution among small- and large-scale farmers (Chavagne 1988). In 1970, Lambert published a pamphlet, "Les paysans dans la lutte des classes" (Peasants and class struggle), that articulated the links between capital, agri-business, and the predicament of newly self-identified paysans. In Lambert's writings we see the beginnings of a new kind of Leftist paysan-identified discourse that laid the groundwork for the discourse from new paysan movements and the Confédération Paysanne that emerged in the mid-1980s. In particular, Lambert clearly articulates the theme of the paysan as part of a broader international struggle of workers, both industrial and agricultural. In a pamphlet he wrote for the Confédération Paysanne in 1968, Lambert states, "A different international division of labor is indeed possible; it will involve industrial as well as agricultural products. The redistribution of wealth, work, and the fruits of our labor will be more rational under a socialist system . . . and this [system] will be neither just nor possible until it is global. All struggles against capitalism, regardless of their size, all lead to the ultimate realization of this goal." That same year, Lambert and other members of the FNSEA's youth wing formed the paysan-based union Paysans-Travailleurs (Paysan-Workers). The Paysans-Travailleurs's slogan, "La terre, outil de travail" (The land, our working tool), signals Lambert's attempt to express solidarity with other workers' movements that were burgeoning at the time. The cover of the Paysans-Travailleurs' journal, *Vent d'Ouest* (West wind), in February 1970 read, "La terre notre outil, le lait, et tous nos produits, notre revenu, voila ce que nous devons défender pour vivre" (The land is our tool, milk and all of our products are our revenue, thus we must protect these things in order to live). In Paysans-Travailleurs actors redefined farming in Marxist terms, signaling a dramatic departure from the discourse associated with the JAC. Paysans-Travailleurs clearly flagged the emergence of a new kind of explicitly paysan identity, an attempt to reclaim and redefine the term, positing it against modernist terms promoted by the FNSEA such as *exploitant* (business operator) or *chef de l'entreprise*. Reclaiming the term *paysan* was a clear strategic move on the part of Lambert and Paysans-Travailleurs. By fusing notions of the paysan and the worker, the union redefined the farmer as part of a larger workers' struggle while also restoring value to the idea of the premodern paysan living and working independently of investment capital, a global market, and an agro-foods industry. Central to the agenda of the Paysans-Travailleurs was the idea of the paysan's right to work. According to those in the Paysans-Travailleurs, paysans had a right to work as farmers that superseded the right to private property. In particular, members of Paysans-Travailleurs fought for a right to sufficient lands, earnings, and levels of production needed to sustain what they called the paysan way of life.

In 1972, the year of a major strike over milk in France, the Paysans-Travailleurs formally broke with the youth wing of the FNSEA — and with the FNSEA itself. In so doing, the union claimed that there were irreconcilable differences between the antiproductivist agenda of Paysans-Travailleurs and the industrial agricultural unions. It is worth noting that not all paysan-identified farmers broke with the industrial agricultural unions. Many individuals continued to remain within the FNSEA, attempting to reform it from within by creating pressure groups such as Interpaysanne (Inter Peasants), an internal paysan pressure group. For a time, such groups provided paysan-identified farmers within FNSEA a space for critical internal debate and discussion. Ultimately, those working within pressure groups grew frustrated by their efforts. Many were weary of fighting what they saw as a losing battle and joined the antiproductivist paysan unions that were steadily gaining force around the country.

MAY 1968 TO THE LARZAC: TOWARD A NEW SOCIAL MOVEMENT

The new paysan movements were strongly influenced by the events of May 1968, which brought together students, workers, and, ultimately, farmers with a potent critique of postwar capitalism (Confédération Paysanne 1997, 72). In May 1968, France saw the biggest general strike the country had ever seen. The events began in Paris as students at Université de Nanterre (Nanterre University) protested problems of overcrowding and neglected infrastructure. Protests also centered on questions of sensibility: by promoting a more solidaire or mutualistic rationality, students openly rejected a perceived hierarchical structure of the university system. As student protests unfolded, workers from across the country were inspired to join forces with students to contest unfair wages and working conditions. Industrial production throughout the country stood still for three weeks as trade union committees occupied factories across the country. The entire town of Nantes in western France was governed by a trade union committee that negotiated terms of industrial and agricultural production. Farmers there were central to the May events in Nantes as they negotiated, for instance, the price of foods they had produced themselves. For a short time farmers had the autonomy to determine their own wages and the value of their products.

Many in the JAC saw connections between their own struggles and those of the striking students and workers. From 1968 onward, a new kind of paysan-identified activism emerged that brought the new paysan movements together into a coalition with a variety of new actors, including workers, traditional sheep farmers, antinuclear activists, and war resisters (Bové 2001).

In 1973, Bernard Lambert (former member of JAC) joined coalition-based movements such as the Larzac (named for the Causse du Larzac plateau), in southern France. The Larzac was a movement in which local sheep farmers resisted the French military's plan to expand a military base. This enlarged military operation was to stand on farmland crucial to raising sheep for ewe's milk — necessary for the production of Roquefort cheese (Bové 2000). It is worth noting that Roquefort cheese has controlled origin status, meaning that it derives its brand and value from the geological and meteorological features of a relatively small region of a rocky and arid plateau in southern

France. By increasing the base from three thousand to seventeen thousand hectares, the military threatened to destroy the Roquefort producers' livelihoods. Desperate for support, Larzac smallholders did something they had never done before: these previously nonpolitical farmers asked for the assistance of actors (many of whom were nonfarmers) from outside their local agrarian world. They reached out to groups of radical young paysan farmers, such as Bernard Lambert and members of Paysans-Travailleurs. These actors were more than willing to support the Larzac farmers in their struggle. Slowly a coalition formed consisting of local sheep farmers, members of Paysans-Travailleurs, and machinists from a local watch factory. In addition, sets of politicized antiwar resisters joined the struggle. These actors were mainly conscientious objectors and army deserters who opposed France's military policy during those years. Many of these antiwar activists were deeply affected by the events of May 1968 and felt generally disenfranchised from the French socioeconomic system that had since swung back in a conservative direction. Among these war resisters was José Bové, only seventeen years of age when he joined the Larzac struggle.

At the height of the movement, a network of more than two hundred Larzac committees circulated throughout France as well as Germany and Great Britain. From the movement's beginning, it was simply called the Larzac, and it continues to be referred to as such today. While resisting the government's assertion that there would be no new construction on Larzac lands, the Larzac movement initiated a two-year project to build a sheep barn out of stone — on land designated for a military base — using collective construction methods associated with the region's history. This building project grew out of a network of an otherwise disparate group of actors: local farmers, paysans, factory workers, and antiwar resisters.

In 1975 Larzac farmers encouraged the paysans from Paysans-Travailleurs and the antiwar resisters to take over empty farms not yet occupied by the army. As the people remained on the land, many transformed themselves into radical sheep farmers (Bové was one of them). These actors began to see protecting the production of ewe's milk for Roquefort cheese as an act of political resistance to militarism and the dominance of industrial agriculture. These farmers illegally occupied and worked the sheep farms for five years. Finally, in 1980, the new Socialist government under President Mitterrand succumbed to popular pressure and granted the farmers ownership of the land. To this day, most of the original antimilitary activists who occupied the Larzac land still work there, producing ewe's milk for Roquefort cheese (Bové 2001). This crosspollination of movements went both ways. As antiwar activists took up the struggles of small farmers, paysan farmers also joined the struggle against nuclear energy and militarism. From 1974 to 1980 farmers in the new paysan movements joined antinuclear protests in Brittany, illustrating the links between capital, agri-business, and nuclear power (Bové 2001).

The new paysan movements that led to the Confédération Paysanne constituted an eclectic mix of political and spiritual philosophies. Many French youths touched by 1968 were influenced by anarcho-syndicalist ideas associated with Peter Kropotkin, Michael Bakunin, and Pierre Proudhon. They were also influenced by the anarchists of the Spanish Civil War, many of whom immigrated to southern France after the war and joined the movement. These influences are significant because they point to a Leftist, but not solely Marxist, approach to social and political change. Although there was a distinct presence of labor and work discourse at this time, there was also something new emerging that surpassed a labor-centered model of organizing.

As Nash (2005) suggests, social movements surface in diverse cultural settings as new actors invent novel expressions for their causes. These new alignments of actors assumed global proportions in subsequent decades as French paysans came to understand their struggle in increasingly international terms. The new social movement associated with the Larzac was deeply antiauthoritarian, critiquing not just hierarchies of class but all forms of hierarchy. This eclectic movement included groups of disenfranchised students as well as unemployed youths who saw a bleak future for themselves under the status quo (Aubineau 1997). Also special to this new French social movement was its reliance on a discourse of nonviolence. While the new paysan movements were first influenced largely by a blend of Catholicism and Marxist theory, their vision expanded during this time to synthesize strategies associated with new social movements in the United States, such as the civil rights, antiwar, and ecology movements. Many in the Larzac movement identified with the pacifist philosophy associated with Tolstoy, Gandhi, Martin Luther King Jr., and César Chávez (of the U.S.-based movement of Mexican farmworkers).

The Larzac had a distinctively postindustrial sensibility. Each group within the movement shared a sense of disempowerment by the rapid industrialization of the country. Some in the movement challenged the industrialized agricultural sector. They saw it as ruinous to a robust rural way of life for French paysans. Unemployed and disenfranchised youths in the Larzac fought against a postindustrial French landscape. Having relocated much of its industrial infrastructure to the Global South (where labor is cheaper), France now presented a bleak future for rural and urban youths who could not even look to the industrial factory as a site in which to build an economic future for themselves and their families.

FARM CRISES AND REORGANIZATION

While the 1970s saw the emergence of exciting new political networks in France, it was also a decade dominated by a series of agricultural crises that intensified already existing tensions between small- and large-scale farmers. These crises enhanced a paysan-identified consciousness that demanded rights to land and farm subsidies while critiquing an industrial and export-based agricultural system. The year 1976 was particularly hard on paysans. French wine growers faced price drops due to an influx of imports from Algeria and Italy brought about by postindustrial trade deregulation. Drought in the north and west of France plunged many small farmers into deep debt to agricultural cooperatives and national lending agencies, such as Crédit Agricole. At the peak of the crisis in 1978, a former member of the JAC, Jean Cadott, conducted a hunger strike against Crédit Agricole. Invoking the Gandhian tradition, Cadott mobilized hundreds of paysans in the Ancones region, which in turn led to the formation of a protest group called "Des paysans et la dette" (Farmers in debt) (Confédération Paysanne 1997, 9). In 1980, French paysans confronted yet another crisis. Two farmers in the south of France had made a public complaint regarding their cooperative's demand that they use banned hormone-based feed. In response, the consumers' union called for a nationwide boycott of veal from France. Within eight days the price of the meat plummeted, devastating paysans for whom problems of overproduction had already led to severe price drops.

Lambert and Paysans-Travailleurs played a key role in framing and articulating the struggle. In particular, Lambert was able to link the problem of hormone-based feed to a broader question of industrialized agriculture. In 1981 Lambert wrote in a pamphlet called "Vent d'Ouest," "Veal production is just one example; all intensive production follows the same schema." The veal crisis represented a major turning point in the new paysan movements.

For the first time, paysans understood the potential impacts that consumer groups could have on the agricultural market. Increasingly, the new paysan movements would try to ally themselves with consumer groups by coordinating campaigns together and adopting consumer discourse on quality that would be taken up again by the Confédération Paysanne.

LEAVING THE FNSEA: A NEW ERA OF ORGANIZING

During this period of crisis, paysans who had remained within the FNSEA stepped up their contestation to the union's policies. Tensions reached a crescendo in 1978 when the FNSEA expelled members of Interpaysanne, accusing them of having an incompatible agenda. For many in the new paysan movements, the expulsion of Interpaysanne members crystallized the need to form a new majoritarian agricultural union outside the FNSEA. In June 1981, local and regional Paysans-Travailleurs groups who had broken with the FNSEA came together to form the first national union of paysans, called the Confédération National des Syndicats Paysans (National Confederation of Paysan Unions). The next year they established a second paysan-based union, the Federation National des Syndicats Paysans (National Federation of Paysan Unions). By 1983 this new union represented a significant counterpower to the FNSEA, polling 15 percent of the seats in the chamber of agriculture.

For the founders of these new paysan unions, the FNSEA came to represent the symbol of industrial agriculture. For many, the FNSEA was an accomplice to the French and European subsidy apparatus. It was also perceived as integral to the French agro-foods industry, industrially oriented cooperatives, export agriculture, and major lending institutions that deprive paysans of adequate capital to remain solvent (Confédération Paysanne 1997). In 1980, despite their differences, the two new national paysan unions joined forces with the FNSEA to contest the quota system for milk production across Europe. The quota system represented Europe's attempt to resolve problems of overproduction that had been mounting since the mid-1970s. All three unions demanded an exemption for small-scale dairy farmers (those producing less than one hundred thousand liters annually), asserting small farmers' rights to production and requesting that the quotas be directed toward large-scale producers (Confédération Paysanne 1997, 7). Despite their efforts, the milk quotas of the 1980s led to a dramatic restructuring of the French dairy world. As members of the new paysan movements predicted, in just ten years half of milk producers in France disappeared (Pochon 1997). By imposing production limits regardless of farm size, milk quotas devastated small dairy farms that depended exclusively on milk production for survival. Following the milk crisis, the new paysan movements focused on problems of land rights and investment capital (problems mainly related to farm size and scale), as well as on general problems associated with overproduction.

THEORIZING THE NEW PAYSAN MOVEMENTS: POLITICAL ECOLOGY, SCIENCE STUDIES, AND SOCIAL MOVEMENT THEORY

It is valuable to look at the rise of the new paysan movements through a theoretical lens. In particular, political ecology, science studies, and social movement theory may enhance an understanding of the new paysan movements. These theoretical approaches are also central to understanding the Confédération Paysanne and other international movements. The first theoretical approach that I find central to this study is political ecology. As a subfield within anthropology, political ecology transfers nineteenth-century-based ecological thinking into a contemporary context (see Blaike and Brookfield 1987; Escobar 1996b; Leff 1995; Peet and Watts 1993, 1996; Raymond 1998; Raymond and Bailey 1997; Robbins 2004; Rocheleau 1995; Wolf 1972; Yapa 1996). Contemporary trends such as transnational capital, identity politics associated with new social movements, and rising awareness of ecological problems have created a need for innovative ways to contextualize ecology in an ever-changing cultural, political, and global landscape (Paulson and Gezon 2005).

In France, groups such as the Larzac, the new paysan movements, and the Confédération Paysanne are not generally framed in ecological terms. The domesticated nature that constitutes agriculture worlds is what Neil Smith refers to as a "socialized nature" (1981). Ecological discourse that focuses on nature per se is not native to France. Instead, agrarian social movements are seen as struggles over land, work, and quality of life rather than disputes over nature. Despite the fact that actors in this study do not see themselves in ecological terms, the framework of political ecology is crucial to locating the struggles over land and agriculture in a transnational context (see Thomas-Slayter and Rocheleau 1995; Walker 2005). Political ecology encourages us to position social movements that emerge around agriculture within international contexts of institutional power. In France we see how groups such as the Confédération Paysanne engage supranational agencies such as the

World Trade Organization, the World Bank, and the International Monetary Fund—as well as a host of nongovernmental organizations around the world (Robbins 2004).

I draw from a specific trend within political ecology to interpret the events discussed here. Poststructuralist political ecology (see Escobar 1992, 1996a, 1996b, 1998, 2002, 2005a) analyzes social interactions within rural zones by integrating a post-Marxist perspective with a poststructuralism informed by Foucault's notions of discourse, power, and governmentality. By post-Marxist I mean that my analysis of paysans, for instance, extends beyond orthodox Marxism to understand how they negotiate forms of power that lie past centralized domains such as the state and capital. In this story power is a dispersed thing, circulating through networks that include civil society actors (such as paysans or consumer groups) as well as the rural spaces in which actors generate, contest, and accommodate conditions of everyday life. Poststructural political ecology owes much to Foucauldian-based discourse theory. Drawing from this approach, I contextualize language and action within fields of political and economic power. I pay attention to the ways in which actors such as paysans or government officials construct their discourses about farming, GMOs, and everyday life. Politicized discourse analysis provides critical insight into the collaborative worldviews of actors negotiating particular cultural and political terrains.

In investigating the French case, I look to political ecologists such as Lakshman Yapa (1996), who demonstrates the discursive dimension of agricultural practices. According to Yapa, the Green Revolution, as a product of development discourse, promoted notions of "miracle seeds," hybrid seeds that promised to dramatically increase productivity in the Global South and put an end to hunger. For Yapa, these seeds embody "the paradigms of development and the epistemology of poverty" (1996, 70), as well as the social relations of production embedded in the seeds' production. In a similar fashion, the genetically modified organisms that circulate through this book tell stories about the beliefs, values, and practices of the corporations, scientists, and farmers who produce them. Stories about GMOs echo those of the Green Revolution. Actors are moved to see GMOs as vital and central to agricultural development.

For the political ecologist Dianne Rocheleau, rural spaces are always discursively inscribed with social relations (1995). As Rocheleau suggests, struggles over agriculture are never purely conflicts over resources. In the

French case, paysans' struggles for land are always deeply rooted in sets of cultural values about small-scale agricultural practice, social solidarity, and notions about how and when to engage with social movements or unions. The political ecologist Arturo Escobar (1996a) locates contemporary actors' understandings of rural realities that can be contextualized within a post-industrial condition. For Escobar, paysans' defense of cultural rights associated with traditional farming practices represents resistance to what Escobar calls the "eruption of the biological" (1998, 85). This explosion emerges at a moment of history in which capital and technoscience bodies target biological realms such as agriculture (or biodiversity) as key sites for capital accumulation (Rabinow 1996). Escobar is particularly interested in exploring the discursive features of political ecology. In much of his work, he examines how government and corporate bodies deploy discourses about rural zones that veil or normalize their agendas in order to discreetly marshal control over resources, groups of peoples, and land areas. I examine how various actors frame their narratives about land and agriculture, always noting the ways in which particular sets of political, economic, and cultural commitments and priorities are embedded in actors' discursive strategies. Discourses on sustainable agriculture provide a good example of the kind of discursive veiling that occurs as actors construct politically motivated narratives about agriculture. For Escobar, discourses on sustainable agriculture conceal the desires of powerful institutions to sustain capital, rather than land areas engaged in particular forms of agriculture (1996a, 49). By producing new ways to understand land areas as places needing-to-be-sustained, powerful institutions such as corporate and regulatory agencies normalize their own instrumental practices that are designed to protect the very land areas that they place in peril.

I also glean insight into the French case by looking to the work of the political ecologist Enrique Leff (1995). His discussion of "alternative production rationalities" clarifies how communities engender locally specific meanings surrounding their own production practices. I draw on Leff's insights as I examine the ways in which paysans and other smallholders construct alternative production rationalities — rationalities of solidarity — that justify the existence of paysans in an industrial agricultural system that renders their work expendable. According to Leff, within every instance of production, agricultural or otherwise, there is a societal rationality at play. I hope to render these sets of rationalities transparent, revealing ways of seeing the world that are always embedded in actors' agricultural practices. I am drawn to a poststructural approach to political ecology because it is explicitly anti-essentialist. According to these theorists, there is no single universal understanding of nature or agriculture, because each set of actors articulates its own meanings. Escobar's idea of the "plurality of natures" is particularly useful as I navigate through the many different cultural understandings of land, rural spaces, and agriculture that surface in the French story (1996b, 4). According to Escobar, an antiessentialist approach is "a necessary condition for understanding and radicalizing the field of contemporary social struggles over the biological and the cultural" (4). The plurality of notions of rural life among actors in this story are always embedded in social struggles over agriculture.

A politically engaged science studies framework is central to understanding the peoples and things that constitute social movements (Woodhouse et al. 2002). One particular science studies approach, actor-network theory (ANT), is generally used to examine processes of technoscientific innovation. I find this framework useful in mapping the various entities that both produce and circulate through social movements generally. ANT is an epistemological framework developed by Bruno Latour, Michele Callon, and John Law (see Latour 1986, 1987, 1988a, 1988b, 1991; Callon 1986a, 1986b, 1987, 1997; Law 1987, 1992; Law and Hassard 1999). Exclusive to this approach is its attempt to transcend the realist-constructivist binary by asserting that the world cannot be reduced to either real (material) or socially constructed (cultural) components of networks that constitute social movements. I look to ANT to shed light on the material and cultural artifacts that helped shape the struggle surrounding GMOs in France. ANT sheds light on the universe of organisms, tools, and other nonhuman entities that often present unanticipated effects and consequences within social movements. ANT is unique in that it rests on a notion of symmetry—the idea that all networks are animated in a mutualistic fashion by sets of both human and nonhuman actors. In this story, some nonhuman actors (actants) assume the form of inorganic tools, texts, technologies, and objects related to technoscience and agriculture. Other actants may be organic in nature, such as genetically modified cells, seeds, and plants that constitute GMOs. Yet other actants in this study are particular foodstuffs, such as Roquefort cheese, which played a powerful role coproducing the series of events that led to the Confédération Paysanne's rise to popular attention. The French GMO controversy could not have unfolded without the key actants that surfaced, often posing surprising and inscrutable effects. These actants' ambiguity and their ability to instill uncertainty into the hearts and minds of their antagonists helped make this whole story possible.

Notions of actants and symmetry — central to ANT — provide those who study social movements an alternative from the circular nature of social constructivism (see Latour 1998). Social constructivism frees us from a deterministic and essentialist worldview, one that sees cultural phenomena as the effect of biological or historical law. Yet social constructivism has a shortcoming. If we see all cultural phenomena as representing merely the effects of social action (activity driven by humans), then we confront the fallacy of circular reasoning: if social phenomena generate more social phenomena, how do we explain the heterogeneous and complex nature of social phenomena that lies beyond the realm of human action? The idea of symmetry allows us to bring discussions of social movements beyond social constructivism. By appealing to notions of symmetry, we look at how actants that lie (at least partially) outside human realms of control and determinacy affect the nature and outcome of social movements.

There is thus symmetry between the farmer planting the genetically modified corn seed (the seed itself as well as the chemical inputs sold in a kitlike system along with that seed). The farmer, the GM seed, and the agrochemicals, together, coproduce GM corn. Other sets of actors and actants in this symmetrical story include the science lab, the scientist, the corporation producing the seed, and the state bodies making policy about GMOs. Also part of this social movement network are the paysans that contest GMOs. ANT also rests on an appreciation of the inseparability of notions such as science and technology. The term *technoscience* is often invoked within ANT as a way to express the overlapping nature of scientific and technological enterprises. A GMO is constituted by scientists and laboratories, as well as by myriad technological instruments and microorganisms. GMOs constitute technoscientific entities.

While ANT has been criticized for being economistic and managerial (Singleton and Michael 1993), some also deem it apolitical (Star 1991). By attributing degrees of agency to nonhuman actants devoid of human responsibility, critics assert that the framework supports a worldview based on ethical relativism. I will follow an argument by John Law that suggests that when human actors take action, they always act politically (Law 1992). While actants such as GMOs or Roquefort cheese do not operate autonomously in an ethical-political field, the human actors engaging with these actants are always doing so in a context of social hierarchy, inequality, and geopolitical power. ANT helped me to pose a set of key ethnographic questions that are deeply political and ethical in nature. I do not ever suggest that genetically modified seeds act alone. As this story clearly explains, all GMOs are co-produced by human actors and nonhuman actants that always exist within fields of power. It is up to those who use ANT to take a critical and political stance toward all of the actors and actants that flow through the networks they study.

While ANT is often criticized for being apolitical, there are other science studies approaches that I feel are highly political—yet unable (or unwilling) to admit so. There is a branch of what I call applied science studies that is used by powerful institutions to monitor and shape various public behaviors related to technoscience. It is important to briefly discuss this wing of science studies—which is so different from ANT—because actors involved in applied science studies were central to shaping the opinions of both powerful institutions and lay publics regarding the activists opposing GMOs. With the term *applied science studies* I refer to that body of science studies scholars who provide powerful institutions (state, corporate, scientific, and so on) with information about public perceptions of new technologies such as GMOs. Those involved in the applied wing of science studies might benefit from examining the instrumental and potentially harmful nature of their work. For instance, applied science studies researchers examining science-related social movements often misperceive and misrepresent social activists (Marris 2001; Wynne 1992). The researchers may portray actors, such as those in the Confédération Paysanne, as hypocritical, irrational, or coolly manipulative. For instance, applied science studies agents often depict actors who are opposed to eating GM foods but may smoke tobacco as irrational. Science studies agents often frame various publics' engagements with science as erratic or inaccurate "public perception" (Levidow and Carr 1997; Marris 2001; Wynne 1992). Public perception theorists (a subset of science studies researchers) see themselves as educating irrational publics about the low risks associated with GMOs.

A politically engaged science studies approach would include in its object of inquiry the public perceptions industry itself. The term *public perception industry* points to that set of actors and practices that use science studies as a tool to monitor and analyze various publics' engagements with contemporary technoscience practice. Actors central to the public perception industry include social psychologists, anthropologists, and sociologists funded to survey public perceptions of new technologies such as GMOs. As a technique of governance, the public perceptions industry assists corporate, state, and supranational bodies to align public behavior with the objectives of powerful institutions. In my own research, I met many well-meaning scholars involved with the public perception industry. Too often, while providing detailed studies about public engagements with technoscience, they unknowingly did a disservice to the very publics they sincerely wished to serve. Many in the public perception industry often portray anti-GMO activists as pushing a deeper political agenda. In doing so, they fail to appreciate the political currents running through all debates about science. Those who regard activists as simply using GMOs to fight for a broader cause trivialize actors' earnest concerns with the social and biological implications of an agriculture dominated by GMO technology. The assertion that actors use science debates to push political agendas is indeed problematic. Science always entails a political set of cultural practices. Activists such as Bové and members of the Confédération Paysanne are indeed fighting for a broader political cause—one that includes and transcends GMOs. They are fighting for a new solidarity-based logic that would create a more humane and ecologically balanced world.

A politically engaged science studies approach recognizes and legitimizes actors' critiques of systems of power embedded in technoscience endeavors. It explores actors' disenchantment with powerful institutions that appear more concerned with garnering profit and power than with nurturing the humane and ecological potential of technoscience itself. When studying questions of technoscience related to issues such as agriculture, science studies can find its complement in political ecology approaches. Political ecology locates new technologies such as GMOs in fields of social and economic power. Political ecology tends to study down, as researchers explore the worlds of actors with less power than themselves. Studying down reveals how sets of disenfranchised actors such as paysans comprehend, contest, and accommodate new technological regimes—on the ground. And science studies tends to study up (Nader 1969). Science studies researchers often study actors within powerful institutions, such as scientists, science policymakers, and public perception agents. By studying up, science studies offers a crucial understanding of powerful expert actors who are often absent from traditional political ecology approaches. Studying up plays a potentially key role in democratizing and demystifying knowledges about the various cultures of technoscience production at this historical juncture. When a political ecology approach meets a science studies approach, a more dynamic and complete picture comes into being. In addition to examining actors who produce technoscience knowledge, we study the ways actors engage with these knowledges on the ground. By studying both up and down the power ladder, we appreciate the broad network of actors who produce, circulate, contest, and appropriate technoscience practice. In so doing, we can uncover the broader logics of instrumentalism and solidarity that flow among the empowered and disempowered actors in the movements we study. Moving beyond reductive portrayals of irrational or politically manipulative activists, we begin to convey the humanistic impulses that often drive social movements. Consequently, we can better understand the complex ways that actors on the ground engage with and contest powerful institutions, such as science bodies, corporations, and supranational agencies.

Finally, I add to my toolkit social movement theory. In addition to using political ecology and science studies frameworks, this book looks to social movement theory to analyze actors and events that surface throughout this story. While social movement theory is an emergent and heterogeneous body of ideas, most scholars who engage this set of studies look beyond Marxist or labor-centered theories about social change in order to comprehend processes that motivate actors in civil society to form social movements. Pioneers of social movement theory, such as Alain Tourraine (1988, 2000) and Ernesto Laclau and Chantal Mouffe (1985), assert that cultural reality — not just material reality — is central to driving society and social change. As post-Marxists, they move beyond the binary of base-superstructure from an econocentric view of the world to one that incorporates issues of race, gender, and other cultural forms of identity. Tourraine in particular examines new sets of actors struggling against a variety of powers that dominate worlds perceived as instrumental. Tourraine posits the social movement as the space in which actors today resist a rationality of instrumentalism that links markets to communities, and ends toward means (1971, 95). As Tourraine suggests, the paysans in this story cannot be reduced merely to workers fighting the capitalist system. Although they do in part identify with class-based theories of social change, they also fiercely engage with what it means to be a paysan at this precise moment of history. Their cultural identification with peasant and indigenous groups around the world attests to the rise of a new multifaceted historical subject. The paysan struggle is not just to overthrow capitalists who control agri-business. The actors are also searching to construct a world built out of a new set of cultural identities, epistemologies, and alternative visions.

For the theorist Sonia Alvarez, "cultural politics" highlight the political implications of local meanings and practices often viewed as marginal by powerful institutions dominated by Western hegemonic thinking (1998). Paysan cultural politics shaped new notions of food and agriculture that counter those promoted by the global agri-foods system. Social movement theory also studies the epistemological processes embedded in social movement activity. Tourraine and other theorists ground their research in notions of historicity, the process through which actors create new societies by engendering new forms of knowledge (1971). According to the social movement theorist Boaventura de Sousa Santos, researchers should analyze actors' collective attempts to use social movements as spaces to promote alternative epistemologies that counter dominant ideologies embedded within powerful institutions (2007). As de Sousa Santos suggests, it is necessary to examine the way that paysan knowledges challenge the logic of capital-driven global food systems. Paysan savoir faire is not only an assertion of cultural identity, but a crucial expression of an episteme eclipsed by capitalist hegemony. The theorists John Law and Annemarie Mol (2000) encourage thinkers to consider these social movements as multiplicities, rather than being born of a single epistemology. For Mol, the current complex movements studied by social scientists are constituted by "neighboring" worlds that overlap and coexist at a single moment (2000, 10). In the same vein, the theorist Janet Conway (2004) asserts that social movements are robust forums for knowledge production. Conway's work sheds light on how both local and global social movements provide arenas for popular education, often by offering workshops and courses that address alternative organizational strategies and processes. Conway draws inspiration from the antiglobalization movement of the 1990s and early 2000s. She underscores the importance of street theater, popular education, and cultural transformation as key modalities in social movement work. Building on this theme, theorists such as María Isabel Casas-Cortes, Michal Osterweil, and Dana E. Powell (2008) explore social movement as sites where actors produce crucial counterknowledges. These innovative researchers explore online and journal debates as a few arenas in which actors engaged in social movements generate and circulate new understandings of local and global justice (2008).

Theorists of social movements are often obliged to challenge taken-for-granted boundaries between research subjects and objects (Casas-Cortes, Osterweil, and Powell 2008). For example, social movement researchers are often engaged in on-the-ground knowledge production. While they study the beliefs and practices of social movement actors, these actors studied often teach them about movement building, strategy, and vision—as well as providing detailed critiques of specific societal problems. A politically engaged and self-reflexive theory of social movements renders transparent these pedagogical moments that occur in the everyday life that flows between actors generating and researching social movement activity.

The social movements in this story are indeed sites of knowledge production. The Confédération Paysanne provides popular education by creating a farm school for new paysans entering the farming way of life. In addition, the union deploys a variety of educational forums such as workshops, conferences, demonstration rallies, and trials, as well as a variety of media, to educate those outside the agricultural world about the need for paysan agriculture and about the instrumental logics that flow through neoliberal systems of global trade.

Conclusion

This chapter periodizes the Confédération Paysanne, locating the union within the broader historical context of the new paysan movements. Two key events during the nineteenth and twentieth centuries inform the dramatic reconfigurations of French rural life and culture. As rural zones became increasingly depopulated and agriculturally focused during the peasantification of France, smallholders found themselves in an increasingly untenable position in an increasingly industrial agricultural system—particularly in the period following World War II. Framing emergent discourses of powerful institutions during these transitions as techniques of governance underscores how government and corporate bodies work in concert, discreetly disciplining rural populations to conform to particular political and economic models for rural development during these key periods.

The rise of the new paysan movements and the Confédération Paysanne represents a collective systemic disenchantment with an instrumental rationality that began to increasingly pervade the French agricultural world during the glorious thirty. The modernism associated with the JAC was marked by solidaire rationality, a concern with humanistic notions of elevating mankind. Yet it was also marked by an instrumental rationality of productivist agriculture, one that assumed a prominent place in the discourse and practices associated with the FNSEA and its youth wing. For Confédération Paysanne founders, the FNSEA epitomized the instrumentalism of agriculture, symbolizing aggressive capitalism itself. Distinguishing itself from the modernist FNSEA, the new paysan movement built on a solidarity-based antiproductivist discourse that it drew from its roots in the JAC. The new paysan movement created a broad humanist vision that went beyond the domain of agriculture. Since its inception, its members dreamed of becoming "more" than activist farmers. They also wanted to become part of a broader social project. The JAC and the later new paysan movements provided forums for young French rural youths to begin to critically examine challenges presented by a French and European agricultural system that determined that their existence was extraneous to the goal of agricultural productivity. The merging of Catholic Marxism, 1968-styled anarcho-syndicalism, and Gandhian philosophy formed a sensibility that is distinct to the French postindustrial paysan. Seeking not only survival within an instrumentalized agricultural system, the new paysan movements and the Confédération Paysanne sought a solidarity-based vision of a rural world built out of a logic of social justice rather than profit-seeking productivism.

3

The Confédération Paysanne

Philosophy, Structure,
and Constituency

On April 29, 1987, the paysan movements of the 1970s and 1980s came together at a meeting in Rennes to form the Confédération Paysanne. While drawing in individuals remaining with the FNSEA, the Confédération Paysanne also brought together members from a range of other paysan organizations. As a new social and political entity, the Confédération Paysanne represented a rare synthesis. This new union emerged as a hybrid entity, one composed of a complex set of histories and discourses of agriculture that over the next decade would become solidified into a coherent agricultural vision that the union calls Agriculture Paysanne (Paysan Agriculture). In an attempt to convey some of the union's unique flavor and sensibility, I carried out numerous formal and informal interviews with union staff, leaders, and members from 1997 to the present, in person and by phone. In the middle of a conversation, I'd just pop out my little notebook and jot down the words of my interlocutors.

Chapter Three

Marxist and Anarcho-Syndicalist Underpinnings: Decentralization,
Autonomy, and Internationalism

The Confédération Paysanne attempts to distinguish its own political approach from that of other agricultural unions — particularly the FNSEA, its
primary rival. In particular, union members criticize the FNSEA's attempt to
portray all French farmers as sharing a common class interest. As the Confédération Paysanne saw it, class divisions among FNSEA farmers became increasingly polarized as the glorious thirty wore on — and it ended with a dramatically bifurcated agricultural world. The emergence of the new paysan
movements represents what the Confédération Paysanne calls the rise of
"union pluralism": the notion that different agricultural unions express divergent class-based vision and goals (Confédération Paysanne 1997, 45). The
myth of class unity was central to the Confédération Paysanne's decision
to abandon attempts to reform the FNSEA from within. No longer necessary were autonomous pressure groups such as Interpaysanne or Paysans-
Travailleurs, whose members often attempted to convince FNSEA leadership
to attend to the particular concerns of smallholders. When paysan groups
finally broke with the FNSEA, they finally committed to building a union that
would completely represent their interests. That union was the Confédération Paysanne.

Rejecting the FNSEA's modernist idea of *exploitants* (familial entrepreneurs), the founders of Confédération Paysanne created a Marxist-influenced
union of workers that posited agriculture as a social project rather than just
a profitable rural profession. For the Confédération Paysanne, the paysans'
mission extends beyond the production of food: its mission is to reinvigo-
rate and restore rural zones by repopulating such areas with multiple small
farms as well as other modes of rural social and material production. Central
to this objective is a Marxist-based discourse on the paysans' "right to work"
that can be traced back to narratives developed among the JAC. The Confédération Paysanne rejects a national and international agricultural form
of governance that deprives paysans access to land and other means necessary for farming. By asserting the paysan and the rural world as a dignified and crucial social sector, the union demands for its members adequate
social security, insurance, and maternity benefits comparable to workers in
other sectors (François Dufour, personal communication, June 12, 1998). In
addition, the Confédération Paysanne aims to create a majoritarian union of

worker- and paysan-identified farmers. The union's ultimate objective is to eliminate the need for agri-business-oriented unions such as the FNSEA by changing farm policy in both France and the European Union.

Another ongoing mission at the union is to prepare for elections held every six years at the nation's chamber of agriculture. During these elections, between forty-five and forty-eight seats are won by various agricultural agencies seeking to control chamber policy that affects three million individuals and fifty thousand professional organizations. There is a local chamber of agriculture in each department (county) in France, totaling ninety-four chambers. When I met the union in 1997, they proudly controlled 20 percent of the seats in the national chamber of agriculture. Their ongoing goal is to step up this percentage, winning the country over to their own model of paysan agriculture.

THE LEGACY OF ANARCHO-SYNDICALISM: DECENTRALIZATION, AUTONOMY, AND LEADERSHIP STRUCTURE

Unlike many Marxist-based movements, the Confédération Paysanne is committed to decentralized forms of organization. Power is distributed as equally as possible among both individual members and regional subsets of the union. An interesting caveat: a vast majority of union members do not identify as anarchists. Yet while the union does not explicitly articulate anarchist goals and vision, it dialectically retains anarchist values by implicitly incorporating a sensibility of decentralization and autonomy into its organizational structure. The Confédération Paysanne indeed takes pride in being decentralized, democratic, and less bureaucratic than hierarchical organizations such as communist unions and the FNSEA. As a decentralized entity, the Confédération Paysanne has members throughout France. The union expresses its commitment to local autonomy by granting local departmental Confédération Paysanne branches a great deal of freedom in managing their local affairs.

Unlike most unions or organizations of its size, the Confédération Paysanne has no national president per se (an expression of its anarcho-syndicalist roots). Instead, the central governing body of the Confédération Paysanne is the national committee, a group composed of twenty-six representatives from twenty-two regions of the country. To maximize member representation and participation, regions with larger constituencies, such as the Pays Loire or Bretagne, are granted three representatives each, rather than one or two (François Dufour, personal communication, November 4, 1999). Again, in the spirit of decentralization, the union convenes in different regions each year. Hosted by local members, this annual congress is the forum in which the national committee elects a set of national representatives (secretaries). These national secretaries serve for relatively short periods of time, allowing for broad participation. The national committee consists of between five and nine national secretaries and generally about ten treasurers. At the national congress, the national secretaries elect a general secretary—someone in charge of managing departmental bodies as well as maintaining relationships between the Confédération Paysanne and other unions and associations.

Instead of having an executive director or president, the national secretaries elect a key union spokesperson, called the union speaker (*porte parole*). The union speaker serves as the public face of the Confédération Paysanne and is empowered to speak on behalf of the union as key press liaison. While the press and public often erroneously refer to the speaker as the union's "leader" or "president," the Confédération Paysanne makes it quite clear that the power of the union speaker is limited in scope. The speaker assumes his or her role for a relatively short period (four to six years) and is recallable. The Confédération Paysanne speaker has relatively limited autonomous decision-making power. All union decisions are made in a participatory, democratic, and decentralized fashion, deploying the greatest amount of membership consultation possible. Yet the speaker is generally a charismatic figure; speakers are expected to help shape the union's overall vision and morale, while presenting a forward-looking face to the public. The speaker's key responsibility is to increase the union's public visibility and power. Historically, each speaker brings his or her own distinctive temperament and style to the job.

During the period of 1997 to 2000, in particular, I carried out countless formal and informal interviews with union members. Sometimes interviews occurred spontaneously, over a cup of coffee in a café at lunchtime. Other interviews were scheduled and took place at the union headquarters or in the homes of union paysans.

In nearly all of my interviews, I would ask paysans how they perceived various speakers of the union. When discussing former union speaker Guy Le Fur, for instance, I was struck by how many described him as "shy, modest, yet fierce." Paysans tended to describe another former union speaker,

François Dufour, in similar terms. Mostly, actors experienced Dufour as "outgoing, engaging, and able to get things done." In keeping with the Confédération Paysanne's nonhierarchical sensibility, a good speaker is one who leads by example, skill, and enthusiasm rather than by exerting authority or coercion over others.

The Confédération Paysanne highly values being a good comrade, working hard for the union, and getting along well with others. During their four-year terms, the national secretaries spend two to three days a week at the Confédération Paysanne's office in Bagnolet, just outside Paris. In order for the union to function effectively, the national secretaries (hailing from across the country) must be able to get along in a convivial way. Representatives perceived as egotistical or shirking duties are often criticized informally for failing to place the needs of the organization before personal priorities. While at the Confédération Paysanne, national representatives share a small dormitory inside the office building. They prepare meals collectively in the Confédération Paysanne's small but lively kitchen and spend time together in the common living and dining room. Together they celebrate political victories, birthdays, and holidays when they are together in Paris, miles from home, often holding raucous parties filled with good food.

National secretaries have an arduous job that often entails a weekly commute to Paris (up to twelve hours by train). Each Monday or Tuesday, national secretaries leave their families behind for three to four days to work intensively with other national secretaries in Paris. For all of this, they receive a relatively modest stipend, which places degrees of hardship on their families both personally and economically. In order to partially compensate national secretaries during their absence on their farms, they are reimbursed for hiring replacement farmworkers. When examining the workload and commitment of the national secretariat, it becomes clear that union members sign on for this job not out of a desire for money, ease, or power, but out of a deep sense of commitment to the union.

CONFÉDÉRATION PAYSANNE INTERNATIONALE

The Confédération Paysanne's international and humanist orientation makes it a bit of a historical anomaly in French rural history. For almost a century, France has perceived its rural zones as a parochial and romanticized "world apart," whose constituents share a conservative backward sensibility. Due to its roots in the JAC, the Confédération Paysanne has a distinctive political vision and orientation. The union holds internationalism and humanism as core values, striving to be tightly integrated into international networks. Even before the Confédération Paysanne was born, members of the new paysan movements recognized the need for international worker solidarity for both philosophical and strategic reasons. Strategically, the need for such unity is clear. This is an age when agricultural policy is shaped by international bodies such as the European Commission, which determines the EU's Common Agricultural Policy and the WTO. The Confédération Paysanne understands that power does in fact lie in numbers. The union is fiercely committed to working with other groups of smallholders to fight against powerful institutions that make policy about agricultural practice.

In 1986, just a year before the founding of the Confédération Paysanne, the new paysan movements founded a Europe-wide network called the Coordination Paysanne Européenne (European Peasant Coordination), with headquarters in Brussels. To this day, the European Peasant Coordination contains eighteen smallholders in farmer and rural organizations from eleven European countries (e.g., Switzerland, Austria, and Germany). In addition to addressing problems associated with the European Common Agricultural Policy and the WTO, the European Peasant Coordination also addresses such food controversies as GMOs, hormones, and antibiotics used in raising livestock. It was through engagements with the European Farmers Coordination that the Confédération Paysanne broadened its network of international contacts with peasant and indigenous groups in the Global North and South. Early in its history, the union realized that groups around the world shared similar concerns related to trade liberalization, land rights, and problems associated with industrial agriculture. In 1986, unease among these groups peaked when the General Agreement on Tariffs and Trade (which later became the WTO) decided to include food and agriculture in its treaties on free trade for the first time.

For many members in the Confédération Paysanne, the idea of including policy on food and agriculture in free-trade agreements was devastating. Such a maneuver could mean that agricultural trade and production would be organized around neoliberal lines on an unprecedented international scale (Bové 2001, 92). Most crucial, individual states would lose the power to generate their own food-related trade policies to protect their own markets. Additionally, poorer countries would be obliged to lower their own tariffs while accepting a large percentage of imports from the United States and the EU. Bringing food and agriculture under free-trade policies meant grave consequences for southern countries at a time when northern countries were responsible for exporting 80 percent of food internationally. The flooding of southern agricultural economies with cheap, government-subsidized foods from the North is referred to as "dumping" (Wise 2004). Such dumping devastates local rural economies of poor countries unable to sell their own food at home and renders it impossible for these countries to compete in a global market.

To address such concerns, the Confédération Paysanne and the European Paysan Coordination joined together to found La Via Campesina (The Peasants' Way) in 1993. La Via Campesina grew to become an international organization consisting of smallholders, agricultural workers, rural women's groups, and indigenous organizations (Desmarais 2007). In addition to fighting problems of dumping, La Via Campesina fights other issues associated with free trade and industrial agriculture generally, as well as focusing on the implications of GMOs for smallholders and indigenous groups worldwide. La Via Campesina's network is vast. It extends into every continent in Europe, North America, Central and South America, Asia, and Africa. Its key organizations include the Confédération Paysanne, the Karnataka State Farmers' Association from South India (which represents ten million farmers and is responsible for leading militant anti-GMO direct-action campaigns), and the Brazilian Landless Movement. The Brazilian Landless Movement is mainly responsible for supporting landless peasants in occupying and farming dormant farmlands in addition to assisting peasants by creating other social and educational programs.

La Via Campesina's mission was further clarified and solidified after the historic meeting in Marrakech, Morocco, in 1994, when the General Agreement on Tariffs and Trade was formally transformed into the WTO. With the WTO in place, individual states lost even more rights to refuse dumped or other unwanted foodstuff imports from WTO member countries. Under WTO policy, states may only refuse food imports when they are able to scientifically prove risk-based evidence that foodstuffs jeopardize a state's population or livestock. The cost (and feasibility) of generating such scientific proof is usually beyond the means of poorer countries. Consequently, the WTO remains largely unhindered in maintaining its power to enforce this policy.

Conf. Culture: Paysans, Salariers, Class, Ethnicity, and Gender

The Confédération Paysanne built its modest headquarters just outside Paris in the small suburb of Bagnolet. The office is housed in an old stone building that the union renovated in the early 1990s, freeing up three good-sized floors that were fashioned into a series of airy and well-lit offices. The feeling of the building is very "1968": colorful, cheerful, humorous, with brightly colored walls covered with various amusing Confédération Paysanne campaign posters. Everywhere bulletin boards are filled with newspaper articles featuring union activities, agricultural news, and witty political cartoons designed by the Confédération Paysanne's signature political cartoonist, Samson. While the headquarters is clearly a place where people come to do hard work, the space also communicates a feeling of not taking oneself too seriously. There is an air of light and witty humor that runs through the constant stream of jokes that fill the halls and political art covering the walls. There is a small and bustling kitchen on the building's main floor where there are almost always a few paysans and staff talking and laughing together, smoking cigarettes or sipping coffee at a wobbly table with a yellow plastic tablecloth. Office doors are generally swung open, creating an informal and welcoming atmosphere at the union, which insiders refer to as "La Conf."

The headquarters in Bagnolet also houses the Confédération Paysanne's monthly magazine, *Campagne Solidaires*. In addition, Bagnolet is home to the team that runs the Association Federal pour la Development de l'Emploi Agricole et Rural (Federal Association for the Development of Rural and Agricultural Employment). Those in and outside the union refer to this project by using the acronym FADEAR. The FADEAR is an education and outreach project by the Confédération Paysanne that develops curriculum on agriculture for paysan youths and for new farmers entering the union. In the yard behind the building stand two small prefabricated structures. These buildings provide spillover space for larger meetings. In the winter, these buildings are chilly and damp, heated with small space heaters. With no extra monies to expand or upgrade the union's building structure, members and staff tough it out on cold winter days, sipping hot coffee and wearing extra sweaters to keep warm.

It is worth noting that the union faces ongoing economic hardship, and this is apparent in the infrastructure of the union's national headquarters.

With scarce funds to create a lavish or formal-looking building, the Confédération Paysanne makes do, creating a space that is inviting, cheerful, and down to earth.

CONFÉDÉRATION PAYSANNE CONSTITUENCY: PAYSANS AND SALARIERS

Confédération Paysanne culture at the Bagnolet headquarters is a hybrid mix of individuals hailing from different classes, ethnicities, sexes, and agricultural backgrounds. At any given moment, the Bagnolet office is overflowing with Parisian organizers raised in urban middle-class families, hippie *néos* (new farmers), and more conservatively dressed *purs porcs* (literally *pure pigs*—farmers perceived as longtime committed farmers), who are descendants of the JAC who hail from generational farm families.

The two major sets of actors at Bagnolet are paysan representatives and salariers. *Salariers* is the Confédération Paysanne's term for permanent staff; those salary-earning nonpaysans who work at the union. At the center of the staff structure are seven key organizers in charge of coordinating administrative issues with the general secretary. Each key organizer is in charge of directing a particular set of ongoing campaign areas, such as agriculture, livestock, the environment, and society at large. In addition to the seven key organizer positions, there is a staff of fifteen working in the office, including a general office worker and three individuals who publish *Campagne Solidaires*.

Confédération Paysanne paysans and salariers represent two different institutional subcultures, each with its own set of cultural norms and practices. For instance, paysans tend to wear clothing with a rural feel, such as pullover wool sweaters with worn-looking jeans and work shoes. Salariers tend to dress quite differently. While their attire is informal by Parisian standards, men tend to wear ironed button-down shirts, urban and fashionable jeans, and more formal dress shoes. Women adopt a slightly *intello* (slang for intellectual) or funky look by wearing urban chic clothing or sporting a dressed-down hippie style. Because many paysans are raised in rural areas, they tend to have strong regional accents. In contrast, salariers tend to have Parisian accents. Differences between paysans and salariers are often class based as well. Many salariers were raised in middle-class families and have the French bachelor's and master's degrees in fields such as environmental studies, communications, and agricultural science. While some paysans also have advanced degrees, others chose nonacademic paths (preferring to go right into farming) for professional or economic reasons. What is significant here is that while salariers may have greater educational and class privilege than many paysans, paysans hold the power in the union. Confédération Paysanne leaders occupy higher status in the organization and are the employers and evaluators of salariers' work.

Yet the Bagnolet headquarters, like the Confédération Paysanne itself, strives to create a nonhierarchical structure and work atmosphere. Since my first formal and informal encounters with union actors in 1997, I have been continuously impressed by the distinct sensibility of the people who flow in and out of union headquarters. Relations between salariers and paysans are generally informal and congenial, and most salariers describe the work environment as "relaxed, stimulating, and rewarding." Most salariers report pride in working for a cause they believe in and express an earnest respect for the paysans for whom they work. In general, paysans and salariers tend to *tutoi* each other, using the informal *tu* (you) in both formal and informal conversation—a practice atypical in professional office settings in France. Also atypical, many paysans and salariers will *faire des bises* (offering each other kisses on each cheek) upon greeting or saying good-bye to each other at the beginning or end of the day. Some paysans who hail from the south of France offer four consecutive kisses on alternating cheeks, as is customary in that part of the country.

Despite these informalities, the organizational boundaries between salariers and paysans are extremely clear. Just as salariers always refer to Confédération Paysanne members and representatives as paysans, paysans refer to nonpaysan staff as salariers. As one salarier said to me, in 2005, "Well, in a way, we're all salariers, we're all workers [*ouvriers*], we all work here, but the paysans, well, they're really our employers. It's their union and we work for them." Lunchtime is a moment when the distinction between paysans and salariers is most visible. Paysans and salariers, who work side by side all morning, dine at separate tables in the restaurant near the office. One salarier explained to me, "The paysans like their privacy, they like to talk among themselves about issues that they are working on. . . . We have separate interests in the end." Once, when I asked various paysans why paysans never occupy salarier positions, many said things to the effect of "The boundaries are clearer when salariers are not paysans." Paysans regard salariers as culturally different. On several occasions I heard paysans bemused about how strange it was that a salarier—so involved in union issues—was raised in an urban setting. At other times, paysans discussed the agricultural lineages of various salariers, noting how they had parents, grandparents, or uncles who farmed in the recent past. Many paysans often referred to such lineages as a way to explain these salariers' commitment to the union's goals and vision. Allusions to salariers' agricultural roots seemed to be a way to locate salariers within the union's landscape, providing degrees of fictive kinship within the organization.

However, for some salariers with more dubious agricultural roots, establishing one's place within the union can be challenging. Anne-Marie B., a salarier who had worked at the union for several years, articulates: "What is strange is that I live in Paris, work in agriculture, and yet no one in my family is from the country. When the paysans ask what region I come from, I'm a bit ashamed to say. I have to say where my grandparents are from. My grandparents are real Brittany stock; they live in the country. You can really have a problem here if you don't have family that works in agriculture. The paysans think it's harder for you to understand the paysan situation. They don't know if you'll really understand."

WHO IS THE CONF.? CLASS, EDUCATION, AND AUTHENTICITY

The Confédération Paysanne does not keep statistics on the agricultural or social and ethnic backgrounds of its members. However, over the years, I have been able to construct a loose profile of the kinds of individuals who constitute the union's leadership and membership. In the end, I found that while there was no single "Confédération Paysanne type," there were a few sets of characteristics shared by many. Most active members in the union are in their mid-thirties to forties. Many of the older members (those over fifty) grew up in the JAC and moved through the various new paysan movements that led to the formation of the Confédération Paysanne. While some younger members do not share this history, they seem to take pride in the union's self-constructed origin story. The union makes it a priority to document and relate its history to newcomers to the organization. The union has several orientation notebooks that clearly document the union's history. These three-ring binders are continually added to and brought up-to-date as the union's story evolves over time.

Usually Confédération Paysanne members constitute part of a farming couple or family. Farming is indeed often regarded as a family activity, one that includes spouses, members of an extended family, and children still living at home. According to most union members, however, most of their own children do not plan to continue farming for economic reasons. Instead, many children of union members plan careers in other domains that will eventually lead them to a French city relatively far from home. When I asked the children of Confédération Paysanne farmers themselves (during farm visits) why they might choose not continue the farming lifestyle, most replied with an emphatic, "It's hard work!" Older children (teenagers and older) also often expressed that agricultural life is too uncertain. Rather than resenting their children's choices, Confédération Paysanne members seem to put their energies into drawing upon French youths who contact the union expressing interest in taking up a farming way of life. The union has a rigorous program designed to assist new farmers and dedicates considerable time and resources toward cultivating a new generation of paysans who would otherwise be turned off from farming in a difficult rural economy.

In terms of educational background, most Confédération Paysanne members completed *lycée* (high school) and passed the final exam (*baccalauréat*). Unlike most of their parents, many paysans in the Confédération Paysanne continued on to higher education in their late teens and early twenties, sometimes receiving the French equivalent of a bachelor's degree in agricultural science at local universities or through correspondence courses. Many union members often chose for personal or financial reasons to move directly from lycée into farming.

At times I noticed an uneasiness regarding the relationship between class and educational background among union members, particularly on the leadership level. Pierre T., a former national secretary (and a man quite active in the union during 1997–2001), reported an interesting situation. In his youth, Pierre earned an engineering (*ingenieur*) degree in agricultural science. In France the term *ingenieur* has a very different meaning from the purely technical term *engineer* in U.S. English (Shinn 1978). One earns an engineering diploma from either an independent school of engineering or high-status institutions called *grandes écoles*. French engineering schools foster academic-industry collaborations where students learn management skills, often central to their future careers. In France, engineer is a title that enjoys similar (or superior) status to doctor in the United States. One can become an engineer in a variety of domains ranging from social to technical science. Once they have become engineers, individuals are granted entry into the elite domains of French society, where they may work in industry, government, or higher education. Pierre T, now in his mid-fifties, hails from a family of smallholders and identifies strongly as a paysan. During an average year, he spends about a third of his time working as an agricultural consultant in Africa, another third teaching courses on agricultural science at his local university, and the last third working on his own homestead with his wife and close family friend on a smallholding of about ten hectares. According to Pierre, "It's hard sometimes at the union. Sometimes you get the feeling others sort of doubt your commitment to be and act like a real paysan. 'Is he an ingenieur or a paysan?' some people ask. For me, though, there is no problem. I know what I am."

For Pierre, matters became even more problematic when his daughter was selected into the single most elite engineering university in the country, an institution whose graduates are granted entry into the highest echelons of French society. Most graduates of this school become key leaders in domains of industry, science, government, law, and education. When Pierre's daughter was accepted, Pierre became a main topic of conversation among many paysans at the union who joked and bantered about the paysan status of Pierre and his family. Many wondered aloud whether Pierre was a "real paysan" or if he was a "professor" or an "international expert" instead. When I mentioned the possibility of visiting Pierre's home for a weekend at a Confédération Paysanne meeting, a national representative turned to me and advised, "If it were me, I'd visit a real paysan. We don't know quite *what* Pierre is!" While I did not observe explicit anti-intellectualism among union members, I did observe moments of confusion and slight irritation during discussions surrounding the class and identity status of particular paysans who had greater access to powerful institutions such as international development agencies or prestigious universities. The more members perceived Pierre as enjoying extra monetary or institutional status outside the paysan world, the more they struggled to identify with his class and cultural identity.

Most Confédération Paysanne members identify as working class, having been raised in modest economic milieus. Some were raised in farm families, inheriting family smallholdings of various sizes from parents or relatives. Others hailed from families that rented parcels from large landowners and lived a kind of yeoman farmer existence that may have lasted for generations. From the time they were children, many knew they would follow in their parents' footsteps to become farmers.

NÉO-RURAUX MEMBERS OF THE CONFÉDÉRATION PAYSANNE

A considerable number of paysans did not descend from farm families. Confédération Paysanne members have a term for individuals who adopt a paysan way of life as adults: *néos-ruraux* (neorural), or *néos* for short. Néos constitute a minority at the Confédération Paysanne. Some of the older néos (in their fifties or sixties) had been active in antiwar movements associated with the Larzac in their youth. Other older néos may have had no history with the Larzac, but they may have become disenchanted by urban life after the events of May 1968 and looked to farming as a more meaningful way of life. While néos like José Bové fall into the former category, those such as René Riesel (a key union activist) fall into the latter. According to Riesel, after the events of 1968 came to a close, he saw no other option but to turn to the country to "escape the disaster that had become his capitalist-crazed country" (René Riesel, personal communication, October 2, 1999).

Whenever I inquired into the existence, number, or even the idea of néos among Confédération Paysanne members, I was met with dismissal or slight irritation. Paysans are critical of the idea of unity among farmers at the FNSEA who did not share class interests. Conversely, at the Confédération Paysanne, actors seem to assume that all union members share the same class interests and thus forge another kind of unity — one that downplays differences among the agricultural histories of its members. As François Dufour (a former union speaker) stated quite succinctly during a speech he gave on April 16, 1998, "We are not concerned with paysans' pasts, but with paysans' survival." The kind of union unity suggested by Dufour seems to be both encouraged and largely achieved. Since the first historical coming together between paysans who descended from farm families (often called purs porcs among paysans) and néos in the Larzac movements, there has been a tendency to downplay such differences in the name of union solidarité. Thus even in informal public settings I found little open discourse among Confédération Paysanne members regarding the agricultural backgrounds of particular paysans. Yet in private, actors' interest in the status of actors like Pierre demonstrates that at least some members of the Confédération Paysanne often hold discussions about individuals' paysan status. The néo-ruraux I encountered reported feeling well integrated into the union. However, they often described life in the broader agricultural community, beyond the Confédération Paysanne, as being sometimes difficult, particularly at the beginning of their farming careers. Many néos will joke about how it took twenty years to prove to neighboring farmers (farmers outside the Confédération Paysanne) that they were "serious" paysans.

In terms of religion and ethnicity, most Confédération Paysanne members would identify as white and were raised Catholic. During my years of studying the union, I encountered one farmer of Jewish and Arab descent, René Riesel—a man who had been a national secretary. To my knowledge there have been no other (or at least very few) Confédération Paysanne farmers of Arab or African descent (Arabs from Algeria or Morocco and Africans from Cameroon or the Ivory Coast represent the two largest minorities in France). While Riesel reports never feeling openly discriminated against for being Jewish (he was elected into the national committee in the mid-1990s), he said he was continuously conscious "that everyone was aware that [he] was 'the Jew' at the Conf." (personal communication, October 2, 1999).

As with whiteness in such countries as the United States, French Catholicism is a normative, unmarked ethnic and religious identity that renders all non-Catholics (white or of color) "other." As adults, many Confédération Paysanne members who were raised Catholic are nonobservant, rarely attending church or requiring their children to attend church. Others seem to have blended the JAC sensibilities of their youth with progressive Gandhian nonviolent philosophies, loosely identifying with the liberation theology associated with Latin American social movements.

Another commonality among many Confédération Paysanne members (particularly among those over forty) is that many have spent time in parts of French-speaking Africa. Many in the Confédération Paysanne chose as youths to opt out of military service, performing civil service in agriculture in France's former colonies. Many speak of these experiences as opening their eyes to the harsh realities of peoples in the Global South. Paysans also report feeling a sense of solidarity with the farmers they met and came to know in Africa. As one Confédération Paysanne farmer put it, "I went to Africa to help these poor farmers. But in the end, it was they who helped me. They taught me how to see the world in a new way entirely." The decision to perform military civil service in former French colonies is directly linked to many Confédération Paysanne members' roots in the JAC. These rural youths were following the modernist directive to become worldly by seeing lands beyond France, and they were following a religious mandate to help humanity through service and labor. In turn, Confédération Paysanne members' international work during their early twenties also represents actors' desire to assert their international solidarity with agricultural workers from other countries, a mandate articulated in Marxist teachings associated with the JAC. But, as many Confédération Paysanne members mentioned to me, they found their experiences in Africa to be quite humbling; they felt that they had been enriched by the experience.

GENDER AND HETERONORMATIVITY AT THE CONF.

Gender at the Confédération Paysanne constitutes a complex set of dynamics and questions that continue to elude my full understanding. At the headquarters in Bagnolet, the national leadership of paysans is predominantly male. Among the salariers, however, there is gender parity, with both men and women holding powerful positions. On the local level, women in the Confédération Paysanne play an active role on the family farm. In addition to taking on a range of arduous agricultural tasks, they often manage family finances and maintain the daily rhythms associated with caring for children, overseeing chores, and maintaining family life. In addition, out of economic necessity, many women work part time off the farm (working in cafés, driving school buses, or working in offices in nearby villages or towns).

A common complaint I heard from women in the Confédération Paysanne was that they felt left out of major decision-making meetings and bodies — on both the local and national level. Many shared similar anecdotes about having to watch what they say during local, regional, or national meetings. Many expressed anxiety about being perceived as too forceful by male comrades in the union. Other women reported the problem of facing angry husbands at home after meetings. According to several women in the union, they feared being reprimanded for being too bold in public, thus shaming their husbands. Over coffee one morning at a farm visit, the union member, Agnes P., said to me, "Why even bother saying anything at a meeting? You know if you disagree with your husband in a public meeting, you're going to get yelled at when you get home."

Finally, while some women do manage to be active in the union on a local or regional level, few participate on the highest level of leadership. The national secretariat is overwhelmingly male. When asked about this dynamic, men and women in the Confédération Paysanne reasoned that, because being a national secretary pulls farmers away from their families for up to three nights a week for three to four years (to work at the headquarters), the job was simply beyond a woman's reach. Women are assumed to hold primary responsibility for parenting children at home, so they are thought unable to spend extended or frequent periods away from home. Of the three women who were national representatives (of whom I am aware) since the union's formation, one was single with no children. The other two were older with adult children who no longer lived at home. For many wives of national representatives, the familial decision for the husband to become a national representative is regarded as both an honor and a significant sacrifice. As Laurence G., the wife of a representative, said to me, "It's like you just say, 'Good-bye, see you in four years!' You never see each other . . . and it's hard on the kids too."

Alongside a gendered dynamic at the Confédération Paysanne leadership, there also exists a related heteronormative ambiance. Homosexuality is generally not publicly discussed at the Confédération Paysanne, and I encountered no openly gay or lesbian couples or individuals in the union. This is not uncharacteristic of many Left-leaning (not to mention Right-leaning) organizations in France. While France is generally politically tolerant of homosexuals on a national level (it legalized civil unions in 1998), there remains a palpable awkwardness regarding homosexuality on a cultural level (Copley 1989). While I did not get the impression that Confédération Paysanne leaders would openly ostracize or criticize a gay or lesbian paysan, I could also appreciate the difficulty that a homosexual union member would have in coming out within the organization.

Conclusion

The Confédération Paysanne represents a hybrid entity. The union constitutes a distinctive and heterogeneous set of discourses and actors that have created novel understandings and practices of French agriculture. During the union's first decade, we see it begin to clarify its vision and objectives, introducing them to the world of French agricultural policy. This is when we see the union develop and present a coherent agricultural program, Agriculture Paysan. By contextualizing the Confédération Paysanne within a broader Marxist and anarcho-syndicalist historical milieu, we can better appreciate the organization's tendencies toward internationalism and decentralization. In turn, by locating the union within the history of May 1968 in

France, we can gain a clearer understanding of the union's special whimsical and witty culture and sensibility. The union represents a special coming together of various sets of actors, each located within fields of power, such as class, gender, and history. Yet despite the diversity of its constituency, the Confédération Paysanne proves capable of maintaining a clear and coherent image of a union with a set of shared solidaire objectives regarding how to reorganize the rural world according to a more solidarity-based logic.

4

Union Activism & Programs

Early Campaigns and
Paysan Agriculture

The Confédération Paysanne's Approach to Direct Action

BREAKING THE "VIOLENT PAYSAN" STEREOTYPE
AND WORKING INSIDE THE SYSTEM

A common sight on the French evening news is a group of farmers blockading a main highway by forming a train of trucks filled with potatoes. One often sees, towering before the blockade, an enormous smoldering pile of dripping, burning tires. When considering spectacles surrounding French farmers, most French viewers make no distinction between FNSEA and Confédération Paysanne farmers. This is largely because most French citizens have little awareness of the dominance of large-scale farmers and the diminished status of smallholders. For most French audiences watching the news, the image of the angry and desperate French farmer is a monolithic icon—a humorous yet pathetic caricature held lovingly, and regularly patronizingly, in the French imagination. Over the years, the Confédération Paysanne has worked to distinguish the Confédération Paysanne paysan from the notion of the "cute little peasant" *petit paysan*, promoted by the FNSEA. In the press, the FNSEA often uses the term *paysan* when describing members' violent tactics such as burning stacks of tires in the middle of highways. By describing FNSEA activists as paysans, the FNSEA diverts attention away from the fact that the vast majority of FNSEA farmers are large-scale industrial growers. They also veil the machinations of power in which the FNSEA administration itself devises the destructive direct actions that they in turn blame on their own petit paysans (old-time) who, in reality, have little power or presence within the powerful union. Members of the new paysan movements have reclaimed the term *paysan*, redefining it in radical and prideful terms. According to many in the Confédération Paysanne, FNSEA farmers continue to regard themselves as modernist entrepreneurs, only invoking discourses on the paysan when seeking to garner sympathy from public bodies and audiences.

In popular French consciousness, paysans are generic, small-scale farmers who inhabit a rustic rural past, living in a world that no longer exists. The term *paysan* has both romantic and pejorative connotations, summoning up bucolic nostalgia as well as rural ignorance, crudeness, and isolation from the modern world. According to many Confédération Paysanne leaders, the FNSEA has always exploited popular understandings of the paysan, using the image of the romanticized old-time petit paysan to justify its tactics and to garner popular sympathy in the media (Basson 1997). The FNSEA is perceived as portraying petit paysans as *casseurs* (thugs) who destroys property to get their own way. According to the former Confédération Paysanne spokesperson François Dufour:

> The FNSEA has always used "les petits paysans" [poor smallholders] in their demonstrations. They would put them in the front of the actions, so the media could see them and they would encourage them to break things, like to go to the prefecture of the police and to break public property. This way, the FNSEA tried to look like a union of old-time paysans that would get a lot of media attention and would also stimulate sympathy on the part of French citizens who see the paysans fighting to survive. The irony is that they used the paysans like this at the exact same time that they were trying to eliminate them from the union. They used them to get media and to portray themselves as paysans with whom citizens should feel solidarity. The message was, "You need the paysans; they're here to feed you; support our struggle!" (Dufour, personal communication, April 11, 1998)

For many Confédération Paysanne farmers, such as the former national secretary Guy Le Fur, the Confédération Paysanne needs to challenge this distorted image of paysans. According to Le Fur, the Confédération Paysanne must actively work to transform the stereotype of the paysan as a casseur— a country bumpkin living outside society who comes to the city to cause a ruckus: "We need people to understand that we are not just people who want to break things. We are rational people trying to create a more intelligent approach to agriculture" (Le Fur, personal communication, October 27, 1997).

In an attempt to enhance the distinction between the FNSEA and the Confédération Paysanne, many members seek to avoid direct action that might be misperceived by the public as being aggressive and foolish. Instead, some in the union opt for a policymaking approach—one that entails working within government bodies to change them from inside. In the late 1990s there was a quiet but palpable tension between older and younger members of the Confédération Paysanne regarding political strategy. Purs porcs (farmers perceived as longtime committed farmers) who had come through the JAC movements preferred lobbying powerful institutions such as the ministry of agriculture. This policymaking approach ironically is not unlike that of the FNSEA, which works closely with government bodies and is continuously making alliances with politicians and industry agents who benefit the union. At the other end of the spectrum is the relatively young direct-action wing of the Confédération Paysanne, which, embracing the spirit of 1968 and the Larzac, favors nonviolent direct action. It is crucial to emphasize that these two wings are not monolithic and have considerable overlap; many Confédération Paysanne members are engaged in both lobbying and direct-action activity.

Many in the union seek to lobby the French government to break the FNSEA's nearly exclusive role as the key consulting body within government forums. In 1990 the Confédération Paysanne won the right to sit on a limited number of commissions on farming policy at the local and national level as a result of a new governmental decree. In 1997 the Confédération Paysanne (along with all farmers' unions) won full rights to be represented on farming policy bodies due to a law passed by the Socialist government (Bové 2001). These new rights allowed the Confédération Paysanne to participate in drafting new laws on farming, and it is increasingly consulted on major policies by the ministry of agriculture.

NONVIOLENT VERSUS VIOLENT DIRECT ACTION: SYMBOLIC ACTION AND FARMS OF THE FUTURE

Among Confédération Paysanne members who promote direct action there is a general embracing of a nonviolent, Gandhian-influenced model of resistance. Many of them critique the FNSEA for historically using harsh or violent forms of direct action (e.g., the blockade incident). FNSEA direct actions frequently cause significant and costly property damage. On many occasions, FNSEA members have smashed large windows of government buildings or ransacked the ministry of agriculture offices, literally tossing office furniture out of windows and destroying filing systems by emptying their contents out the window as well.

Alternatively, the Confédération Paysanne promotes nonviolent direct actions, events that are often dripping with irony and media-ready symbolism. Many Confédération Paysanne actions entail creating a "farm of the future" on the site of an offending government or corporate body. Generally speaking, farms of the future require paysans to haul farm animals and large sacks of dirt and hay to a given site. After laying out the dirt and hay, union members set up model farms, usually in urban centers, to create an anachronistic, comical effect. Farms of the future often resemble little petting zoos with lambs or foals, and urban children have an opportunity to feed or touch the animals. Farms of the future almost always culminate with a picnic in which paysans spread out blankets upon which to enjoy a feast of artisanal breads, cheeses, wines, pâtés, and fruits brought from various regions of the country (Bové, personal communication, November 11, 1999). Such direct actions are intended to demonstrate what a postindustrial farm could look like.

I attended several farms of the future, but one stands out to me most. It took place a few blocks from my apartment in the 1st arrondissement of Paris in the fall of 1998. The union planned a conference focusing on the upcoming meeting of the European Commission on Agriculture—the body that creates what is called in France the Politique Agricole Common (Common Agricultural Policy). The policies issued by the commission are similar to those established by the U.S. farm bill.

This particular farm of the future was set up at the Place des Muses in the esplanade near Paris's first American-style shopping mall, Le Forum des Halles. The location was symbolic. Since 1183, Les Halles had been Paris's largest central traditional market. It was demolished in 1971 to make way for an underground and aboveground modern pedestrian shopping mall. In its heyday before 1971, Les Halles was a shelter for the country's national merchants traveling to Paris to sell their wares. People who remember Les Halles often speak nostalgically of enjoying its busy and bright atmosphere—usually in the early hours of the morning—after attending theater or the opera. Parisians wearing suits and gowns would dine at little stalls at Les Halles (set up primarily for working merchants) where they'd enjoy bowls of onion soup. All around, workers in the meat or poultry industry hung carcasses and prepared produce for the next day's market. For centuries Les Halles was known as "the stomach of Paris." Le Forum des Halles (the mall) is truly a postindustrial entity. Unable to compete in the new market economy based largely on supermarkets and the agro-foods industry, Les Halles was transformed into Le Forum des Halles just as the paysans were transformed into agriculteurs or disenfranchised smallholders. The Place des Muses, the center of the outdoor mall, features a set of sculptures and an ornate marble fountain. It is a site usually full of hip-looking students, tourists, and young people zooming around on skateboards. Others at the Place des Muses may loll along the wall of the fountain munching on hamburgers from McDonald's or slowly licking scoops of ice cream from Ben and Jerry's.

To attend the farm of the future, Confédération Paysanne members traveled from all over the country. As is often the case at such events, for many this trip represented their first excursion to Paris. Confédération Paysanne organizers set up a small tent by the fountain where a series of representatives of consumer, ecology, and farmers' groups held small meetings on the implications of European agricultural policy for paysans. Outside the tent, across from the fountain, stood the union speaker François Dufour with his twelve-year-old daughter. Together they had traveled from Brittany to set up a farm of the future, complete with horse, goat, lamb, and chickens enclosed in a makeshift wooden fence. Along the surface of the concrete floor, Dufour and his daughter scattered bales of hay and several bags of soil. Amused passersby would stop and pet the animals, pose questions, and generally enjoy the strange ambiance of a small farm plopped in the middle of a Parisian square on a sunny October afternoon.

Other Confédération Paysanne members had set up a small, spontaneous farmers' market to sell mostly farm-raised grilled lamb, cradled between rough pieces of homemade bread. These sandwiches were consumed eagerly — mostly by Confédération Paysanne members attending the demonstration. These delicacies featured artisanal roasted lamb slapped between bread without garnishes. For my part, I tried to down my sandwich quickly while the delicious but greasy meat soaked straight through the bread. As I sat fumbling with my meal, a few older paysan men sat and watched me, laughing good-naturedly. In vain they tried to instruct me in the proper way of consuming the meal and avoiding a messy disaster.

One image stands out to me still. Outside the tent, sitting along the fountain, was a line of older paysans in their sixties or seventies, wearing woolen berets, heavy hand-knit sweaters, and rough-hewn workpants and shoes. The men sat along the wall, speaking in strong southern accents, passing back and forth golden baguettes, speckled tubes of homemade salami, wedges of cheese, and bottles of red wine in dark-green bottles. As the men reclined along the wall, they studied passersby in a bemused yet polite fashion, as if they were watching a strange but intriguing film. In turn, young Parisians skating by, with headphones and spiky hair, looked equally politely yet bewildered at the older men, as if they too were watching a fascinating film from another era. The scene reminded me of preindustrial paysans and postindustrial urban youths studying each other, as if trying to determine the answer to a historical riddle.

The idea of a farm of the future — a mainstay of the Confédération Paysanne's demonstrations — emerged from the union's desire to promote itself as a wholly modern organization with a forward-looking vision of agriculture. According to many Confédération Paysanne members, the union must distinguish itself from the FNSEA's large-scale industrial agriculture. In addition the union must also differentiate itself from romantic back-to-the-landers with whom union members do not identify. For paysans, such farmers represent a small-scale antimodern agriculture, one promoted by *ecolos* (slang for *ecologists*), "back-to-the-land hippies," or right-wing smallholders. According to many in the union, these farmers tend to promote a politically reactionary and *passéist* (past-oriented) vision of agriculture that begs for a return to an idealized (and nonexistent) rural past.

The farm of the future serves two purposes. It attempts to "remind city dwellers that small farmers are here and haven't gone away" (François Dufour, personal communication, April 16, 1998), and it also suggests that farmers can be modern and progressive while also promoting a model of agriculture that is safe, clean, and small enough in scale to allow for a robust and widely populated rural world (Guy Le Fur, personal communication, September 9, 1999). The Confédération Paysanne has thus staged several farms of the future in busy Parisian squares, or, on a few occasions, even (illegally) inside the walls of McDonald's restaurants. Other times members of the Confédération Paysanne have brought livestock to symbolic sites of contestation, transporting sheep to Montparnasse, goats to Bercy, or chickens into the offices of government and corporate lending agencies. Once, when contesting government policy on milk production, the Confédération Paysanne led a cow first to the Louvre and then to the Museum National d'Histoire Naturelle (National Museum of Natural History). The goal of this tour was to "show Parisians that real cows do still exist—before they end up only in museums" (René Riesel, personal communication, October 12, 1998).

Paysans frequently refer to two Confédération Paysanne actions that specially emblematize Conf. sensibility. In April 1992, Confédération Paysanne members emptied a bag of chicken feathers on a top executive of the Pohlmann Corporation (a German industrial chicken producer). This action protested the construction of a massive chicken farm outside Paris (with more than five million chickens). It is worth noting that this feathering was symbolic. The feathers rested on the executive only long enough to snap a picture—union members did not tar him. After feathering the corporate agent, Confédération Paysanne national secretaries reclined on the grounds of the chicken farm to picnic and conduct a formal meeting of the national committee. At this gathering, the union demanded that the government create a law (that eventually passed) requiring producers of more than three hundred thousand chickens to attain preapproval by the town prefect before opening an operation that would put small poultry producers out of business (Basson 1997). Another memorable action took place in November 1996, when 250 paysans occupied the office of the director of the Association Générale des Producteurs de Blé et Autre Céréales (French General Association of Wheat and Grain Producers) in Paris. Paysans herded six cows into the office one by one and demanded that farm subsidies be brought back to levels set before the European Commission on Agriculture lowered them dramatically. There is an iconic Confédération Paysanne poster featuring this action. I spotted it in many Confédération Paysanne members' homes and at the headquarters in Bagnolet. In the poster, government agricultural officials are seated wearing three-piece suits along one side of a table, as if in a press conference, and holding papers and notebooks. Standing across from the officials is a small crowd of white and black Holstein cows. Across the top of the poster, an understated yet hilarious headline reads: "Visit to the Wheat and Grain Association" (Baudry 1997, 25).

With these types of actions the Confédération Paysanne demonstrates its ability to develop media-ready images that communicate a politically potent and entertaining message. The Confédération Paysanne regards its direct actions as nonviolent because they generally cause minimal or incidental property damage and are symbolic (and ironic) in nature. At worst, the actions cause degrees of humiliation for the symbolic heads of powerful institutions such as the Pohlmann executive. They tend to leave behind a bit of animal manure and straw, but Confédération Paysanne members are sure to remove it all at the end of the action.

EARLY CONFÉDÉRATION PAYSANNE CAMPAIGNS: PAC, GATT, AND REFORMING FRENCH POLICY

In the 1990s, in addition to addressing the domestic problems of paysans, the Confédération Paysanne's activism focused on reform of European agricultural policy and issues of free trade. Union members addressed issues of agricultural subsidies and burgeoning international discourses on food sovereignty that emerged in the late 1990s. In 1992, the newly reformed European Common Agricultural Policy intensified inequalities among European farmers, removing limits on farm subsidies to large-scale farmers. This policy led 85 percent of farm subsidies to be distributed among 20 percent of farmers (the large-scale ones) (Pochon 1997, 116). Confédération Paysanne activists protested these reforms, demanding at minimum a limit on subsidies received by large-scale farmers and a more just redistribution of farm-based aid.

Throughout the decade leaders of the Confédération Paysanne called for the European Common Agricultural Policy to include a production quantum, a limit to the aid each farm receives, regardless of size. This request was based on the fact that for decades bigger farms received more aid, destroying smallholders in the process. In addition, Confédération Paysanne farmers demanded a subsidy repartition that would allow for the existence of eight hundred thousand French farms instead of the tiny fraction of that number that now peppers the French countryside. Needless to say, that demand has yet to be met.

During this time, the Confédération Paysanne also challenged the General Agreement on Tariffs and Trade, bolstering their claims about food by appealing to newly emerging discourses about the rights of local communities to determine their own agricultural policy. On December 4, 1993, union paysans joined eight thousand other smallholders from across Europe to travel to Geneva, carrying a banner that for the first time read *Souveraineté alimentaire* (Food sovereignty). Although the precise origin of the term is unclear, it began circulating through international smallholder forums in the early 1990s. It was formally adopted as a core principle in 1996 by La Via Campesina. What is fascinating about food sovereignty discourse is that it throws a wrench in trade-related food discourses that frame agriculture and its products as mere commodities. When viewed as a fungible commodity, the products of agriculture come under the jurisdiction of discourses of free trade, food risk, food safety, and food security. Departing from this instrumental rationality of agriculture that runs through these discourses, food sovereignty discourse is based on a solidaire rationality. Many of the world's smallholders demanding food sovereignty seek the right of individual countries to determine their own food policy—while fighting neoliberalism in general (Holt-Gimenez and Peabody 2008).

Confédération Paysanne's Agricultural Vision: Paysan Agriculture

CONFÉDÉRATION PAYSANNE'S PROGRAM: PRODUCE, EMPLOY, AND PRESERVE

The Confédération Paysanne's agricultural program represents a distinctive elaboration of many of the values derived from the solidaire rationality that originated in discourse associated with the JAC. Again, paysans remaining within the FNSEA tended to identify with the instrumental rationality of a productivist and capital-driven agriculture. In contrast, founders of the new paysan movements and the Confédération Paysanne identified more with a solidaire rationality of agriculture. According to this vision, the Confédération Paysanne must promote a spirit of solidarity between all smallholders seeking to create a robust and solidarity-based rural world.

In the 1980s and 1990s, the Confédération Paysanne printed its key slogan, "Produce, Employ, Preserve," on all union pamphlets, stickers, banners, T-shirts, and posters. These three words represent the three prongs of the Confédération Paysanne's program during this period. Each term in the slogan is framed in a square and paired with a particular image. *Produce* is illustrated with a field of grazing sheep, summoning an image of agricultural production that is small scale and pasture based, rather than an image associated with the industrial feedlot. The Confédération Paysanne's insistence on production reflects the union's belief that there is still a need for a small farmer who not only gardens the landscape, preparing an appealing countryside for passing tourists, but also a paysan who produces food for citizens. The Confédération Paysanne's programs attempt to reverse the productivist trend by restructuring the rural world based on a postindustrial model: a rural zone overflowing with robust small-scale farms. The image accompanying *employ* is a circle of women and men holding hands, symbolizing solidarity among paysans as workers struggling to establish farming as a viable option for all paysans. Here we see an insistence not only on production—growing food as an end in itself—but also on wage-earning employment, the right to use one's talents and skills to earn a livable wage. The term *preserve* depicts a childlike drawing of clouds, trees, and hills surrounding a bucolic farm. It is worth noting that the Confédération Paysanne portrays preservation in a way that diverges from many non-French environmental understandings of conserving wildlife or wilderness by protecting it from human activity. Here the paysan preserves the countryside by knowing, caring, and transforming land into a productive and meaningful landscape. The idea of nature as agriculture has specific meaning in the French context. Through words and images, the Confédération Paysanne establishes the paysan as producer and manager of the rural economy—as well as steward of the countryside whose cultural expertise preserves the land for future generations.

PAYSAN AGRICULTURE: MODERN AND SOLIDAIRE

The terms *employ*, *produce*, and *preserve* are also incorporated into the union's agricultural vision, known as Paysan Agriculture. At the union's founding meeting in Rennes in 1987, the Confédération Paysanne presented this vision, calling it "a necessity for a society that is both modern and based on solidarity" (Aubineau 1997, 107). The Confédération Paysanne links together what Raymond Williams calls keywords (1976), such as *modern* and *solidarité*. In bringing these words together, the union discursively established a notion of rural solidarity that is progressive rather than antimodern. Like the farm of the future, the union's idea of Paysan Agriculture implies a forward-looking model of agriculture that produces food while also supporting the lifestyles of other worker-identified smallholders in France and around the world.

Between 1987 and 1998, the Confédération Paysanne refined the definition of Paysan Agriculture, presenting it again in December 1998 in the form of a public document that can be found on the union's website, "L'agriculture paysanne: Une agriculture qui respecte le paysan et répond aux attentes de la société. Charter Agricole qui respecte le paysan et répond aux attentes de la société" (Agriculture Paysanne That Respects the Farmer and Meets the Needs of Society). This charter assumes the form of ten principles. Each principle represents the Confédération Paysanne's public rejection of policies related to European agriculture policy as well as those promoted by free-trade agreements. The following principles, promoted by the union, advance an alternative model to industrial farming and the agro-foods industry.

TEN PRINCIPLES OF PAYSAN AGRICULTURE

1 Providing production and distribution that allow for the maximum number to work as farmers, earning a viable income.

2 Forging solidarity with farmers in Europe and throughout the rest of the world.

3 Respecting nature by ensuring its use by future generations.

4 Promoting diligent use of rare resources.

5 Providing transparency in all relations of purchasing, production, processing, and sale of agricultural produce.

6 Ensuring the good quality, taste, and safety of produce.

7 Providing farmers' maximum autonomy.

8 Forming partnerships with others living in the countryside.

9 Maintaining the diversity of animals, plants, and land for both historic and economic reasons.

10 Being mindful of the long-term and global context. (My translation)

In the Ten Principles of Paysan Agriculture there is a solidaire rationality of agriculture that is traceable to the JAC and new paysan movements. Half of the principles (numbers 1, 2, 7, 8, 10) are drawn from such values as the right to work, international solidarity, autonomy from corporate and capitalist control, solidarity (and potential coalition) with other nonpaysan rural groups, and a concern for future generations and the world at large. These five principles articulate the Confédération Paysanne's aim to establish agriculture as a distinctly social and political activity. For the Confédération Paysanne, notions of agriculture must be understood in the context of human rights and social solidarity. Paysan Agriculture even reaches beyond the domain of farming to touch on issues of justice regarding the need to restore the vitality of rural life. The union's emphasis on both futurism and internationalism distinguishes it from parochial ruralist organizations that are antimodern, antiprogress, regionalist, or nationalist.

PAYSAN AGRICULTURE VERSUS SUSTAINABLE AGRICULTURE

The ten key principles of Paysan Agriculture reflect a divergence from other alternative agricultural discourses such as those on sustainable or organic agriculture. When related to foodstuffs, the terms *sustainable* and *organic* tend to emphasize the degree to which agricultural production methods are chemicalized and thus potentially harmful to peoples and environments. Questions of production scale (farm size), farm wages, or quality of life for people living and working in agrarian areas are largely ignored in sustainable and organic discourses on agriculture. For decades, the Confédération Paysanne has been committed to developing and promoting its own distinctive vision of agriculture. According to several of the Confédération Paysanne leaders I interviewed, the term *sustainable agriculture (agriculture soutenable)* is not a "French idea." Many Confédération Paysanne members went as far as rejecting the term *soutenable* because it was simply a direct translation of an English term that couldn't be accurately translated to French. As such, it "could not relate to the specific situation and concerns of French paysans" (François Dufour, personal communication, April 11, 1998). If pushed to use the term, Confédération Paysanne members attempted to put a French spin on it, coining phrases such as *agriculture durable* (durable agriculture) or *agriculture raisonable* (sensible agriculture). As one Confédération Paysanne leader said to me, "What is sustainable agriculture? No one really knows. It's very unclear at times and does not always include the social and political element. We need our own term to describe our own vision. The term *agriculture durable* is better than *agriculture soutenable*. But neither has precise meaning for our cause." The FNSEA uses the term *agriculture durable* to fit into the Anglophone framework. Many Confédération Paysanne members think both terms, *durable* and *soutenable*, were coined by those in non-French, specifically Anglo-dominated, contexts. Union members seemed wary of joining a perceived inchoate chorus of actors asking for different and even contradictory visions about what an alternative agriculture would be. In contrast, Paysan Agriculture offers union members an inimitable contribution to international discussions about agriculture, one that carves out a definition that cannot be contained under the rubric of sustainability (Andre Serat, personal communication, November 18, 2000).

An interesting finding: The Confédération Paysanne website as of 2012 features a significant archive of press releases, articles, and other Confédération Paysanne–related texts. When I did a search for "agriculture soutenable," only four links appeared. When I punched in "agriculture durable," I found seventy-three links. When I entered "agriculture paysanne," 384 links sprang out before me, indicating the relevance and meaning of the term within relation to the union's vision and goals.

Discourses on sustainable agriculture do indeed have a special history, quite distinct from the Confédération Paysanne's discourses on agriculture that emerge from the new paysan movements. While it is not in the scope of this book to untangle the complex and multifaceted history of notions of sustainability, it is worth noting that *sustainable development* or *sustainable agriculture* are keywords. As Williams suggests, such keywords are endowed with uncommon histories and objectives. In addition to reflecting new understandings of land, people, food, and nature, they also constitute new understandings and practices through their own networks of usage (Williams 1976). The keyword *sustainability* emerges in the early 1980s as a way to talk about stemming the tide of ecological breakdown in the Global South. Discourses on sustainable development were first cited in a formal document in 1983 by the Bruntland Commission, a team of advisors to the United Nations considering increasing problems of global resource depletion and environmental degradation. While many people today associate sustainability discourse with grassroots local movements, it is worth noting its historical ties to agents within powerful institutions. According to Arturo Escobar, discourses about sustainability were heavily promoted by northern nongovernmental organizations in the early 1990s (Escobar 1996, 52). While such organizations strove to address problems associated with the industrialization of the Global South, they also played a role in legitimizing and actually sustaining capitalist practices (Escobar 1996a). For Escobar, discourses and practices surrounding "sustainability" represent a "reinvention of nature as environment" that allows capital, rather than nature, to be sustained (1996a, 49). Corporate and regulatory agencies seeking to protect nature from unsustainable practices often end up protecting the very capitalist system that destroys lands and peoples. For Escobar, sustainability discourse colonizes lands, species, and people according to an instrumental logic, rendering them "efficient" for the advanced capitalization of nature (see Escobar 1992, 2002, 2005).

PAYSAN AGRICULTURE VERSUS ORGANIC AGRICULTURE

It is crucial to note here that the "nature" invoked through Paysan Agriculture is quite different from the instrumentalized nature-as-environmental-resource suggested by much of sustainability or organic discourse. Within the logic of paysan agriculture, the idea of nature is inseparable from the solidaire rationality extended to peoples and cultures associated with particular agricultural zones. Out of the ten key principles, just a third actually invoke the term *nature*. However, here nature represents a rationality that expresses solidarity with future generations. The other more indirect reference to nature (the ninth principle) represents a call to maintain diversity of animal and plant species for distinctly social reasons that were determined "historic" and "economic."

The Confédération Paysanne's idea of nature as agriculture does not poise nature against the idea of society. For the Confédération Paysanne, agriculture is a form of nature, a domain of work within a larger sociopolitical context. Confédération Paysanne discourse puts an unusual spin on the Western town-country dichotomy locked firmly into the popular imagination. For the Confédération Paysanne, agriculture is a domain equally imprinted by discourses of work and class, continuous with labor movements associated with the urban world. In its emphasis on production scale, Paysan Agriculture is also distinct from notions of organic agriculture, which have a different history. The term *organic agriculture* first grew to prominence within Northern Europe in the nineteenth century, later resurfacing in the 1960s as part of the back-to-the-land counterculture in the United States. As Michael Pollan points out, U.S.-based organic movements of the 1960s and 1970s (which later spread to Europe) suggested a more holistic societal vision (Pollan 2006, 141). We could say they were grounded in a solidaire rather than instrumental rationality. The sensibility originally associated with organic agriculture was one that rejected big business and consumer capitalism (associated with junk food) and sought an alternative, more community-based and rural lifestyle that would accompany an alternative food system.

In 1998, when the USDA created federal standards for organic farmers, it instrumentalized organic agriculture, reducing it to a set of technical criteria that could be easily operationalized by large industrial growers as annexes to their nonorganic enterprises. "Big organics" has become the fastest-growing sector in the agricultural market internationally (Pollan 2006, 158). Today, two large-scale organic producers generate close to 90 percent of all organic produce grown in the United States. Once again, large-scale agriculture crowds out small-scale growers, "even" in the domain of organics. The Confédération Paysanne, however, did not necessarily anticipate the co-optation of organics by large-scale agribusiness. At a meeting of the national committee at the Confédération Paysanne in 1999, I mentioned that organic agriculture was on the verge of being appropriated, or overtaken, by large-scale industrial growers in the United States. Everyone in the room looked at me with disbelief, laughing and shaking their heads. "Why should we be surprised?" asked one of the national secretaries, as he took a sip of coffee from a small, thick mug. "They'll take everything they can."

The Confédération Paysanne emphasizes production scale, so the union has never regarded organic production methods as a necessary component of Paysan Agriculture. As a social rather than environmental or technical concept, concern for agricultural scale is an expression of social solidarity; it reflects a collective desire to increase the overall number of farmers able to be employed in a given region or country. According to most union members, proponents of organic or sustainable agriculture fail to recognize issues of scale as a social as well as ecological issue. According to Dufour, the French government bases subsidies on the number of farm acres or workers. In so doing, it penalizes farmers with limited acreage and a small family workforce. It is this lack of concern for small-scale farmers that has led to a situation in which 50 percent of paysan husbands or wives work off the farm. Needing additional income to survive, farm families work in factories, drive buses, or work in retail. If lucky, each family can afford to support one full-time worker on the farm (François Dufour, personal communication, October 12, 1998). For Dufour, the smaller the size of the average French farm, the greater the number of individuals able to farm and receive aid. Dufour reflects, "Big farms take all of the aid and make it impossible for small farms to survive." As the Confédération Paysanne member André Aubineau writes in his brief history of the Confédération Paysanne, "There are those, on modestly sized farms, who decide to remain small in order to respect their neighbor, in order to allow young farmers to set up new farms for themselves" (1997, 107). Once again, the Confédération Paysanne represents a sharp departure from other alternative agriculture models in Europe or the United States that promote organic agriculture as the primary alternative to productivist farming. In fact, only a minority of Confédération Paysanne farmers use organic farming methods. While many regard it as too expensive and impractical, others view it as a bourgeois endeavor, focusing instead on the broader social context surrounding small-scale farming.

In France, debates about food are framed by paysans in primarily agricultural terms. In contrast, in the United Kingdom, Northern Europe, the United States, and Australia, consumer-driven ecology groups primarily rally the cause. The emergence of Confédération Paysanne farmers as key symbols for postindustrial agriculture (and the anti-GMO movement) is linked to local understandings of nature, culture, and agriculture.

NO NATURE, JUST CULTURE: THE FRENCH CASE

Anthropologist Marilyn Strathern has contributed significantly to our understanding of nature as an idea that is constructed in particular ways by specific peoples. In her canonic essay "No Nature, No Culture: The Hagen Case" (1980), Strathern explores the nature-culture binary as a distinctive Western way of organizing reality. Challenging structuralist notions of nature and culture as a universal (and gendered) binary, Strathern's crosscultural study of the Hagen peoples of Papua New Guinea demonstrates the extent to which the nature-culture dualism, as well as discrete notions of nature and culture, is a distinctly Western configuration.

In my research, I have found France to be home to a distinctive nature-culture framework. In combing through the considerable international literature on food quality, an interesting pattern emerges: Actors in Britain, Northern Europe, and Australia tend to frame GMOs as unnatural. In contrast, French actors tend to reject GMOs as noncultural.

In determining GMOs as noncultural, French actors presented an unusual configuration between nature and culture that departs from the classical Western nature-culture dualism. Yet before I further explore notions of a "French nature," a caveat is necessary: there is no monolithic French understanding of nature and culture. As a country composed of multiple subcultures, regions, and dialects, French understandings of nature are complex and uneven. Keeping this complexity in mind, it is still useful to point to a trend in France to construct notions of nature and culture in a unique way. French understandings of nature revolve around two primary Western approaches to ordering the nature-culture binary. First, the nature-culture binary is grounded in notions of nature as presocial rather than social. Second, the nature-culture binary is based on the idea of culture as either essential or processual.

Again, the nature-culture dualism is indeed a Western construct organized in two primary ways, presocial and social. Many in the West posit nature in opposition to culture, but others in the West construct nature in more social terms. In the latter case, nature stands in historical continuity with culture, as the two ideas are linked together in the idea of agriculture. For example, German romanticism of nature in the nineteenth century portrays nature in presocial terms, as wild and pristine in association with untouched areas (such as the Black Forest in Germany or the American wilderness). In contrast, French romanticism of nature tends to portray nature as *le terroir*. The untranslatable term *terroir* signifies in France a unique agricultural area that has distinctive soil and weather conducive to producing particular food or potables (Morgan, Mardsen, and Murdock 2006). In le terroir, meteorological and biological features of particular land areas are interwoven with the savoir faire of the artisanal producers to create, for instance, Roquefort cheese or Champagne.

In the German case, while Western notions of a wild or presocial nature percolated throughout the colonial period, they were taken to a new ideological level in the nineteenth-century nature romanticism of Germanic theorists such as Ernst Moritz Arndt and Ernst Haekel. In 1815, Arndt published *On the Care and Conservation of Forests*, which condemned deforestation associated with dawning industrial practice, calling for a harmonization between nature and culture that could be achieved by recognizing nature's "connectedness" (Staudenmaier 1995, 6). Decades later, in 1868, the zoologist Ernst Haekel coined the term *ecology*. In his book *The History of Creation*, Haekel describes ecology as the study of a nature deemed pure and primordial (Haekel 1868). For Haekel, ecology and nature were defined in opposition to society, which he regarded as inherently foreign, corruptive, and degrading (Mosse 1964, 29).

Unlike Germanic associations between a presocial nature and a primordial national identity, France tends to associate a presocial nature with that which is not French. For most French people, the idea of nature as wilderness signals a romanticized idea of that which is exogenous and exotic. In nearly every interview I conducted with actors in a variety of forums, narratives of wild nature (*nature sauvage*) did not refer to the French territory. Rather, wild nature was what led actors who could afford it to visit places and peoples in France's French-speaking former colonies, such as Cameroon and Senegal, or the colonized worlds of the United States or Australia. When speaking of nature in the French context, actors invoked romantic notions of spaces associated with traditional agricultural practice. This social understanding of nature represents an implicit collective recognition of what the theorist Neil Smith refers to as the social production of nature (1996, 49), the socialization of nature through human activity or labor. For many French people, going back to nature means returning to a particular agricultural region (*terroir*), returning to one's rural or agricultural roots (Hervieu 1996b). Today, many people in France continue to own a small country home inherited from agrarian grandparents or other relatives. For those who do not have country homes, many participate in France's well-established agrotourist industry, visiting country inns (*gittes*) that allow French tourists to "commune" with their rural pasts (real and imagined).

In my discussions with actors regarding the French anti-GMO movement, they would often appeal to reified notions of a "French nature" in their attempts to explain why the ecology movement is less prominent in France than in the Anglo-Saxon countries. Similarly, they would explain why French people have a special relationship with food or agriculture. For Pascal R., a key researcher at France's Institut National de la Recherche Agronomique (National Institute of Agricultural Research), the question of ecology is different in France because of France's lack of nature:

> You see, there is no nature in France. There are still some valleys, some ravines, and a few forests, but they are quite small, just a few hectares. The environment in France is a product of systems of human practice and so you can't treat the environmental question like you can in other countries, the Anglo-Saxon countries. The ecologists have to see nature in a different way. When they see a wild plant, for instance, they understand that behind this plant is a farmer, and the conditions in which this plant will live is a system of relationships between farmers, the government, and what happens on the European level, in Brussels. (Pascal R., personal communication, September 25, 1999)

If nature means a presocial wilderness, then France has none. In interactions with farmers throughout the country, I found so many who took pride in explaining to me how every inch of the countryside is fully used and made productive. On several occasions farmers who had heard of U.S. farming— where there are large areas of unused land surrounding farm plots—took great pleasure in bringing me to the edge of one of their fields to show how the field was cultivated right out to the road. "No room for nature here!" exclaimed one union paysan from Normandy, pointing to the tidy edge of his field of sugar beets growing nearly flush with the roadside. "You might have room to spare over in the Midwest, there," he said. "But here, we use every inch of nature that we can."

While French notions of nature are deeply social, they are also processual rather than essentialist. Once again, the dividing line tends to fall between French and Germanic ways of constructing the nature-culture dualism. In the West there are two primary understandings of culture, one based on the Germanic notion of culture as *Kultur* (inherited essence), and one on the French notion of culture as process (*cultiver*) (Pandian 1985, 30). French understandings of culture as cultiver find their origins in the preclassical Latin term *cultus*, which has two meanings, one material and one semiotic. On the one hand, cultus refers to the cultivation of the material or biological world. *Culture* is the term both for an agricultural crop and for the microorganisms used in the fermentation process required for making cheese and wine. On the other hand, cultus implies the idea of developing cultural knowledge. To be cultured is to be cultivated. It means one has developed an appreciation of cultivated things, such as French wine, cheese, literature, or philosophy. In turn, the eighteenth-century French notion of civilization, derived from the Latin *civis* or *civilitas*, is linked to the idea of cultiver, to the idea of modern progress as a universal process of development. Rather than constitute a national or cultural essence, civilization represents a developmental process, a model of upward mobility constituted by stages of human development (Pandian 1985). French understandings of nature and culture represent a distinctive understanding of the Western nature-culture dualism. Instead of there existing a fundamental tension between nature and culture, the two categories are understood as two dimensions of one continuous process of development that entails the nurturing of both material and semiotic worlds. Again, instead of a binary between nature and culture, France is marked by a binary between culture and nonculture, between people and things that are cultivated and not cultivated.

Even though the Confédération Paysanne does not rely heavily on romanticized notions of nature, the way that the union relates to politically charged discourses on nature is significant. The Confédération Paysanne's invocation of the keywords *nature*, *rare resources*, and *diversity* (principles 3, 4, and 9) reflects its attempts to enter international environmental forums that became increasingly salient in Europe and internationally during the 1990s (Gupta 1998). During this time French, European, and international environmental forums began to calculate the environmental implications of postwar intensive agriculture. Consequently, they began to produce new sets of meanings and practices that have had significant implications for the rural role of paysans.

On the European level, the Common Agricultural Policy engendered new norms related to nature and environment that greatly affected paysans. European policies emerged that attempted to engage paysans in maintaining the resources and infrastructure of rural areas. European-driven subsidies encouraged paysans to engage in such projects as improving problems related to rural water pollution or helping to restore deforested and poorly maintained areas that were increasingly vulnerable to natural disasters (e.g., fires). Perhaps most significant, European policies surfaced that attempted to persuade paysans to address the decreasing aesthetic tourist appeal of the French countryside (Perigord 1996, 37). By introducing the category of "agro-environment," the EU launched three hundred new rural development projects in sustainable development, giving priority to projects that supported a "diversified countryside," one that restores traditional forms of agriculture such as Provençal terraces and animal husbandry in the mid-mountain region. Such agro-environment projects reflected the EU's hopes to increase the aesthetic as well as environmental robustness of rural domains that had become increasingly depopulated and left in a state of disrepair. On the French level, the General Directive No. VI implemented European agro-environmental policies, offering paysans subsidies for planting environmentally appealing crops, such as sunflowers, and raising livestock more extensively and in a more spacious manner. In addition, paysans began to receive government subsidies for engaging in agricultural restoration of the nation's rural heritage (*patrimoine rural*) by planting trees, managing ponds and streams, and restoring old bridges, fences, small historical churches, and walls (Perigord 1996, 37).

In 2005, I was visiting a Confédération Paysanne family in southern France when sunflowers were in full bloom. I was contentedly riding shotgun next to Marcel L., a Confédération Paysanne member and descendant from a long line of small farmers who had at one time farmed a diversified set of crops. As I looked out over the dazzling fields, I waxed poetic about the endless acres of brilliant swaying sunflowers. "You think this is beautiful?" Marcel asked me, horrified. "Don't you?" I responded, embarrassed at what had clearly been a faux pas. "When I look at a field of sunflowers," Marcel continued, "all I see is a European policy gone wrong, an EU policy that pays paysans to grow fields of pretty flowers for tourists, rather than food. We get extra points for 'environmental beautification,' extra subsidy monies for planting fields full of sunflowers." As the rural sociologist Bertrand Hervieu suggests, the idea of countryside is important not only to foreign tourists but to French citizens themselves who, particularly since the postwar era, have stepped up a romantic and idealized desire for an attractive rural sphere. A poll from 1994 found that French citizens strongly supported the idea of subsidizing French farmers for maintaining "the aesthetic value" of French rural areas (Hervieu 1996a, 23).

While intensive farmers are in charge of large-scale production, paysans are increasingly (yet still minimally) subsidized for maintaining a countryside that is appealing to tourists (Hervieu 1996b, 7). Many founders of the Confédération Paysanne have conflicting sentiments regarding agroenvironmental policies. While many embrace beautification subsidies as a necessary source of revenue in a competitive agricultural economy, others regard them as a government maneuver to further marginalize paysans, trivializing their political goals while transforming them from active producers to gardeners (*jardinières*) who work practically for free.

MULTIFUNCTIONALITY AND CONSUMER QUALITY: NEW CONFÉDÉRATION PAYSANNE OBJECTIVES?

Many founding members of the Confédération Paysanne contest the reduction of the small-scale farmer to a gardener and maintenance crew member for the tourist-oriented countryside. In turn they have a profound distaste for the "multifunctionality concept" — the promotion by political bodies of the diversification of rural tasks and practices beyond the domain of food production. While multifunctionality also means practices of "adding value" to farm products such as milk or meat by producing artisanal cheeses and pâtés, the notion of subsidized rural restoration and stewardship is also central to multifunctionality.

The ten principles of Paysan Agriculture reflect the union's attempt to address questions of multifunctionality. In the ten principles, we see environmentally oriented keywords such as *nature, rare resources,* and *diversity.* In using these keywords, the union expresses its ambivalent desire to establish itself as a powerful conduit of French and European agricultural policy.

In addition to the ten principles of Paysan Agriculture, the charter has a section that specifically refers to multifunctionality. For instance, the section "Farming to Serve Society" concludes with the statement "To respond to the needs [of society], farming produces two types of goods: commercial goods such as foodstuffs and noncommercial entities including the environment and landscape." The Confédération Paysanne's decision to distinguish between "two types of goods" signals a slight shift in discourse from the union's earlier emphasis on rights to production and fair wages. While Confédération Paysanne literature frames this new role of stewardship as essential to its overall environmental vision, many within the union still have a cynical view of the multifunctionality idea. The former Confédération Paysanne national secretary Réné Riesel, in particular, speaks quite candidly about what he calls the "museumification" of the paysan who "plays the multifunctionality game by becoming a little showpiece in the countryside" (Riesel, personal communication, October 17, 1999). For Riesel, paysans in the union are often too willing to participate in European agri-environmental policy, becoming "gardeners rather than farmers, failing to truly fight industrial agriculture and capitalism." But there are other Confédération Paysanne farmers who see multifunctionality as a necessary means to sustain paysans until a different European policy can be created that will restore the real role of the paysan — to produce.

In addition to incorporating discourses on multifunctionality, the charter also conjures consumer-oriented discourses on food quality. Out of the ten principles, two (numbers 5 and 6) address consumer concerns such as transparency and quality in the production process. The keyword *transparency* (principle 5) is often found in politicized circles. By the 1990s, the term (clustered together with *quality* and *safety*) had become a keyword in governmental, consumer, scientific, and corporate circles during the food scares associated with productivist agriculture crises that began in the 1970s with the first hormone-treated veal affair and continue today in crises surrounding hormone-treated beef, mad cow, and GMOs. Transparency became the symbol of a food-production chain that was visible and traceable, and one in which consumers could receive plain and honest communication. The inclusion of the term *transparency* in the ten key principles (as well as in general Confédération Paysanne consumer-oriented discourse used in the press) conveys the union's tactical decision to align paysan discourses with those of consumer groups.

Conclusion

Carving out a new rationality of activism, production, and quality of food and life proved challenging for the Confédération Paysanne during its first decade. The union has always had a distinct activist style, and it achieved its goal of creating Paysan Agriculture as a model of a postindustrial agriculture that offers more than organic or sustainable agriculture while remaining an alternative to the industrial agricultural model. The union is not a monolithic entity. It is full of heterogeneous sets of objectives and strategies. While one tendency is more reformist in nature, seeking to use policymaking bodies as a primary site for social change, another wing of the union draws from a tradition of Gandhian-influenced nonviolence and direct action. The direct-action styles within the union are generally amusing, symbolic, and highly creative.

Paysan Agriculture is the central node within the union's broader vision where nearly all actors' objectives converge. Paysan Agriculture constitutes an alternative postindustrial response to the industrial model, establishing more solidaire production rationality. Whereas Paysan Agriculture generally offers a solid and clear set of principles, the union's stance in regard to issues of multifunctionality and ideas of transparency remains ambiguous. Discourses on multifunctionality allow the union to indirectly assert a culturally acceptable rationality for its own existence within an agricultural system that otherwise regards smallholders as expendable.

5

We Have Always Been Modern

Toward a Progressive
Anti-GMO Campaign

Defining a Position on GMOS

SEARCHING FOR THE CONFÉDÉRATION
PAYSANNE'S POSITION ON GMOS

When genetically modified crops and seeds began arriving on the
shores of France and throughout the rest of Europe in the fall of 1996,
it was not Confédération Paysanne members who first greeted them.
Instead, Greenpeace France confronted the ships rushing through the
Normandy waters. While the Confédération Paysanne was aware of
the new agricultural technology (particularly genetically modified
milk), the question of genetically modified staple crops had yet to
stimulate sufficient debate within the union to move members to take
decisive action. About a decade earlier, in the late 1980s, the union
learned about the introduction of r-BST in the United States (r-BST is
milk made from cows injected with a genetically modified growth
hormone). Union paysans were uneasy to see Monsanto celebrate its
product's ability to increase milk production in an era that already

had milk quotas due to overproduction. The arrival of r-BST provided cause for some union members to question the purpose of the technology. Why develop a product to increase milk production when small-scale dairy farmers have all but disappeared because of milk's overabundance?

Despite growing concern, the union's position on GMOs remained unclear through the late 1980s and early 1990s. René Riesel, Confédération Paysanne's former national secretary, remembers his own initial ambivalence. For Riesel, r-BST was indefensible. But as for the new genetically modified staple crops, he and many others in the union were less certain about the agricultural implications. As progressive Leftists, many in the Confédération Paysanne did not wish to be considered *retrograde* (antimodern or reactionary) by opposing a new scientific technology. In particular, they did not want to be seen as critical of a technology that promised to solve environmental problems associated with agriculture and end world hunger. The union's ambivalence was not helped by the fact that in Europe it was *ecolos* (French slang for *ecologists*) rather than paysans who initially contested the technology. Ecolos had a reputation for being reactionary, so many in the union wondered whether GMOs were a romantic bourgeois cause taken up by environmental groups. The Confédération Paysanne has endeavored since its inception to distance itself from visions of a closed-off parochial rural world — one that is often associated with rural villages that collaborated with the Vichy government during World War II. "If we just rejected the technology outright," said Riesel, "we could be seen as reactionary. And we wanted to avoid that" (personal communication, October 11, 1999).

GMO NEWS FROM THE GLOBAL SOUTH: MORE NEWS IS BAD NEWS

In early 1997, just a few months after the Greenpeace action, the Confédération Paysanne decided to launch its own anti-GMO campaign. This decision was facilitated by two factors. First, the union was engaging in international dialogues on GMOs among peasants and indigenous organizations in La Via Campesina (cofounded by the Confédération Paysanne in 1993) who had been fighting GMOs for several years. Second, the union was discussing GMOs with members of the French Alliance for Consumers, Ecologists, and Paysans, established in 1992. Consumer groups within the alliance were beginning to express intense concern about GMOs. The alliance's unease surrounding GMOs prompted the union to look more strategically at GMOs.

Paysans had learned from previous experience: they needed to be attentive to issues addressed by consumers' groups.

In addition to networking with French consumer groups, the Confédération Paysanne locates its anti-GMO campaign within a broad national and international movement of peasants and indigenous groups questioning and fighting the genetic modification of agricultural crops. Indeed, the union's new anti-GMO campaign would be part of a broader geographical, historical, and informational network that had been developing its own agricultural discourse for several decades. There had been an emerging solidaire rationality not only of agriculture but also of notions of technoscience, environment, and free trade. This rationality eventually crystallized in 1999 around the anti-WTO demonstrations in Seattle, which consolidated the newly emerging antiglobalization movement.

Beginning in the 1980s, international environmental organizations associated with such publications as the Malaysian magazine *Third World Resurgence* and the British journal *The Ecologist* and such organizations as the Canadian Rural Advancement Foundation International had been developing a cultural and economic critique of GMOs. From the Earth Summit in Rio de Janeiro in 1992 to the demonstrations in Seattle in 1999, critiques of relations among the Global North and South, international peasant movements, and discourses on sustainable development and food sovereignty were central to what would later become an international alter-globalization agenda. GMOs would be located within the broader rubric of global capital, global peasant movements, trade deregulation, and international environmentalism.

The Confédération Paysanne has strong ties to La Via Campesina. One of the largest groups in La Via Campesina is the Karnataka State Farmer's Union, the farmers' union in southern India. This union was garnering international attention and support for spearheading a powerful campaign against GMOs. At this time the Internet was being made available to actors outside academic and industrial networks in France. This allowed the Confédération Paysanne to receive daily reports from Karnataka farmers for whom the question of GMOs was inextricably tied up in neoliberal policies surrounding free trade and agriculture. According to Karnataka farmers at this time, GMOs meant farmers increased their reliance on agro-chemical companies that monopolize the sale of expensive patented genetically modified seeds and their requisite chemical inputs. In addition, the Karnataka farmers believed that genetically modified crops had dire implications for future agricultural biodiversity. After learning of these concerns, Confédération Paysanne actors considered the fate of paysans if a few multinational agro-chemical companies monopolized the patents for a dramatically reduced seed supply. News about a corporate and global monopoly of agriculture began to circulate through global networks of smallholders and indigenous groups internationally. Perhaps most salient for Karnataka farmers (and for the Confédération Paysanne) was the fact that GMOs threatened to put an end to seed saving, an agricultural practice that has thrived across cultures since the beginning of agriculture at least ten thousand years ago (Shiva 1993b). Historically, farmers save seeds from the most productive and adaptive plants, planting them to enhance the next year's crop. Saving seeds is also a form of cultural solidarity and reciprocity as farmers exchange seeds annually with others in their communities. In addition to providing forms of mutualism and agricultural productivity, seed saving promotes the development of seeds acclimated to particular geological and meteorological zones (Gupta 1998, 55).

When Confédération Paysanne farmers learned about biological patenting, an issue highly publicized by both the Indian activist Vandana Shiva and Karnataka farmers, concern among paysans grew. Once a seed is patented, farmers lose the right to save, reuse, or exchange seeds with other farmers. Patented seed becomes a form of intellectual property protected by state property law, as well as by international agencies such as the WTO. At home in France, Confédération Paysanne members watched small French seed companies disappear as they were bought out by large agro-chemical companies investing in agricultural biotechnology. Within five years, such large conglomerates rendered small seed companies obsolete. With the disappearance of small, regionalized enterprises capable of cultivating seeds for particular French terrains, the paysans saw a dire future. Paysans (as well as large growers) feared that they would be forced to depend on a few major multinationals to provide expensive and inflexible sets of seeds and inputs that may not be even be well suited for their own particular geographic zones.

The Confédération Paysanne's decision to create an anti-GMO campaign also emerged out of dialogues that surfaced between members of the Alliance des Paysans, Ecologists et Consommateurs (Alliance of Peasants, Ecologists, and Consumers). Central to this alliance were branches of international ecology organizations such as Greenpeace France or Écoropa who were also members of the alliance. These groups had been developing their own critiques of GMOs for several years before the Confédération Paysanne launched its campaign (Goupillon 1996). However, ecology and environmental groups lacked wide public support in a French political milieu largely dominated by political parties and unions. They were unable to sufficiently popularize their sociopolitical critique of GMOs, relying, often unknowingly, on hegemonic risk-based arguments to bolster their claims.

Écoropa is a European ecology organization with its strongest support base in France. During the early years of the union's anti-GMO campaign, Écoropa was an interesting player in the French GMO controversy. Écoropa drew its legitimacy at least in part from its ties to the well-respected journal *The Ecologist*. Yet both Écoropa and *The Ecologist* were rumored to be financed by the brother of the renowned French right-wing ecologist Teddy Goldstein. Écoropa's alleged relationship to the Goldstein family raised the suspicion of many in the alliance regarding the underlying political orientation of Écoropa itself.[1] Yet despite these reservations, the Confédération Paysanne could not ignore the news about GMOs as *The Ecologist* and Écoropa relayed information from India to Europe regarding the potential implications of GMOs. Like La Via Campesina and Écoropa, actors who publish *The Ecologist* also had direct ties to Indian agricultural politics. Shiva, for instance, published widely in *The Ecologist* and also had links to Écoropa. Shiva is renowned as one of the first international public science intellectuals to publicize the plight of Indian farmers opposing GMOs from the 1980s onward. Through Écoropa's presence in the alliance, the Confédération Paysanne had access to communiqués with Shiva. Such information sharing helped solidify the Confédération Paysanne's appreciation of the implications of GMOs for paysans.

The Risk Phase of the Confédération Paysanne's Anti-GMO Campaign

A LEG UP FOR GMOS: DEREGULATION, THE LAW OF SUBSTANTIAL EQUIVALENCE, AND BIOLOGICAL PATENTS

Throughout my research, many have asked why the United States has consistently invested so intensely in developing and exporting GMO-related technologies internationally. While the answer is not simple, I can say that it becomes clearer when we consider the postindustrial condition faced by the United States in the 1980s. That was when the United States was confronted by a potential postindustrial wasteland and initiated a search for new sites for investment capital. As the Global North had relocated much of its industrial infrastructure to the Global South in the 1970s and 1980s, an economic crater widened in the U.S. landscape. Venture capital thus sought sources of new production for capital accumulation within the United States. While U.S. investors flocked to burgeoning service and retail sectors (associated with big-box stores, megachains, and so on), as well as to informatics and computerization, they also set their sites on the promising new area of biotechnology (Heller 2001b). The Reagan and Bush presidencies left behind a legacy of stepped-up neoliberalism and environmental and health deregulation. It was in this context that governmental actors vehemently supported the fledgling biotechnology industry in the United States (McMichael 2004). To this end, the government passed a law that would establish GMO foodstuffs as "substantially equivalent" to their non-GMO counterparts. The rule of substantial equivalence entails that genetically modified seeds and cultivars are identical to non-GMO varieties, thus requiring GMOs to follow no special regulatory protocols. Substantial equivalence guaranteed investors in agricultural biotechnology that the new products would be not be subjected to regulations in a competitive agricultural market that ordinarily demanded special labels and product-safety testing. Thus, GMOs would require no labeling or rigorous scientific testing by the Department of Agriculture or the Food and Drug Administration for product safety. Any testing that would take place would be mainly for public relations purposes (proving the safety of the products). This research (and there has been little of it) would be conducted or financed by the biotechnology companies themselves.

While substantial equivalence represented a regulatory coup, the biotechnology industry received yet another leg up. In 1980 the U.S. Supreme Court ruled in favor of biological patents (Kaplan 2004). In the case, a scientist at General Electric named Ananda Mohan Chakrabarty had designed a genetically modified bacterium able to absorb crude oil. According to General Electric's lawyers, this bacterium could be an environmentally friendly way to solve the problem of oceanic oil spills such as the tragedy of the *Exxon Valdez*. Even though the genetically modified bacterium proved useless in cleaning up oil spills, the court ruled that the bacterium could be patented.

For the first time in history, biological organisms could be patented as "technical inventions." This decision rested on the Court's assertion that genetically modified organisms would not be patented per se. Instead, the genetic information within the genetically modified organism's DNA would be

decoded, catalogued, and ultimately patented. Thus, from the 1980s hence-
forth, all GMOs and their offspring would contain patented genetically modified information (Shiva 1993b).

WHY RESISTANT GENETICALLY MODIFIED SEEDS?

Biotechnology companies do also produce a few antifungal crops, but
the 1980s and early 1990s saw the dispersion of the first (and still the only)
generation of genetically modified crops to circle the globe. These crops (including corn, canola, and soy) mainly consisted of two "resistant" varieties.
The Bt variety of GMOs are genetically engineered to resist certain agricultural pests. Bt GMOs contain a soil bacterium, *Bacillus thuringiensis* (Bt), that
produces proteins toxic to agricultural pests such as beetle larvae as well as
moth and butterfly caterpillars that feed on cash crops (e.g., fruits, vege-
tables, corn, potatoes, and cotton). Bt was first discovered in 1901 by Japa-
nese scientists who were studying dead silkworm larvae. U.S. industry first
commercialized Bt-based pesticides in 1958, and Bt had captured 95 percent
of the U.S. biopesticide market by 1989 (Swadener 1997). The second group
of GMOs are genetically engineered to resist or tolerate substantial spray-
ings of Monsanto's popular herbicide Round-Up. By making the plants tolerant to Round-Up, farmers were now able to use doses that would usually
kill the treated crops. The GMO, called Round-Up Ready, also provided another function: Monsanto avoided an economic downfall when its twenty-
year patent for the Round-Up herbicide expired. Once Monsanto's patent on
Round-Up expired, any agro-chemical company could develop its own version of the same chemical compound. By patenting a Round-Up Ready genetically modified seed, Monsanto could ensure its exclusive dominance over
the product. By the early 1990s, Monsanto developed a "kit-packaging" marketing strategy that legally requires farmers to purchase Monsanto's chemical inputs when buying Monsanto's genetically modified seed (Bhabha 2007).
I call this approach the Microsofting of the agricultural economy: just as customers must buy Windows when they buy many PC computers, farmers must
buy chemical and other inputs when they buy genetically modified seed.

By the fall of 1996, U.S.-based Monsanto (now joined by Swiss-based
Novartis) began to export resistant-variety seeds and foodstuffs processed
with GMOs to European markets. By early 1997, just as the Confédération
Paysanne joined the international fight against the new technology, the
French public was becoming increasingly aware of GMOs. Due mainly to a

French network of consumer groups, scientists, and green-leaning politicians (the Socialist and Green Parties had just joined forces to elect Lionel Jospin), the GMO question began to take the French press by storm.

CORN CONTROVERSY: RISKY OR NOT?

A controversy began to emerge around a set of contradictory decisions made by the French government associated with the potential risks of three varieties of Novartis corn. Unlike the United States, Europe does not have the same law of substantial equivalence. Products issued from GMOS must be tested for approval before being considered for commercialization. Due to France's generally positive position in regard to GMOS at that time, Novartis selected the French Committée de Génie Biomoleculaire (Committee on Biomolecular Genetics) to test the genetically modified corn. The committee recommended the corn for government approval. However, just a few months later Novartis and the French scientific community were shocked when the French government rejected the committee's recommendation. In March 1997, Prime Minister Juppé publicly announced that he would not approve the three varieties for cultivation on French soil. When Prime Minister Jospin came to power soon after, he baffled the public entirely. Having run on a Socialist and Green ticket, the public expected him to assume an anti-GMO position in accordance with the Green program. Yet instead of complying with Juppé's decision to ban the corn, he decided to accept the genetically modified corn in the spring of 1998. Members of ecology, farmers', and consumers' organizations felt surprise and disappointment. They felt that Jospin and Dominique Voynet (the former leader of the French Greens and the incoming environmental minister) had betrayed them by taking a pro-GMO position.

Central to the public controversy were the risks associated with one variety of the Novartis genetically modified corn. This variety in particular contained antibiotic resistance markers (used in producing the corn) that could theoretically transfer to the digestive tract of humans or animals consuming the product. The corn controversy launched what I refer to as the risk phase of the French GMO debate. During the first period of the debate (1997–99), actors both for and against GMOS (paysan, ecology, and consumer activists as well as media and public officials) tended to emphasize the health and environmental risks, focusing particularly on questions of antibiotic resistance. Other risks included the allergenicity of genetically modified foods, the potential gene flow between genetically modified and non–genetically modified plants growing in open-air field trials, and the possibility of increased weed and pest resistance of genetically modified crops (and their non–genetically modified neighbors).

The Confédération Paysanne followed this risk trend. Whereas the union had clearly developed a broad analysis of the social and economic issues associated with GMOs gleaned from international circles, its initial public platform tended to emphasize the scientific rather than social or economic discourses that circulated through the union. For the first two years of the anti-GMO campaign, the union assumed a riskocentric stance, publicly raising questions of food safety and environmental harm and invoking the expertise of scientists to promote the cause. While Confédération Paysanne literature did also incorporate a broader solidaire rationality, members' public actions relied heavily on risk science to support their claims

TENSIONS IN THE UNION:
HOW TO FRAME GMOS? WHAT KIND OF STRATEGY?

The Confédération Paysanne's initial struggle to publicly frame GMOs was linked to underlying concerns regarding the union's relationship to French discourses on modernity. Like Riesel, many Confédération Paysanne leaders originally worried that taking a public stance against the technology could present the union in a reactionary or antimodern light. The early phase of the Confédération Paysanne's anti-GMO campaign was indeed fraught with attempts to confront ongoing cultural stereotypes about the rural world and paysans as closed off, conservative, and antimodern. In addition to the modernity question, the union addressed questions of political strategy because there existed two distinct yet overlapping wings of the Confédération Paysanne.

Guy Le Fur sought to put his energy into reforming government bodies from within. Particularly during the earlier period of the union's anti-GMO campaign (1997–99), Le Fur was weary of engaging in direct actions. Wanting to protect the union's image, he saw that direct action could reinforce stereotypes of paysans as *casseurs* (thugs), marginalizing the union in the eyes of the public. Le Fur looked to policy and advisory bodies related to agriculture as key sites for popularizing the paysan cause. In contrast to Le Fur stood the direct-action wing, which was headed up by actors such as José Bové and René Riesel. To Bové and Riesel, direct action was crucial to the

anti-GMO struggle. Direct actions represented a way to attract media attention within France while establishing the union as a central player within the
broader national and international networks. It is important to note that tensions between modernity and antimodernity or between policy and a direct-
action strategy were never discussed in my presence in official Confédération
Paysanne contexts. It was during informal discussions with Confédération
Paysanne members that I became aware of the multiple and contradictory
notions regarding technoscience, activist strategy, and the relation between
the two that existed within the union at that time.

Another unspoken tension within the union regarded whether it should
present a scientific (risk-based) or a more political perspective of GMOs.
Nearly all union members shared a solidaire rationality of agriculture, science, and the world. Yet they did not share the same view regarding how to
strategically present a solidarity-based rationality when it came to publicly
discussing the GMO question. The union's riskocentric stance is an instance
of instrumental rationality. Supporters of this position generally promoted
a policymaking reformist approach, seeking to avoid publicly denouncing
GMOs across the board. Instead, they sought to judge each genetically modified product on a case-by-case basis by appealing to available scientific information. On the other hand, the more solidaire stance on GMOs was advanced by the union's direct-action wing. Actors in this group asked for a
total ban or moratorium on GMOs. They were troubled by risks associated
with the technology, but their primary frame was social because they regarded GMOs as representing a socially unjust form of agribusiness. For these
actors, a case-by-case approach would fail to directly address the cultural,
political, and economic implications of the new technology. From both my
formal and informal interactions with various actors, it was clear that both
paysans and salariers were well aware of differences of opinion within the
union in regard to how to frame and approach the GMO issue. Yet I was often
surprised by the lack of overt tension or disagreement within the union itself.
In general, members tended to get along well, and divergent viewpoints surfaced more or less off the record. I heard many comments similar to the one
made by this salarier during lunch one day in 1998:

> Some people at the Conf. are against GMOs not because of the risks, but be-
> cause corporations are making a profit. They make pretty much the same
> statements as the Conf., they see things the same way, but they say things

a bit differently. They just draw different conclusions. Réné Riesel, for example, he is against corporations, he thinks we should ban GMOs completely. Then there are other people like Guy Le Fur; he has a different position. He thinks there are good and bad GMOs. But in the end, they do all think pretty much the same thing.

While most paysans did tend to "think pretty much the same thing" and shared a general solidaire rationality of GMOs off the record, they often disagreed on how to publicly articulate this sentiment. While many sought to emphasize more scientific arguments, appealing to risk claims, others emphasized impacts on social and biological fabrics around the world. During this first riskocentric phase, the former tended to win out as actors drew heavily on the authority of science experts to bolster their GMO-related claims (see table 1).

In February of 1997, the Confédération Paysanne published its first pamphlet on GMOs, "Technologies génétiques: Pour un moratoire sur la mise en culture et la commercialisation pour l'application du principe du précaution" (Genetic technologies: For a moratorium on cultivation and commercialization and for an application of the precaution principle) (Confédération Paysanne 1997). The pamphlet presents a signature solidaire rationality of agriculture and discusses the potential negative implications of genetically modified crops for paysans. In particular, the pamphlet emphasizes the role of GMOs in destroying paysan autonomy by increasing dependence on large seed and chemical companies as well as infringing on rights to reuse farm seed. A few features make the pamphlet particularly striking. Even though it puts forth a predominantly solidaire framing of GMOs, it strongly emphasizes notions of progress and a pro-science perspective. In turn, the pamphlet presents a substantial section on risk. Yet, overall, the document also showcases a particularly heterogeneous repertoire of solidaire discourses, by far more diverse than what other French NGOs (ecological, agricultural, and consumer) were presenting in 1997.

It was shortly after the Confédération Paysanne announced its GMO campaign that I met up with the union at the Parisian Salon de l'Agriculture in March 1997. While every progressive consumers' union or ecology group had a pamphlet or leaflet on GMOs, the Confédération Paysanne was the only organization at the salon to advance such a broad analysis that took political, ethical, and economic issues into consideration. It was for this reason that I

Table 1. Solidaire rationality and instrumental rationality

SOLIDAIRE RATIONALITY	INSTRUMENTAL RATIONALITY
No particular concern with the union's modern image.	Deep concern with protecting the image of the union as modern and forward-looking.
Emphasizes effects of GMOs on peoples and cultures with whom the union expresses solidarity.	Emphasizes the effects of GMOs in regard to scientifically provable environmental and health risk.
Tends to gravitate toward a direct-action and internationalist approach to French and international agricultural policy.	Tends to gravitate toward a lobbying approach that focuses on changing French apparatuses, concentrating on GMO-related risk.

decided to study the Confédération Paysanne. Standing there at the Parisian Salon de l'Agriculture, I was thrilled to be talking about the fate of agriculture and small farmers around the world with Marie-Agnes Fouchet—then a national secretary of the union. I was struck by the similarities between the union's discourse and the one that had influenced me back in Vermont. Looking back now, it is clear that while I did not share the exact same viewpoint with the union, we had been affected by discourses on neoliberalism and global justice traceable to the budding alter-globalization movement (first spearheaded by Indian activists).

After the salon, I took the Confédération Paysanne materials back to my apartment in Paris to study them more closely. Poring over the texts, I noticed a glaring disparity between the breadth of the pamphlet (written mainly for farmer and consumer audiences) and the narrowness of the Confédération Paysanne's public discourse for the general press. At this time, Confédération Paysanne representatives who were interviewed publicly tended to emphasize notions of risk. In particular, they invoked the precaution principle, a code of conduct used in policymaking circles across Europe on matters of science and technology innovation. Union members also drew from consumer-oriented discussions of quality and public safety.

Within the leaflet's pages were several narratives that expressed the union's concern about being misperceived as antiscience. On the first page, written in bold (in the middle of a discussion on the potential impacts of

GMOs on farmers' seed practices), is a slightly revealing caveat: "Defending the savoir faire of traditional paysans and the immemorial right of the farmer to choose his own crops has nothing to do with a backward [passéist] vision of agriculture" (Confédération Paysanne 1998, 3; my translation). Following this caveat, the pamphlet presents a series of arguments regarding the systemic problems associated with GMOs such as issues of seed saving, corporate-driven science research, and the potential impacts of the technology on developing countries. Following this broader, more politicized discussion, the pamphlet takes on a more instrumental tone, promoting a risk-oriented case-by-case approach: "Certainly, some utilizations of genetic technologies can be beneficial to the environment, providing a better quality of life for man, specifically if they can better control pests or plant illness not easily managed by sustainable methods. It is only by looking case by case, after an exhaustive study of the middle- and long-term consequences for the environment and human health, that the Confédération Paysanne will consider these innovations as instances of progress—and on the condition that [GMOs] will not lead to the development of a destructive productivism" (5). These stipulations signal ambivalence and disagreement among various union leaders about voicing a critical and systemic position on GMOs. Within the union, some actors were concerned about how to present an anti-GMO stance while protecting the Confédération Paysanne's modern public image. The union's decision to embrace a case-by-case approach is derived from its modernist roots, which are traceable to JAC and to Marxist discourse, which equate technology with progress. It is also tied to the union's fear of being regarded as passéist or retrograde—French terms that roughly translate to the English *backward*. From 1997 to 1999, the union heavily promoted Paysan Agriculture as a modern and forward-looking form of agriculture. Confédération Paysanne representatives and salariers alike expressed concerns of reinforcing stereotypes of the Confédération Paysanne as a union of ignorant *ploucs* (hicks) fearful of scientific innovation.

Because the term *plouc* appears often in this text, it deserves at least a brief discussion. Paysans often use the term *plouc* to describe how they imagine the public sees them. While the term's precise origin is unknown, most paysans believe it comes from the idea of the "stupid Breton," or the "stupid guy from Brittany." A powerful French stereotype is of Brittany filled with overcrowded farmhouses containing innumerable family members. At one time, Bretons inhabited *paroisses* (parishes). Somehow the term *plusier* (many) fused with the idea of paroisses to form the odd-sounding word *plouc*. Brittany is one of the last regions in the country where residents maintained a distinct language and culture. And many were punished for doing so — even as children. Many paysans I met from Brittany described being abused by schoolteachers who forced students to wear a heavy wooden board strung with cord around their necks. A large *B*, for Breton, the pre-French dialect of the region, was carved into the board. Having the wooden *B* hang from one's neck was a humiliating reprimand for speaking in Breton during school hours. People who live in Brittany are ridiculed to this day as the symbol of an antimodern and backward refusal of a progressive French society.

The plouc stereotype made the paysans wary of going public with their position on GMOs. The paysans were aware that the modernist FNSEA had yet to adopt a public stance in regard to GMOs, so the Confédération Paysanne was skittish about going out on a limb in the broader unionist milieu. After all, they were the only leading farmers' union to take a public stance on the new technology.

The union made it clear that it was critical of particular cases of GMOs, so the Confédération Paysanne avoided being perceived as antiscience or antimodern. And by appealing to the precaution principle, the Confédération Paysanne invoked a socially legitimate and modern discourse on technoscience that promotes vigilance regarding innovation. The precaution principle helped the union present itself as simultaneously forward thinking and critical of a new technology.

LA BATAILLE DE LA VILLETTE

The Confédération Paysanne faced tensions while protecting its modern and progressive public image. In the winter of 1998, the French government announced it would hold a public debate about GMOs at the Cité de la Villette, a public museum, conference, and entertainment complex located just outside Paris. The debate was publicized in several newspapers and on the radio as the government's attempt to respond to the public's request for consultation and discussion regarding GMOs. The committee that planned the event invited scientists, industry officials, government agents, and social scientists viewed as supportive of the technology. It also invited representatives from ecology and consumers' associations who had publicly voiced criticism of GMOs. Upon hearing of the list of invitees (mainly through informal networks), many in anti-GMO groups in Paris deemed the impending debate scandalous. In the weeks before the event, I met with activists in various forums who said the debate was a botched governmental response to public outcry. According to these actors, the government had failed to consult key leaders or incorporate them in anti-GMO associations into the event. Thus the debate was denounced by many weeks before it ever took place.

I attended the debate with an intern at the Confédération Paysanne, curious to see if the forum would successfully stimulate public debate on GMOs. As I entered the enormous ultramodern auditorium, I took my seat in the packed audience. On the stage sat a panel of well-dressed white men behind a sleek black table. Behind the row of seated men, an enormous video screen hung, concert style, to be used for slides or film. It would also magnify the image of presenters reading their papers at the podium. For the first thirty or so minutes, men rose and took to the podium to read papers deemed tedious by those sitting around me. Across the audience I could hear people rumbling audible remarks such as "Ooh la la" and "Ça fait casser les oreilles!" (This is so boring!) during each paper reading. Then in the middle of a paper presentation, an unexpected turn: a series of eggs zoomed through the air, projected from unidentifiable sources. Eggs and shells splattered across the presenter and the screen, leaving the blurred image of experts standing dazed on stage. For several seconds I watched the wavering form of a man in a suit, apparently disoriented, trying in vain to remove egg from his face with wilted drooling sheets of his own papers. The audience exploded with shrieks of horror and surprise (more "Ooh la la!"). Alongside the many cries of "C'est quoi ça?" (What is this?) rings of laughter developed as people ducked to avoid the ever-flying eggs.

While the eggs soared, a series of anonymous and nondescript audience members rose to their feet holding sheets of paper. One by one they read inchoate yet discernible statements of outrage about the need for real public debate about science. Each individual read his or her paper in a slow, determined, monotone voice, decrying the debate as nothing but a sham or a false substitute for public consultation. Finally, the egg throwers and the orators took their seats.

Sitting in the audience, I could not help but be impressed by one thought: had this event taken place in the United States, police or security would have removed the orators and egg throwers within seconds. Perhaps even some kind of charge would have been pressed. However, nothing of the sort took place here. The egg throwers and orators were allowed to remain in the theater once the event resumed. The egg toss and speeches lasted about seven minutes or so. At some point, a woman wearing a bright-red skirt suit smoothed her hair into place and walked onto the stage. Smiling calmly, she called for a brief intermission. During this interlude, everyone bustled about, chatting with friends and colleagues about who could have planned such a spectacle. The most remarkable thing to me was that following the intermission, the debate resumed as if absolutely nothing out of the ordinary had just occurred, and no one on stage made a verbal reference to the preceding events. Following their cue, the audience returned to their plush seats and listened, this time more quietly, to the rest of the presentations. A few presenters did make jovial allusions to the remaining eggshells stuck to the desk or to the screen still dripping overhead. Others just rose in good cheer, happily rifling through their papers.

When the event was over, ushers hurried the crowd out of the building. There was no lingering in the center's grand entryway to socialize as audiences usually do after a show or presentation. Once out of the building, people scattered down to the metro, engrossed in lively conversation. For weeks afterward there was significant buzz in Paris as experts and activists alike attempted to determine who was indeed responsible for what had been baptized La Bataille de la Villette (The Battle of Villette). After a few days, it was simply referred to as La Bataille.

A week later, I attended a meeting at the French equivalent of the U.S. Department of Agriculture. The Institut National de la Recherche Agronomique (French National Institute for Agricultural Research) had a special office for social and political affairs headed up by a Left-leaning social scientist whom I will call Michel Beauvent. Beauvent often held impromptu meetings, after hours, from five to seven, at his office in Paris. Calling these meetings *cinq a sept* (five to seven) was a humorous play on words. In France, *cinq a sept* is an expression for an after-work romantic tryst. The meeting's comical name communicated Beauvent's desire for participants to meet and discuss political ideas in a relaxed, informal, and enjoyable atmosphere. Beauvent always served wine and assorted salted nuts (a proper before-dinner snack) to please his guests. Beauvent invited individuals to attend five to sevens whenever he felt that pressing agriculture-related matters surfaced in France. Being invited to a five to seven was regarded as a marker of political or intellectual status, and most actors attended if they could. Beauvent always emphasized at the beginning of each meeting the informal nature of the gathering as well as the fact that the arena was meant to stimulate discussion rather than solve problems or make formal policy recommendations.

Beauvent was one of my key informants, and he was an ongoing source of crucial cultural and political information. I was delighted to be invited to my fourth five to seven. Beauvent invited twenty or so intellectuals, activists, industry agents, and government officials as well as a Confédération Paysanne salarier, a union organizer who worked on the GMO question. Beauvent explained that we had gathered to analyze the events of La Bataille. As usual, Beauvent offered his guests refreshment. But this time his offerings had a droll twang. Clear glass bowls of hard-boiled eggs were placed around the small office room—along with the usual fair of wine and salted nuts. I was surprised to see many participants actually nibbling on the eggs, as hard-boiled eggs are not a typical food item offered to guests at a meeting or any social engagement. By giggling as they bit into the peeled eggs, participants seemed to be demonstrating an air of good humor. Many even dabbed their egg with bits of salt while laughing in a jocular, almost cynical way about the whole affair.

After much informal gossip and discussion, Beauvent called the group to take their seats around the room. Perhaps the most prestigious guest was Guy Paillotin, the president of the Institut National de la Recherche Agronomique. After several people in the room offered comments regarding the possible originators and meanings of La Bataille, the room quieted as Paillotin began to speak. I could feel the union's salarier squirm next to me as Paillotin made numerous allusions to the Confédération Paysanne's responsibility for La Bataille. As Paillotin spoke, he appeared bemused and slightly patronizing, chuckling that it was "good for paysans to express their discontent with the overall situation."

The next day, at a Confédération Paysanne meeting, the salarier informed the paysans about Paillotin's comments. "It was clear, though," the salarier stated, "that he saw the egg throwing as the work of unsophisticated people; he saw it as the work of paysans. I was really upset by it." Union members were not responsible for the egg throwing. One paysan at the meeting expressed outrage, declaring, "We have so many scientific arguments at our disposal. Why would we resort to tactics like that? We are not casseurs! Those kinds of acts just heighten prejudice against us." There were nods of agreement. All seemed agitated and outraged. Participants at the meeting reached immediate consensus that the union must immediately send a letter to Paillotin, demanding an apology. After several weeks of waiting, the union finally received a two-sentence note from Paillotin. For union members, the state official had delivered a delayed and weak response. They found Paillotin's brief narrative dismissive and insulting. For weeks union members made frequent references to Paillotin's insult. They commented on the overall political and social milieu in which paysans must continually differentiate themselves from chauvinistic stereotypes such as ploucs who would disrupt a public meeting by throwing eggs.

Sitting among the paysans, I could feel for the first time the weightiness of their desire to be seen as intellectually and politically sophisticated. This small crowd of paysans, generally so quick to laugh at any absurdity, found no humor in the stories surrounding La Bataille. With no cultural room for humor, the paysans hunkered down to consider how to redeem the union after learning those at the five to seven laughed along with Paillotin about paysans needing to express themselves by throwing eggs. For many, using scientific arguments about GMOs was the key antidote to counter the public's perception of paysans as childish ploucs who knew no better than to throw food at people in power.

Confédération Paysanne Victory: Guy Le Fur and the Report for the Conseil Économique et Sociale

A BRIEF HISTORY OF LE FUR AND OVERVIEW OF THE REPORT

Guy Le Fur was a key figure during the riskocentric phase of the union's anti-GMO campaign. A founding member of the union, Le Fur appealed to risk in promoting what he called a progressive GMO critique. During the time when Le Fur prepared a government report on GMOs, he was a hog farmer in his late forties. Le Fur lived with his family in Brittany, making the three-hour commute to Paris several times a week to carry out union responsibilities. A tall man of slight build with shortly cropped silver hair, Le Fur is a presence that commands respect and admiration, and he speaks and laughs with a quiet modesty. Although he is soft spoken, Le Fur is a powerful public speaker and respected as a union founder and a passionate fighter for social justice. After coming of age in the JAC movement, Le Fur joined the youth wing of the FNSEA and later the main FNSEA, eventually becoming a president in his county's branch. Le Fur was among the many in the new paysan movements who believed for many years that the FNSEA could be reformed from within, and he was at first reluctant to abandon the majoritarian union to create the Confédération Paysanne (Guy Le Fur, personal communication, October 27, 1998).

Le Fur describes finding it hard to simply leave the FNSEA, allowing agribusiness to continue its dominance. Yet in 1982, Le Fur had no further choice when leaders in the FNSEA labeled Le Fur a dissident. That year he had written a report on the need for the government to create subsidy adjustment for farmers working in difficult geographic zones. After learning of the content of Le Fur's report, FNSEA leaders officially blocked him from presenting it at a national meeting. Having labeled him a union dissenter, they then pressured him to resign. Demoralized by FNSEA politics, Le Fur was eager to find another forum in which to further the paysan cause. That year, he went on to found a small paysan-based union in his region. A few years later, in 1987, Le Fur went on to become a key founder of the Confédération Paysanne. He was elected to serve as a Confédération Paysanne national speaker between 1989 and 1993. In 1994, Le Fur became the Confédération Paysanne's chief liaison to the French Conseil Économique et Sociale (Council on Society and Economics). The council is an advisory body in Paris. It is composed of representatives and groups that speak on behalf of various sectors of French society. When preparing policy on a particular topic of social or economic concern, the government looks to the council to provide a comprehensive report on the issue. If the report is approved, the council publishes and circulates it in book form throughout a range of policymaking circles. A report composed by a council appointee is expected to inform state policymaking in a significant way. Le Fur's appointment at the council marked the first time the Confédération Paysanne was to be represented in a major government advisory body. In addition to granting prestige to the union, this appointment signaled a challenge to the hegemony of the FNSEA in the council. Le Fur's presence at the council signaled the moment when the Confédération Paysanne became a major player in a national policymaking forum. In 1997, Le Fur decided that he would take on a most challenging mission: he would write a proposal to create a key council report on GMOs.

The story of Le Fur and his report for the Conseil Économique et Sociale is one that demonstrates the power of language, knowledge, and power in producing particular kinds of subjects, identities, and practices (see Foucault 1976). Throughout the report-writing process, which I witnessed, I noted the ways a written text—a linguistic inscription—can exert a discursive power that is distinct from economic or political power waged by powerful institutions. Through writing the report, Le Fur and the Confédération Paysanne were seen in a light new by actors in the FNSEA and other powerful institutions. By the end of the project, Le Fur and the union had new subjectivities: they were regarded as modern, intellectuals, and competent authors.

The stakes surrounding the report were indeed high. The Conseil Économique et Sociale conducts research on topics of social concern and presents reports that are consulted each time the government passes a national orientation law (*lois d'orientation*). In short, an orientation law is similar to a national act in the United States that lays down the basic principles for government action in a given field. For instance, the U.S. Department of Education created the American Recovery and Reinvestment Act of 2009, whose objective was to recover funds in order to allocate services to children and youths with disabilities. Similarly, in France, national orientation laws are created by various government bodies in order to clarify the rationale surrounding a course of action in a particular domain of society. Among its 247 members, the council maintains a balance of workers, business owners, and members of major civic associations. The council is divided into eighteen working groups and twelve sections, and activities are organized around issues such as agriculture, technology, environment, and workplace.

Perhaps it was his history in the FNSEA that drove Le Fur to write the report for the council. When the FNSEA blocked Le Fur from presenting his controversial report twenty years earlier, it turned him into, in his words, "a fighter." Now at the council he would work tirelessly for months, doing whatever he could to prepare a report of the best quality that would not be shot down. Council protocol requires interested parties to first conduct a pilot study, and then, if the study is approved, to compose an official report. The project to create the pilot study and then the report represented a grueling year-long endeavor involving intensive research and writing. In addition to commitment, it required the mobilization of an elaborate network of experts on agriculture, technoscience, and GMOs. Le Fur was responsible for assembling a set of actors in domains of economics, molecular biology, law, and agricultural science. He was also responsible for meeting with heads of consumers associations, environmental organizations, public science bodies, and government agencies. His goal in each meeting was to extract as much information on GMOs as he possibly could. Le Fur also headed up a GMO research team at the union, which included key members such as Valentin Beauval and José Bové. The individuals who worked most mightily on this yearlong project were Le Fur and Julie Audren, a young expert in agricultural science hired by the Confédération Paysanne. The third member of the team was Maria Garcia, an agriculture specialist "on loan" from the council to assist Le Fur and Audren in learning how to compose the report. Together, Le Fur, Garcia, and Audren became a solid trio, working long days and evenings, confronting a tense political climate at the council every day. I was fortunate enough be allowed to attend many of the meetings held by Le Fur at the Confédération Paysanne's office and at the council itself.

As Le Fur predicted, FNSEA leaders, also working within the council, were openly hostile opponents of Le Fur and his team. Upon learning of the Confédération Paysanne's attempt to establish itself as a competent and equal presence in the council, the FNSEA members expressed concerns (off the record) that the Confédération Paysanne would take a strong political stand on GMOs. According to FNSEA officials, this would force the FNSEA to take a public stand on GMOs before they were prepared to do so. So far the FNSEA had yet to adopt a formal or public position on the GMO question. According to Le Fur, FNSEA representatives tried to sabotage the trio at every step of the way. Their objective was to prevent Le Fur from presenting the pilot study and, ultimately, the council report on GMOs. When FNSEA representatives in the council's technology working group first learned of Le Fur's proposal, they challenged the scientific expertise of Le Fur and the Confédération Paysanne. They went as far as insisting that the more "technically sophisticated" FNSEA leaders should be selected for compiling the report instead. In the end, the council partially ceded to the FNSEA's wishes, dividing the GMO report into two parts. The first half was to be compiled by FNSEA representatives in the council's technology working group. This half would address both medical and agricultural uses of GMOs. The second half of the report was to be composed by Le Fur, who would also be placed in the council's agriculture working group. The scope of Le Fur's report would be limited. He would be permitted only to cover the agricultural applications of GMOs in France. When Le Fur received news about how the report was to be divided, he was enraged. Yet when I asked him about how he would proceed, Le Fur flashed a wry and quiet smile, saying, "Yes, they're ridiculous . . . but

I am always up for a fight. Our report will be narrower in scope, but it will be better. We'll just have to do a better job than they!" (personal communication, November 19, 1999).

For months the Confédération Paysanne's team worked endlessly, combing through various drafts and rigorously debating the report's content. They negotiated a series of compromises they would have to make. Le Fur was forever troubleshooting, anticipating criticism from the FNSEA members who would inevitably be present in the council's agricultural working group. While abridging the text to avoid a stalemate, the team was determined to include key points of importance to the Confédération Paysanne, such as the potential impacts of GMOS on French smallholders. In each meeting there were negotiations regarding what to include or how far to push particular issues, such as the ethics of patenting life. While no one ever stated outright that the report could not be too radical, there were frequent discussions about not appearing too negative, and about the need to draw, as much as possible, from scientific arguments.

If the council ultimately accepted Le Fur's report, this success would symbolize the Confédération Paysanne's position within the broader political landscape. It is important to note that the objective in writing the report was not to present the Confédération Paysanne's position on GMOS. As Le Fur stated, "This is not a Confédération Paysanne report; it is a report for the council composed by a representative of the Confédération Paysanne. It must be of the utmost quality" (personal communication, April 19, 1998). During numerous conversations with members of the trio and the research team, actors described the report as a potential triumph over chauvinism, in addition to a symbolic victory over the FNSEA. According to Garcia, in preparing the report, Le Fur faced considerable antimodernist prejudice: "After the first part of the report came out, a member of a FNSEA leader comes up to me and says, 'I'm sorry to have to admit that the report's quite good. I wasn't expecting such high-quality thinking.' And what he's really saying is that he thinks Guy is not capable of doing things correctly, because Guy is from the Confédération Paysanne. They judge him without knowing him. The Confédération is seen as a bunch of ideologues who are oppositional, antiprogress, not very intellectually cultivated. And so Guy has to be careful to work harder than other reporters" (personal communication, October 22, 1999). In July of 1999, the Confédération Paysanne finally saw victory. Le Fur's report of nearly three hundred pages was published under the title *La*

France face au defi des biotechnologies: Quels enjeux pour l'avenir? (France facing the biotechnology challenge: What are the stakes for the future?). The report was unanimously accepted by the council and was described by council administration as exhaustive, detailed, and scientifically accurate.

THE SYMBOLIC MEANING OF THE REPORT

Looked at one way, the text was what Foucault would call a disciplining technology (1976) of governance, enticing its authors to voluntarily conform to a rationality of government when it came to science. Because it is written in the bureaucratic style of a government agency publication, the report uses an instrumental logic of cost-benefit analysis. The report considers, for instance, the risks or advantages of particular applications of GMOs, framing them in such terms as economic risks, legal consequences or liabilities, and health and environmental risks.

In the report's conclusion, Le Fur summarizes the technological, economic, and agricultural implications of GMOs, asserting the technological benefits that they could provide. He also stresses the importance of France supporting its own biotechnology industry and the need to further study the agricultural risks. In general, the report presented a generally positive picture of GMOs, depicting the technology as controllable, inevitable, and a new site for French agricultural research. By being swayed to paint an optimistic portrait of GMOs, Le Fur was perhaps ceding to the pressures of the council. When we look more closely, however, the picture becomes far more complex. By writing the report, Le Fur (and the union) were both disciplined and empowered. Although they were coerced to align themselves with the objectives of powerful institutions, they were also able to establish themselves as budding brokers within a governmental body. Often after council meetings I'd meet Le Fur and his team at a little café where Le Fur, Audren, and Garcia would drink coffee or wine, laughing about the day's various foibles and triumphs. Despite their palpable frustrations, they clearly felt proud of the work they were doing.

When the report came out in book form, it received little press coverage. It ended up falling a bit flat, making few, if any, waves in either official or activist circles. Le Fur surmised that "it didn't really help that it came out right in the middle of the summer when people were thinking about vacation" (personal communication, September 26, 1999). According to the Confédération Paysanne and others in policymaking circles, the report had little political impact. It ended up having minimal effect on policymaking surrounding GMOs. Yet neither Le Fur nor the Confédération Paysanne appeared disappointed. In contrast, Le Fur reported a feeling of triumph that the report was overwhelmingly accepted at the council. He also took enormous pride that, in the end, the text incorporated many points important to the union, including "the potential impacts of GMOs on farmer autonomy and on farmers in developing countries" (personal communication, November 17, 1999). The report, the product of considerable compromise and negotiation, contained elements of a solidarity-based view of GMOs that might not have ever been presented to a public advisory body.

After a year of intensive study and research, Le Fur and the rest of the Confédération Paysanne research team had become self-taught experts. They proved themselves capable of nuanced reflection in a variety of technical as well as social and economic domains. For the Confédération Paysanne, the report had particular meaning. The text demonstrated the intellectual abilities of paysans in a broader sociopolitical context. The council report did have cultural weight, and it embodied the Confédération Paysanne's ongoing struggle to establish itself as a major stakeholder in governmental bodies, and as a union of competent political actors capable of intellectual accomplishments.

Conclusion

When considering the union's historical and cultural ambiance, it is easy to appreciate actors' initial hesitance in taking a public stance on GMOs. Clearly the union hoped to appear modern and forward thinking. But it also sought to express a solidaire rationality of agriculture that stands at odds with the instrumental rationality surrounding GMO technology. As time went on and union members consulted activists in the Global South, many in the activist wing began to gain confidence in the validity of their own anti-GMO position. While still relying on riskocentric arguments during the first phase of the French debate, the union also continued to fortify its solidaire critique. This solidaire rationality would become more pronounced on a public level after 1999 in a way that no one could have ever imagined.

The union's solidaire rationality of agriculture was crucial, but gaining acceptance in French policymaking circles was also a key objective. Le Fur's report circulated through networks of experts, activists, and powerful institutions, transforming each actor who produced it. As a form of governance, the text both disciplined and empowered its authors. While Le Fur and his staff made many instrumental concessions, they also used the text as a mechanism to establish the Confédération Paysanne as a legitimate player within a larger political machine.

6

The Trial of the GMOS

*Deploying Discourses from Risk
to Globalization*

The Confédération Paysanne's anti-GMO campaign is a story of an alternate production rationality that gained ascendancy within a debate about food and agriculture. It is an account about how this alternate rationality represents a counterhegemony that opened a space for a solidaire as well as an instrumental rationality of agriculture and science. Actors in the Confédération Paysanne began to speak more publicly about GMOs, venturing increasingly outside the dominant discourse of risk. Their success in popularizing a solidaire rationality is linked to a kind of cultural clout the union was able to cultivate that established its members as paysans rather than scientific experts within the broader anti-GMO network. The Confédération Paysanne's first major anti-GMO direct action, The Trial of the GMOS, gained José Bové and the union public attention and credibility sufficient to popularize an alter-globalization perspective to advance a broader solidaire rationality of agriculture in the public domain.

The Confédération Paysanne's Direct-Action Wing

JOSÉ BOVÉ AND RENÉ RIESEL

Key figures in the Confédération Paysanne, such as Guy Le Fur, emphasized a lobbying approach, choosing to reform existing political bodies to inform agricultural policy. While Bové and René Riesel commended Le Fur's triumphs, they add a complementary approach to achieving the union's objectives. By promoting a direct-action strategy, these leaders drew from the Confédération Paysanne's roots in Paysans-Travailleurs, the strike of May 1968, and the Larzac. The union was never split into two camps, though. Bové even joined Le Fur's research team in preparing the report for the Conseil Économique et Sociale. Bové appreciated the symbolic meaning of the project, and he went to great lengths to research and to provide information to Le Fur regarding GMOs' relevance to French agriculture. By the same token, union leaders unanimously decided to publicly and financially support the direct actions spearheaded by Riesel and Bové as they unfolded after January 1998. Even when expressing concerns about reinforcing the image of paysans as casseurs, the union stood by its members when they took a direct-action approach.

The Confédération Paysanne's direct-action campaign began in January 1998 in the southern town of Nérac. The campaign continued through the spring of 1999 in a series of "crop pulls," culminating in an anti-McDonald's action headed up by Bové in August 1999. Bové and Riesel eventually parted ways over ideological differences at the end of that year. But for a period of time, these two potent personalities played a major role in putting into place an alter-globalization critique of GMOs that would eventually influence not only the activist terrain in France but the international arena as well. The two activists share much in common. Bové and Riesel, both *néo-ruraux* (those born outside the paysan world), were influenced by the events of May 1968. Then they turned to the farming life in their youth after being alienated by French postwar political and economic culture. For Bové, his dissatisfaction with French society originally stemmed from a rejection of militarism. For Riesel, the culture of consumer capitalism engendered a kind of cultural emptiness associated with late-modern society (Polanyi 1957; Polanyi and Pearson 1977). For both actors, the paysan identity represented an attempt to build a more meaningful way of life. Rural living provided a potent vantage point from which to understand and change the world.

RENÉ RIESEL: SITUATIONIST PAYSAN

I first met Riesel in February 1998 at the Confédération Paysanne's headquarters during his last days as a national secretary. I had heard a lot about Riesel at the union. Mostly I had been impressed with discussions regarding his intense political conviction, fierce intelligence, and passionate personality. Riesel agreed to an interview, and sat across from me at a table at union headquarters, chain-smoking hand-rolled cigarettes. His speech was rapid-fire, tinged with a southern accent. Riesel rattled off paragraphs, rather than sentences; he was so immersed in his own narrative that he barely made eye contact. I was impressed by what I perceived as a roiling set of contradictions. Riesel was humorous and ironic — yet dead serious in his conviction on political matters. He had a warm and engaging smile, but also a darting fervent look as he delivered stories about his life or about his critiques of the union. While firmly committed to the union, he also criticized it for not pushing its goals far enough.

At the time of the interview, Riesel was a short muscular man in his late forties with a ruddy complexion and sporting a goatee and roughly shorn jet-black hair. He was usually dressed in old jeans, hand-knit sweaters, and a pair of worn leather clogs. Riesel was constantly in the process of either rolling, lighting, or extinguishing a cigarette. He was born in Algiers in 1950 and is the son of Jewish immigrants. His mother, a Sephardic Jew, was raised in Algeria, while his father grew up under the Austro-Hungarian Empire and became a watchmaker and jeweler. Riesel's father was a communist, nurturing in Riesel a critique of the capitalist system. Riesel's father met his wife after moving to Algeria in the early 1940s, seeking asylum from Hungary's increasingly anti-Semitic political climate. After the Algerian war, when Riesel was twelve, the family moved to Paris, where Riesel attended high school for a brief time. He recalls being teased for being an Arab. He was often the target of ethnic epithets, being called a *pied noir*, a pejorative and racist French slang term for Algerians that suggests they are people with black or dirty feet. When recalling the insults, he smiled wryly, saying, "What do you want? Of course I was happy when kids didn't see me as truly French. I hated the French." At sixteen, Riesel became increasingly disenchanted with public school. He dropped out and was drawn toward various anarchist and communist circles. It was then that he began a lifelong engagement with revolutionary ideas and the communist movement. After participating in the Congres Anarchiste (Anarchist Congress) in 1967, Riesel briefly attended the University de Nanterre. At that time, Nanterre was a cultural and political center that wildly excited Riesel.

At Nanterre, in the spring of 1968, Riesel broke with the Communist Party and became the youngest member of the infamous anarchist group Les Enragés (The Enraged Ones). Les Enragés was a small but powerful group of five activists who banded together with the Situationist Internationale (Situationist International), an even more powerful group of anarchists who developed an avant-garde critique of postwar consumer-capitalist France. Building on the philosophy of Guy Debord, the Situationist Internationale members saw their mission as helping French society discover the spectacular abomination that postwar France had become. For Debord, "spectacular society" was forged out of notions of progress and modernity, ideas that translated into forms of modern technology, architecture, consumer capitalism, entertainment, and the media. According to Debord, under late capitalism, "The Spectacle" comes to increasingly dominate the sociocultural landscape and reduces humanity to a passive consumer and viewer of the machinations of capitalist society itself (Plant 1992). To put an end to the meaningless spectacle of society, the Situationist Internationale members created counterspectacles in churches, classrooms, sidewalks, and cafés through street theater, graffiti, and art installations in city squares. The sensibility was often absurd. A man and woman might lie down naked inside a public fountain, imitating its nude sculpted classical figures. Or they might paint sayings like "L'université, c'est la peinture," "University is paint," across the walls of an old university building. Together, the Situationist Internationale and Les Enragés were responsible for providing much of the sensibility, aesthetics, and theory behind the events of May 1968 (Plant 1992, 73).

Riesel was soon elected president of the Committee de L'Occupation de la Sorbonne (Occupation Committee of the Sorbonne) on May 14, 1968. This committee was charged with overseeing the ongoing occupation of the Sorbonne by students, workers, and others involved in the May events. One month later, he joined the Situationist Internationale, becoming a fervent member until his exclusion in 1971. When reflecting on his time in the group, he laughed, recalling, "What was truly great about the Situationist organization is that eventually, everyone was expelled—just the way the communists expelled their members. We even sent letters to people who were never even members of the Situationists, informing them of their expulsion."

In contrast to the authoritarianism of the Communist Party and scientific Marxism, Les Enragés and Situationist Internationale emphasized free association, nonorganization, and artistic and "libidinal self-expression" as antidotes to the perceived lifelessness of a highly consumerist society (Plant 1992, 75). The revolution, they believed, would be fought spontaneously as workers, students, and everyday people realized what a boring spectacle postwar society had become (Debord 1967). During the major strikes and demonstrations of May 1968, Les Enragés and Situationist Internationale helped shape the mass mobilization of workers and students who, in an unprecedented alliance, called for a set of major reforms in such domains as factories, retail stores, and universities. Even though May 1968 was marked by sets of material demands, the events were distinct because they incorporated earlier psychological and aesthetic movements such as surrealism, Dadaism, and Freudianism, forming a potent activist cocktail. Both groups encouraged creative acts of spontaneity such as writing poetry on factory and university walls, occupying theaters for sites of debate, and constructing street barricades out of pillows and couches while prancing around the streets in fanciful costumes.

When I asked him about his current political identity, Riesel recalled that while his ideas had matured over the years, he still mostly identified as a Situationist. "If I agree with *anything*," Riesel said, chortling, "I guess I still agree with Situationism. My political analysis is still very much inspired by the ideas associated with May 1968." When the events of May 1968 came to a close, Riesel reports he fell into a depression, and "hid out" in Paris until the age of twenty-two. In 1972, he and his common-law wife, Françoise, moved to the country with Françoise's young son from a previous marriage. They decided to become farmers. "I had to leave," Riesel said. "You had the feeling that life had disappeared completely from Paris. Les Halles was being turned into a shopping mall" (personal communication, October 10, 1998). When Riesel and Françoise left Paris to become néo-ruraux, Riesel asserted that they never identified with the more romantic back-to-the-land movements that emerged in France in the early 1970s. For Riesel, such movements were influenced by the hippie ideologies of U.S. Americans. He found such trends politically unappealing in their naïveté and lack of analysis of "the system." His decision to move to the country was not particularly political or idealist; it represented a personal attempt to remove himself from a "deadening Paris in the wake of 1968" (personal communication, October 18, 1998). Riesel expressed cynicism for French ecologists that did "the hippie back-to-the-land thing, trying to bring life back into the rural." For Riesel, such movements are "ridiculous, because at this point in history, the rural can never really be more than an annex to the global market."

Riesel and Françoise moved with their son to the southeast near Papillon. Riesel described the area as economically depressed and arid. It was a region where sheep farming was practically the only agricultural option. They also decided to raise sheep to protect the land from the kind of disuse that resulted in disastrous forest fires. After ten years, Rene and Françoise tired of living among what Riesel describes as "parochial and inhospitable villagers suspicious of young out-of-towners who wanted to farm. . . . These villagers preferred to sell unused land to wealthy Germans to build their summer houses." In 1983 Riesel and Françoise moved to Lozere, a nearly deserted area in southwestern France, tended mostly by sheep farmers: "This time we showed up with our sheep and things went over much better. Now we looked like farmers. You should see it there, though. It's like Siberia, a very difficult place to farm and live, but the community is much more welcoming; far less xenophobic" (personal communication, October 18, 1998).

Riesel joined the regional body of the Confédération Paysanne in the early 1990s. In our discussions, he emphasized that he did not decide to join the union out of political idealism: "I joined the union because I wanted some form of political affiliation after years of isolation in the rural world." From the beginning, Riesel had concerns regarding reformist aspects of the Confédération Paysanne's political agenda. When he finally joined the union, he said, it was because he ultimately supported its "overall agricultural policy." In 1994 Riesel was elected a national secretary. He describes his first two years as a national secretary as generally positive and stimulating. During this time he fully committed to playing a defining role in the Confédération Paysanne's anti-GMO campaign, working side by side with Bové, a fellow activist and sheep farmer.

The second part of Riesel's term, however, proved problematic. During his last year as a national secretary, tensions mounted when Riesel could not fulfill his responsibilities. When union leaders learned that his absence was due to family illness, they expressed sympathy, finally understanding why Riesel was unable to consistently make the weekly journey to Paris. Yet criticisms of Riesel mounted once again following an anti-GMO action he planned with Bové in the town of Nérac. The criticism was not necessarily about the action itself, but about the fact that Bové and Riesel had conducted the action without first consulting the union. Riesel, in turn, often expressed critical feelings of the Confédération Paysanne. According to Riesel, the Confédération Paysanne's major limitation was that it "fell prey to popular discourses surrounding democracy." For Riesel, underlying the Confédération Paysanne's reformist approach is a belief in social democracy and the power of transparency to democratize knowledge about GMOs:

> At the Conf., we diverge on the issue of democracy. They believe that if things [about GMOs] are decided transparently, then they can distinguish between good and bad GMOs. There are some who think that genetically modified rice is good in certain situations in the Third World, etc. But really, [GMOs] are a question of man's place, how the whole of life is becoming marginal and artificial, how we are slowly becoming a society in which the circulation of commodities becomes the sole important thing, and how men become but a support for this system. Little improvements, little reforms, just reinforce the situation. (Personal communication, October 18, 1998)

Riesel has a critique of what he calls *citoyenité* (citizenism), which he regards as endemic to the culture of the politically correct. According to Riesel, popular discourses on citizen participation, notions of organizing from the bottom up, and the new flurry of political organizing on behalf of formal associations is constitutive of a welfare state in which "citizens act to make life more tolerable within an otherwise intolerable system." The Confédération Paysanne fits within this kind of "accommodating milieu" (personal communication, October 18, 1998).

In many of our discussions, Riesel reported feeling ideologically isolated within the union. His deeper political ties were to a group of intellectuals in Paris whose analysis and sensibility trace back to May 1968. The group chose to go by no name and rejected a stable form of membership and organizational structure, consistent with its ties to Situationism. The group functioned as a loose cluster of individuals who shared similar political concerns. They met often to plan various forms of direct action and to participate in writing and publishing leaflets, pamphlets, and a monograph series, including a series on GMOs written by Riesel. Riesel introduced me to members of this group, and I met regularly with them during my time in Paris. I found the dozen or so members of this group to be intellectually stimulating, good humored, and passionate, ranging in age from seventeen to seventy.

For hours, we would lounge around the Parisian apartment of some former Situationists, drinking coffee, smoking cigarettes, and cheerfully arguing over various political issues. At some point in the meeting (often a day-long affair on a Sunday), we would find ourselves in someone's kitchen, preparing a fancy, oddly shaped pizza, or cooking up a chicken or two for dinner. It was this activist group that convinced Riesel to become active on the issue of GMOs in 1998. Group members recalled spray-painting a series of anti-GMO messages on symbolic and powerful institutions in Paris. They seemed to take pleasure in the fact that no one seemed to have any idea who was responsible for the enigmatic anti-GMO graffiti (which was written at a time when most people in Paris had no idea what a GMO was). Some also surmise that this group organized La Bataille de la Villette.

JOSÉ BOVÉ: FROM THE LARZAC TO NÉRAC

Like Riesel, Bové was a key actor at the Confédération Paysanne in launching the union's direct-action campaign. Anytime I mentioned my interest in GMOs, union members would ask, "Have you spoken with Bové?" I first met Bové at the Confédération Paysanne headquarters. The former national secretary now often traveled to Paris from his farm in southern France to assist Le Fur in shaping the report for the Conseil Économique et Sociale. At first Bové seemed wary of meeting me, the woman whom he called "the American student." He laughed wryly at the idea of a U.S. American anthropologist studying farmers from the Confédération Paysanne. He was even more put off when I informed him that I had a research fellowship at the Centre de Sociologie de l'Innovation (Center for the Sociology of Innovation). Being a doctoral fellow at the Centre meant that I was stationed at one of Paris's most elite engineering schools, which had close ties to the French government. "So you're a little spy," he smiled dryly. He warmed up slightly when I told him a bit about my own activist history in the U.S. ecology movement. He became even more welcoming during a lunch break one day when I told him that I too had participated in anti-McDonald's actions. At lunch I had overheard him describe some of the anti-McDonald's actions he had been organizing. Sitting beside him, I responded with genuine enthusiasm. I described similar movements in Vermont, where activists worked long and hard to keep the chain out of their towns. One day, following a meeting, Bové presented me with a gift, a short book that he found interesting written by Paul Aries. *A Little Anti-McDo Manual: For the Young and Old* (1999) analyzes McDonald's from what I'd call a perspective that anticipates the anti-McDonald's sentiment that would grow around the emerging alter-globalization movement a few years later.

I was continually impressed by Bové's political sense of humor. For several years he had been constructing farms of the future inside various McDonald's restaurants with other paysans in his area in southwest France. Within minutes, about twenty paysans would quickly scurry into the restaurant, spreading topsoil and a few farm animals onto the floors to the surprise of workers and locals eating burgers. After setting up the "farm," he and the other union paysans would put down blankets and picnic baskets, readying to enjoy their lunch on the floor. For about thirty minutes they would recline, passing back and forth bottles of wine, wheels of cheese, and blocks of pâté. Such a lengthy action would be unthinkable in the U.S., where police would arrive at the scene ready to arrest activists immediately. But in France, there is a public culture of respect surrounding union members generally. Police know that it makes for bad press to show state authorities such as the police displaying aggression toward union leaders and members.

Bové is a short man with a muscular build. He has red cheeks and a Fu Manchu mustache that he often combed with his fingers as he spoke. Like Riesel, Bové is a smoker. At any given moment he was attending to some aspect of pipe smoking. After removing the tobacco from a worn leather pouch, he fit the tobacco into the pipe with a small metal instrument, stirring, lighting, puffing, and relighting. Bové's pipe smoking effectively punctuated and slowed down his otherwise pistol-speed delivery of bold articulations. It also seemed to disarm others who encountered him, as he always seemed somewhat distracted by his ongoing attention to the pipe. Dispersed throughout his confident assertions, Bové would flash a warm smile, exhaling a plume of sweet-smelling smoke, speaking slowly and forcefully, with authority.

Like Riesel, Bové is a néo. He laughed when telling me the profession of his parents: molecular biologists who work at the Institut National de la Recherche Agronomique (French National Institute for Agricultural Research). After he first learned about the GMO issue, Bové was surprised when he found out the technology was based on the field of molecular biology — though his parents worked in issues of human, not plant, genetics. Bové was born into a middle-class Catholic family in Bordeaux. When he was four to seven, Bové lived with his family in Berkeley, California. His parents were engaged in scientific research at the University of California, and he remembers having a pleasant time attending an American elementary school. After returning to Paris, he completed elementary school and Jesuit high school. At seventeen, Bové decided not to attend university as planned and instead moved back to his family's home in Bordeaux. Like many in his generation, he had been enchanted by the events of 1968. He was subsequently dismayed with mainstream French capitalist society and looked elsewhere for inspiration and direction.

At seventeen Bové was inspired to join the antiwar movement as a conscientious objector. To avoid the draft, he hid in a southern farming village. It was there that Bové discovered a Catholic pacifist movement called L'Arche (The Arch). L'Arche was a rural religious community based on Gandhian principles of active nonviolence. Of the ten L'Arche communities scattered through France, one was engaged in the antinuclear and antiwar movements. The L'Arche community that Bové joined was located fifty kilometers from the region known as the Larzac. According to Bové, L'Arche was the first organization to make contact with Larzac farmers. Upon learning of the struggle of Larzac farmers, L'Arche sought to support the farmers' fight against the government's attempt to confiscate their lands to expand a military base. According to Bové, the fact that L'Arche was a religious organization gave cultural legitimacy to the traditional Larzac farmers. L'Arche provided a cultural bridge between the antiwar movement and the Larzac farmers' movement. It was L'Arche that encouraged local priests and bishops to join the struggle of the Larzac farmers. According to Bové, once religious authorities decided to publicly support the farmers' struggle, L'Arche was able to legitimize the antinuclear dimension of the movement. L'Arche opened the door for nonfarmers such as political activists to become part of the struggle. Bové recalls:

> As soon as religious authorities recognized the resistance, Larzac paysans started accepting people from the outside. But in general, Larzac paysans made the decisions. Everyone else listened and gave their support. The antiwar activists, antinuclear activists, anarchists, extreme Leftists, [and] ecologists were there to help, not to lead. Suddenly it seemed, over one hundred towns expressed their support. For the first time, people came together around a common theme, transcending their differences. There was a radical element that hadn't been introduced before into the paysan milieu. The

movement really helped solidify the paysan struggle that led to the formation of the Confédération Paysanne. In 1973, Bernard Lambert came to Larzac, and Paysans-Travailleurs became a national movement. (Personal communication, November 2, 1999)

In 1976, along with his then wife, Alice, and their newborn daughter, Bové
joined the paysans in the struggle surrounding the Larzac. For more than
a year, activists had begun occupying abandoned farms bought by outside
speculators. Bové and Alice took up residence in an empty farm and began
raising sheep. In this endeavor, Bové drew from the farming expertise he
had acquired two years earlier when hiding in a rural village as a conscientious objector.

For five years Bové and his family illegally squatted on the Larzac farmland along with many other paysan families. But then in 1981, François Mitterrand and his Socialist Party came to power in France. Responding to popular pressure, Mitterrand granted the squatters permanent ownership of the
land. But the former squatters wanted to do more than simply divide the land
among themselves into private parcels. Instead they decided to share the
land collectively. According to Bové, the Larzac squatters sought to demonstrate the possibility of a solidaire logic of agriculture. They wanted to show
the potential of collective ownership of land and a solidarity-based way of
life: "When granted the land, we decided to manage it collectively, showing the Socialist government that there was another way to manage land. We
had fought for the paysan right to work the land, not to own it. We formed a
contract with the state in which seventy-five farms would collectively own
the land, about one hundred people in all. And over the years, most of us are
still involved in sheep farming" (Bové, personal communication, November 2, 1999).

After winning the right to farm the Larzac land, Bové entered yet another
set of struggles. Beginning in 1986, Bové began a nearly decade-long campaign against the Roquefort industry, which had established a production
minimum for producers of ewe's milk. A major triumph came later, in 1994.
That year, Bové led the Confédération Paysanne's fight for the right to representation in industry bodies that determined such norms as price setting for
ewe's milk. This campaign was particularly significant for the union because
this right had been historically enjoyed exclusively by farmers in the FNSEA.
During the 1980s and 1990s, Bové was also a key union representative in the

Sydicat des Producteurs de Lait de Brebis (Sheep's Milk Producers' Union), a body that negotiated regularly with the Roquefort industry for a fair price and production minimum. Bové played a central role in the union, working not only on a regional or departmental level but also on a national level. Bové served as a Confédération Paysanne national secretary while also becoming leader of the union's national committee on sheep milk production. In addition he played a key advisory role in Le Fur's council report on GMOs in 1997.

Like many others in the union, Bové shifted his focus slightly when he became more aware of GMOs in the mid-1990s. Bové learned of the GMO question through the Confédération Paysanne and international networks. Bové was an active member of both the Coordination Paysanne Européenne (European Peasants Coordination) and La Via Campesina, and through these groups, he learned of the potential impacts of GMOs on small farmers worldwide. In 1997, Bové began to participate in some initial anti-GMO actions in his local region, focusing mainly on crop pulls of genetically modified fields that went barely noticed by the media. In France, there is a law that requires transparency regarding the location of field trials of GMOs. Each town cultivating genetically modified crops as experimental field trials is legally obligated to publicize the precise location at the town prefecture. Walking through fields to uproot genetically modified crops (engaging in a crop pull) thus became a logical and practical form of nonviolent direct action by members of the Confédération Paysanne during 1997 (and it continues to this day).

Crop pulls serve as symbolic actions that aim to draw media and public attention to the existence of GMOs in local and national contexts. In preparation for the crop pull, Confédération Paysanne farmers inform the police in advance, alerting them of the exact time and place of the crop pull, and summon the media. They trudge through fields carrying large garbage bags, filling as many as possible. Crop pulls usually culminate when the participants load the garbage bags onto tractors and haul them to the center of a village. In a spirit of celebration, activists then drop the bags before the building of the town prefecture. I was always amazed by the relaxed sensibility that flowed through the event, beginning to end. In the United States, in contrast, such actions would prove nearly impossible and quite dangerous. Field trials of genetically modified crops are considered private information and their whereabouts are classified. Most U.S. Americans do not engage in crop pulls because they constitute a felony in many states. Activists could also risk their own personal safety if caught by armed police in the fields. There was only one crop pull in U.S. history that was executed successfully. And even this one is little known outside the small U.S. anti-GMO movement. It took place early in the U.S. movement, in 1987. One night, just outside San Francisco, an anonymous group of ecological activists pulled out a field of genetically modified strawberry plants. Scientists at the University of California had inserted into the plant's genome a gene for frost resistance that they removed from the DNA of a cold-water fish. The hope was to design a strain of strawberries that could grow in very cold climates. Frost-resistant strawberries were never successful or commercialized. Yet the image of this genetically modified entity lives on as a mythical icon of GMO history. It remains a mainstay in the repertoire of anti-GMO activists globally. At nearly any demonstration against GMOs there are activists dressed up as creatures that are half strawberry and half fish.

The French crop pull remains a source of fascination to me. I am amazed that union members actually call the police and media before crop pulls. I find it even more incredible that activists go about their business in the middle of the day, while police stand by, doing nothing to deter their activity. When I would ask Bové about the candidness of the event, he simply replied, "Why bother doing a crop pull if no one sees it?"

The Trial of the GMOs

By the late 1990s, Bové and Riesel had spent considerable time together in the union and various sheep farmers' organizations. They also shared a similar analysis of agriculture, capitalism, and GMOs. By the end of 1997, the two decided to plan an anti-GMO action come January in southern France that would target Novartis's genetically modified corn, the GMO that stood front and center of French political controversy. On January 8, 1998, Bové, Riesel, and about one hundred union paysans entered a Novartis storage plant in Nérac (in the Lot-et-Garonne region). After splitting several sacks open with knives, the paysans let loose three tons of corn across the floor. The paysans then sprayed piles of golden kernels with water hoses found in the facility. Bové and Riesel were subsequently arrested, along with the Confédération Paysanne activist François Roux.

News of the arrests and the incident was met with mixed sentiments at

149

Confédération Paysanne headquarters in Bagnolet. I remember, months afterward, discussing with Confédération Paysanne leaders and salariers Bové and Riesel's decision to execute the action. Guy Le Fur admitted that when he first heard of the action, he was a bit concerned: "Things like this have to be done carefully, they take careful planning. Or else we end up looking like rioters [casseurs]" (personal interview, May 11, 1998). For the union speaker, François Dufour, his initial apprehension stemmed from the fact that neither Bové nor Riesel had contacted Confédération Paysanne leaders for consultation before taking action: "They simply decided to do it and that was that" (François Dufour, personal communication, May 11, 1999). For one salarier, a key organizer of the Confédération Paysanne's anti-GMO campaign, news of the action spelled chaos: "After learning of the event, it took weeks to prepare an entire press kit and to figure out how to deal with all of the inquiries, all of the press. It would have been good to have had some notice." Despite the reservations of various actors, I never sensed outright condemnation or rancor among anyone at the union. Most seemed generally bemused by the work of Bové and Riesel and never questioned whether the union would support them. "They are our men and we will support them" was a common refrain I heard from leaders such as Le Fur and Dufour. Although the Confédération Paysanne contains divergent viewpoints on strategy, it remains unified when supporting its members.

THE RISK SIDE OF THE TRIAL: A DEBATE ABOUT SCIENCE

Soon after their arrest, Bové and Riesel set about considering a discursive strategy for the upcoming trial. They designed an action redolent of the ironic and symbolic sensibilities of their forebears in the new paysan movements and the absurdist activists of May 1968. In a spirit of the ridiculous, the two activists named their own hearing the Trial of the GMOs. They would not allow the court to contest the legitimacy of their own actions. Instead they turned the event on its head. Bové and Riesel were to challenge the legitimacy of agricultural biotechnology itself. By the trial's end, the three who were arrested received a suspended sentence of several months of imprisonment. For Bové and Riesel, however, their "loss" in court and the resulting suspended sentences were of little consequence. Triumph lay in the abundant media following their arrests. For weeks, news stories spun out in the press publicly presenting the duo's provocative set of GMO discourses. The trial itself was suspended in a tension between two logics, one solidaire and one instrumental. Bové and Riesel consistently drew upon a solidaire logic that openly criticized corporate greed and that demanded dignity and autonomy for paysans across the globe. But they also relied heavily on the instrumental expertise delivered by scientists who were summoned to support their cause.

The Trial of the GMOS is an excellent case for applying ANT, particularly the question of how nonhuman actors, actants, always play a central role in debates about science. ANT is a framework generated over time by a series of theorists interested in studying the process of technoscience innovation and contestation (see Latour 1986, 1987, 1988a, 1988b, 1991; Callon 1986a, 1986b, 1987, 1997). ANT transcends the realist-constructivist binary, which suggests, for instance, that risks related to GMOS are either real or socially constructed (not real). Within the rubric of ANT, the Bt corn that was debated in the trial is indeed a real object in the material sense. But it is also real as a cultural object. While Bt corn is material, composed of biological germ plasma, it is also the result of cultural-scientific enterprise. Like all human inventions, Bt corn has both material and cultural dimensions that are equally physically real and socially constructed. As a hybrid material and cultural object, Bt corn is also an actant. While lacking the conscious agency of a human, the Bt corn nonetheless demonstrates a nascent ability to act in particular ways. As an actant in this story, Bt corn shaped the French debate about GMOS by presenting previously unimagined effects and consequences within the greater network of actors engaged with GMOS. Bt corn has the ability to confound experts with its undeterminable effects. It is precisely the corn's ability to generate confusion that drove the Trial of the GMOS. The Bt corn's indeterminate implications on health and environment moved sets of actors to mobilize around the corn. If Bt corn induced absolute scientific certainty about its unanticipated effects, there would be no Trial of the GMOS. There would be no national controversy at this time. By failing to present certainty, Bt corn acted on the humans in the GMO network, inciting them to speak for or against it with great rigor.

At the trial, the actor-network notion of symmetry was at play. Symmetry is the idea that human and nonhuman actors together coproduce networks such as social movements. On the one hand, we see human actors such as scientists, farmers, and legal and media agents. On the other hand, there is the Bt corn. While the human actors argue for or against the corn, the corn acts upon various actors' sense of certainty, uncertainty, moral understandings, and so on. Although a sack of Bt corn never took the stand at the trial, its name was invoked endlessly as it played upon actors' sense of what is real and unreal, risky and nonrisky, and right and wrong.

To defend the farmers (and to defame the Bt corn), Bové and Riesel generated a network of recognized Parisian scientists. Bové and Riesel convinced a set of prestigious scientists to take the day-long journey to the southern town. In particular, they invited the molecular biologist Gilles-Eric Seralini of the Centre National de la Recherche Scientifique (French National Center for Scientific Research). In addition, they invited the biologist Jacques Testard from the Institut National de la Recherche Agronomique (French National Institute for Agronomic Research), and Richard Lacey (British microbiologist and specialist in BSE or mad cow disease). In numerous press releases following the trial, Lacey was quoted as discussing the risks associated with the Bt corn, calling for the judge to consider a "logic of precaution" (Marris et al. 2004, 7).

Along with Bové and Riesel, the Bt corn coproduced a major press event, again drawing the media in with notions of uncertainty. Together the activists and the corn invoked media agents to cover a trial in which various actors discussed the degree of Bt-related risk. Arguments of risk and precaution saturated the general discourse. On January 10, 1998, *Le Monde*, France's most popular newspaper, published an article describing the action as an attempt to "alert the public about the dangers that could affect the health of humanity by transmitting resistance to certain antibiotics" (Da Silva 1998; my translation). *La Dépeche*, a popular news magazine, also ran a series of articles during the week of the trial. In one story, the magazine featured a cartoon in which a journalist interviews a scientist whose face is half corncob, half human. The caption reads, "You're *sure* transgenics pose no risk?" (Levalier 1998; my translation).

During the trial, scientists and farmer activists alike invoked previous science crises to bolster their claims about the risks associated with GMOs. In particular, a contaminated-blood scandal from the early 1990s surfaced as a central theme running through the testimony of Riesel, Bové, and the invited scientists (see Hermitte 1995). This contaminated-blood scandal began in 1991. The scientific controversy was set in motion when the journalist Anne-Marie Casteret published an article in a popular news magazine showing that France's national center for blood transfusion knowingly administered potentially contaminated blood to patients between 1984 and 1985. In this tragic affair, French scientists allowed blood they knew to be potentially contaminated with HIV to enter the pool of donor blood used in public hospitals for transfusions. When tried in a court of law, it was found that the scientists failed to use available U.S.-patented tests capable of determining the blood's safety. The accused scientists admitted that they were waiting to use soon-to-be-released French tests. Unfortunately the French tests were patented too late for some blood recipients. After several French citizens tested positive for HIV, the country was in an uproar as citizens considered the moral and rational authority of French scientists. The deeper meaning of the contaminated-blood issue linked, in the mind of the public, issues of power, self-interest, and science. For our purposes here, it also illustrates the role of a nonhuman actant (such as blood) to animate a scientific debate born out of uncertainty. In this historic case, the public saw scientists who made decisions so their hospitals would receive monies for using a French, rather than a U.S., technology (Hermitte 1995, 3). In the mind of the public, scientists had acted like businesspeople, putting profit before human health. Like the Bt corn, the contaminated blood was more than a mere symbol or passive socially constructed thing. The blood, along with the scientists, coproduced a good deal of illness, death, confusion, and public mistrust in science bodies.

At a key moment during the trial, the defense lawyer Marie-Christine Etelin turned to the tribunal. In a solemn voice, she asked the judges, "What would *you* have done in 1984 or 1985 in responding to doctors who had destroyed bags of contaminated blood?" (Etelin 1998). Etelin compared the destroyers of the Bt corn to the few scientists who did indeed save lives by destroying bags of blood that were potentially contaminated. The contaminated blood, as an active nonhuman actor, played upon the consciences of those in the courtroom.

A news article in *Libération* (France's second major newspaper) on January 11, 1998, featured a photograph of the Confédération Paysanne's banner in Nérac that read, "1985: Contaminé, 1998: Transgené" (1985: Contaminated, 1998: Transgenized). Again, by comparing nonhuman actors such as Bt corn with contaminated blood, the paysans framed GMOs as not only a problem of science and risk but also a problem of a science corrupted by negligence linked to self-interest and power. Without the element of unanticipated effects—generated first by blood, and then by corn—the network comprising the trial would have had little impact.

It is also important to look at the theme of modernity that continually surfaced during the trial. In keeping with the union's ongoing concern about its modern status, the question of the Confédération Paysanne's progressive sensibility was in full bloom. In February 1998, *La Dépeche* published an article by Claude Julien, the former chief editor of the journal *Le Monde Diplomatique* and a popular French Leftist intellectual. During the trial, Julien wrote the article "C'est nous qui sommes les modernes" (It is we who are modern). In the piece, Julien declares, "It is *we* who are modern, because we seek, in this democratic society, a real public debate on genetically modified products" (February 1998) (my translation; emphasis added). The term *modernity* reverberated a good deal throughout the media coverage of the trial. In Julien's statement, for instance, he uses the ecumenical *we* to show solidarity with the paysans who took action against GMOs. In so doing, Julien challenges the idea of the backward paysan, asserting instead the modern and rational position of those who destroyed the corn. Julien thus emphasizes the Confédération Paysanne's ability to bring a rational analysis to its consideration of matters of society, democracy, and science.

During a Confédération Paysanne meeting about a month after the trial, I presented an anxiously awaited copy of a *New York Times* article that covered the trial (an item that Le Fur and Bové had requested I bring to union headquarters and translate) (*New York Times*, February 9, 1998). After a friend sent the article to me in the mail, I rushed it over to the union office. In my excitement to see the union featured in the *New York Times*, I did not even wait to read the article in advance. I sat reading from the paper among the paysans in the meeting room, translating as I went. All around me, paysans hung on every word, apparently pleased to see the union's name printed, for the first time, in a major U.S. newspaper. After reading the usual narrative about how the group entered the Novartis plant, scattering containers of seed, I paused. I was stunned to hear myself read, "And then, the group of farmers proceeded to urinate on the corn." As my voice trailed off, a thick curtain of silence fell over the room. A while later, paysans at the table began a round of head shaking and a chorus of "N'importe quoi!" (They'll do anything at all!). Finally, the Confédération Paysanne leader Valentin Beauval exclaimed, "Great! We finally get mentioned in the *New York Times*, but it's for pissing on corn! That's how they think of us, not as people who know the science, the risks, but as ploucs!" Beauval's comment crystallized the union's sentiment completely. According to the paysans in the room that day, not just France but the entire world saw the Confédération Paysanne as a bunch of ploucs. Once again, the Confédération Paysanne was portrayed as a group of antimodern paysans who fear rational science, throw eggs at science experts, and piss on genetically modified corn. This is why the union relied on discourses of scientific risk during this phase of its anti-GMO campaign. Risk allowed the union to assert its status as a modern and rational player in an international science debate.

THE ANTIGLOBALIZATION SIDE OF THE TRIAL:
A DEBATE ABOUT PROFIT-SEEKING SCIENCE

While relying on discourses of risk and science, Bové and Riesel also publicly introduced a new set of discourses about GMOs that went beyond instrumental notions of risk. They presented to the national and international press their own solidaire expertise as paysans and union workers uniquely situated to speak about GMOs. So in addition to summoning knowledges related to genetic science, they asserted their own authority in matters of global capitalism, cultural homogenization, and the global implications of industrialized agriculture on rural and indigenous peoples. In so doing, the two paysans established themselves and the Confédération Paysanne as a dynamic and politicized site in the broader national and international anti-GMO network. By introducing the union's solidaire rationality of nature and agriculture, the two paysans distinguished their position from naturalistic discourses of ecology groups such as Écoropa. Écoropa in particular, in its anti-GMO pamphlets and media communications, had tended to present a romantic and essentialist discourse about GMOs transgressing natural orders, allowing man to play god, or impinging on the pure world of nature. To the Confédération Paysanne, nature is not wild or presocial. The union promotes a socialized nature whose value is historical, cultural, aesthetic, and economic. For Bové and Riesel, nature-as-agriculture provides paysans with a viable and productive way of life. Linking questions of nature to issues of labor and capital resonated with many in the budding alter-globalization movement in France and internationally.

What is also distinctive about Bové and Riesel's discourse during the trial is that they invoked the French worker in relation to GMOs. They framed this worker as a small-scale farmer struggling to survive in a competitive international agricultural economy. In so doing, they called for citizens to support the struggle of a French union—something French citizens are accustomed to doing. Even today, while many in France express frustrations with the day-to-day inconveniences associated with union strikes, barricades, and demonstrations, the public regards trade unions as integral to French society. Trade unions are generally regarded as a legitimate voice in public debates about labor as an active and constitutive force in social and political life. French unions tend to enjoy degrees of asylum from harsh treatment by French courts or police. It is rare that union members face police brutality when engaging in union activity that entails breaking a law. Union members are also generally exempted from severe jail sentences and fines. By framing paysans at the trial as workers treated unfairly by agro-chemical corporations, Bové and Riesel challenged the exploitation of French citizens by a capitalist system driving science. At the trial, Bové and Riesel point out that citizens' tax dollars are spent to support public institutions seeking economic profit rather than promoting societal benefits.

It is useful here to return briefly to the contaminated-blood scandal. In this case, we see a science question move beyond the risk discourses associated with contaminated blood. Similarly, in the trial, we see a science issue move beyond risk discourse. Through the discursive framing by Bové and Riesel, we see a science question transform into a discussion of the ways in which powerful institutions such as corporations or governments use science to maximize their own status and profit. By challenging the validity of industrial agriculture and of profit-seeking science research, Bové and Riesel demystified genetic science research. They transformed GMOs into a mode of production worthy of public scrutiny. In so doing, they indirectly disrupted hegemonic notions about science as a wholly objective pursuit, standing outside the domains of society and self-interest.

BECOMING KEY PLAYERS IN THE EMERGING ALTER-GLOBALIZATION MOVEMENT

For months after the event, news of the trial circulated through Internet-based alter-globalization listservs and websites, as well as through print-based magazines and journals. In celebrating the trial, international activist media hailed the "French farmers" who were heading up a new anti-GMO movement in Europe. Despite the fact that the world press remained ignorant of the differences between large- and small-scale "French farmers," Confédération Paysanne members took satisfaction in the first major action in their campaign.

During the trial, the union carved out a unique position on global politics economics that resonated with the alter-globalization movement percolating within France and abroad. In France, the alter-globalization movement during the late 1990s focused on issues of GMOS as well as popular intellectual critiques of neoliberal economics. The union summoned the testimony of members of ecology and consumer groups to strengthen its support base. In so doing, they enhanced the credibility of groups such as Greenpeace France and Écoropa. Groups that stand outside the existing system of political parties or trade unions often have difficulty being recognized as potent political actors. As such, they are historically unable to win broadbased support. At the trial, the Confédération Paysanne gave credibility to French ecology groups while also strengthening the union's ties to international anti-GMO movements associated with Écoropa and the British journal *Ecologist*. The union received a big boost when Écoropa invited one of the most prolific activist writers on the issue of GMOS, Vandana Shiva, to the trial. Shiva flew to France to testify against GMOS, presenting her own solidaire perspective. At the trial, Shiva spoke out against the "commodification of life" by biological patents and against the disenfranchisement of peasants by multinational corporations seeking to patent and monopolize global food production (Shiva, personal communication, July 7, 1998).

In the news stories following the trial, journalists often mentioned Shiva's involvement. The idea of a scientist traveling from India to France to testify on behalf of paysans was intriguing. Several articles in popular magazines such as *La Depeche* described Shiva as having come to France to "speak on behalf of the Third World" (a claim that Shiva herself would never make) (Agence France Press, January 21, 1998). While such statements were inaccurate and politically problematic, they did underscore the international character of the Confédération Paysanne's struggle and demonstrate the global nature of its support base.

As the year following the trial wore on, it became clear that the direct action and its media-rich aftermath had helped the Confédération Paysanne further cement its place within France's budding alter-globalization network. That year some union members began to engage with the prestigious intellectual and political journal *Le Monde Diplomatique*. Dufour began writing for the journal on a range of political issues, reinforcing the new image of the Confédération Paysanne as the union of paysan intellectuals. At the end of 1998, Dufour became vice president of a French-based organization founded by a group of French thinkers associated with *Le Monde Diplomatique*. This organization was called Association pour la Taxation des Transactions Financières et pour l'Action Citoyenne (Association for the Taxation of Financial Transactions for the Aid of Citizens). To this day the group is exclusively known by its punchy acronym, ATTAC.

Founded in December 1998, ATTAC's first objective was to demand taxation on all national and global financial transactions. The rationale was twofold. First, the group sought to establish a development fund for paysans and other groups marginalized from the market system. Second, the group's founders yearned to stem the tide of stock market speculation that was driving the neoliberal economic system. ATTAC is a remarkable French organization. It has greatly succeeded in attracting considerable numbers of members and garnering media attention. But most interesting is that it is the first French-initiated grassroots social movement to attain the magnitude and status of an international organization. French politics tends to orbit around state-sponsored parties and unions. Associations outside this structure are generally limited, articulating power on the local or regional level, serving as interest groups rather than constituting international political forces. After its initial focus on financial speculation in France, ATTAC expanded its purview to address a range of issues related to neoliberal economics in countries throughout Africa, America, Asia, Europe, the Middle East, and North Africa. Today ATTAC members are active in more than forty countries throughout the world, organizing around supranational organizations such as the World Trade Organization, the World Bank, and the International Monetary Fund. In addition, ATTAC has generated campaigns to end Third World debt and free-trade zones. ATTAC also works to halt the privatization of water and other public services in the Global South by multinational companies. As the organization itself attests, ATTAC promotes a solidaire rationality, aiming to "propose concrete alternatives to neoliberal orthodoxy based on solidarity (www.attac.org/en/what-attac, 6).

Julien, at the Trial of the GMOs, presaged and perhaps facilitated the cooperation between the Confédération Paysanne and the Leftist intellectuals who ultimately founded ATTAC. Renowned for his alter-globalization editorials, Julien testified on behalf of the arrested, articulating a clear anti-neoliberal message. Throughout the trial, the Confédération Paysanne thus asserted itself as a key passage point within international networks for organizations seeking a symbolic intermediary that could represent both the Global North and South. Through the work of Bové, Riesel, and others in the Confédération Paysanne, the French paysan emerged in the popular imagination as a hybrid entity: the French paysan was now symbol of the post-industrial peasant located within, yet disenfranchised from, powerful sites of capitalist accumulation.

Conclusion

In the Confédération Paysanne's riskocentric phase of direct action, the union appealed to instrumental discourses of risk. At the same time it also became the first group in France to publicly present a solidarity-based critique of GMOs, highlighting the linkages among capital, science, and agriculture. While Riesel and Bové were concerned with protecting the union's modern status and allying themselves with key scientists, they also began to articulate a discourse of paysans and workers that established the Confédération Paysanne as a key node in the emerging national and international alter-GMO movement. Despite dilemmas over modernity and strategy, the Confédération Paysanne became the first French organization to have the cultural credibility to generate a public debate on GMOs. The Confédération Paysanne was not, however, the first French organization to launch an anti-GMO campaign. But the union was the first that proved capable of popularizing the debate, increasingly adding a paysan discourse into the mix as time wore on. After 1999, the Confédération Paysanne was able to foster enough cultural clout to promote an anti-GMO and alter-globalization perspective that resonated with the French public.

7

Caravans, GMOS, & McDo

The Campaign Continues

What happens when French scientists and farmers collide in a debate over GMOS? What kinds of conflicts emerge when each side proves unable to appreciate the other's understanding of the meaning of genetically modified crops? In the spring of 1999, Confédération Paysanne members join forces with farmers from southern India to publicly demonstrate that GMOS are not just a problem of scientific risk, but a crisis regarding the fate of international rural peasantry. As we shall see, when union members and Indian farmers destroy GM plants under experimentation by French scientists, chaos ensues. For French scientists, it is irrational to destroy studies that could prove GMOS risky. But for the farmers in this story, the rationality for sabotaging the experimental GMOS came out of a solidaire rationality, rather than one based on instrumental risk.

A Caravan from Paris to Montpelier: From a
Drowsy March to a Wild Ride

THE CARAVAN COMES TO PARIS

In April 1999, the Confédération Paysanne offered to host a stop on a five-hundred-person intercontinental caravan tour of Europe and, later, the United States. The caravan's mission was to protest neoliberal global economic policy that was disenfranchising indigenous and peasant groups around the world. The Karnataka State Farmers' Association, the largest agricultural union in India, played a major role in organizing the caravan. As groups of the caravan dispersed throughout Europe, a group of one hundred Indian farmers was scheduled to spend five days in different parts of France for demonstrations related to issues of neoliberalism, farm policy, and GMOs. To understand the caravan more broadly, it must be placed within the context of the Peoples' Global Action, a significant yet informal network of alter-globalization activists from the Global North and South. Peoples' Global Action sought to draw attention to such problems as free-trade agreements, which it perceived to be harmful to the world's poor. Peoples' Global Action is not an organization per se and, consequently, it has no formal members, spokespersons, or leaders. Instead, it is a network that allows various groups throughout the world to communicate and organize conferences, protests, and gatherings related to global inequalities associated with neoliberal trade policies. The idea for Peoples' Global Action emerged during a meeting held in 1996 by the Zapatista Army of National Liberation, which was formed by Mexicans living in the state of Chiapas. The Zapatistas' initial uprisings in 1994 (and ongoing struggle) focused on a collective demand for a wide range of issues, including cultural autonomy, access to farmland, and freedom from the harmful practices associated with neoliberalism and free-trade agreements. In 1996, Zapatista organizers made a public call for the first gathering (*encuentro*) of international grassroots movements; they were to come together in the Chiapas jungle to discuss urgent aspects of their struggle against neoliberalism. The Zapatistas were astonished when more than six thousand activists from more than forty countries arrived, determined to create an international network capable of fighting globalization gone awry.

In 1997 a second encuentro took place in Spain. Representatives from grassroots organizations such as the Brazilian Landless Worker's Movement and the Karnataka State Farmers' Union met to discuss peasants' rights to farmland, as well as the problem of GMOs. In 1998, yet another encuentro gathered in Geneva, Switzerland. It was at this meeting that activists decided to formalize their network, calling it the Peoples' Global Action. Seeking to avoid the socialist-Marxist trend on the Left to build hierarchical, rigid parties, the network is loosely structured. Yet the Peoples' Global Action is organized around five key themes: anticapitalism (anti–free trade), hierarchy (patriarchy, racism, religious fundamentalism), direct action (rather than lobbying or reforming powerful institutions), civil disobedience (taking illegal action in the name of social justice), and decentralization and autonomy.

The Karnataka farmers initially suggested the caravan, and it was co-organized with Peoples' Global Action. Significantly, the Confédération Paysanne joined the international alter-globalization movement by hosting the caravan in France. Here we see a shift. Since 1987, the union had primarily promoted the cause of French paysans against European agricultural policy. Then a decade later the union's anti-GMO campaign led it to join forces with international groups facing deterritorialization and economic marginalization. Together, they began to forge international, mobile, and hybrid political alliances as they struggled against neoliberalism (see Featherstone 2005).

Paris was scheduled as the caravan's first of three stops in France. The small committee at the Confédération Paysanne charged with preparing events for the three-day Parisian stint was unprepared to house, feed, and organize one hundred Indian farmers. René Riesel had volunteered to be the point person and organizer. Yet due to a family health crisis, he was unable to be present in Paris during the weeks leading up to the caravan's arrival. In his absence, an inexperienced group of community volunteers (including me) and union salariers tried as best they could to prepare for the caravan's arrival. Union organizers were overwhelmed with the idea of preparing for the arrival of nearly one hundred farmers. To take care of housing, a few days before the caravan's arrival, a salarier at the Confédération Paysanne asked a group of young anarchists if they could use the large abandoned building where the youths were squatting just outside Paris. The squatters agreed to share their quarters, but they warned of their humble offerings. This group of about ten young people slept on rolled-up blankets. The cement floors of the old factory buildings were gritty and cracked, and the squatters made do with no electricity, running water, or flush toilets. Seeing no other alternative, union organizers and volunteers spent the days leading up to the Indian farmers' arrival by sweeping, scrubbing, and preparing the squat as best as they could.

When buses finally rolled into the anarchist squat, looks of disbelief and astonishment flashed from the faces of the people behind the vehicles' windows. Occupying a different cultural universe, the anarchist youths, along with union activists, smiled with wild abandon, shouted excitedly, "Les Indiens!" when they saw their awaited guests. While the French greeters at the squat were thrilled to meet a group of "Indiens," the Karnataka farmers themselves looked slightly mortified at their first glimpse of a bare-bones abandoned warehouse located just outside postindustrial Paris. Descending tentatively from the bus, the caravan farmers appeared horrified to face the group of scantily dressed punk and hippie youths. They looked even more despondent when they noted the crude accommodations. Many farmers expressed disappointment when they learned that they would be sleeping on cement floors using only thin mats as padding. They were stunned to find that their lodging consisted of buildings with pipes and wires sticking out in all directions. To make matters worse, the union had been able to round up only two portable toilets, two working sinks, and no showers. These accommodations were to be shared by one hundred people. Fresh drinking water and food supplies had yet to be hauled in from Paris by teams of volunteers.

I met the president of the Karnataka State Farmers' Association, Mahantha Devaru Nanjundaswamy (known within the movement as Professor Swamy, or simply Swami), just minutes after he stepped off the bus at the squat. I was asked to bring him a bottle of water by a Spanish member of Peoples' Global Action who was working closely with Swami during the caravan's voyage through Europe. I ran off to a union car that contained bottled water and handed one to Swami, apologizing that it had become hot inside the car. He nodded with a quiet, dignified smile, saying, "Water is water." Swami was a short small-boned man, and his fine-featured face was dominated by a large pair of wire-framed glasses edged in gold. His features were flanked between a boxy green cotton cap that he always wore and a coarse grayish beard. Over his shoulder he slung a long green bolt of cloth with his union's insignia printed at the bottom. The cloth acted sometimes as a kind of scarf, sometimes as a shawl, but mostly it sprawled over one shoulder and down his back. Swami spoke in a careful quiet manner, commanding immediate attention and respect from the (mostly male) members of his union who generally surrounded him, appearing eager to serve and please him. As the leader of the Karnataka State Farmers' Union, Swami assumed a central position of leadership in the five-hundred-person caravan traveling across Europe that spring. I was grateful to conduct several interviews with him, and he discussed the meaning of the caravan and his views on neoliberalism and agriculture. During his stay, I was also asked many times to translate for Swami, facilitating communication between him and non-English-speaking paysans such as Riesel.

About thirty minutes after the caravan's arrival, tensions began to mount. While I was working to further prepare the squat for its new inhabitants, caravan members took me aside. Misreading me as a European—but not a member of the union—they looked to me despondently, as if I could somehow solve their problems: "We expected to meet traditional French paysans. Or at least well-groomed Parisians." Assuming I had a position of power or authority, they beckoned for a better alternative to what the squatters had to offer. I summoned union paysans, who did their best to allay the concerns of the caravan farmers. The union paysans explained that things hadn't quite gone as planned. The first night was awkward as it became obvious that neither the squatters nor the union members had prepared ample or appropriate food for the caravaners. Finally a group of paysans drove into Paris, taking with them a long list of groceries requested by caravan women. At about nine o'clock the paysans returned from Paris with provisions. Within minutes, caravan women set to work, preparing regional delicacies that did not appear until about ten-thirty that night. During this first meal together, paysans and anarchists mingled with caravan members as they sat together on the floor devouring a late-night meal. Despite the disorganization and late hour, the ambiance improved as the group enjoyed their dinners, sitting on the scrubbed cement floor in small circles.

Caravan women and men sat in separate clusters while eating and performing other activities. This gave me the opportunity to speak with women about issues that were often intimate and sometimes disturbing. That first night, I learned that the women occupied a distinctly separate sphere from the men in the group. When not attending meetings or direct actions, women gathered together, often singing, laughing shyly, and exchanging stories about their lives. Men tended to gather in small groups, a good distance from the women, playing cards, smoking, or discussing various political matters. In speaking with the women that night, we used English as a common language. Usually, some woman around me knew enough English to translate for the others. For hours we kept afloat an often-scattered set of conversations. I observed the many women reclining along the crumbling floors, wearing glowing silk saris or decorative cotton ones. I came to understand that the fabric of the women's saris often (but not always) indicated their particular class or caste. I did my best to make sense of the contrasting contours of this group of people differentiated by sharp dynamics of differing cultures, languages, classes, and professions.

While many of the French organizers referred to everyone in the caravan as les Indiens, the group was far from homogeneous. About four-fifths of the participants were members of the Karnataka State Farmers' Union and came from southern India. But they were individuals from across a strongly stratified society, which is divided along lines of gender, class, professional status, and caste. The rest of the participants hailed from many countries throughout southern Asia, including Pakistan, Sri Lanka, Bangladesh, Bhutan, and Nepal. Many of these actors came as representatives of farmers' groups, indigenous associations, workers' councils, women's cooperatives, and organizations of the unemployed.

TENSIONS MOUNT: GENDER, CLASS, AND POWER

My decision to spend a good deal of time with caravan women during their three days in Paris was informed by several factors. Their stay in Paris took place during an unseasonable heat wave. I found it difficult to cover myself as effectively as the caravan women did. For many men in the caravan, my tank tops or fitted T-shirts signaled an invitation for flirtation that on a few occasions erupted into outright sexual harassment. One evening, harassment churned into physical assault when a young man from the Karnataka union forced me into an empty bus, where he pinned me down on a seat, declaring that he would "have me." When a group of older men finally heard me screaming in the bus, they rushed in to pull me out. After offering me a vague and hurried apology, the older men chided the young man, threatening to report the event to Swami—which, to my knowledge, they never did. Nearly each member of the caravan inquired about my marital and parental status. Learning that I was unmarried and childless made matters worse. And my youthful appearance probably did not help to establish me as a thirty-something woman worthy of respect. But the more I spoke with women, it became clear that they also remained vigilant in regard to the men on the caravan. They reported the need to travel in pairs when going off to the bathroom or even moving from one building to another.

The caravan was co-organized by the Peoples' Global Action, which asserts itself as an antipatriarchal movement. When I mentioned this to women on the caravan, one spoke for the group, laughing at me: "Oh, the men act here as they do at home. Just because we fight against [free] trade, doesn't mean the men will respect women." Indeed, despite their status as members of a political caravan, many women expressed that the men often treated them as badly as they would treat them in their own country. Many women were married but traveling without their husbands. Their sponsoring organizations could only pay for one woman representative. So I often heard, "Being seen as a woman alone is like being seen as a whore. [The men] can say or do to you whatever they want." When I asked women what Swami had to say about their treatment on the caravan, they generally laughed, saying, "He is so respected. He's a leader, a professor. But don't forget that he's a man! He doesn't want to hear a word about it." As a cultural anthropologist, I did my best to contextualize this masculinist (and at times violent) environment and focused on understanding as much as I could about who and what the caravan was. The female squatters and Confédération Paysanne members, on the other hand, had a different approach. They tended to admonish the offending caravan men, writing them off as *jouers* (players). Sometimes they would threaten to inform Swami of the men's transgressions. I was struck by the way many men and women (both within and outside the caravan) perceived Swami as a source of discipline. Many imagined him as a masculine force who could control or punish men for treating women badly.

Another set of tensions began to surface during those three days in Paris. Within hours, paysans from the Confédération Paysanne began to look accusingly at many of the members of the caravan. In particular, they scrutinized several farmers from the Karnataka union, determining them to be "upper class." Pulling me aside, union paysans exclaimed in horror, "Look at their hands!" Lacking agricultural savoir faire, I looked at the hands of the men and women ambling about, dazed by their new surroundings. I found their hands illegible. I did, however, get the message. One paysan, a national secretary, ran up to me, eager to let off steam: "They came saying they're paysans, but they're not. Most are wealthy landowners who've never worked a field in their lives. They have paysans work for them. They just wanted a free trip to Europe!" When questioned directly by one bold Confédération Paysanne youth, a young Karnataka farmer turned to me, asking me to translate. Showing us his hands, he said to me in English, "You're right, my hands are not the hands of a hard worker because I have been studying abroad this year. But usually I am hard at work on my father's farm." Unimpressed, the Confédération Paysanne farmers shook their heads in disgust, muttering an exasperated, "N'importe quoi" (Nonsense).

Riesel finally arrived at the squat a few hours after the caravan rolled in. Riesel was the primary organizer of the caravan's voyage to Paris, so several union members gathered around him. They wanted to let him know how they'd been tricked by the fake paysans. "We've talked to many of these guys," one young man said, "and not one of them has a small farm. They have huge enterprises. They might as well be [FNSEA] farmers." Riesel squinted at the union men, taking a long drag of his thinly rolled cigarette. Then he exhaled, "You can't know who all these people are. Have you gone around and taken a poll on each single one? They're from an enormous union. Of course there are some who aren't paysans. Their system is different from France. But they've haven't come all the way here for nothing! They've come to fight the G8. It's not your job to play cop [*flique*]." At that, Riesel walked away from the group of men and began getting to work to help get the squat ready for night.

Several hours later, after dinner, I sat down next to Riesel. I too wanted to ask him about the matter. He turned to me with impish eyes and a sardonic smile: "Oh, my dear Chaia, we're all paysans, aren't we? You're a paysan, as you study paysans and write a book. I'm a paysan, a Situationist paysan. Too bad! Let them all be paysans. All I know is these Karnataka people organize some fierce demonstrations. They burned an entire building containing GMOs in southern India just a month ago. That's paysan enough for me." What I find striking in Riesel's words is a thread of Situationist absurdism strung into his understanding of identity. Riesel indirectly acknowledges the limits and instability of all identities, including that of paysan. By including me, an anthropologist from the United States studying French paysans, in the identity world of union paysans, he illustrates the often untenable dimensions of identity that surface as actors cling too heavily to them. In a way, Riesel is saying, "If I, a Situationist, can call myself a paysan, then who am I to judge others?" There is also a bit of instrumental logic running through

Riesel's solidarity rationality. Riesel appeared willing to engage what could be called a strategic essentialism (Spivak 1990). While recognizing the limits of identities, such as paysan, he also saw such forms of identification as effective in bringing disparate groups together to fight a united cause. Riesel's ironic smile and statement suggested his clear understanding of what matters to him politically. Detached from the romantic view of paysans — or peasants generally — as inherently virtuous, Riesel articulated what he values most in the activists with whom he works: the ability to join forces to fight destructive forms of power and the audacity to take dramatic action to accomplish a group's goals. Riesel respects activists with daring. Identifying more as a revolutionary than a paysan, Riesel was inspired by farmers who would set fire to a corporate building that housed injustice. Thus, his solidarity aligns more with actors willing to confront power directly than with actors who identify as paysans.

One further note on the term *paysan*: When speaking of any smallholder — from France or internationally — union members tended to refer to the individual as a paysan. While union members know that the term *paysan* has specific cultural meaning in France, they nonetheless extend the term to any smallholder in any culture. For the purposes of this book, I use the term *paysan* only when referring to union members. I also use it when quoting union members as they refer to other smallholders. In all other cases, I refer to farmers outside the Confédération Paysanne as either peasants (if the actors use an equivalent term in their own language), smallholders, or family farmers (when I speak about a specific set of smallholders in the United States).

MORE TENSIONS OVER A FAILED MARCH

Union organizers planned a series of actions and press events in Paris that they hoped would draw significant media attention. The paysans planning the caravan's activity during those days imagined a robust series of happenings, the kind they had seen in international journals featuring the bold Karnataka farmers burning down buildings and bringing thousands of demonstrators into the streets. Paysans had seen images of thousands of Indian farmers marching in Bombay, waving broad green strips of cloth (their union's color). In photographs the Karnataka farmers looked fierce, dedicated, and militant.

I too was enthralled to see what would unfold during the caravan's three days in Paris. I had heard about the Karnataka farmers for years and was excited to speak with Swami about his union's style of demonstrating. In one interview he described his union's first major anti-GMO protest in December 1992: "About three hundred Karnataka farmers were at the bottom entrance of the offices of Cargill Seeds [a division of the U.S.-based multinational]. Then about seventy-five of us entered the offices. We promised that our protest would be nonviolent. We dumped several walls of file cabinets; we tossed stacks of papers through the office window. They fell like snow. Then we went back to join the others outside the building. We lit matches and threw them onto the piles of papers in the street. All around us, traffic came to stop." "We lit a 'bon fire,'" he laughed dryly. "*Bon fire* is a good term," he smiled at me mischievously. "It comes from the French *bon feux*, or good fire. We were there to cremate Cargill. We want to cremate them all, Monsanto too" (Swami, personal communication, June 16, 1999). The next year, 1993, two hundred thousand Karnataka demonstrators marched in New Delhi to demand that the Indian government denounce the Dunkel Draft on the Trade Related Intellectual Property Rights section of the General Agreement on Tariffs and Trade (GATT). Swami in particular had criticized the Dunkel Draft, asserting the right of every farmer to produce, improve on, and sell seeds. For Swami, the production of genetically modified rice — a staple crop on which all Indians depend — would mean the loss of farmers' resources and property (Gupta 1998, 292).

Despite the Karnataka farmers' reputation for organizing impressive events, the first two days of the caravan's Parisian stay proved uneventful. The press conferences and rally that took place in the financial section were poorly organized, and at each one both French organizers and members of the caravan failed to arrive at the right place and time. Haplessly, these events took place with little audience or press. Both French and caravan actors appeared hot, tired, and frustrated with each day's labors. Most paysans held out hope that at the very least they would be able to pull off a high-profile march to the Eiffel Tower, where caravan members were to publicly demonstrate against neoliberal global economics. With one hundred caravan members and at least twenty French organizers, they would surely generate critical mass to draw attention and excitement.

What followed instead was a disastrously low-profile stroll through Paris. Riesel and others had asked caravan members to show up at a particular Parisian square at noon. But by one o'clock, only about seventeen members had arrived. At two o'clock, union paysans decided to go ahead with the march. Yet there were only about twenty caravan members joined by ten or so paysans and volunteers who had finally made their way there. Despite the small number, those present were ready to take to the streets. During the quiet promenade through Paris, a few Karnataka farmers tried their best to engender enthusiasm. From time to time during the nearly two-hour march, some took their cue from Swami, enthusiastically swirling their signature green cotton cloths above their heads in a circular fashion. While marchers shouted Karnataka union slogans in their native tongue, passersby on the streets offered back looks of confused annoyance. Most caravan members walked distractedly, talking casually among themselves, pointing to various sites in the city that called their attention. Along the way, a few radio and television reporters stopped a marcher or two, asking to film or interview them. But, overall, union paysans determined the event a media flop.

The march was to culminate in a rally held in a small park behind the Eiffel Tower. Union paysans had prepared a modest sound system and invited various Parisian activists to speak. Yet with so few present, the rally turned into a small impromptu meeting. About ten men from the caravan sat around Swami on the grass, nodding their heads gravely as he spoke. The union had prepared a picnic lunch of bread, cheese, bottles of wine, melon, and lots of water bottles to allay the day's dragging heat. Those in the caravan who chose not to join the group sitting with Swami lounged yards away. These individuals sat on blankets provided by the union, waving away the heat with their hands. From time to time, a few men and women would scurry off to buy ice cream from local vendors scattered around the tower. At one point, two young paysan men sidled up to me to speak in confidence. "Look at them," one said, pointing to a group of caravan members snapping photographs of each other before the tower. "How can they take pictures of such a thing? Don't they know it's a symbol of imperialism?" The other echoed his friend's outrage, asking, "What are they, tourists?"

For weeks leading up to the arrival of the caravan, many Confédération Paysanne members had clearly romanticized the caravan as a group of exemplary paysans. Many were patently disappointed to be faced with a group whose internal power dynamics were becoming increasingly clear. As one young paysan said to me that day, "Many of these people are of the upper class in India. They aren't workers like paysans. They've come here on vacation!" During the picnic lunch, there was talk among caravan members and paysans about why so few from the caravan had made it to the march. One woman in the caravan said to me, "The rich in our group are locating Parisian electronics stores, buying cameras and laptop computers that are cheaper here." The poorer members of the caravan, many of whom represented women's peasant associations and workers' cooperatives, reclined on the lawn, gazing up admiringly at the shining tower. "Of course they're out shopping," said a young woman from a small rural village in Sri Lanka (through a translator). "They have so much money. Back home, they wouldn't so much as look at us, let alone share a bus with us as we're doing now!" Comments about stratification within the group were abundant. Women who saw me as a sympathetic and neutral individual within the group shared stories about what life was like for them as poor women both at home and on the caravan. A young woman from Bangladesh described being sexually accosted when walking alone at sunset to fetch water for her family: "If you are seen alone, without a man to protect you, you are nothing but a prostitute and you deserve what you get." Other comments were more about questions of class and caste stratification. An Indian woman from the untouchable class commented about the odd situation presented by the caravan: "In India I would be the servant of many of the people here. I would not even be able to prepare their food, though, as I'm not pure. But on the bus here, I even sit on the same seat with an elite woman. I eat the same food and we sit at the same meetings. We all know it is fake, though. If we were at home, they would not look at me." The caravan was a temporary disruption of the social orders that members maintained at home. What struck me was that no actors pointed to political contradictions between the broader goals of the caravan and the stratified social systems back home. In these women's narratives, fighting neoliberalism was not necessarily linked to fighting forms of social stratification such as class or caste.

As the Peoples' Global Action held gender equality as one of its key values, it was interesting and disturbing to see that gender inequality was never discussed, at least during my time with the caravan. It was difficult to determine why the women failed to make these connections. Was their social structure was so hegemonic, so taken for granted, that they were unable to challenge it consciously? Or did these women simply not want to discuss these contradictions with male members of the caravan? Also noteworthy was the sharp contrast between the members of the Karnataka union and the Confédération Paysanne in terms of cultural and organizational style.

The Confédération Paysanne openly celebrates its nonhierarchical and decentralized structure and lacks an authoritarian leader. In this way, the union shared much in common with a post-Marxist body like the Peoples' Global Action. In contrast, the Karnataka union is explicitly hierarchical. If the union speaker François Dufour was jovial, down to earth, and approachable, Swami was cool, genteel, and distant. His mere presence seemed to wield a tremendous degree of intellectual and political power.

Several times during their stay in Paris, caravan members would hear news that Swami had called for a formal assembly. Whether the gathering was held at the squat or in a Parisian park, they arranged themselves around Swami in a specific order. While top-ranking male union leaders flanked his sides, other men took their places beside these men, standing in order of marked status. As many members of the Karnataka union explained to me, the smallest and poorest farmers in the union were always positioned farthest from Swami at such meetings. As for caravan women, they knew never to sit in close proximity to Swami. Instead, they served as audience, along with poor or undistinguished men. Their job was to prepare food for caravan men and to listen intently when Swami spoke to the group.

The meeting Swami called for that day behind the Eiffel Tower was to address reports he had heard about tensions among caravan members. He spoke intermittently in English and in a few other South Asian languages. He delivered a lecture slowly, deliberately, in philosophical terms. Expressing disappointment in the group's behavior, he discussed the need for the group to show solidarity and project a dignified image of the Karnataka State Farmers' Union to the rest of the world. "Those who are off buying computers," he said, looking down, "are acting selfishly. But we must remain unified in our mission." During his oration, he commanded tremendous attention from the small group gathered around him. The men nodded and applauded furiously at each point he made.

The Paris experience provided a window into the complexity and heterogeneity that constitute the cultures of various peasant groups. Unlike progressive groups that emerged in France post-1968, the Karnataka State Farmers' Union emerged from a radically different cultural and political context. As a postcolonial formation (Gupta 1998), the Karnataka State Farmers' Union sprang from a country marked by years of colonialism and centuries of hierarchies of class, caste, religion, and gender. The Indian union also emerged from a tradition of Gandhian grassroots movements. While these movements promote active nonviolence, they are marked by culturally specific practices of hierarchical leadership and organization. As I noted in Paris, while many members of the caravan expressed to me degrees of dissatisfaction with the organization's hierarchical style, they spoke off the record and never publicly. Despite glaring cultural differences, leaders such as Riesel were committed to working collaboratively with the Karnataka activists. Increasingly, many members of Confédération Paysanne came to understand the necessity of negotiating differences in organizational styles and structure while working to build an international movement.

BURNING PLANTS, GOING SWIMMING

After the caravan's uneventful Parisian stay, Riesel invited about twenty Karnataka farmers to accompany him to the southern city of Montpelier to participate in a small but ultimately significant direct action. For Bové and Riesel, this particular direct action reflected a significant shift in strategy. As Riesel explained, "For us, the trial was about the multinationals, the role of Novartis in pushing genetically modified corn on us. This time, our target was public research in the hands of corporations" (personal communication, October 18, 1999). For months before the direct action in Montpelier, Riesel had joined with Bové and other union members to destroy open-air field trials. They had also taken action against greenhouse studies of genetically modified plants in several sites in Montpelier. But the action conducted by Riesel and the Karnataka farmers elicited the greatest public response.

On June 5, 1999, Riesel invited a group of caravan members from the Karnataka union to join Confédération Paysanne activists in sabotaging experimental genetically modified rice growing in a research greenhouse facility. The research was the property of two French-based science institutions. The first, called CIRAD, is the Centre de la Recherche Agronomique pour le Development (Center for Agricultural Research for Development). CIRAD focuses on developing agricultural plants useful for what CIRAD actors call "developing countries." The second science institution at issue that day was the Institut National de la Agronomique (National Institute for Agricultural Research). The latter tends to concentrate its energies on developing agricultural practices for various areas within France itself. At the time of the caravan, most individuals active within anti-GMO networks were aware that agro-chemical corporations sought to patent and commercialize GMO equivalents of key staple crops internationally. While corn, soy, and canola were the center of concern for small growers in the Global North (as well as in Brazil and other southern countries), the development of genetically modified strains of rice caught the attention of Indian activists. It is for this reason that CIRAD — with its southern focus — was chosen as a key site for demonstrating against GMOs. CIRAD scientists, it was rumored, were developing a strain of GM rice. According to Shiva and Swami, allowing private corporations to patent rice varieties could have dire impacts on biodiversity and seed-saving practices among India's many peasant rice cultivators.

For Riesel, the goal of this particular action in Montpelier was to enter and sabotage a greenhouse laboratory growing genetically modified rice. CIRAD's mission was to create a variety of genetically modified rice that would be helpful to developing countries. Rejecting this view, Riesel and the Karnataka farmers saw taking symbolic action together as a crucial step against CIRAD and its funder, Cargill. They would demonstrate an international refusal of genetically modified rice. Riesel stated to me before the action, "We did [the action] with the Indians to show symbolically that this is not just about France[,] . . . to show that this is about globalization and about turning the world into merchandise. Rice is not merchandise. It is nature, food, and it is an important crop in the developing countries" (personal communication, September 19, 1999). Swami and the Karnataka farmers were eager to conduct an anti-GMO protest on French corporate soil. Blending Confédération Paysanne and Karnataka sensibilities, the farmers entered a Center for Development greenhouse, removed trays full of genetically modified rice plants, and tossed them into a pile on the greenhouse lawn. Dancing and singing around the plants, the Indian farmers waved their green union shawls. At some point during the dance, the farmers decided to engage in their signature act, "cremating" GMOs. After dousing the plants with alcohol, they lit the pile of greenery on fire. Around this relatively small group of people stood a few policemen who merely parked themselves around the demonstrators, observing the events. The press, notified of the action beforehand, was on the scene, snapping photographs and interviewing various activists. After the activists stamped out the small fire with their feet, the action was over. The group of Karnataka farmers and Confédération Paysanne paysans then proceeded to stroll down to the ocean for a picnic and a bit of swimming. While Karnataka women sat on the sand in their saris, the men lifted their pant legs and waded into the frothy waves. Confédération Paysanne farmers (men only) stripped down to their undershorts and dove eagerly into the waves.

The action was followed by much media frenzy. According to Riesel, he did not anticipate the amount or degree of public attention so easily won. Confédération Paysanne members had worked hard to generate media attention around the trial. But this time, with almost no effort, a flood of media soon poured into national papers about the action. As Riesel said, "It's amusing to see how the media liked to describe us little farmers, peasants from France, working together with little Indian peasants to destroy big and powerful scientific research" (September 29, 1999). Upon learning that their research materials had been destroyed, the enraged scientists went to the press and to legal forums. For weeks following the incident, a heated exchange tore through French newspapers. While many French scientists tended to publicly denounce the action, various environmental and consumer groups defended the Confédération Paysanne.

A TALE OF TWO RATIONALITIES

The rice action, as well as other actions that summer, signaled a collision between the hegemonic risk frame and an emerging alter-globalization frame. While biologists evaluated the rice primarily in terms of environmental and health risks, Confédération Paysanne activists framed it in terms of paysan survival and neoliberal globalization. Once again, an instrumental rationality bumped up against a solidaire worldview. Scientists from the public research bodies conducting the studies regarded risk as an exclusive frame for thinking about the rice. Many of these scientists were unable to think about risk as a frame (one among many), and so were unable to consider nonrisk frames as potentially legitimate. This rice affair is a tale of two rationalities. According to a calculative and instrumental rationality of risk, the Confédération Paysanne's action was illogical. According to a solidaire rationality, however, the action made complete sense. In a spirit of social justice, the farmers danced around the pile of genetically modified plants, tossing matches into the pile as they clapped their hands and sang. They were celebrating their symbolic attempt to put an end to a form of agriculture that they saw as dangerous to paysans all over the world.

The term *irrational* surfaced as a potent keyword reappearing in academic and popular news articles covering the incident. From the riskocentric perspective of the scientists conducting the study, it was irrational for the farmers to tamper with their experiment. These scientists could not under-stand the farmers' motivations. If farmers were concerned with the envi-ronmental and health risks associated with genetically modified rice, why would they deter a study that could potentially support their goal to ban GMOs on scientific grounds? When interviewed, scientists from CIRAD such as Michele Dufar asked bewilderedly, "Didn't the Confédération Paysanne ask for studies of the risks associated with these plants?" (personal commu-nication, September 20, 1999). After all, the Confédération Paysanne itself had summoned scientists to the trial in Nérac to speak about such risks just a year before.

A biologist from the National Institute for Agricultural Recherche (French National Institute for Agricultural Research), Marie Chevre, publicly ex-pressed outrage in France's key Leftist daily (*La Libération*, June 7, 1999). In the interview she decried the "irrationality" of Confédération Paysanne farmers who destroyed risk-related research. A colleague of Chevre, the biologist Jean-Benoit Morrell, explained to me: "They, the Confédération Paysanne, say they are concerned about this technology, but how can that be true when they destroy research that is investigating potential risks? Clearly, they have another political motivation for doing this" (personal communica-tion, September 10, 1999).

Riesel and the other farmers there that day thought the action was quite rational; it was completely consistent with their overall perspective. While they were earnestly concerned about dangers associated with GMOs, the risk factor represented but one problem among a myriad of equally pressing social and political issues related to GMOs. For Riesel, in particular, the Montpelier rice action constituted a rational attack on a technology associated not only with potential threats to health and the environment but also with the harms of globalization, corporate-financed research, and a model of postindustrial agriculture that endangers local agricultural economies throughout the world.

Bové and the Anti-McDo Action of 1999

Heated debates in *La Libération* and in the scientific community over the Montpelier rice action continued through the summer of 1999. The event marked a media success for the union and stimulated even more public dis-cussion about GMOs than the trial. Yet while the rice affair received a good amount of national and international attention, the public might have forgotten the action by summer's end. But in August a truly big news story about the union would hit the press. A series of events were sparked off by an anti-McDonald's action that serendipitously allowed the Confédération Paysanne to enter the national and international spotlight. Having captured the media's attention, the union was able to establish a clear link in popular consciousness between GMOs and neoliberalism that would indirectly challenge the hegemony of science based on instrumentalist risk.

The trial and the Montpelier rice actions represented major coups for the union's anti-GMO campaign. Yet those two actions would pale in comparison with what was to come. After a now-infamous anti-McDonald's action, the Confédération Paysanne finally cultivated a frame for GMOs in a way that would deeply resonate culturally with the French and international public. In August 1999, Riesel was working to strengthen ties between the union and the growing international alter-globalization movement. He flew to India to participate in a Peoples' Global Action meeting hosted by the Karnataka State Farmers' Union. During the same time, Bové planned a local action a few days before he was to go on a family vacation. The demonstration was another in a series of actions in McDonald's in his region. Bové had been leading anti-McDonald's actions for years, conducting farms of the future in many of its restaurants throughout the southwest. For Bové, McDonald's was a potent symbol of globalization gone awry. According to Bové, "McDo crystallized everything that was wrong with the global food system" (October 12, 1999). It is worth noting here that *McDo* is French slang for McDonald's. The anti-McDonald's action in August was intended to send a particular message. At the Confédération Paysanne's annual national congress in April in Vesoul, union members discussed the question of how to respond to the WTO's decision to punish Europe for banning hormone-treated beef.

And thus enters yet another nonhuman actor into this story: hormone-treated beef. The question of hormones in French meat has a history that dates back to the 1970s. Since that time, the union has been aware of the negative reception to hormone-treated beef by French consumer organizations. Fearing beef boycotts, which could harm French farmers, the Confédération Paysanne worked with other farmers' groups to lobby the EU to ban hormone-treated beef among European producers. Many in the union worried that the WTO would regard a European ban as an illegitimate form of protectionism. Trade officials use the term *protectionism* when they believe a country is refusing to import a certain product based on its desire to shield its own domestic markets from a stream of less-expensive or more-valued imported products—a event that could weaken the importing countries' markets. The WTO frowns on protectionism, but it will at times permit a country to ban the importation of a product if that product can be considered a health risk. As there is still little scientific proof that hormone-treated beef is harmful to those who eat it, the WTO determined the European ban to be protectionist.

Hormones had already proved themselves to be key actants in food-related social movements. In the 1970s, they had the sway to stop consumers from buying farmers' products. Hormones would also rile up the WTO and U.S. President Clinton. In many industrial livestock systems, farmers either add growth hormones to animal feed or inject the hormones into animals' bodies. Such practices have become routine in the United States among industrial farmers encouraging rapid and bulky growth of beef cattle (Schell 1985, 57). These hormones invoked distinctive responses from various sets of actors in France. Some members of science, farm, and consumer bodies publicly stated that hormones are unnecessary and unhealthful both to the animals and to the humans who eat them. They asserted these beliefs despite a body of scientific evidence that could impress the WTO. Other sets of actors, mainly in farmers' and consumers' groups, rejected hormone-treated beef due to questions of taste. According to many actors I interviewed, hormone-treated beef has an inferior *gonflé* (puffed up) or *pâle ou liquide* (watery taste). Like Bt corn, hormone-treated beef is thus another nonhuman actor that induced a range of responses from actors in this story. While some actors expressed uncertainty and confusion, others articulated disgust and anger. In any case, hormone-treated beef is indeed an actant, spurring human actors to take legal action and to engage in public demonstrations.

In 1997 the WTO lifted the de facto ban on hormone-treated beef to Europe that had been in place for decades. In 1998 the Dispute Settlement Body of the WTO took action. The Dispute Settlement Body is generally called upon when member-states of the WTO have trade disagreements. Pressured by the United States, the Dispute Panel Body announced that it would give Europe fifteen months to lift its ban on U.S. hormone-treated beef. The deadline, May 13, 1999, came and went. European leaders defied the WTO, keeping the ban intact. In retaliation, the WTO sanctioned Europe for rejecting the hormone-treated beef. The sanction entailed a 300 percent customs sur-charge on nearly one hundred European agricultural export products. Many of these products were luxury products such as fine cheese that are central to the local economies of many farmers throughout Europe.

PUTTING THE BEEF QUESTION IN CONTEXT:

A BRIEF HISTORY OF THE WTO

To more fully understand the French beef affair that led to the anti-McDonald's action, it is key to clarify the broader historical context sur-rounding the wto. The union's decision to create a direct action against the wto reflects its general sentiment about neoliberalism, free trade, and indus-trial agriculture generally. Groups such as the Confédération Paysanne view institutions such as the wto as part of a problematic Bretton Woods system that world leaders put into place during and after World War II. The wto is a multinational decision-making body. As such, delegates of member-states determine policies that have implications for peoples and markets world-wide. Supranational institutions such as the wto, the International Mone-tary Fund, and the World Bank are often poorly understood (or patently unknown) by those around the globe whose everyday markets and cultural practices are dramatically touched by them. Yet, as we have seen in this story, there do exist actors, such as those in the Confédération Paysanne, who at-tempt to understand and engage with such institutions. In recent years, the wto has become a potent locus for actors to express disenchantment with the Bretton Woods system, associated with the neoliberal system itself.

Although I cannot provide a fully detailed discussion of the wto in this text, I will try to succinctly outline some of the wto's main history and features. I hope to shed light on the place and meaning of the wto in the minds of alter-globalization activists. The wto's history began during World War II. Before the war, trade relations between various nations were gen-erally bilateral; leaders between two trading countries reached their own agreements privately and independently. In other words, when one country sought to develop trade relations with another, the two simply made a con-fidential trade policy. Sometimes the agreements stabilized economic rela-tions between trading countries. At other times, disputed contracts engen-dered political conflict. In 1944, during World War II, leaders of the allied nations came together at the Bretton Woods Conference in New Hampshire (in the United States). Leaders discussed the need for a supranational body that could peacefully govern trade between nations at the war's end. Ideally, these trade discussions would transcend the economic interests of particular countries. According to Bretton Woods leaders, trade agreements would sometimes be plurilateral — involving the trade interests of a limited set of countries. But Bretton Woods officials hoped for increasingly multilateral agreements — ones that would be accepted by a major set of countries with key markets. Such plurilateral or multilateral agreements, it was believed, would assist national leaders to develop trade policies in a more systematic, transparent, and diplomatic manner.

At its first meeting, many at Bretton Woods promoted the idea of creating an international trade organization to be guided by the United Nations. But the United States (and a few other countries) did not support the idea of a formally structured organization whose agreements would be binding. Thus, in 1948, leaders formed the GATT. The GATT would not be an organization per se, but it would constitute a series of trade conferences that would in turn generate policies on importation and exportation between a large number of countries. The GATT thus became the de facto supranational trade organization.

In addition to looking to questions of postwar trade, those at Bretton Woods knew that significant monies would be required to rebuild a war-torn Europe. Postwar Europe would need to revive its markets and productive capacities; it would require significant loans to recover physical and financial infrastructure. Thus, the Bretton Woods leaders founded two other institutions that today are called the World Bank and the International Monetary Fund. Like the GATT, these lending institutions would also be supranational bodies. Their missions would be to remain politically neutral as they provided funds to stabilize a postwar Europe.

Under the GATT system, seven sets of negotiations cycled between 1948 and 1994. Each meeting cycle was called a round, and often a round named for a city or country in which the trade meetings took place. The eighth cycle, called the Uruguay Round, began in 1986, just one year after the Confédération Paysanne was born. That year the union watched critically, noting how those participating in the Uruguay Round were seeking to allow wealthy northern nations to expand trade agreements into new areas of production. Those areas would include agriculture, intellectual property rights, and services.

Taking a step back, it is vital to note that the Bretton Woods system is composed of two overlapping phases. As we have just seen, the first phase

(1948 to 1958, roughly speaking) focused primarily on lending funds to northern industrialized nations for economic recovery. By the end of the 1960s, when this project was largely accomplished, Europe was once again a set of wealthy nations, ready to participate in GATT meetings.

After first assisting Europe in successfully rebuilding itself with funds from the Bretton Woods system, the system had a second objective: to develop southern nonindustrialized nations. The second phase of the Bretton Woods system would prove far more problematic than the first. Again, during the first phase of the Bretton Woods system, nations borrowing monies were relatively equal in term of power. They were also mainly Western nations that had already been using the capitalist system for hundreds of years. Once recovered, European countries quickly reestablished themselves as industrially dominant northern nations. The second phase of the Bretton Woods system, however, is still being played out on an uneven field. During this period (roughly 1958 to the present), the Bretton Woods system has targeted largely agrarian societies in the Global South. Many of these nations, ranging from countries in Africa to southwestern Asia to Latin America, were former colonies of the newly reempowered European nations. Once decolonized, they began their ongoing struggle to establish themselves as autonomous political, economic, and cultural entities. According to many in the alter-globalization movement, the Bretton Woods system failed to support a robust set of newly independent southern nations. Instead, many feel it set in motion a complex economic, political, and cultural dynamic of social inequality that continues today.

To further clarify, it is useful to examine two critical problems that arose during the second postcolonial phase of the Bretton Woods system. Trying to reestablish their own infrastructure, industry, and agricultural systems, impoverished countries borrowed monies from such supranational bodies as the International Monetary Fund and the World Bank. Subsequently, they faced high interest rates, soaring debt, and increased destitution that in turn led their leaders to look to the Bretton Woods system for more monies. As a result, these new debtor nations found themselves unable to sit as equals during international trade negotiations. To address the debt problem, leaders of the Bretton Woods system introduced structural adjustment programs in the late 1970s. Through structural adjustment programs, Bretton Woods agents began to grant new loans or reduce debt—if poor countries would fully capitulate to a neoliberal economic system. *Neoliberalism* is a term used to describe an economic system that promotes minimal state intervention in private enterprise. Otherwise stated, a neoliberal approach assumes that state regulation of private corporations hinders a nation's overall economic growth. According to a neoliberal model, states should reduce as many production or trade-related regulations as possible. While this laissez-faire approach seems reasonable enough to some, to others it enhances social inequality in an era when northern nations seem to benefit substantially more from the system than poor southern nations.

The neoliberal structural adjustment programs ask leaders of poor countries to agree to free market programs that bring about increased privatization, deregulation, and reduced trade barriers. According to many in the Confédération Paysanne, structural adjustment programs are unjust forms of coercion. As Bové says, "Yes, they [the Bretton Woods system] are happy to reduce debt and give help to developing countries [*pays en voie de développement*], but everyone knows what it really is. It's blackmail [*C'est le chantage*]" (personal communication, November 6, 1999). In some cases, powerful institutions require debtor nations to accept trade agreements that lead to the dumping of cheap northern products and services onto their own fledgling economies. Reproductive health also often falls into the purview of structural adjustment, as poor countries are obliged to implement family-planning programs that are often incompatible with local and cultural reproductive practices. Often, powerful institutions compel nations in debt to lower labor or environmental standards for multinational corporations that have set up shop in their countries. Other structural adjustments include debt-for-nature swaps. In such exchanges, Bretton Woods institutions pressure poor countries to trade off crucial natural resources either to lower debt or to increase their access to new loans. Such resources include waterways crucial to agriculture and everyday hydration, fertile land areas, forested areas rich in biodiversity, and tourist-rich shorelines also central to nations' fishing economies. Issues such as structural adjustment and free trade have been central to the Confédération Paysanne since its inception. Many were concerned when, during the Uruguay Round, leaders of the GATT decided to place staple agricultural products (often referred to as bulk products or grain commodities) into the trade system. Among other things, this meant to union members that increased dumping would occur in the Global South.

Intellectual property agreements would allow biotechnology corporations to further lock in GMOs as a primary form of global agricultural production. Agricultural biotechnology depends on intellectual property rights; without such rights, Monsanto, Novartis, Cargill, and other corporations cannot patent their seed-input packages. If unpatented, such products would be available to any manufacturer, and corporations would find it impossible to maintain dominance over the agricultural biotechnology market. The entry of services into the GATT was also of great concern to the Confédération Paysanne. In the 1970s and 1980s, when industrial capitalism underwent a dramatic period of restructuring, union members witnessed the service industry become a primary target for capital accumulation in many wealthy industrialized nations. Many in the union wondered about the future implications of cultural products being owned by private corporations and traded in an international market. Considerable discussion took place in the union regarding the fate of local and cultural autonomy of peoples across the globe.

During the Uruguay Round, the union watched telecommunications services become a lucrative tradable commodity. In turn, the financial sector became a key site for investment as wealthy nations began to build their own banks, lending agencies, accounting firms, and other financial services in other member countries. Entrepreneurs noted the potential for poor countries to become major tourist sites, so the GATT assisted wealthy nations in establishing new forms of rural, urban, and ecotourism services in other countries. Private corporations also targeted transportation as an effective site for commodification. Since the 1980s, privately owned buses, airplanes, and car services have increasingly been sold to both tourists and general publics in new locations around the world. Wealthy nations also began to sell juridical services such as legal training and consultation. At the same time, private companies constructed their own primary, elementary, and secondary schools within poor countries, making profits in the educational sectors there. Private corporations began to put on the market healthcare services around the world as private firms from the north set up high-priced clinics, hospitals, and pharmacies. Unfortunately, many of these state-of-the-art facilities would be accessible only to the elite classes living in poor nations.

Environmental services also emerged as a leading source of revenue for many countries participating in the Uruguay Round. Trade experts put into place international environmental standards and regulations, and private corporations benefited from these policies by creating firms that could sell to poor countries consulting and technical services that would allow them to stay up to code. Prevention-related technologies for flooding, earthquakes, and droughts are a key set of commodities being sold by wealthy nations around the world. Although the causes of such natural disasters as hurricanes are controversial, many in the alter-globalization movement link these problems with what they call the climate crisis. Whether these disasters are "natural" or created by global warming, many of these events occur within impoverished nations, requiring leaders to look once again to Bretton Woods agencies to help them reduce structural damage and human suffering. Private corporations from wealthy nations also sell to newly industrialized countries services that are designed to curb vehicle emissions, reduce noise, and protect landscapes. Wealthy nations also profit from retailing sewage, refuse, disposal, and sanitation services to poor countries. Certainly, many services sold to impoverished nations are necessary. Yet many in the Confédération Paysanne (and in the alter-globalization movement generally) wondered if a flood of Western service commodities could drown out countries' abilities to maintain or strengthen their own culturally appropriate and affordable ways of life.

The union's apprehensions about the Bretton Woods system continued into the 1990s. On April 15, 1994, no one in the union was surprised when members of the GATT met in Mexico to sign the Marrakech Agreement. This agreement finally established a new trade-based institutionalized organization, the WTO. While the GATT represented a series of trade meetings that ended in treaties, the WTO would constitute a permanent structure that is capable of establishing binding multilateral agreements.

To return to the question of hormone-treated beef, we now have a better understanding of why those in the Confédération Paysanne would react negatively when they learned that the newly refurbished WTO had come knocking on their door, so to speak. In 1997, just three years after the creation of the WTO, the union was dismayed when the WTO changed its policy on hormone-treated beef. The GATT leaders had made a plurilateral agreement that exempted Europe from importing beef treated with hormones, but in 1997 leaders of the WTO canceled the exemption, demanding a multilateral agreement.

THE ORGANIZATION DISCIPLINES EUROPE: NO BEEF, NO ROQUEFORT

In retaliation for Europe's refusal to import U.S. hormone-treated beef, the WTO placed a heavy surtax on luxury foodstuff, including Roquefort cheese. When French sheep's milk producers learned that Roquefort cheese would be included in the list of surtaxed high-end foods, they had reason for deep concern. The cheese already sold in the United States for more than thirty dollars a pound. At nearly ninety dollars a pound, it would become unaffordable to many American retailers, restaurants, and consumers who would normally buy the extravagant cheese. Roquefort is a high-stakes commodity in France. And perhaps most important, the cheese has controlled origin status. This means that it is produced only by sheep farmers in one small region of south-central France called the Avéyron. Like many products of le terroir, Roquefort is central to maintaining the local economy. Today, more than thirteen hundred workers (farmers, processors, and so on) depend on Roquefort that is destined for domestic and foreign markets. A drop in sales could devastate an entire region of the country.

For those unfamiliar with Roquefort, I will give a brief yet inclusive overview of the history and production methods associated with the cheese. The cultural practices and meanings surrounding Roquefort offer insight into the reasons why it is so valued by many members of French society. In France, Roquefort is known as "the king of cheeses." The term *Roquefort* is derived from the region's ancient local dialect, Occitan, which calls the cheese *rocafort*. The cheese is white, with a texture that is both creamy and slightly crumbly. Running through the cheese are its famous threads of blue-black mold that pack the cheese with an unparalleled tangy punch. Unlike many French cheeses, Roquefort has no rind and every part of its wheel is edible. In general, wheels of Roquefort weigh between two and three kilograms and are ten centimeters thick.

The cheese dates back to 79 AD. In 1411, King Charles VI granted the people of what was then called the Region of Roquefort a monopoly over the cheese. He determined that a cheese could only be called Roquefort if it had ripened in the region's unique caves. Centuries later, in 1925, Roquefort became the first French product to achieve controlled origin status. This means producers must conform to a strict set of protocols to make a cheese branded with the Roquefort label. Controlled origin status guarantees a select group of French farmers the right to label and sell the cheese, preventing others from copying or imitating the product for a lower price. Roquefort embodies notions of le terroir, the distinctive culinary and geographical dimension associated with particular regions in France. When combined with the traditional savoir faire of the French artisanal producer, terroir wines, cheese, or pâtés attain the status of products of French high culture (Hervieu 1996b, 24). The idea of terroir means that for champagne to receive controlled origin status, it can only be produced in the Champagne region. Burgundy wines can only be produced from grapes grown in Bourgogne.

Roquefort can only be produced by using the milk of sheep that have grazed on grasses from the south-central regions of France known as the Aquitaine, Languedoc, the Pyrenees, Provence, and Corsica. The cave walls of Mont Comblaou (where the cheeses age) are marked with porous streaks, known as *fleurines*. These caverns allow an inimitable form of ventilation necessary for the cheese's maturation. The caves also sustain a temperature of about 50 degrees Celsius, and 95 percent humidity. Roquefort is spotted with *Penicillium roqueforti*. The mold itself is a cultural artifact, centuries old, imbuing the cheese with its distinctive "stinky" savor. Roquefort producers cultivate this mold by placing loaves of wheat and rye bread onto planks in the humid caves. After several weeks, the producers scrape mold from the bread and subsequently inject it into the cheese. In addition, other mold spores float into the cave, blowing through the fleurines, fixing themselves to the cheese. Once the Roquefort producer has cultivated the cheese with mold, he or she mixes it with salt. The young cheese then sits on old oak planks for a minimum of three months. Once it is fully ripe, Roquefort producers wrap the cheese in foil to prevent it from contacting air.

I relate these details because many people in the United States are unaware of the rich set of cultural practices associated with the cheese. In fact, I have found that many in the country confuse Roquefort with the idea of blue cheese in general, often using the terms *Roquefort* and *blue cheese* interchangeably. What many Americans do not know is that blue cheese is any cheese made from the milk of cows, goats, or sheep that is cultured with the mold *Penicillium*. Blue cheeses are usually speckled or streaked with blue, gray, or green mold, and they generally have a salty pungent flavor. Since the term *blue cheese* is simply a descriptor for a generic category of cheese, it can be produced by any individual, in any part of the world. Blue cheese has no relation to any combination of particular climates, soil, grasses, milk, mold, or caves. Because the United States annually imports about 440 tons of Roquefort, this market is crucial to Roquefort cheese producers. The professional association of Roquefort producers met with Jean Glavany, France's minister of agriculture, to appeal for help. Glavany responded that he was powerless to reverse the WTO's decision and promised only to do what he could to pay for a publicity campaign that might help the farmers' cause (Bové 2001, 93).

Along with other farmers in local sheep's milk associations, Bové decided to take action. The paysans planned a direct action that would hopefully draw France's attention to the trade policies of both Clinton and the WTO. After learning that a McDonald's restaurant was in the initial stages of construction in Millau (a small town in the Avéyron), the paysans determined the site as good as any for a direct action. Congregating at the construction site, the paysans symbolically sabotaged the building under construction. While some hammered away at a few tiles on the half-finished red roof, others pulled down the construction sign. With signature Confédération Paysanne humor, the activists said to the press on location that day that they were "dismantling" (*démontant*) the restaurant the way one would carefully dismantle a bomb. Despite the metaphor, Bové later described the action as having a light and congenial feeling. Families with young children picnicked on the rocky grounds of the construction lot. Meanwhile other paysans held an informal presentation for a few members of the local press who had decided to show up that day.

For many, particularly those outside Avéyron (and beyond France), the dismantling was confusing. Why, many wondered, would sheep's milk producers protest a McDonald's? Was the union simply expressing an anti-American spirit by protesting a symbol associated with the United States? In press releases and interviews, Bové and others tried to articulate the links between hormone-treated beef sold by the U.S.-based McDonald's, and the exorbitant export tax on Roquefort cheese that could devastate the local community. According to Bové, "We tried to make it clear: it was industrialized agriculture against local artisanal agriculture. We were protesting a symbol of industrialized agriculture, not the U.S." (personal communication, June 19, 2000). Here we have two nonhuman actors at play. On the one hand, hormone-treated beef summons negative sentiments about industrial agriculture. On the other hand, Roquefort cheese wafts up generally positive regional and national feelings about nonindustrial agriculture. Roquefort did many things that day at the McDonald's construction site. In addition to catalyzing activists to remove tiles from the building's roof, paysans painted the slogan "McDo Defora—Gardarem Roquefort!" (McDo out, Roquefort in!) across the building's half-built roof. The paysans wrote their slogan in

Occitan, a southern dialect of the traditional region known as Languedoc. Since the 1980s, it has been popular for activists in the southwest to voice political demands in Occitan. While some elders in the community were still familiar with Occitan, the dialect had been virtually driven out of circulation by national educational efforts in the postwar era. Occitan thus came to constitute a symbol of regional and local identity against national or international powers (Lem 1999, 18).

The cultural and biological flair of Roquefort cheese also had the power to draw upon networks established more than twenty years earlier during the Larzac movement. When Bové and other farmers in associations for sheep's milk producers announced the action, they were not surprised when three hundred paysans—and supporters—showed up at the McDonald's that day in mid-August. August is a period in France when much of the nation enjoys its summer vacation. Bové did not make the McDo action take place on his own. It was Bové and his symmetrical ally, Roquefort. The action brought together people from the original Larzac struggle while also embodying the sensibility of the Larzac. Farmers stood side by side with nonfarmers, fighting a power they perceived as instrumental. In the minds of the paysans that day, they were fighting state power that once reduced farmland to military bases and food to industrial commodities.

"ONLY AMERICANS WOULD TREAT A UNION MAN LIKE THAT!" NATIONAL AND INTERNATIONAL SUPPORT FOR BOVÉ

When I explain my research topic to friends in the United States, many say, "Oh yeah, I heard about the French guy who drove his tractor into a McDonald's." When I ask where they heard this story, they will reply by saying something like, "I read it in the papers." After which they'll continue, "Can you imagine what it must have felt like sitting there eating a hamburger as this guy plows into your table? He should have been put away for life!" I have heard many such comments over the years. Slowly Bové's story morphed into a kind of international urban legend. Such narratives reflect two things: a predilection in the United States for stories about crazed, lone individuals committing odd crimes in strange places, and a lack of understanding in the United States about the plight of small farmers generally. Just as no tractor ever plowed into a McDonald's restaurant, the lead character in the McDo tale was not a guy going postal. In recent U.S. history, popular imagination is indeed fixated on the figure of the alienated individual (usually male) disenchanted by society who just loses it and commits a senseless and destructive crime. This individual is often depicted as roiling with rage, gunning down ordinary people in schoolrooms, post offices, and workplaces before placing a pistol between his own teeth. But in the French McDo story, there is neither violence nor a solitary irrational individual. The main characters in this story are union farmers who, in French society, are generally granted degrees of respect and asylum from harsh punishment.

French farmers from the FNSEA are known for breaking windows of public buildings and blockading highways for hours with piles of smoldering tires. These events are widely depicted on the nightly news. Yet rarely do FNSEA members leave the scene with more than a slap on the proverbial wrist. The day after such an action, FNSEA leaders find themselves sitting in tidy government offices, engaging in rounds of negotiations with powerful policymaking bodies. Few French citizens will pass picket lines, and even fewer would approve the harsh treatment of unionized workers demonstrating for fair wages or prices.

It is this cultural context that makes the story of Bové's arrest and imprisonment so remarkable. After conducting farms of the future in McDonald's restaurants for years without ever receiving a serious charge, Bové and his local community were shocked when he and several others were arrested and jailed for conducting this particular demonstration. According to Bové, the severe charges were not merely the result of the McDo action. Instead the charges served as retaliation on behalf of a young new judge in Millau. This judge had been presiding throughout the summer of 1999, a summer of, in the judge's estimation, an unending series of paysan-led crop pulls topped off by the Montpelier rice affair. Determined to punish Bové for the anti-GMO actions, the judge ordered Bové and the six others under arrest an unusually high bail and charge (José Bové, personal communication, October 27, 1999). Unknowingly, the judge's actions set in motion a surprising chain of events that forever transformed the French GMO debate, putting Bové and the Confédération Paysanne on the international map along the way.

When the bail orders were actually served, Bové and his family were vacationing in southern France. Upon his return a week later, Bové learned that he would have to wait for up to one week in the local prison for his bail hearing. After fulfilling his one-week stay, he was informed that the bail would be twenty-five thousand dollars—a sum the union would be obliged to pay in order for him to be released. Bové decided to remain in jail for two more weeks to await a second hearing at which the judge would determine the charges. As Bové reflects, "I figured I'd already spent a week [in prison], I might as well wait another two for the charge hearing. . . . Besides, I'd realized that we were getting pretty good media by my being in there." The French press widely covered the story of Bové's sentencing, jail stay, and unusually high bail. This news hit a cultural nerve that, within weeks, catapulted Bové to the status of national martyr and hero in the French and international alter-globalization movement. According to Bové, "The French don't like to see a farmer or a union man put in jail like that for such a small thing. They saw the high bail and charges as being more like the American system. They said, 'That's how Americans do it, and we're not Americans'" (personal communication, October 27, 1999).

Another nonhuman actor became central to the anti-GMO network: a photograph of a smiling Bové with handcuffed fists raised above his head. This photograph was made possible by a local police officer who was leading Bové from a police car to prison. The officer charged with this task was a local who knew Bové personally and was sympathetic to his cause. In the police car, Bové had asked the officer to remove the cuffs from where they were bound behind his back. He explained that if bound in the front, he could raise his cuffed hands for the media waiting outside the police car. Bové knew what a splendid picture this would make (José Bové, personal communication, October 29, 1999). This photograph hit the front page of many national and international newspapers and appeared in television reports. The photograph was an actant in the fullest sense of the word. It acted upon the French public, stimulating sympathy, moral indignation, and national pride at the sight of a French union man and paysan, grinning with dignity in the face of national and international authorities. Had the photograph been a lackluster snapshot of Bové being shoved into a car with hands behind his back, it might have produced an entirely different set of cultural meanings.

MCDO AND GMOS: TYING THE TWO TOGETHER

With the help of Roquefort and the photograph, Bové was suddenly renowned for the McDo action rather than the GMO issue. He then decisively determined to seize the opportunity to advance both causes. While Bové did not explicitly attempt to counter science hegemony associated with risk discourse, he explained to me that he wanted to illustrate the links between

GMOs and globalization. As Bové explained, "In every interview after McDo, I would talk about GMOs. . . . It was an opportunity to make that link clear in people's minds, that GMOs and McDo were really two aspects of the same problem[,] . . . that multinationals, the WTO, that capitalism, are controlling everything from culture to food" (personal communication, October 29, 1999). Drawing on both paysan and alter-globalization discourses, Bové continued to reframe GMOs and McDo as examples of "globalization and a decline in quality of food and life both in France and throughout the world."

The success of the McDo action in bringing the Confédération Paysanne national attention led the union, on an organizational level, to more publicly endorse and promote the anti-GMO campaign first spearheaded by Bové and Riesel. Bové's public endorsement by the Confédération Paysanne and by the key French anti-globalization group ATTAC also marked the beginning of the end of the Bové-Riesel duo. Upon his return from India a week after the McDo incident, Riesel was dismayed by what he perceived as "a serious change in the strategy and discourse" that the two had been developing for the two previous years (Riesel, personal interview, November 2, 1999). Within weeks following the McDo action, Riesel publicly resigned from the Confédération Paysanne, explicitly distancing himself from Bové. Riesel expressed his disappointment about the McDo affair in an open letter to Bové during Bové's imprisonment. He later published a book that, as he said to me, sharply criticized Bové for "selling out the anti-GMO campaign to Confédération Paysanne moderates and to the reformist alter-globalizationists as well" (personal communication, November 8, 1999).

As Riesel receded from the public GMO controversy, Bové rose to become the central figure associated with both the French anti-GMO and anti-globalization movements. To this day, few are aware that Riesel was at one time a main force in the union's campaign. In the spotlight, Bové largely succeeded in reshaping the debate. Scientific risk still clearly remained a key frame for thinking about the technology. Yet, increasingly, the media, activist groups, public researchers, and even government officials broadened their discourse. They included in their GMO narratives questions ranging from biological patents and the fate of small farmers in France to the homogenization of cultures globally by neoliberal-style capitalism. Many even tied the question of GMOs to the WTO.

Bové had become a cultural folk hero domestically and internationally, symbolizing French resistance to perceived processes of commodification in domains of food, language, music, and business. The media often drew attention to Bové's hybrid identity as the son of French scientists and a paysan. Journalists, industry officials, and government agents often challenged his status as a real paysan. Despite these disputes regarding his real identity, Bové enjoyed tremendous acceptance by the French public. After 1999, Bové became a key figure in the French and international alter-globalization movement, speaking and organizing in countries from Mexico to Brazil, and he accepted a post as a regional director in La Via Campesina in 2000. Perhaps most interesting is that he soon became a hero to many in the U.S. alter-globalization movement. He was celebrated mightily in the United States just months after his release from prison.

LA MALBOUFFE: SYMBOL OF TASTELESS GLOBALIZATION

Bové's rise to stardom was accompanied by an unusual anti-GMO discourse that strengthened his position as key spokesperson for national and international anti-GMO and alter-globalization networks. The centerpiece of Bové's discourse was *la malbouffe*, literally meaning "bad food," which he equated with GMOs, McDo, and all products of globalized culture and industrialized agriculture. *La malbouffe* is a slang term that translates imperfectly into "bad chow" or "junk food." For Bové, the term symbolizes everything distasteful about globalization, ranging from the cultural homogenization associated with McDonald's fast food to the industrialized agriculture associated with hormone-treated beef or GMOs.

While popularized in France with Bové, the term *la malbouffe* itself was coined in 1981 by Stella and Joel de Rosnay in a short and little-known book titled *La malbouffe* (1981). Bové, a self-taught scholar in the politics of food, had read the book years before 1999 and invoked the term during and after the McDo action for lack of a better word. To uncover the more subtle meanings of Bové's *la malbouffe*, we must first understand the meaning of *la bouffe* itself, an affectionate colloquial term referring to food in general, from which the English word *buffet* is derived. *La bouffe*, bringing together notions of pleasure, tradition, and French cuisine, really has no translation in English.

To be cultured in France is to be cultivated, or to have good taste. The meaning of taste is of course twofold, as both food and people may be understood as being cultivated or tasteful. While a food is well cultivated when it is produced according to regional agricultural traditions, a cultivated individual is capable of recognizing and taking pleasure in food considered cultured and good tasting. Within this cultural-culinary universe, la malbouffe represents the antithesis of cultural pleasure and cultivation. It signals that which is not traditionally cultivated, that which lacks cultural expertise and history—and thus that which has no taste (literally and figuratively). By pronouncing McDo, GMOs, and hormone-treated beef as incidents of la malbouffe, Bové created a story. He generated a salient symbolic synthesis of the cultural and agricultural features of globalization gone wrong. And by looking at this story through the lens of symmetry, we see that McDo, GMOs, hormone-treated beef, and the photograph of Bové in handcuffs also worked to coproduce the celebrity of Bové.

In referring to la malbouffe, Bové invokes and solidifies his agricultural authority and cultural expertise. As a producer of sheep's milk for Roquefort cheese, Bové is linked to an actant that is a particularly potent cultural symbol. Roquefort integrates notions of biology, geography, and cultural expertise. As a product of le terroir, the cheese embraces all parts of the artisanal process, from the bacterial cultures used in Roquefort production to the historical cultures of local farmers. Reflecting upon the evocative power of le terroir and of Roquefort in particular, Bové asserted wryly, "Clinton made a big mistake when he chose to mess with Roquefort. He didn't know what he was dealing with. It means something to French people" (personal communication, October 29, 1999). By proclaiming GMOs an instance of la malbouffe, Bové translated a debate about scientific risk into an overtly political debate about food quality, paysan survival, and neoliberal trade policy. In so doing, he shifted the site of discursive authority from the objective and scientific risk expert standing outside culture and history to the intensely engaged paysan expert standing for culture and history.

Conclusion

The historic anti-McDo action that took place in the southern French town of Millau did not just happen out of the blue. In this case, we see how tensions between public scientists, private corporations, and peasants from France and India snowballed into an impressive force that led a local judge in Millau to harshly punish paysans for their anti-GMO and anti-McDo activities.

From his prison cell, Bové asserted the contradiction between instrumentalized agricultural products such as hormone-treated beef and McDo hamburgers and artisanal and traditional products such as Roquefort cheese. In so doing, he laid bare the clash between an instrumental and *solidaire* rationality of agriculture.

For the heirs of the Larzac legacy, Roquefort symbolized a logic of solidarity that brought farmers and nonfarmers together to fight against militarization, privatization, and political domination generally. Roquefort stood for quality food and the right of the world's smallholders to work together to protect both food and a *paysan* way of life.

8

Operation Roquefort, Part I

Traveling to Washington, D.C.

In September 1999, the Confédération Paysanne was challenged to build on the momentum generated by the McDo affair. In the months following the McDo affair, government and media actors did their best to deter the union from garnering more popular attention and support. Despite these attempts, the union took charge of its own self-image, devising ways to keep the Confédération Paysanne on the minds of the public both inside France and internationally. Bové in particular continued to appear in various media outlets, and the union allowed a major French publishing house to create a book about the Confédération Paysanne's and Bové's roles in the McDo action. This book ultimately became a national bestseller, further solidifying Bové's and the Confédération Paysanne's positions in a national debate about food, globalization, and the place and meaning of paysans in French life. In November 1999, the union sent a delegation of paysans to Washington, D.C., and Seattle for the WTO meetings, where they would serve as witnesses (*témoins*) to the official hearings. In Seattle, we see the union advance another set of key objectives: to promote popular support for Bové and the union's postindustrial model of agriculture.

Building Momentum and Heading to the United States

CULTURAL DEPICTIONS OF BOVÉ: FROM ASTERIX TO TARZAN

After August 1999, Bové had become a truly iconic French figure. He was often portrayed as a French David taking on the Goliath of international finance. He was also frequently portrayed as one of the characters in France's famed cartoon *Asterix and Obelix*. Like Bové, Asterix le Gaulois sports a blondish Fu Manchu, heightening the symbolic similarities between the two common men who dared challenge a superpower. The character Asterix is often merrily plowing through various exploits with ancient Romans during the time when Rome occupied France. Similarly, the figure of Bové was depicted as taking on corporate America, neoliberalism, and everything that threatened French identity. Bové was thus presented as an intractable Gaulois. He was seen as a headstrong Frenchman, willing to protect French tradition against impending Europeanization. Bové's popularity rose during a time when France was preparing to exchange the French franc for the euro. Such transitions were topics of heated debate. Many feared that French culture would dissolve into an increasingly integrated Europe and a neoliberal global economy. The ubiquitous cartoon image of Asterix as Bové constituted a key nonhuman actor in the French anti-GMO movement. The cartoon figure stirred warm humor and sympathy among Bové's supporters. It also spurred a cynical brand of mirth among opponents who sought to see him as nothing more than a harmless comic strip buffoon.

In addition to comparing Bové to Asterix, politicians and the media often associated Bové with a passing media fad. During and after the McDo affair, French media experts and politicians predicted that Bové would not maintain his popularity as a public figure. According to these actors, Bové's élan would prove as fickle and ephemeral as the French media itself. Such predictions served as a warning to union organizers. Many paysans sat together in countless meetings, determined to strategize how to maintain the Confédération Paysanne's media momentum. Keeping Bové's popularity afloat was their primary objective following the summer of 1999.

The authors of *La fabrication de l'information* (Manufacturing information) critique the French media for "fabricating personalities" in a reckless manner (Aubenas and Benassayag 1999, 44). In particular, the authors refer to the case of Tarzan, a French member of a truck drivers' union who captured national attention in 1992. After leading a heroic national strike headed up by truck drivers, Tarzan rose to instant celebrity. Within days, the truck driver's face had appeared in every major paper and on the evening news and major television shows. However, after just a few short weeks, Tarzan's popularity faded. He disappeared back into a media abyss as quickly as he had come on the scene.

At the peak of Tarzan's celebrity, there was a media frenzy that focused on a historic meeting between Tarzan and the French prime minister (Deluchey 1992, 32). The covers of news magazines and papers flashed images of Tarzan preparing for the encounter. Most photographs featured Tarzan in an elite Parisian clothing store being fitted for a high-priced suit. Saturated in class discourse, these images were a discursive technology for disciplining the truck driver. Powerful institutions such as the state and media were hard at work marking his person with symbols associated with class precisely to emphasize Tarzan's inferior standing. The French populace considered a meeting between an uneducated truck driver and the prime minister both amusing and unsettling (Debons and Le Coq 1997, 56). Unlike the U.S. media, the French media rarely promote folksy images of down-to-earth politicians. In the United States, many television viewers were happy for George W. Bush to appear on the nightly news wearing a cowboy hat, making small talk with locals in a Texas bar. In contrast, French officials rarely publicly present themselves dressed in the attire of working people. If they meet with union representatives, for instance, government officials wear their usual tailored suits, while the union leaders dress up as best they can.

Tarzan discourse was abundant during the post-McDo period in France. In mid-September, the French press often asked Prime Minister Jospin for his opinion on Bové. In response, Jospin made frequent classist and patronizing comparisons between Tarzan and Bové. In numerous interviews, he referred condescendingly to "the brief and sad story of Tarzan" (Aubenas and Benassayag 1999, 46). At the time, many in the Confédération Paysanne wondered if Jospin's comments belied his concern about the potential power of figures arising from outside the formal political party system. "Perhaps Bové really is seen as a threat," said many in the union when I questioned them on Jospin's references to Tarzan. Others in the union also wondered if Jospin hoped that Bové would simply fall from the limelight of the political media.

In my own fieldwork, I noted frequent Tarzan references in interviews with actors in French scientific, industrial, and governmental bodies. Such Tarzan discourses minimized and normalized the Bové affair, reducing it to a hoped-for passing spectacle. For such actors, Bové was nothing but another Tarzan; Bové's affair would surely have little lasting cultural or political impact.

Aware of what was called "the Tarzan effect," the Confédération Paysanne began to strategize soon after the McDo incident how to build upon Bové's celebrity to draw media and public attention to the union's broader objectives. Everyone at the union knew that this endeavor would prove daunting. Bové and the Confédération Paysanne devised ways to deploy Bové's icon status as a charismatic individual while making sure to emphasize his role within the union and within wider international struggles. By linking Bové the individual with the Confédération Paysanne as a rising powerful farmers' union, Bové and the union hoped to secure the longevity and potency of union programs and vision. The Confédération Paysanne thus sought to present Bové as a member of the union rather than its leader. To that end, Bové and the union speaker, François Dufour, stood side by side at meetings and photo shoots. Despite their efforts, the media often ignored Dufour and pointed their cameras and microphones at Bové instead. To the general French (and international) public, Bové's status within the Confédération Paysanne was ambiguous. No longer a national secretary, Bové held no formal high-profile position in the union. Regardless, the press regularly referred to Bové as the union's founder, leader, or president, further confounding various audiences. The press also often portrayed Bové as a charismatic individual who acted singularly during the McDo action. If the Confédération Paysanne did not play its cards carefully, the visions and objectives embedded in the union and in the McDo action risked being obscured.

In August 1999, Decouverte, France's premier publishing house, approached Bové to cowrite a book about Bové intended for a public audience. In discussions at the union, Bové and others contemplated how to create a book that would further the union's long-term presence and goals — while building on Bové's popularity. Finally, Dufour and Bové requested that the book be based on interviews with both Bové and Dufour. This, they hoped, would help demonstrate Bové's location within the greater union. While Decouverte's editors did feature Bové a bit more heavily, the union achieved its goals. The book *Le monde n'est pas une marchandise* (The world is not for sale) (Bové and Dufour 2001) portrays Bové as but one member of a larger union and agenda. When the union considered how to present Bové in the context of his U.S. voyage, it was clear to all in the Confédération Paysanne that the trip would be a forum in which Bové and Dufour would transcend the lone-actor image. Whenever possible, Bové and Dufour would appear together as members of a broader farmers' union with broad-based vision and goals. Bové and Dufour could be seen in many photographs taken after McDo, standing side by side, fists raised together, presenting a united front.

ONE DELEGATION, ONE TRANSLATOR, MANY PAPARAZZI,
AND SEVERAL POLITICAL GOALS

In November 1999, a few months after the McDo incident, the Confédération Paysanne made plans to send a delegation of farmers to the United States for a double mission. First, the group would travel to Washington, D.C., to meet with the National Family Farm Coalition. Afterward, the delegation would attend the WTO meetings in Seattle as legal observers (*témoins*). In Seattle, the Confédération Paysanne delegation would meet with international peasant and indigenous organizations, building on the momentum to generate a robust alter-globalization movement. The Confédération Paysanne delegation destined for Seattle consisted of a group of nine union members including Dufour, Bové, others arrested at the McDo action, and a few local supporters from the Millau area. The Confédération Paysanne was also accompanied by Gilles Marchaud, who was assigned by Decouverte to cowrite the book of interviews with Bové and Dufour. Since Bové's trial, Marchaud had been mainly focusing on Bové, camping out on Bové's farm near Millau and shadowing him as he went about his daily activities. Marchaud was actively preparing for what promised to be a best-selling popular book that outlined the Confédération Paysanne's objectives that came to the surface during the McDo affair.

In addition to Marchaud, a group of about thirty other journalists from France and other parts of Europe had also camped out on Bové's farm during the months after August. Many of these journalists would form an entourage around the delegation to the United States. During the voyage, the delegation came to affectionately call this group of journalists "our paparazzi." The delegation integrated the journalists into various aspects of their daily lives during the trip, creating an easy-going, fun-loving feeling among the whole group. I wrangled my way into the delegation as well. One evening in Paris, just a month before the delegation left for the United States, I attended an informal planning meeting at a café across from a train station from which Bové was to depart later that evening. As the group discussed the trip's details, I asked if anyone in the delegation spoke English. Bové explained that he had spent a few years as a young child in the United States, but had little left of his rudimentary English. "Need a translator?" I asked. Over the past several months, I had been honing my translating skills in various activist forums. Bové looked around the table at the others in a bemused fashion. "I won't cost a thing," I added. After a round of approving nods from others, Bové relit his pipe and exhaled a thoughtful plume of sweet smoke: "We can only pay your expenses on the ground in the U.S. You'll have to fly yourself there." As I had planned return home around that time for Thanksgiving anyway, I was set to go.

The union's planning committee began to determine the objectives of the voyage. The central goal would be to evaluate the WTO's impacts on peasant and indigenous groups globally. Established in Marrakech, the WTO was in its fifth year. In Seattle, the union would have ample opportunity to meet with other organizations to assess the effects of the trade body on actors on the ground. They would also meet to strategize how to address the issue of trade deregulation. To the Confédération Paysanne, the situation appeared dire for smallholders across the world, particularly in the Global South. In poor countries, governments are generally unable to provide subsidies to farmers. Without subsidies, local farmers cannot afford to buy or rent land. Thus, land is open to foreign investors who buy vast areas in southern countries. This land is used mostly for plantation agriculture whose products are for export. As a result, smallholders have little access to lands for local agricultural production, and communities go hungry. One paysan leader, Marcel Dupuis, said, "Most decent land in poor countries is taken over by foreign multinationals for their own use. There's land in poor countries—paysans just don't get subsidies to farm it" (personal communication, January 15, 2007).

In addition, the Confédération Paysanne was greatly concerned with the problem of dumping. Crises in such countries as the Philippines had become emblematic of the predicaments of small farmers who were self-sufficient for centuries before their governments began using lands for export agriculture. The WTO required the Philippine government to lift tariffs (import taxes) on foreign rice. Such tariffs were designed to protect the country's local rice economy. Once the tariffs were lifted, powerful countries began to dump their heavily subsidized rice on Philippine markets. Dumped rice is less expensive on the local market than locally produced varieties. Dumped foreign rice wiped out both the subsistence and local market economies. Needless to say, the Philippines is no longer self-sufficient in rice production (Glipo 2003, 2).

The Confédération Paysanne also focused on how to preserve the world's seed and plant biological diversity. For decades large seed companies had bought out or replaced local and regional distributors across the globe. These local seeds were the result of seed-saving practices by farmers who had developed plant varieties tailored specifically for local climates, soil conditions, water availability, and local food practices for thousands of years. As these cultivars are wiped out and replaced by large seed corporations, there is a devastating reduction in seed and plant biodiversity. Corporations promoting export-oriented agriculture put their eggs in one basket, relying on a limited array of seeds to keep their monoculture plantations going. Relying on few, rather than a multitude of, seeds makes farming a risky business. With fewer seed varieties to choose from, a nation's key crop can be wiped out by unanticipated pests, drought, or other agricultural dangers. Fewer seeds in the hands of the world's farmers generates agricultural vulnerability and rigidity. If and when a corporate-owned seed fails, local farmers will have few seed options to choose from. Problems of biodiversity have dire implications for the economies, cultures, and autonomy of rural peoples around the world.

The Confédération Paysanne's delegation also planned to meet in Seattle with members of La Via Campesina, including Professor Swami, Mexican farmers, and peasant groups from other countries. A central question these groups would discuss was whether agriculture, as a mode of production, should be included or excluded from future free-trade negotiations. Should food be treated as a fungible market commodity like any other? The Karnataka State Farmers' Union and other groups from the Global South took a radical stand. Not only did they demand to get agriculture out of the WTO, but they also sought to abolish the WTO entirely. According to Professor Swami, "The World Trade Organization is inherently unethical and thus unable to be reformed" (personal communication, June 18, 1999). The Confédération Paysanne, along with other groups, proposed to reform the WTO. Such groups hoped to modify the WTO's current platform based on free trade to one based on fair trade. According to the fair-trade proposal, the WTO would promote fair prices for exported agricultural goods — prices that would eliminate the problem of dumping. In a fair-trade situation, the WTO would not be permitted to destroy the agricultural economy of nonsubsidized poor countries. Also, a fair-trade vision asks for tariffs on imported products as well as livable wages for smallholders and rural peoples everywhere. The Confédération Paysanne called for the United Nations to establish an international tribunal charged with monitoring the WTO. It would evaluate trade practices and disputes on a case-by-case basis.

U.S. PERCEPTION OF BOVÉ—AND OF FARMING ITSELF

Upon arriving in Washington, D.C., the delegation became aware for the first time of Bové's stature as an international icon. Whether he was walking down the street in D.C. or dining in an Ethiopian restaurant, passersby cheerily called out to him, smiling and waving, asking if he was indeed "the farmer who blew up a McDonald's." Throughout the trip, union members did their best to ask that journalists pair Bové with Dufour whenever possible during press conferences and photo shoots. Attempts to present Bové as but one member of the union proved unfeasible, though. The media was interested only in Bové. In the United States Bové had captured the attention of many on both sides of the political divide. Conservative and mainstream media tended to frame the McDo event as anti-American. According to this view, Bové was a French food snob shaking his finger disapprovingly at McDonald's, a symbol of American populism. Progressive Americans tended to take a different position. Most in the United States were unaware of Bové's history as a member of a French farmers' union and as a paysan. Instead audiences viewed Bové through the cultural lens of the rugged American individual. Bové was seen as a strong-minded individual taking a stand against the excesses of a neoliberal system. At the time when U.S. audiences learned of the McDo action, there was considerable anticorporate sensibility running through the United States, so Bové was regarded as a regular guy fighting the corporate system (like Ralph Nader or Michael Moore).

The content and meaning of Bové's McDo action were indeed poorly understood by U.S. audiences. Nonetheless, many Americans seemed delighted by the idea of any individual taking on a multinational corporation. In U.S. newspapers, narratives about the action had become a series of strange urban legends. While one paper described Bové as single-handedly driving his tractor into a McDonald's restaurant, another would report that he alone had blown it up. In contrast, Bové's action had an entirely different set of meanings for American small farmers. For such actors, Bové and the Confédération Paysanne were simply smallholders taking on agribusiness. Many American farmers shook their heads incredulously at all the attention Bové and the Confédération Paysanne were able to muster. They seemed to admire the French paysans a great deal, wondering why American citizens did not seem to respond to farmers in the same way.

Culture Clash: Paysans Meet American Family Farmers and the D.C. Police

MEETING THE NATIONAL FAMILY FARM COALITION IN D.C.

Before traveling to Seattle for the WTO meetings, the delegation decided to spend several days in D.C. with representatives of the National Family Farm Coalition. Meeting with the National Family Farm Coalition was part of the union's ongoing commitment to understanding and supporting the struggles of diverse rural peoples in the Global North and South. Founded in 1986, just a year before the Confédération Paysanne, the National Family Farm Coalition represents farmers and rural groups from thirty-two states in the United States struggling with conditions of postindustrial economic recession in rural communities. Like the Confédération Paysanne, this organization fights for fair farm prices and is against the corporate control of agriculture.

It is worth noting some important differences between the Confédération Paysanne and the National Family Farm Coalition. While both organizations follow a collaborative response to postindustrial agriculture, they share different historical and discursive contexts. For instance, actors from the National Family Farm Coalition do not use terms such as *peasants* or *small farmers*. Rather, they chose a term more culturally evocative in the U.S. context: *family farmers*. In the 1980s the term *family* emerged as a keyword in the U.S. vernacular. According to Raymond Williams, keywords emerge at particular historical junctures, reflecting and producing specific sets of cultural meanings (1976). During the 1980s, the keyword *family* was paired with words such as *values*, *Christian*, and *focus*. And we came to see new phrases and organizations surface such as the *Christian family*, *family values*, and Focus on the Family. The Religious Right still deploys the term *family*, contrasting it to terms it regards as negative, such as *abortion*, *homosexuality*, *premarital sex*, *teen sex*, and *divorce*.

The National Family Farm Coalition was established during the heart of the Reagan and Bush presidencies. This was a time when the term *family values* formed a potent discourse associated with white Christian morality. The National Family Farm Coalition is by no means a right-leaning or specifically Christian entity. Yet members knew implicitly that the term *family farmers* would convey a more culturally salient set of meanings than the term *small farmers*. By using the term *family farmers*, the organization hoped to garner public sympathy for small-scale farmers edged out of the U.S. agricultural economy. According to Bill Christison, family farmers, unlike large-scale industrial farmers, "might be seen as people who valued their families enough to maintain a farm that could keep farm families together" (personal communication, November 20, 1999). The term *family farm* assumes particular meaning in a society that romanticizes the heteronormative Christian family as the crucial foundation of a virtuous society. The Confédération Paysanne adopted the term *paysans* for cultural reasons as well. As we have seen, the French populace tends to romanticize and alternately patronize the idea of French peasants. In France, the term *family* holds a different set of meanings. The right wing in France tends to emphasize neoliberal economics and a xenophobic discourse on immigrants or guest workers. The French term *paysan* has cultural clout in France, invoking feelings of nostalgia. The term *family* has little resonance with the populace in general.

As the Confédération Paysanne is a trade union, it is endowed with a certain degree of status, legitimacy, and visibility with French society. In contrast, the National Family Farm Coalition is a lobbying organization that acts as a networking body, bringing together twenty-four grassroots organizations in thirty-two states. It also works with international organizations such as La Via Campesina, focusing on supporting small-scale agriculture globally. The National Family Farm Coalition's main objectives are to advocate for U.S. small farmers to receive credit from loaning agencies, to secure fair-trade prices for small farmers, and to change the U.S. Farm Bill so that it supports farmers outside the agri-business system. The National Family Farm Coalition also invokes discourses on food sovereignty in its fight against international trade policies that it sees as devastating to food producers around the world.

While the Confédération Paysanne was the product of French social movements associated with the Larzac, the union retained a mutualistic set of values and structures. In contrast, the National Family Farm Coalition came together as an advocacy-lobbying body based in D.C. Consequently, the

National Family Farm Coalition has a structure that is hierarchical and centralized. The coalition has a president who has degrees of decision-making autonomy, in contrast to the Confédération Paysanne spokesperson, who is only articulating the views of the union. The National Family Farm Coalition's past president, George Naylor, represents a single charismatic figure. He was featured often in news stories and films about farming in the United States, especially Michael Pollan's book *The Omnivore's Dilemma* (2006).

Despite the differences between the two organizations, they share a strong political affinity. Both groups, for instance, prioritize the GMO issue. That week in D.C., the National Family Farm Coalition presented its "Declaration on Genetic Engineering in Agriculture," scheduled to be released just before the meetings of the WTO. The declaration represented the first attempt by a group of U.S. farmers to publicly present a stance on agricultural biotechnology. Standing before the press, the coalition members presented a statement of principles developed by thirty-four farm groups comprising the Farmer-to-Farmer Campaign on Genetic Engineering. While we were in D.C., I had the opportunity to speak with many members of the National Family Farm Coalition. They expressed tremendous excitement over the French anti-GMO movement and about the Confédération Paysanne in general. Aware of the union's new international profile, they were thrilled to have delegates at their press conference. In particular, a leader from the National Family Farm Coalition asked Bové to stand by coalition leaders when they presented their declaration at the press conference. They hoped Bové's presence would allow them to draw more media attention to their anti-GMO campaign.

"DOES THE UNITED STATES HAVE AN ANTI-GMO MOVEMENT?"

Many people in the United States often ask whether the country has produced a strong anti-GMO movement. When responding, I generally explain that my study is not comparative in nature and I lack the authority to speak on behalf of the U.S. movement. I am aware that many groups in the United States have generated anti-GMO activity. Yet this movement is limited in time, scope, and popular support when compared to the French case. The U.S. anti-GMO movement arrived on the scene in the late 1980s, but by the early 2000s, the relatively small spate of activism and lobbying had died down. The movement was originally spurred by a small network of ecology initiatives such as Greenpeace, Friends of the Earth, and the Biotechnology Project at the Institute for Social Ecology. It was also born out of groups that rose specifically to stop GMO technologies, such as the Pure Foods Campaign. It is not within the rubric of this book to explore in full the reasons why the United States did not generate a powerful anti-GMO movement. Yet my hunch is that it has much to do with a complex set of cultural, political, and economic features associated with U.S. agriculture.

In addition to features of U.S. agricultural history, the distinctive relationship among U.S. corporations, media, science officials, and government bodies is central to the question of a U.S. anti-GMO movement. The U.S. government's support for a biotechnology industry led to a culture of deregulation and nonlabeling of foods processed with GMOs. Unlike in Europe (and most countries globally), the United States pronounced it illegal to label GMO foods. In addition, U.S. corporate and government bodies mustered the power to inform the content and direction of mainstream media, which sparsely reports on GMOs. Also, the absence of a popular Leftist culture in the United States made it difficult for American activists to garner popular sympathy and support. In the French case, the Confédération Paysanne represents the rise of a union of paysans with whom the country shared degrees of sympathy and identification. The paysan of the Confédération Paysanne attempts to become the symbol of the protection of French food and culture. Members seek to establish themselves as experts on a food culture that is very different from the food cultures that exist throughout the United States.

The tragedy of the American small farmer followed nearly the same trajectory that France experienced during the same time period. Yet the history of the American small farmer contains nothing comparable to a new paysan movement or a union with the stature of the Confédération Paysanne. The absence of such popular farmers' movements in the United States reflects a complex set of cultural and political questions. However, perhaps France's historical relationship to notions of French peasantry, the power of French trade unions, and the place and meaning of food in French society opened, at least in part, a cultural space for an anti-GMO movement to emerge in France. When hearing of the French case, many Americans have asked, "What would be the equivalent of the Confédération Paysanne in the United States?" The answer is that there is no analogue to the Confédération Paysanne in U.S. agricultural history. The United States is a product of European colonialism, the dispossession of American Indians, and a protracted and lasting cultural legacy of slavery. The history of U.S. land use is marked by colonial land grabs and speculation by a wealthy slave-owning and land-owning class.

If the United States has no figure comparable to the feudal French peasant, then what is the symbol of the primordial, original farmer in America? Surely, the symbol of the "traditional" American farmer is not the American Indian who invented agriculture in the southwest nearly ten thousand years ago. Nor is it the African American slave whose sorrowful labor allowed the country to generate considerable wealth associated with both agriculture and industrial production. Rather than the Indian or the slave, the symbol of the foundational American farmer is a white man in overalls caring for livestock and growing crops. This small-scale diversified farmer is the character children learn about in preschool when singing "Old MacDonald Had a Farm." In popular consciousness, the icon of the American farmer is a white, wholesome, humble, and rugged American individual grounded by traditional Christian values (Heller 1999, 42). Many of those who first occupied the American colonies took up an agrarian lifestyle, engaging in cattle ranching or setting up farms for food or cotton production. Many who could afford to chose to buy slaves who did much of the work on plantations, both big and small.

When they could, the founding citizens of the United States preferred enterprises such as industrial corporations and banking to agriculture. Until relatively recently (the 1970s and onward), U.S. agriculture was not a site for major capital accumulation. While many U.S. elites owned large plantations, they tended to invest their money in ventures that allowed them to develop the American ruling class. Over the next several hundred years, slavery was abolished and wealthy landowners in the agricultural sector hired tenant or migrant workers to farm their land. Many smallholders in both the U.S. north and south continued as before, cultivating their own lands, often looking to family labor to keep the farms going. Meanwhile, the U.S. productive sector became more industrial. Many U.S. immigrants coming through Ellis Island often remained in the northeast to work in mills or factories. Among the immigrants who were racialized as white, many went on to accumulate wealth by starting retail companies or forming corporations. Some in the United States can trace their lineage back to the early colonial settlers who lived agrarian lives. However, many U.S. citizens are the descendants of immigrants who began their American lives as industrial or mercantile laborers, never engaging with the agricultural sector at all. Unlike most Americans, many French citizens can trace their agrarian roots back two or three generations. In contrast, the United States is home to many who have no cultural memory of an agrarian America. For those in the United States who live outside the agricultural belt of the Midwest (or other agricultural centers), agriculture is an abstract and remote concept.

U.S. industrial agriculture gained steam in the 1970s, as it did in France. Again similarly to the French situation, the U.S. farm bill targeted large-scale industrial producers as the recipients of farm subsidies. As a result, the size of American farms grew larger, while the number of farms dropped dramatically. By the 1980s, smallholders were largely edged out of the agrarian economy. When the farm crisis peaked in the 1980s, many Americans gazed sympathetically at their TV screens depicting images of the tragedy. Certainly, they felt compassion while viewing otherwise stolid midwestern farmers covering their tear-stained faces as they sold off the last of their farm equipment. When learning of the story about the plight of the family farmer, all Americans could do was weep. Despite the authenticity of Americans' empathy for the small farmer, there was little historical or cultural continuity between those learning of the crisis and those living it.

As for the status of trade unions in the United States and France, the differences between the two countries are noteworthy. Since the agreement between labor and capital following the U.S. economic depression of the 1930s (Harvey 1991), there has been little trade unionist tradition embedded in American culture. The U.S. Left lacks the backing of a powerful union system, a Left-leaning political party, or even a set of progressive grassroots movements robust enough to inform U.S. food or farm policy. It is in this context that U.S. smallholders found themselves poorly equipped to fight agribusiness on such a grand scale. When the Confédération Paysanne delegation arrived in the United States, members were acutely aware of their American conservative critics. Yet they were also cognizant of a significant support base among American small farmers who looked to them for inspiration and support.

ROQUEFORT: LOST IN TRANSLATION

Despite the best intentions of all involved, cultural clashes abounded between the French farmers and the American farmers. One vignette illustrates the different food cultures associated with the Confédération Paysanne and the National Family Farm Coalition. This incident took place at a dinner reception hosted by the National Family Farm Coalition on behalf of the Confédération Paysanne in the basement of a small restaurant. The dinner was after a daylong press conference held with farmers from both groups. Serving as translator for the evening, I assisted the two groups in formally thanking each other for a productive day and expressing gratitude for their mutual support and shared goals. I took a seat next to a National Family Farm Coalition leader. He asked me to assist him in beginning the meal by passing around "the appetizer." It was then that I noticed that a coalition member had opened a wheel of Roquefort cheese the diameter of a pizza and nearly a foot deep. The Confédération Paysanne had bestowed this very expensive gift upon the National Family Farm Coalition as an expression of gratitude and generosity. For the coalition, serving the cheese to the paysans was an expression of gratitude and politeness. They opened the wheel of cheese the way a host might open a bottle of wine to share with dinner guests who had gifted the bottle.

Coalition farmers preceded to hand me small paper plates to pass around to each person seated at the table. Plates were loaded up with thick slices of Roquefort cheese, each the size of two hefty portions of cheesecake. My stomach clenched as I studied the plates sagging beneath the heavy cheese. I considered the painful fact that each portion cost about one hundred dollars. Alongside the weighty chunks of cheese, the servers had placed a few Ritz crackers. Coalition farmers politely received and examined the plates' contents, smearing but a sliver of the cheese onto a cracker. Lifting the cracker to their mouths, many coalition farmers wrinkled their noses, shooting quizzical gazes at other farmers around them. "Blue cheese!" exclaimed several farmers, finally identifying the strong-smelling stuff. Smiling good-naturedly, several added, "Don't care much for blue cheese." There were bewildered looks on the faces of the paysans. They looked down into what they saw as a mountain of Roquefort sitting on a paper plate. Having noted that coalition farmers had made a few remarks about the cheese, they looked to me for translation. "They think it's just any blue cheese," I said. "Some don't really like blue cheese." The paysans silently beseeched me with stunned disbelief. Then the unthinkable transpired. When coalition staff determined the appetizer portion of the meal complete, several rose to their feet, grabbing black trash bags. They politely circled the table, holding the bag out to each individual seated at the table. Farmers dumped plates full of Avéyron gold into the bag. Looks of confusion that had sprouted on the faces of the Confédération Paysanne delegation now morphed into looks of undiluted horror.

For the Confédération Paysanne delegation, there were too many things wrong with this picture. I will attempt to describe at least a few elements that the paysans found particularly disturbing. After the meal, late into the evening, acting as de facto ambassador, all I could do was try to elucidate. We were all sprawled across the snug white couches in the small lounge of our hotel. Confédération Paysanne members sat around drinking wine, trying to figure out how such an awful thing could have happened. "In the U.S., people eat cheese the way one might eat a slab of meat," I explained. They put slices of it onto sandwiches or they grate it over hot meals to add flavor. They eat it in larger portions than in France." "We do that too, with some cheeses," responded Marie-Claude, a young woman in the delegation. She continued, "But to put servings for ten or more people onto one plate! Who can eat that much cheese? Didn't they know it was Roquefort?" "In the U.S., I think only the wealthy would know the cost of Roquefort. The coalition farmers aren't wealthy," I said. "Most of them are from the Midwest. They eat a lot of cheddar, which isn't a delicacy there." "You don't have to be rich to know Roquefort," Marie-Claude added. "They might know Roquefort," I replied. "But mostly, Roquefort is known as a flavor put in salad dressing you buy in the supermarket. Some use it in dipping sauce for barbequed chicken wings." While providing these details, I knew I had lost them completely. The paysans simply ignored my statements, returning to their collective disappointment. "How could they cut an entire wheel like that?" asked Michel, a young paysan from Millau. "Each plate could have served fifteen people," he continued. "Did you see the looks on their faces when they smelled the Roquefort?" asked Pascale, a young woman who was a local journalist from Millau. "They looked like children, smelling it for the first time! How could they throw it away like garbage?" As she spoke, she swung her hand from side to side, flicking her wrist—a common French gesture that signals frustration, annoyance, or disgust. "Ridiculous," Pascale said, nodding her head in the negative. The paysans in the lounge discussed how they thought the Roquefort scenario was supposed to go. After offering the Papillon to the coalition, they assumed it would be carefully divided among coalition farmers to be taken home and shared with friends and family. "We expected they would take it home to please their families for their holiday," Michel offered.

For the paysans, there was yet another riddle to the cheese story. In France, cheese is generally eaten as a dessert, following the meal. When serving a cheese course, the delicacy is paired with artisanal bread and a glass of good wine. "Why would they serve Roquefort before the meal, with crackers?" asked Pascale. In France, crackers are a treat served only before a meal, as appetizers. They are offered to guests in small quantities with salted peanuts or other savory delicacies such as smoked salmon served on tiny, thin slices of buttered toast. Salty appetizers are generally paired with predinner liqueur such as Port or Crème de Cassis. For the paysans, the idea of placing sweet and salty Ritz crackers on the same plate as Roquefort was like eating pickles with ice cream. "Those crackers were sugary sweet," frowned Frédo, another young paysan from Millau. "If you eat Roquefort with something sugary sweet, how can you taste its flavor?" In France, mixing sweet and salty foods is considered to be an "Anglo-Saxon" food practice associated primarily with British cuisine; many find this combination unappealing.

The paysans were also affronted by the size of the cheese portions served that evening. In France, excellent cheese is generally served in small quantities the way one might present a delicate pastry or a fine chocolate truffle. A cut the size of a pie slice might be gifted to a host at a holiday party. The host would subsequently serve the cheese after the meal to many guests. Roquefort, or any good cheese, would be cut into tiny slices, perhaps a half-inch thick. If a host presented Papillon Roquefort to guests, they would be expected to consume it slowly and appreciatively. The host would anticipate guests' comments as they discussed the cheese's particular flavor and texture. In France, while delicacies such as Roquefort may not be accessible to all classes, the general public tends to recognize, desire, and consume such luxuries — at least a few times a year, on holidays or other special occasions.

Even the French government is concerned with Roquefort. State officials are highly committed to cultivating "taste" in the palates even among the youngest of citizens. In an attempt to preserve the nation's culinary heritage (*culinaire patrimoine*), the government sponsors various programs aimed at familiarizing children of all classes with high-quality French foods. In elementary schools throughout the country, children learn about the origin and history of such foodstuffs as Roquefort and pâté de foie gras. Teachers administer small servings of these foods to children as part of a French history curriculum.

The collective horror among the paysans that night was thus not an expression of classism. As members of the working class themselves, the delegation members' dismay stemmed not from a classist gaze but from a culturalist one. In their minds, everyone knows the universal meaning and symbolism of French cuisine. To fully appreciate the meaning of this cheesy affair, some backstory is required. The wheel gifted to the coalition was part of a stock of two hundred kilos painstakingly smuggled by the delegation into the United States, circumventing Clinton's extra tariff that had raised the price of Roquefort almost threefold. The Confédération Paysanne smuggled the cheese as an act of symbolic defiance, displaying the triumph of paysan wit (and their sense of good taste) over international bureaucracy. Roquefort, as a key nonhuman actor in this story, was taking its rightful place at center stage.

While about half of the cheese was illegally flown by cargo planes to D.C., the other half was divided into massive portions and carefully carried by hand in duffel bags by delegates as they climbed on and off the plane. Since their arrival, the paysans had worked hard to ensure the Roquefort would find safe harbor in the United States. They stuffed as much cheese as they could into the mini fridges in their hotel rooms and asked hotel staff to place yet more in the hotel's basement refrigerator. The rest they loaded into coolers they bought at a local Kmart and kept in their hotel rooms, each day faithfully restocking the coolers with bags of ice. While all Roquefort is a delicacy in France, this particular Roquefort was a product of Papillon, the company known in France to produce among the most expensive and highest-quality Roquefort. Papillon is wrapped in satiny black foil with its gold insignia at the center of the wheel.

The Confédération Paysanne smuggled the cheese as a symbol of the dignity and pride of French paysan sheep farmers. In so doing, they took for granted the idea that international rural and indigenous peoples they would meet in the United States would find Roquefort intelligible. When the coalition farmers were unable to culturally index the cheese, the paysans took it as a personal affront. Despite my attempts that night in the hotel to explicate the different meaning of cheese in the United States and France, the paysans seemed unable to shed their shared consternation. Throughout the rest of their stay in the United States, they continued to be mortified by Americans' inability to appreciate Roquefort.

Bové was also lost in cultural translation when it came to comprehending the illegibility of Roquefort for U.S. audiences. During nearly every U.S. press interview, Bové expressed empathy for Americans who would be unable to enjoy Roquefort during their holiday season. He began many talks at rallies and press interviews by invoking the cheese: "We have brought with us to the U.S. Roquefort cheese. It is not fair that because of Clinton, you will not be able to eat such good food during your holiday season." As I had tried to explain to Bové, slices of quality Roquefort were appreciated and affordable only to wealthy consumers. Yet Bové remained earnest in expressing empathy for all U.S. Americans who would be deprived of this special treat during their holiday season.

A few days before Thanksgiving, the group joined with the organization Friends of the Earth to execute a "GMO dump." In this small-scale direct action, paysans tossed foodstuffs processed with GMOs into a large plastic tub before a Safeway supermarket in D.C. The paysans smiled at TV cameras (and at their personal entourage of journalists), dropping boxes of breakfast cereal and bags of corn chips into a dark-green bin stamped with a hazardous waste symbol. During the action, I was readying to take leave of the group for a few days to spend Thanksgiving with my parents and other family in Connecticut. I worked my way through the small crowd of paysans, U.S. activists, and intrigued passersby. I was determined to be polite by kissing each member of the delegation. Alternating from side to side, I kissed each person's cheek four times — as is commonly done in southern France. As I was about to take my final leave, Pascale (a woman in the delegation) rushed over to me excitedly, "José [Bové] said you must absolutely take some Roquefort home to your family for your holiday. Share it with your extended family, everyone!" Out of her own duffel, Pascale lifted a hefty triangle of Roquefort (worth about two hundred dollars) dressed in its Papillon covering. With great care, Pascale had wrapped the exposed areas of the wheel in layers of tin foil. The thought of hauling this weighty cheese through D.C., and on and off a train, was daunting. I knew that no one in my family would have the slightest idea of what to make of the cheese and that much of it would be unappreciated and go bad. Even though I hated to waste Avéyron gold, I knew I had no choice. By the look on Pascale's face, I knew that this was not a gift I could refuse. After thanking Pascale and the other paysans profusely, I returned to my family in Connecticut. For the next two days, I preceded to deliver endless portions of Roquefort all over town to my parents' friends. "This is good stuff—the Champagne of French cheese," I explained, handing wrapped slices of the cheese. "Smuggled in from France, by José Bové himself," I said. With nearly each delivery, my parents' friends thanked me politely for the blue cheese. Then, nearly each one added something that went like the following: "Hey, aren't you studying that French guy who ran his tractor into a McDonald's? If he hates McDonald's so much, then why do the French have so many in their country? They can't get enough of our fast food!"

YOU CAN'T GET ARRESTED; WE'RE OFF TO SEATTLE!

Another vignette crystallizes for me the different political cultures of France and the United States. After a press conference with the National Family Farm Coalition, the delegation decided to check out a few key sites in the city. Delegation members, in addition to "our paparazzi," decided to cross the street and head toward the Capitol a few blocks away. Nearing the Capitol building, the group determined it a perfect site for a group photograph. They arranged themselves before the white domed building, cupping their hands over their mouths, remarking on what a cold day it was. Meanwhile, Dominique, an art activist from Millau, unfurled a beautiful hand-painted cloth banner (*bandrole*) that featured the union's name and logo flanked by a colorful cloudburst and rainbow. Dominique had created the banner specifically for the U.S. trip; with great care, she spread it across the group, asking those in front to gently fold the banner's top edge. Standing in formation, the group smiled widely before its own small crowd of journalists who snapped photographs and shot video of the scene. A few delegates giggled about feeling that they were children, standing for a class photograph. "Say cheese!" shouted one of the paysans in English, making everyone in the group laugh.

Suddenly, as if out of nowhere, about ten police officers arrived, a few on horseback. Striding close to the assembled group, several officers inquired into the group's intentions and informed members that they cannot take photographs of government buildings (an inconsistently applied and controversial policy). As I translated the officers' words, members of the group became outraged and agitated. Bové zoomed up to one of the officers, moving directly into his personal space. With one hand Bové held his smoking pipe. With the other he pointed his finger about an inch from the officer's nose. The delegations' journalists snapped photographs, circling the scene, making sure to capture Bové as he confronted U.S. police. In halting English, Bové said, "We are union people from France. We are able to take a photograph." This was the first time I had heard Bové speak English publicly. It was as if his anger at the situation eclipsed his discomfort with displaying his limited English. The group grew more agitated. French statements of infuriation rang out from all sides. The officer facing Bové looked into his eyes, stating angrily, "You're about to get yourself arrested, sir. If you continue to point your finger in my face, I will arrest you." Bové looked at me with confusion, unable to understand the officer's comment. I explained to Bové that in the United States, you can get arrested for even unintentionally touching a police officer.

Unfazed by the officer's warning, Bové continued his oration, shaking his finger in the officer's face. Huddled around Bové, the rest of the group grew more agitated. Within minutes, more police arrived on the scene. I explained to the police officers that these were peaceful members of a union of French farmers. "They aren't familiar with U.S. policy about pointing fingers and picture taking," I said. "Well, you tell your friend he's about to get arrested," the officer retorted in disgust. "In France, we make photo of anything," Bové said in English. "Well, you can't do it here," replied another police officer, who proceeded to confiscate the group's banner. "You can't take my banner!" cried Pascale in French. The group tightened their grip on the banner. Another officer joined the first in attempting to pry the banner from the group members' hands. Pascale began to sob, giving the officer a slight push. She single-handedly tugged the banner from both officers' hands, clutching the long draping thing against her body. An officer began to make orders for the arrest of Bové and Pascale. "This is José Bové," I said to the officers. "He's an international figure, known all over the world. If you arrest him for such a small infraction, you'll make the city police look ridiculous." "I'm not concerned what the city thinks of us, miss," the young officer said to me hotly. "Tell your friends that if they want to leave here without spending a few nights in jail, they'd better leave now." I explained to the group that we'd better take off. "Not without my banner," pleaded Pascale, who was now down on her knees, bawling, fully distraught. During the confrontation with Bové, two of the officers had forced the banner out of her hands and were holding it carelessly, bending the painted canvas against their uniforms and letting the ends of it drag on the rain-soaked ground.

Bové once again approached the police, this time reprimanding them (in French) for mistreating members of a trade union. The officers looked to me for translation. Before I could get a word out, a member of the delegation yelled, "José, we have to be in Seattle in two days. What if you get stuck in a D.C. jail?" Bové paused for a second and considered the scenario. "Maybe that's not such a bad idea. Imagine the publicity," Bové laughed, taking a drag on his pipe. Finally, Bové turned to me. "No, we need to be in Seattle. Tell the cops we'll leave if they return the banner." Miraculously the entire delegation set off together — with the banner intact. The group whooped and cheered at the shared victory of reclaiming the precious painted thing, expressing horror at the "brutality of American cops" and the police's lack of respect for union peoples. As the delegation gloated and laughed over the matter, the journalists rushed to the group's bus, tapping on laptop computers, busily sending off images of the confrontation. The images would arrive in time to be printed in the next morning's newspapers in France and internationally. The images would depict the juicy confrontation between Bové and U.S. authorities. Later, in the van, Bové and others reflected on the events that had just taken place. "It would have been imbecilic to get arrested in D.C. and never make it to Seattle," Bové admitted, shaking his head as he relit his pipe. Several members of the delegation turned to me over the course of that evening, including the journalists, asking, "Is this what U.S. police are really like? We thought that was just on TV." To each inquiry, I answered gingerly, not wanting to appear too aloof. "That was nothing," I said. "Wait till Seattle."

Conclusion

The McDo affair catalyzed a set of events that would further solidify the union's place in a national and international debate about GMOs and the effect of the WTO on global agricultural markets. The union diverted the French government's attempts to discipline Bové by comparing him to a previous passing media hero. In so doing, it successfully mustered media of its own. These efforts included a best-selling book that featured the union's objectives. When, in November 1999, the union sent a delegation of paysans to the United States, union members navigated their way through a series of internal differences with a U.S. group of smallholders. While in the United States, the union devised strategies to present Bové—whenever possible—with Dufour to promote an image of a union in action, not just an individual. On the ground in the United States, the delegation confronted a series of cultural contradictions. In addition to encountering divergent interpretations of Bové, the delegation met differing cultural understandings of agriculture. The members even confronted contrasting cultural understandings of the meaning of Roquefort cheese and police discipline.

9

Operation Roquefort, Part II

The Battle of Seattle

The Confédération Paysanne's voyage to the United States represented a major media success. Before, during, and after the delegation's trip, the French press was saturated with visual images and
printed texts. Providing a steady flood of information, journalists
portrayed the union as playing a central role in the U.S. and international alter-globalization movement. Bové continued to be followed by "our paparazzi," who, by the time we arrived in Seattle,
had incorporated themselves into the group. These journalists often
dined with the delegation, joining Confédération Paysanne farmers
in the small hotel lobby, where they tended to stay up late, rolling and
smoking cigarettes, drinking coffee or wine, and exchanging endless
humorous tales. This group of French and international journalists
had continuous and intimate access to Bové's comings and goings.
Each day during the voyage and for weeks after, they sent print and
visual media around the world, amplifying the union's presence in
the United States.

A Little Anti-McDo in Seattle?

Upon entering the streets of Seattle, one of the first things that the delegation noticed was several McDonald's restaurants boarded up as if prepared for a hurricane. The group paused before a group of workmen nailing stray slabs of particleboard across the building's windows. One member of the delegation asked if I would tell the workmen that he was arrested in Millau for "the original" anti-McDo action. "Also tell him that is the *real* Bové," the paysan added, pointing to Bové, who was smoking his pipe and squinting up at the boarded windows. After my translation, the workmen laughed and scrutinized our motley group of generally friendly-looking people. "*You're the guys who tore down the McDonald's in France?*" asked a young man with blond shaggy hair, jeans, and a tool belt. The young man informed the rest of the crew, who in turn stared at the delegation in wonder: "Wow, you guys are pretty cool. Good work!"

TO MCDO OR NOT MCDO?

The McDonald's corporation was not the only one alerted to Bové's arrival in Seattle. Several grassroots alter-globalization groups had also heard the news and expressed hope that Bové might stage another anti-McDonald's action in the city. These groups had learned of the McDonald's action over the Internet in various alter-globalization networks; Bové was already a budding celebrity in the small but active U.S. anti-GMO and alter-globalization movements. Many had seen the famous photo of Bové in shackles in Leftist magazines or on the Internet.

Through my affiliation with the Institute for Social Ecology in Vermont, I had ties to a main organizing group in Seattle that week called the Direct Action Network. Brooke Lehman, a key organizer in the Direct Action Network, was an alumna of the Institute for Social Ecology. As an antiauthoritarian organization, the Direct Action Network was planning a nonviolent civil-disobedience protest to take place the morning the WTO meetings were to begin. The Confédération Paysanne, the National Family Farm Coalition, La Via Campesina, and many other groups were traveling to Seattle with the objective of acting as witnesses to the WTO meetings. The organization Public Citizen worked with other U.S. groups to prepare legal protest activities that would include an evening rally featuring high-profile speakers such as Michael Moore, Ralph Nader, and Bové. Public Citizen, along with other groups, also planned other popular events. The morning the trade meetings were to begin, organizers coordinated a gigantic rally to take place in a sports dome that featured central representatives of the alter-globalization movement, such as Vandana Shiva and Professor Swami, members of the National Family Farm Coalition, representatives of various indigenous groups, and U.S. trade unionists. After the morning rally, a massive march took place. Groups of farmers, indigenous peoples, trade unionists, ecology organizations, and alter-globalization activists from all over the world spent at least two hours marching together.

During my week in Seattle, I carried my tape recorder everywhere, often asking activists what had brought them to Seattle and how they saw the WTO. One young woman from Iowa City encapsulated the voices of many when she said, "We're here to show that the world is watching. To show that the WTO is an unjust institution and its members can't just meet behind closed doors, making decisions that oppress people and hurt the environment." Like this woman, many expressed their wish to demonstrate global resistance to an organization they saw as corrupt, unethical, and ruinous to local economies the world over.

Many groups in Seattle had come to participate in legal forums such as city-approved rallies, marches, and press conferences set up by reform-oriented organizations. Yet according to an activist I knew from the United States, more radical groups were going to Seattle to engage in illegal protest that would assume the form of civil disobedience. Civil disobedience is a protest form that is generally, though not always, nonviolent. Some trace the idea back to Henry David Thoreau's essay "Civil Disobedience," written in 1848. Thoreau articulated the idea that citizens have a moral responsibility to demonstrate against laws, taxes, and other state practices (such as slavery or war) that they see as unjust. For Thoreau, when citizens do not take a stand against the immoral actions of their government, they fail to demonstrate civic accountability. Gandhi was not the first to deploy civil disobedience when he led thousands during the Indian struggle for independence from the British Empire. Yet for many, the Gandhian model serves as the prototype for nonviolent civil-disobedience action.

Illegally refusing to pay taxes or abide by draft laws and or participating in illegal boycotts are instances of civil disobedience. Others are designed to interrupt, sabotage, or prevent the functioning of powerful institutions, such as state offices, corporations, science bodies, or universities. By engaging in sit-ins, for instance, activists use their bodies to form human blockades. Such blockades can prevent the passing of military vehicles, police cars, state officials, or corporate agents. Often, sit-ins are conducted at crucial intersections of major cities in order to stop "business as usual" and draw media attention to an issue. In some sit-ins, activists create a circle on the ground by linking arms or using bicycle locks or chains to bind one person to another. The latter strategy is used when activists want to slow down the arrest process, because police are obliged to slowly and carefully use saws to separate activists before arresting and removing them. In the United States, activists in the civil rights movement practiced civil disobedience, and in the 1960s other associated groups took up the strategy, especially for the antiwar movement. Activists would consciously commit illegal but nonviolent crimes in order to raise awareness of social injustice. Civil disobedience is also a strategy used often by members of the Confédération Paysanne and by their predecessors in the Larzac movement. Acts of civil disobedience ranged from squatting illegally on farmland and conducting farms of the future in McDonald's restaurants to pulling up crops of genetically modified organisms and sabotaging greenhouses.

Weeks before leaving for the United States, I received a call from Brooke Lehman, a member of the Direct Action Network in New York City. Lehman had been a student of mine at the Institute for Social Ecology. Aware that I was accompanying the Confédération Paysanne to Seattle, Lehman asked if I would invite Bové to participate in a civil-disobedience action that week in Seattle. "It would be great if it could be directed at McDonald's," Lehman said. Lehman also inquired about the possibility of Bové giving a talk at the convergence center created by the Direct Action Network (a space for activists from around the world to receive a variety of services). Determined to maintain my ethnographic stance, I explained to Lehman that the purpose of my trip to Seattle was to serve as translator for the delegation. In addition, I would be there to observe and participate with the group rather than direct their activities. I could thus neither ask Bové to do an anti-McDo action nor ask him to give a speech at the convergence center.

Based in New York City, the Direct Action Network brought together antiauthoritarian groups from across the country. The Direct Action Network had rented an empty building in Seattle two months prior to the protests. Lehman and other activists had been hard at work to create the convergence center. The center would offer space for presentations by key movement figures and hold workshops to prepare for upcoming direct actions. In addition, it would offer teach-ins and civil-disobedience trainings for the out-of-town activists expected to pour in. Other services to be offered included free vegetarian meals, medical treatment (at a small but impressive impromptu infirmary), legal advice for activists before and after potential arrests, activist meeting space, and a large space where artists could construct banners, signs, and enormous puppets in the style of Bread and Puppet of Vermont.

My role in Seattle was to observe and provide translation for the delegation. Yet just hours after our arrival in Seattle, Bové inquired about a civil disobedience he heard was planned for the first morning of the trade meetings. I explained to him, as best as I could, the history and composition of the Direct Action Network, which was planning the action. I told him that it was indeed possible that civil-disobedience action might be more thoroughly covered by the media than the legal rallies and marches. Unfamiliar with the U.S. political grassroots landscape, Bové would never have chosen to join a group he knew nothing of. A careful strategist, Bové sought instead to build upon ties with a known entity, like Public Citizen. Associated with Ralph Nader, Public Citizen was founded in 1971 as a lobbying group. By addressing the executive branch of government, the Congress, and the courts, Public Citizen has contested unethical practices of the pharmaceutical, nuclear, and automobile industries, among others. Having recently focused on issues of social justice related to trade policies, Public Citizen was an appropriate U.S.-based organization for the Confédération Paysanne to affiliate with. As a broad-based advocacy group, Public Citizen tended to avoid direct connections with explicitly antiauthoritarian groups such as the Direct Action Network. When learning of the Direct Action Network, Bové said that the group was probably unknown or riotous, constituting an isolated and potentially destructive organization. Like many in Seattle that week, Bové had no idea that the Direct Action Network would prove to be a nonviolent organization capable of mobilizing considerable media and political action. It was indeed the Direct Action Network's civil-disobedience action that played a key role in making the Seattle protests a historic event. If it were not for this civil-disobedience action in Seattle, the Confédération Paysanne's anti-GMO and antineoliberal message would have been barely heard across the world.

It was not just the Direct Action Network that sought to help organize an anti-McDonald's event for Bové and Dufour in Seattle. Public Citizen organizers also recognized the potential impact of creating an event that would highlight the plight of small-scale farmers related to international trade. Yet Bové and Dufour were concerned that such an action could reinforce the anti-American image still perpetuated by the mainstream media in the United States. Such a protest, they feared, might lead to an arrest and deportation. While the idea of arrest was not disturbing per se to the two longtime activists, timing was everything. An early arrest could prevent them from participating in and observing the trade meetings or meeting with other groups, including La Via Campesina and Peoples' Global Action. The two paysans also worried that an anti-McDonald's action could send a confusing message to the international media. The McDonald's construction site in Millau had provided the union with a local strategic symbol of global capitalism and industrial agribusiness. Now in Seattle, Bové and the Confédération Paysanne had come to directly protest neoliberal free trade and its implications for small farmers across the globe, using the broadest terms possible. Bové and Dufour considered the matter thoroughly. After much deliberation, they agreed to participate in a small and nonviolent demonstration in front of a McDonald's. But they asked that the demonstration be legal, sending a clear internationalist message.

At noon on the delegation's second day in Seattle, the group sauntered over to a McDonald's designated as a good site for a small-scale demonstration. The original plan was for Bové and Dufour to deliver short speeches about GMOs and food quality to passersby. While they were speaking, the rest of us in the delegation would hand out slices of bread and Roquefort to any who might stop and listen. As the delegation approached the restaurant, they suspected that a much bigger event was about to unfold. Tacked to a telephone poll by a bus stop, Bové spotted a large poster announcing "The Demonstration":

FAMED FRENCH FARMER JOSÉ BOVÉ TO WARN
CONSUMERS OF BIOTECHNOLOGY, WTO AT SEATTLE

McDonald's. José Bové, Jailed in France for Destroying a McDonald's, to Speak at Peaceful Press Conference with Farmers from Asia, Africa, Latin America, U.S. and Europe. Speakers to Condemn McDonald's "Frankenfoods" Bio-engineered French Fries, Beef Treated with Hormones and Antibiotics. Bové to Serve His High Quality Roquefort — Cheese Was Heavily Taxed by U.S. in Retaliation For European Ban on U.S. Hormone Beef.

Looking up at the sign, members of the delegation frowned. "Public Citizen said the action would be a small thing," Bové said curtly. "But look at this, a poster making it sound like a major event." As he spoke, a bit of irritation curled from his lips as he clenched his pipe with his mouth. When the delegation arrived at the McDonald's, Bové and Dufour stood before the doors of the restaurant, each one taking a microphone handed to them by a Public Citizen organizer. Within minutes, a crowd of about one hundred activists appeared. Upon seeing the group of activists, a paysan from the delegation said, "We definitely won't have enough Roquefort for everyone." About ten minutes later, the crowd had grown sizably. Activists were circling around Bové and Dufour so tightly that the delegation's journalists could barely reach a vantage point from which to snap pictures or shoot video. Five minutes after that, the crowd swelled to about four hundred. Within the din of the expanding crowd, no one could hear Bové's and Dufour's respective speeches about neoliberalism, unfair trade, GMOs, and the fight against junk food. Public Citizen organizers recognized the need for a more substantial stage for Bové and Dufour. They also realized that Bové and Dufour were in danger of being accidentally squashed by the adoring mob quickly moving in. "Get them out of there!" a Public Citizen organizer cried. Grabbing his cell phone, the organizer called for a van.

MCDO INTERNATIONALE

I was standing in the crowd, pushed against the boarded-up McDonald's, leaning into Bové and Dufour, feeling claustrophobic. Suddenly, I noticed Public Citizen organizers grab Bové and Dufour. The organizers protectively muscled them away from the McDonald's, through the crowd, and finally to an adjacent street corner where a light-blue van stood waiting. Inside the vehicle were Swami from the Karnataka State Farmers' Union and John Kinsmen and Bill Christison of the National Family Farm Coalition. Public Citizen organizers had summoned these leaders hoping that they too could be incorporated into what was steadily becoming a major demonstration and media event.

Public Citizen organizers, as well as other members of the delegation, became a ragtag security force, maintaining a ring around the van, providing journalists and organizers room to move. Suddenly, someone inside the van had a great idea. A Public Citizen organizer opened the skylight on the van's roof, assisting each farmer to climb up and through, transforming the van's roof into a stage. It was quickly determined that the van's roof could hold only four bodies, which meant that there would be no room for me to join the paysans to translate. Since Dufour spoke no English at all, he opted out. "You go," he said to his friend. This meant that Bové would be speaking publicly for the first time without a translator. Bové was the last farmer to climb out of the skylight. When the crowd of more than a thousand demonstrators recognized Bové, they applauded and cheered wildly. They clearly recognized him by his handlebar moustache and pipe, having seen images of him in stories about Millau. Although unfamiliar with the faces of Swami and farmers from the National Family Farm Coalition, the crowd celebrated the four men. In unison, people began a little cheer, shouting over and over, "Hey, hey, ho ho, farmers rule, not the wto!" The farmers on the van's roof that day made history. Small-scale farmers were actually capturing the attention of alter-globalization activists gathered from across the United States — and from across the world. The farmers were now key symbols of the many who are oppressed by neoliberal trade policy. Perhaps for the first time in U.S. history, small-scale farmers were being regarded as national and international heroes.

This was certainly not the first time a farmer had attracted national attention in the United States. In the 1970s, César Chávez impressed the American public when he organized a workers' strike and grape boycott in California that lasted five years. But the heroes in the Chávez story were exploited farmworkers whose invisible labors were the very engine that drove industrial agriculture. Like Chávez, Bové framed his struggle in terms of labor. He too brought the plight of oppressed farmers into the public arena. Yet while Bové was a small-scale farmer fighting agribusiness, Chávez was a farmworker who owned no land. Chávez was a labor leader, speaking out for farmworkers' rights, especially fair wages and decent living and working conditions. Framing his struggle in a civil rights rubric, Chávez won popular support in the United States at a time when the public was receptive to discourses on civil rights deployed by Martin Luther King Jr. In 1962, along with the activist Dolores Huerta, Chávez cofounded the National Farm Workers Association, which later became the United Farm Workers. This union is the first and largest agricultural organization, active in ten states throughout the country.

While Chávez became a symbol of the exploitation of farmworkers by industrial agriculture, Bové stood for small-scale farmers fighting to end the industrial model entirely. There is an interesting racializing discourse at play here. Chávez and many leaders in the union he cofounded are Mexican Americans and other exploited ethnic minorities. Since that brief period in the 1970s, the U.S. public has not generally imagined the "American farmer" as a person of color. Members of the National Family Farm Coalition are nearly all white. Yet they are certainly not wealthy. White small-scale farmers are generally not as exploited as migrant and other farm laborers in agribusiness. Yet they too are marginalized by the system that promotes industrial agriculture. Seeing the coalition farmers John Kinsmen and Bill Christison standing side by side with members of farm unions in France and India sent a clear message. In Seattle that day, the farmers spoke out for the rights of small-scale farmers struggling to survive in a postindustrial agricultural landscape.

While Chávez successfully captured public attention for his cause, he was a man whose ideas were ahead of his time. In the 1960s and 1970s, when industrial agriculture was ascending as a powerful institution, the U.S. public was not yet sensitized to questions of food quality or production scale associated with agriculture. Americans did not yet understand agriculture as a global system that presents a range of problems that extend well beyond questions of workers' rights. Chávez did shed light on the plight of farmworkers, but the public could not frame agriculture in broader terms as it has in recent years. Even today, the agricultural issue is still generally consumer based, focusing on alternative food discourses such as organic, vegetarian, or vegan foodstuffs (Heller 1999).

Yet the farmers standing on the van's roof that day were helping the public link consumer issues related to food to humanistic and cultural issues associated with small-scale agriculture. As Bové said to me after that day, "People need to see that paysans are real people. If they want good food, quality food, they must support our cause." The crowd assembled in Seattle included an eclectic mix of activists and ordinary citizens who had come to have their say about the state of democracy in corporate America, and the state of global finance generally (see Graeber 2002, 2009). Dotted throughout the crowd was also a smattering of black-clad anarchists, including a small group from Portland, Oregon, dressed in anarchist regalia and identifying with members of the German Autonomen movement of the 1980s. In Europe, when many organizations come together to participate in a political march, they form blocs, or groups, with each group wearing a T-shirt of a particular color. Members of the Autonomen wore black clothes, invoking the black flag associated with anarchism. This is the source of the term *black block* used by anarchists in the United States, who often wear black hats, face coverings, clothes, and shoes when they march (Steinmetz 1994, 61).

Anti-GMO activists were there that day as well. Many were festooned in what had become the iconic anti-GMO outfits. Many wore creative costumes, with some dressed as monarch butterflies, invoking a study by U.S. scientists that showed that monarch butterflies suffered a range of physical problems after ingesting pollen from GM crops. In addition, there was the iconic symbol of the GMO: half fish, half strawberry—a reference to one of the first experimental field trials from years before in California. There were also members of the United Steelworkers of America union, members of indigenous groups, and ordinary U.S. citizens, young and old, concerned about the status of the world's food supply.

Seizing the moment, Bové took the microphone and gazed deep into the crowd, flashing his humble yet mischievous smile. In one hand, Bové held up a large slice of Roquefort cheese; in the other hand, a chunk of bread. Holding the bread and cheese over his head, he boomed into the microphone using his increasingly confident English: "I am a sheep farmer from France and we bring you good Roquefort cheese. . . . We don't want to eat hormone beef and GMO. Americans must not be punished because of Clinton and the WTO. Americans, too, have a right to good food. They should not be forced to only eat GMO, McDonald's, and hormone-treated beef. Together we must fight for no more GMO! And tomorrow, at the rally and march, we will do this nonviolently." Delirious with delight, the crowd chanted, "Hey hey, ho ho, GMOs have got to go!" Such "ho ho, got to go" chants, I have noted, were first heard at U.S. gay and lesbian pride marches during the early 1980s. The repeating 'ho' sound in 'ho ho, homophobia has got to go' proved catchy indeed. Hey-Hey, Ho-Ho chants became popularized during a period when activists were fighting for research on HIV/AIDS. Out of curiosity, I asked about thirty crowd members whether they knew the origin of this chant form. Not one person had any idea. The chant had been reformulated to speak to the issues in Seattle that day.

On top of the van, pipe in hand, Bové broke bread with the other farmers, holding wedges of Roquefort toward the sky as the crowd roared below, spreading out for blocks. As Bové spoke, the delegation fanned out into the crowd, each of us passing out hundreds of slices of bread smeared with

Roquefort. Once again, Roquefort continued its work as a key nonhuman actor, this time creating connections between French activists and U.S. demonstrators intent on learning more about the future of food. The Roquefort acted wildly, shooting invisible arrows of bacterial culture into the olfactory systems of surrounding activists. As we offered Roquefort and bread to smiling demonstrators, they tended to laugh and take the bread, looking slightly confused. "What is this?" demonstrators would ask, smelling the bread with a bit of trepidation. "Why blue cheese?" Aware that most people are unaccustomed to eating food provided by complete strangers, I did my best to explain, at the prodding of delegation members. "It's Roquefort," I explained. "It's a special kind of cheese produced by Bové and other French sheep farmers. The U.S. made the WTO put a huge tax on it so Americans wouldn't buy it. They're punishing France for banning U.S. hormone-treated meat." "Oh," the demonstrators would generally say. "Wow. Thanks. I'll give it a try." Roquefort delighted and stunned some that day. But every tongue or nose that it touched was forever changed. It turned an ambiguous global food fight into something curious and concrete. Most who came into contact with Roquefort in Seattle were "cultured" by the cheese's bacterial culture: they understood that the French farmers were fighting for something — for a food and a quality of life — they cared for deeply.

As we ran about offering bread and cheese to activists, Bové delivered another short speech, this time comparing his sabotage of McDonald's and GMOs to the Boston Tea Party. He referred to the nonviolent direct action Americans took to free themselves from British imperialism centuries ago. Bové invoked the Boston Tea Party during the rest of that week. The reference served multiple functions. By referencing U.S. revolutionary history, Bové expressed solidarity with U.S. activists demonstrating against trade-related imperialism today. In addition, the Boston Tea Party served as a symbol of U.S. hypocrisy, casting Clinton into the ironic role of imperial power, this time punishing a Europe struggling to rid itself of U.S. tyranny.

Here we see the image of GMOs change dramatically. In the first phase of the GMO debate in France and elsewhere, the idea of GMOs was paired with figures of lab scientists manipulating pipettes. But GMOs were steadily undergoing a makeover and were now paired with notions of revolutionaries tossing boxes of tea and peasants sabotaging GMO greenhouses and McDonald's construction sites. Photos and footage of the GMO debate displayed that day in Seattle traveled by satellite back to France and across the world, further destabilizing the science frame that held primacy in the GMOS controversy. Without a scientist in sight to be consulted about risk, Bové stood on the van's rooftop holding up Roquefort for the world to see. He stood between U.S. and Indian farmers, symbolizing a new hybrid identity of cultural expert, family farmer, and international worker, speaking against neoliberalism and for the flourishing of local cultures and international solidarity. I remember standing on the ground, by the van, looking upward. When I traveled to France to conduct my research on the Confédération Paysanne, it never occurred to me that my research site would wind its way back to the United States. I never dreamed that a sheep's milk producer such as Bové could become an international symbol of cultural expertise, identity, and resistance to global capital. I was astounded as I watched chunks of Roquefort cheese make their way into such a forum, meaning so much to so many.

In Seattle, Roquefort continued to serve as an ongoing symbol of French culture and resistance to U.S. imperialism. Papillon circulated through the streets and press conferences, toted around in duffel bags by Bové and the other farmers in its sparkling black and gold foil. Roquefort's charisma moved activists to assist farmers in setting up tables and platters full of oven-baked bread and cheese. The ambiance of sharing inspired reporters to run out to local markets to buy wine as accompaniment. Riddled with blue pockets of bacterial culture, Roquefort was a visual and olfactory reminder of the stakes that had brought activists to confront globalization in both Millau and Seattle. Roquefort stood for culture against transnational capital.

Despite efforts of some U.S. media to portray Bové as an anti-American French nationalist, Bové consistently delivered a clear internationalist message. During his five-day stay in Seattle, Bové strategically appeared in press conferences with coalition family farmers. Cameras flashed as Bové and Christison stood side by side before a table of Christison's Wisconsin cheddar and Bové's Roquefort. Bové was also repeatedly photographed arm in arm with Indian and Mexican farmers from La Via Campesina at the main labor march. In media interviews, Bové stated repeatedly, "McDonald's and GMO are not just American. They are bad food the WTO obliges people everywhere to eat. Paysans, small farmers, can give you good food" (Bové, personal communication, November 19, 1999).

The Battle of Seattle

The evening after the McDo demonstration, we attended a large rally at a major Seattle stadium. After Michael Moore delivered a long and impassioned speech about corporate power, Bové strode onto the stage. Wearing jeans and a worn leather jacket, Bové walked slowly to the microphone and began speaking in a halting, careful voice as the audience struggled to both identify and understand him. Finally recognizing him from that day's action, the crowd of nearly five thousand began to wail with excitement.

In the days following his arrival to the United States, Bové's confidence in his English had grown considerably. In D.C. I served as translator for Bové and Dufour in nearly every interaction with press or members of other farmers' organizations. Once in Seattle, however, Bové took the English gleaned during his childhood stint in California and transformed it into fodder for passionate oratory. While his beginners' English infantilized him slightly, Bové competently conveyed a complex message through a limited vocabulary. Personally, I was accustomed to Bové's rough brazen speech style and southern French accent. His powerful and articulate oratory style in French helped transform him into a hero in France. However, Bové's newly refound ability to express himself in broken English allowed him to speak awkwardly — yet directly — to U.S. audiences. To his surprise, the Americans in the audience found his hesitant English endearing. Bové's increasing ability to speak English stunned all in the delegation. At the Confédération Paysanne headquarters in Bagnolet I encountered only two actors who claimed to speak English "just a little." Among the Confédération Paysanne delegation in Seattle, Bové was the only individual able to speak English with any degree of proficiency. The rest of the delegation admired him greatly for this, as they could utter only a few phrases, generally reserving these utterances for humorous imitations of American passersby.

Bové's willingness to speak English publicly made him available to U.S. audiences in a way that few French activists had ever been. As Bové stood on the stage, calling for fair, rather than free, trade, he garnered tremendous respect. For many gathered there, it was the first time they had seen a French activist, a farmer at that, take center stage at an international protest forum. As Bové closed his speech, he asked all in the stadium to join the peaceful and nonviolent rally and march planned for the next day. These events were to feature Bové and a dynamic lineup of international activists speaking out about the WTO.

Since arriving in Seattle, members of the delegation had questioned me about events planned by the Direct Action Network. I explained that organizers were indeed planning a sit-in. According to Lehman, activists were to gather at four in the morning in front of, or near, the hotel where the trade meetings were to be held. Activists planned to form a great mass of people, assuming the form of a series of tight concentric circles. Fusing themselves together using chain or Kryptonite bicycle locks, they were to form a human blockade. This human obstruction was intended to prevent delegates from entering the building. "We can get up early and go to the lockdown. Afterward, we can attend the rally and march," said one of the delegates. "We don't have to get arrested," she added. "It's going to be the main event this week and José [Bové] should be there to at least witness it."

With Bové moving about the city on his own, the rest of the delegation was unable to discuss the sit-in with him. No longer in need of a translator, Bové was busy attending numerous press conferences and meetings. My primary charge now was to assist the rest of the delegation from Millau that spoke no English. As translator and ethnographer, I was to attend the rally and march rather than participate in the civil disobedience taking place at the center of town. The next morning, the entire delegation wore "No to the WTO" yellow rain ponchos that were being inexpensively sold around town. That week in Seattle was cold and rainy, not uncommon for the last week of November. The group packed layers of sweaters under their ponchos and gathered proudly around the beautiful banner that had nearly been confiscated by the D.C. police. Surrounding the large logo at the banner's center stood a mountain range and a large sun looming over the horizon. The delegates snapped pictures of each other in their ponchos, taking turns holding the banner before heading off to the stadium.

Minutes into the rally, we began hearing rumors that the civil disobedience had taken place as planned in the center of Seattle. We also heard that the police had responded with unexpected brutal force. Ignoring the rally (which took place in English), members of the Millau group posed questions about the sit-in: Were my friends okay? Had they been beaten and arrested? When the rally was over, we set off for the march. Each group preparing to march waited in line, wearing matching T-shirts and carrying a banner. As I stood waiting with the delegation, I worried about the many activists I knew who had participated in the sit-in. At some point, Bové sauntered over to me. "Seems your friends have made quite a mess [*bordel*]," he smiled, conveying that he was indeed impressed. "Your police sound like monsters," he added, walking back to his place next to Dufour.

For nearly two hours, I marched along with the delegation, which marched alongside the Karnataka farmers and a contingency of Mexican farmers from La Via Campesina who each carried bright banners. The march was lively and inspiring. Members of the United Steelworkers of America, anti-GMO activists, and indigenous groups from around the world strode in unison. I was surprised to see so many signs and banners that had explicitly anticapitalist, anti-free-trade messages, such as "Ban capitalism," "Life isn't a commodity," and "Just say no to the WTO." These slogans signaled a new analysis of global economic power that had not been seen in the United States for decades.

When the march finally tapered off, the Confédération Paysanne delegates decided to wander out into town on their own. Bové and Dufour quickly left to attend a meeting with representatives of international peasant and indigenous organizations. It became increasingly clear to the rest of the Millau group that Bové and Dufour were obliged to attend to an agenda largely designed by Public Citizen. With the march over, the Millau contingency would now create its own itinerary. The Millau group decided to venture into the center of Seattle to see what remained of the sit-in. We were stunned to face something reminiscent of a war scene we had only seen on film.

All stores were closed and almost all were boarded up. Streets were emptied of cars or casual pedestrians. Activists ran furtively from one crisis scene to another, usually clutching a T-shirt or another piece of fabric to their noses and mouths. It was clear that they were trying to mitigate the effects of chemical agents flung by police through the city air. On several street corners stood a few lay medics from the Direct Action Network. They were doing their best to assist people who had been doused with pepper spray, tear gas, or nerve gas. These individuals were usually down on the ground, grabbing at their eyes and coughing. The medics did their best to flush their eyes with a preparation of liquid antacid and water. While we had heard rumors of vast property damage done by activists, we saw very little evidence that much had been destroyed or broken. Only one storefront showed signs of sabotage: a Starbucks window looked as if someone had hurled a brick through its center. Otherwise, the city's infrastructure appeared protected and intact. What struck us instead were the contorted bodies walking around in a state of confusion. We saw people wrapping ripped T-shirts or bandanas around arms or wrists to stop bleeding. Several individuals were walking around, head in hands, eyes pressed shut from obvious pain.

We walked through the strangely vacant streets unable to make sense of what had happened, or what had gone wrong. At nearly every corner, police officers positioned themselves in rows of nearly twenty. They wore full riot gear and stood with arms folded and pressed against their chest. In the distance, we could see the remains of the sit-in that had taken place in the early morning. Large cardboard signs lay face down, sagging with moisture in the middle of the street. Strips of banners were strewn across sidewalks. Parts of large street-theater puppets lay eerily on the street, like dismembered bodies. A few gas masks were scattered along the ground, artifacts left behind by young activists who erroneously chose to wear them that day. As many reported later, police officers often ordered activists with gas masks to lift the apparatus, only to spray them straight in the face with tear gas — before replacing the mask. Hundreds of activists and ordinary pedestrians had been arrested and driven out of the city in school buses early that morning. Having been released due to obviously false charges, many had made their way back and were rambling through the streets, looking for friends who might have disappeared or been injured.

An old woman wearing long silver braids pinned to the top of her head wandered around holding the hand of her six-year-old granddaughter. She was looking for the rest of a group with whom she'd traveled from New Hampshire to Seattle. "We were sitting, linked arm in arm with our friends, singing peace songs, and they sprayed [tear gas] right into our faces," she told us. "They could have blinded her," the woman said, pointing to her granddaughter. Their eyes and faces were puffy and red. After each translation to members of the Millau group, they would respond by shaking their heads, muttering, "Pas possible [Impossible]" or "C'est grave, ça [That's serious stuff]."

Other activists were wandering aimlessly, trying to find their way to the convergence center for medical care. From a few blocks away we could hear the sounds of other activists attempting to continue the fight, determined to maintain what they regarded as their right to remain in the streets. Some could be seen speeding away from police squads, hiding around corners or abandoned vehicles. Others were down on their knees as officers beat them repeatedly with billy clubs before dragging them away. For hours, activists sat in school buses rented by the city police, waiting to be brought to jail. One young woman wandered over to us, crying hysterically, looking for her boyfriend. She seemed desperate to tell anyone her story: "They locked us in a bus for three hours. No water or bathroom. Then they drove us to the jail, where we sat for hours in a room where they turned the heat up so high we all felt sick. Then, they'd blast the air conditioning so we'd freeze. Hot then cold, hot then cold, like they wanted to torture us." From time to time, a bold individual would pick off the ground a small canister containing chemical agents that had failed to detonate. Tossing the tiny canister back toward the police, the activist would cover his or her face and run the other way.

RECAP: SEARCHING FOR AIR, AND A TRIP
TO THE CONVERGENCE CENTER

At some point the Millau group members determined they were exhausted and famished. We strode further downtown, where life was slightly less surreal. There were more people on the streets, although they too walked around appearing stupefied. We ducked into a pizza place, the only open restaurant on the block. Over a late lunch, we discussed fragments I had heard from passing activists or from old friends I had seen along the way in the city's center. For almost an hour, I did my best to provide a recap of that morning's events.

It seemed that at first the sit-in had gone well. Activists arrived at the scene at four in the morning, as planned. They sat in their prearranged places, forming concentric circles in front of the entrance to the hotel where the trade meetings were to take place. Others created the same formation at other street junctures, making it impossible for those attending the meeting that day to enter the area. Arms linked, protestors sang peace songs from the civil rights movement and played small hand drums or tiny wooden whistles. At first, the Seattle police force remained calm, standing by. For weeks they had been meeting with organizers from the Direct Action Network. The organizers had briefed the police on the practice of civil disobedience and explained that activists would be conducting a nonviolent sit-in. The officers had been amicable and assured organizers that they would maintain a clear line of communication before and during the protest.

At U.S. civil-disobedience actions such as sit-ins, there is generally a predictable police protocol. First, officers announce to protestors that by remaining in place (blocking an entryway or a passage), they are breaking the law. Protestors are instructed that they may avoid arrest by leaving the area calmly and immediately. This moment of prewarning in a sit-in is pivotal. Many activists plan to participate only in the initial stage of a sit-in in order to demonstrate their moral position related to a specific political issue. Doing so allows for a great number of people to symbolically have their say before the public, press, and political authorities. But not all activists are financially, physically, or psychologically able to subject themselves to the arrest process. Sometimes only a relatively small percentage of those participating in a sit-in have planned to go through the arrest process. Being arrested for engaging in an act of civil disobedience can require considerable time and money. First, activists must go through an arrest process that can last for an entire day. They can then be imprisoned for sentencing for hours or days. If the arrest and charges lead to a trial, this process can be lengthy, requiring frequent costly meetings with lawyers and time in a courtroom. While many poor activists in the United States choose to engage in this process for moral reasons, the consequences can prove onerous. They may lose their job, finances, and so on. And arrests can be physically harmful, depending on the arresting officer. An officer can tug at activists' arms and shoulders, wrenching them behind their bodies. They can roughly drag activists into police cars or buses, jabbing them with billy clubs along the way. Many activists are injured during the arrest process, so older activists and those in ill health may choose not to go through it. Activists who depend on daily medication for mental or physical ailments may find themselves unable to access their prescriptions for days, putting themselves in a dangerous situation. In addition, depending on the state, city, and police force at hand, arrests can be dangerous for women and people of color, who are often more likely to be sexually or violently harassed by officers and prison guards. Queer people are often at tremendous risk of being abused when going through the arrest and prison process. Officers and prison guards are frequently physically rougher with visibly queer activists, and sometimes judges give them harsher sentences. These are just some of the many reasons that activists may choose to support civil disobedience by participating only in the initial stage.

Once those who have chosen to forgo arrest rise to their feet, police generally permit them to leave the scene unharmed. Officers then begin the process of slowly arresting and removing demonstrators who chose to engage in civil disobedience. Brooke Lehman was a key organizer of the direct action that took place that week in Seattle. According to Lehman, on this day in Seattle, an unexpected sequence of events unfolded. The chief of police changed protocol by skipping the first step of officer engagement with the protestors: activists were never given warning to leave in order to avoid arrest (Brooke Lehman, personal communication, November 19, 1999). In the core of the sit-in were activists who planned to face arrest. They had created special equipment for committing a lockdown, a form of direct action where activists either lock their own bodies together in some way or lock themselves to a particular object such as a door handle, fence, tree (in the case of forest-protection activists), or even a motor vehicle. In this case, activists had created thick plastic tubes through which they placed their arms. Also strung through the tubing was a long steel chain that went from the cuff of one activist's tube to the other. The activists were bound together. A lockdown is often a preferred strategy for activists wanting to slow down the arrest and removal process. It can take sometimes over an hour for officers to safely use saws to detach each activist from the other without cutting anyone. At the sit-in in Seattle, only about thirty activists had chosen to engage in the lockdown. They formed a circle in the middle of the other circles formed by hundreds of other activists not planning to be arrested.

According to Lehman and others on the street that day, the police failed to provide activists with the official arrest warning. Police moved straight into the tightly seated crowd in absolute silence. They beat activists of all ages with billy clubs. They also deployed chemical agents. In some cases, they sprayed nerve or tear gas over the crowd's heads, to shower a good number of people. In other cases, police sprayed chemicals directly into the faces of those seated. For the seated activists, this meant being temporarily blinded and enduring great pain and confusion (Lehman, November 19, 1999). They found themselves trapped in a dangerous situation. Many tried in vain to rise to their feet and run. But officers grabbed activists who were rising to leave or standing by as witnesses. Officers beat and sprayed them with chemical agents before hauling them away. Many people that day who never intended to commit civil disobedience found their hands bound behind their backs. At demonstrations, instead of using pricey and heavy metal handcuffs, police often use strong plastic strips not unlike those used to bind trash bags. While such devices are cheap, light, and disposable, they also often prove injurious. Acting in a hurry, officers often bound activists' hands too tightly behind their backs. The plastic strips can impair blood circulation in addition to cutting into wrists, bloodying people and causing great pain. As the young woman had reported to us that day, those who were arrested were then pushed into school buses and driven to jail. Arriving at the local prison, activists were reportedly abused, deprived of bathrooms and medical or legal services. For long hours they were also exposed alternately to extremely hot and cold temperatures.

As the crowd was in the thousands, the police officers were unable to arrest each and every person in the area. Many activists and Seattle residents who had been beaten or sprayed had decided to remain in front of the hotel. They wanted to talk to the press. They sought to protest the police brutality that they had either just experienced or witnessed. Hundreds fled, but hundreds remained in the area near the hotel for hours. All around the streets, we could hear people shouting, "The world is watching; the world is watching!" praying that the media present would capture the scene in its entirety.

I sat with the Millau group in the pizza restaurant, and we discussed our shared terror about the sit-in gone wrong. However, our momentary reprieve was interrupted by screams from a few individuals who were tearing fearfully down the street before the restaurant: "Run!" was all they shouted as they ran, covering their faces with any piece of cloth they could find. Within seconds, everyone seated in the restaurant was assaulted by what could only be described as a wall of sensory pain. Eyes streaming with tears, our throats roared with fire as our muscles twitched and ached. Most of us were instantly overtaken by waves of confusion, ache, and nausea. The restaurant owner snapped into action, ordering each customer onto the street. "We'll be asphyxiated in here!" one member of the Millau group exclaimed as we stood wondering if we should listen to the restaurant owner or head for the street. And so we took to the small avenue before us, running blindly in no particular direction. Unfamiliar with the city, we looked at each other in panic. The Millau group looked at me, pleading, "What should we do?" Out of nowhere a cluster of frantic people ran by yelling, "Run to the water! There's wind!" We indeed followed those running toward the water—having no idea how far away "the water" in Seattle might be. Finally, we reached a kind of boardwalk where a slight breeze wafted off the water. Fresh air poured over us as we began to calm. All around were the sights and sounds of people vomiting, coughing, and crying. Some of us began retching into the dirt. My eyes and throat burned as if I'd inhaled fire. "What *was* that?" asked Fabien, a Millau farmer. "Tear gas, pepper spray, and nerve gas, I suppose," I replied. Slowly we all stood, stunned. "The cops must have tossed canisters just up the street from the restaurant," I mumbled, my throat and eyes raw. We decided to make our way down to the convergence center. Horrified by the situation, the Millau group wanted to learn more about the events of the day and why it had all gone so wrong. The convergence center occupied only a few floors of an abandoned warehouse. Looking around the raggedy and humble center, the Millau group expressed their immediate appreciation for the level of organization. "It's really well orchestrated in here," noted several in the group. "Can you imagine anyone in France being this organized?" several laughed. Along one main wall hung an enormous map of Seattle's center. Organizers divided the map into various pie-shaped sections. Particular activist groups had been assigned to perform lockdowns or sit-ins in various parts of the city center that morning.

We made our way toward the center's infirmary, as several of us needed painkillers for acute headaches and stomachaches that followed our exposure to chemical agents. Several people were lying on cots, moaning and vomiting intermittently. Volunteer medics attended to others, pouring solutions into activists' burning eyes, dressing wounds, and swathing activists' bodies or faces with sterile cloths. One young woman stood in the center of the infirmary, her face bathed in blood, her hair matted. "She needs a hospital," a medic called as the young woman was given a compress and assisted down the stairs to await the car that was to take her to the hospital. "She'll be lucky if she's seen at all tonight," another medic called back, indicating that the overpacked local ERs were unable to accommodate the number of injured individuals making their way to the hospitals. "Ambulances are hard to come by today," shouted someone assisting another medic. As the young woman walked away, she kept repeating confusedly, "I swear, I was just sitting there, we were just sitting on the street, I swear, it was all nonviolent, I swear . . ."

In another wing of the convergence center, organizers were conducting an emergency meeting. They were using a meeting technique referred to as spokesmeeting, in which small groups of activists each select a spokesperson to sit in front of their group. Each spokesperson then constitutes one spoke in a wheel composed of other spokespersons. Many of the participants in the spokesmeeting were part of affinity groups. An affinity group is generally a cluster of six to twelve activists who choose to enter a civil-disobedience event together. While some members may choose to be arrested, others volunteer to act as support on the ground, tracking their friends as they move through the legal system, doing all that they can to assist them in receiving legal and medical services. While some affinity groups are formed on the spot before a mass action, others are groups of people who came together to the action. These long-term affinity groups have been working together for between six months and twenty years.

During the spokesmeeting, decisions were made in a precise manner. When it came time to come to some kind of agreement, spokespersons turned back to their groups for consultation. After the group had come to a conclusion on a particular matter, the spokesperson would turn back again to the larger spokesgroup for further consultation, moving the process along. The spokesmeeting model is central to a commitment to democratic and decentralized organizing associated with many in the alter-globalization movement. Particularly in the United States, this model has become a popular and effective way to combine values of direct democracy with practical methods for decision making among relatively large groups of people. Most recently, the spokesmeeting model was a central form of group organization in the Occupy Wall Street movements that began in September 2011. "Amazing that so many people can work this efficiently together," one member of the Millau group commented. The delegation watched people of all ages move through the convergence center. Some appeared mainstream; others were dressed in an antiauthoritarian style with black ragged clothing, body piercings, and dreaded or messy hair. Older activists, people from forty to seventy, helped lead groups and offer support in a variety of ways.

In another area of the convergence center stood a cluster of six or seven television sets, all tuned to different channels. While watching the sets, organizers communicated by cell phone to other organizers at the Independent Media Center located in another part of the city. Alter-globalization activists created the Independent Media Center as a way to produce their own media coverage of protests as they unfolded on the ground. U.S. activists had been long aware of the mass media's tendency to minimize the size of protest groups while misrepresenting generally peaceful protestors as riotous and violent. To counter this trend, the Independent Media Center (now called Indymedia) invited technically inclined activists to take video and still prints of events taking place on the streets, in addition to interviewing activists on the ground as protests developed. The Indymedia Center made its debut in Seattle. Since that time, activists have created centers all over the world. Indymedia centers constantly livestream video of alter-globalization events and provide edited print, audio, and video coverage. Media produced from such centers is relayed over the Internet to alternative and mainstream news outlets internationally.

Having observed the small media center at the convergence center, the Millau group asked to visit the Indymedia headquarters on the other side of town. As we entered the space, the Millau group was astonished to see how a group of young men and women had set up editing suites where they were hard at work to prepare short news stories to be sent out to the world. Translating for the Millau group, I communicated as best as I could information related to Indymedia staff by Indy reporters. As I translated reports on the activists' stories that were coming into the center, the group stared at me, incredulous to hear about such degrees of police brutality. At the Indymedia center, as at the convergence center, multiple televisions were set up, all tuned to various U.S. news stations. By intermittently translating reports provided by mainstream media and Indymedia, the Millau group was able to note the dramatic disparity between information being sent out to the world. "C'est n'importe quoi, ici [What nonsense here]," said Francoise. "C'est pire qu'en Frence, meme! [It's worse than in France even!]"

BOVÉ AND THE MORNING AFTER

The next morning the delegation all met together for coffee in the hotel. Like everyone in the city (and the world), Bové had learned of the disaster that had taken place the morning before. He was impressed to learn that the Direct Action Network's demonstration was well designed and nonviolent. While enraged by the viciousness of the police, he was impressed with the activists' work. Bové said to me in his sly, subtle way the next morning: "You were right, they did good work. Your police are nasty, though." That morning the Millau group attended a press conference organized by Public Citizen during which Bové would be interviewed. Into a series of microphones Bové declared with disgust, "This is no democracy, where peaceful protestors are beaten. It is shameful to see in the U.S." At that press conference and at many afterward, Bové expressed solidarity with international activists taking a bold stance against U.S. authorities. He denounced the U.S. government for allowing the suppression to continue. His words traveled to France and around the world, bringing global attention to a horrible affair.

During the days after the lockdown, people took to the streets. Many were out-of-town activists who had been brutalized, terrified, jailed, and released. A good many others were ordinary Seattle citizens who had had little previous knowledge of the WTO protest. They had decided to take time off from work to join a collective effort to challenge their city's police force. These days were full of marching, singing, and chanting. By simply occupying the streets of Seattle, people defied police efforts to impose curfews, form roadblocks, and threaten arrest. They were also challenging Clinton's decision to send in the National Guard. According to many, the presence of the National Guard only led to more terror and intense acts of violence directed at U.S. citizens.

"What are they saying?" asked Pascale, after she and the Millau group heard the same chant repeated over and over by protestors. "They're chanting, '*Whose* streets? *Our* streets! *Whose* streets? *Our* streets!'" I said, recording the chants with my tape recorder. When marchers switched to another now-familiar chant, I translated that one as well. "This is what democracy looks like! This is what democracy looks like!" I shouted over the crowd's din. "They're refusing the government's demand that citizens stay off the streets. They are saying that they see this demand as undemocratic." That particular chant, "This is what democracy looks like," became the mantra for that week in Seattle. "We're all fighting for democracy," Pascale added. She smiled sadly at the crowd moving as one organism down the street.

Later that day throngs arrived before a small wooden platform constructed for a farmers' rally scheduled to take place in downtown Seattle by the lake. Crowds waited patiently for Bové to take the stage. People from all over the United States, and from around the world, were moved by his unflinching conviction, his boldness, and his moustache-and-pipe charisma. Perhaps because of his heavily accented and awkward English, many people I interviewed found Bové "charming," "sexy," and "so French." They reported being surprised to see that "French people" were concerned with questions of fair trade or democracy. When I asked about this surprise, many answered, "It's usually people from the Third World, poor people, who are being done in by the WTO."

In all of his interviews and orations during those days in Seattle, Bové artfully linked a series of issues. He made connections between the right of U.S. citizens to peaceful protest with the right of people around the world to determine their own economies and cultures. As Bové articulated that day, the WTO was a threat not just to fair trade but to democracy in general. The WTO was described by many as a "mafia-like" alliance among state bodies, multinational corporations, and supranational institutions such as the International Monetary Fund and the World Bank. Many described this mafia as determined to control the ways of life of the world's population.

Standing among the crowd listening to Bové, I wandered around, interviewing activists, holding out my little tape recorder. Seeing my tiny contraption, people seemed relieved to have somewhere to place their thoughts. "Who knows?" I said, "I might write a book about this someday," I said, trying to reassure them. Many U.S. citizens during those days in Seattle spoke their thoughts into my tape recorder, expressing how inspiring and reassuring it was to see international activists present to speak out against the assault on democracy that they had seen in Seattle. While some interviewees saw Bové as allied with peasants and indigenous peoples in the Global South, many others saw him as representing French citizens, as a witness from a global superpower who would travel back to his country and spread the news about what had happened in an allegedly democratic U.S. city: "Let him tell France, tell the rest of the world, what democracy *really* looks like in the U.S." This was a refrain repeated often into my recorder by members of the French delegation as well as by U.S. activists. But the words were not just directed to the problem of nondemocracy in the United States. According to nearly everyone I encountered, the crisis witnessed in Seattle was perceived as clearly international in character. For so many, the WTO had come to symbolize a malevolent form of neoliberalism; they saw it as a form of nondemocracy that was slowly encompassing the globe.

After spending three days in Seattle, the French delegation traveled as planned back to France. Released from my charge as a translator, I remained in the city for several more days. I joined activists' ongoing fight to challenge police brutality, to free the many activists still incarcerated in the city's King County jail, and to convince the WTO to cancel its meeting. After many days of street marches and demonstrations, activists felt a sense of tremendous triumph when some of these goals were achieved.

During a chilly evening meeting outside the city's main prison, hundreds of activists met in spokesgroups to draw up a set of demands. In particular, the groups sought the release of all activist prisoners, rejecting police accusations that some of the arrested merited harsher sentences than others. As many of the imprisoned were engaging in "jail solidarity," they had refused to provide police and prison officials with their names. In turn, they declined to admit that they had committed any punishable crime that would distinguish them from any other prisoner. Those on the outside also engaged in jail solidarity by conducting a sit-in in front of the prison and chanting their support for hours on end. Toward the end of the evening, at nearly eleven o'clock, the Direct Action Network's legal council announced to the crowd that all prisoners would be released immanently.

That same memorable night, after the good news at the prison, I made my way over to the Westin Hotel, where a late-night meeting was being held by representatives of the WTO. A group of about twenty activists were engaged in a lockdown. They had attached themselves to the hotel's entrance with bicycle locks, attempting to obstruct the entrance as best as they could. Around the front of the hotel were young people drumming and dancing, singing political chants they hoped the trade officials might hear. At issue were rumors circulating about African WTO delegates. Many who had witnessed the trade meetings had told me that delegates from several African nations were being pressured to sign on to particular free-trade agreements they knew would prove disastrous to the peoples of their countries. In unison, activists engaged in lockdown alongside about a hundred others who were drumming, dancing, and chanting, "Africa, don't sign! Africa, don't sign!" After sitting and talking with the activists, I heard screams of joy. "Africa bailed!" a young woman yelled as she ran from the hotel entryway toward the small group. "The delegates from several African nations have refused to sign and so the meetings are done." Deafening cheers rang out as young people pounded on their drums. "That means the meetings are canceled!" called out a young man near the hotel's entrance. "The delegates heard us. We made the WTO cancel their meetings!" No one will ever know if those outside the hotel indeed informed the African delegates' decision to refuse to sign the trade agreements. Yet both mainstream media and Indymedia agreed that the refusal led to a stalemate, which in turn led to the meeting's cancellation.

For many in Seattle that week, it seemed likely that activists' efforts were effective. They challenged perceived injustices associated with the WTO. In addition, they articulated resistance to acts committed by the city and national officials they regarded as violent and undemocratic. Perhaps most important to so many, they communicated support for those within the WTO who opposed the trade body while also publicly contesting the legitimacy of the institution itself.

Conclusion

The visit to the United States provided a window into the key differences between French and U.S. cultures of food, politics, and activism. This text cannot possibly provide an in-depth exploration of all these cultural differences. But it is still useful to examine how such disparities in group cultures surfaced during the Confédération Paysanne's voyage to the United States. In addition, the trip provided the union insights into the heterogeneous and democratic character of an increasingly international movement. A growing awareness of both cultural difference and international solidarity perhaps helped the Confédération Paysanne as it turned next to furthering its own struggle in France. According to Bové, the delegation was moved by the democratic and antiauthoritarian sensibility expressed by the Direct Action Network and other U.S. activists in Seattle. For Bové, what came to be called the Battle of Seattle reminded him of the spirit of the Larzac and the events of May 1968. All three actions opened a cultural space in which heterogeneous sets of actors and objectives could merge in creative new ways. As the delegation departed the United States for France, many members expressed a desire to incorporate this Seattle sensibility into union events that would ensue in France during the coming months.

10

Postindustrial Paysans in a Post-Seattle World

New Movements, New Possibilities

Central to the postindustrial condition is the rise of new oppositional actors resisting a brand of instrumentalism associated with neoliberalism. The instant popularity of Bové's book *The World Is Not for Sale* (Bové and Dufour 2001) spoke to a growing collective malaise in France (and throughout much of the Global North) regarding a perceived reduction of life, nature, food, and humanity to commodities. In an era of increasing deregulation and free trade, actors began to form groups and coalitions, positioning local cultures and natures against multinational corporations and the political bodies working to support global capital. Out of the ashes of a once diverse and richly populated agricultural landscape rose a social movement given new momentum by an international alter-globalization movement that expressed an antineoliberal sentiment around the world. From 2000 to 2003 Bové enjoyed tremendous popularity in France, providing the Confédération Paysanne a much-needed leg up in French agricultural policymaking forums. Following 2004, however, Bové's popularity declined slightly. In a political and economic climate of increasing neoliberalism, Bové and the Confédération Paysanne found themselves striving to popularize their postindustrial model of agriculture and society.

Confédération Paysanne: Enjoying the National Spotlight

UNION SUCCESS AND A COMMANDO-STYLE ARREST

The year 2000 saw the close of Dufour's eventful term as union speaker. When Dufour's run ended, Bové was instated as the new speaker at the union's annual general assembly. After the events of 1999, Bové seemed a natural choice. The Confédération Paysanne is a leaderless body, but the media nevertheless regarded Bové as the leader, and his excellent communication skills and national popularity made him a powerful voice for articulating the union's goals and objectives. During his tenure as union speaker (2000–2003), Bové continued to build on the momentum of the alter-globalization movement, continually expanding the Confédération Paysanne's vision to include an increasingly global, solidaire, and antineoliberal perspective. As Bové's alter-globalization activities are too numerous to name here, I focus on a few events surrounding Bové and the union that struck me as particularly pertinent.

SEATTLE-SUR-TARN

In June of 2000, Bové co-organized an alter-globalization rally in Larzac featuring a crowd of two hundred thousand to three hundred thousand. The event was referred to as Seattle-sur-Tarn (Tarn Valley is in southern France). The reference to Seattle is significant. The Battle of Seattle had set the tone and sensibility for an alter-globalization movement that was emerging in France as well as throughout Europe and the world. Seattle-sur-Tarn took place during the days leading up to Bové's trial for the McDo affair of 1999. As usual, Bové playfully referred to his trial as "the trial of free trade" and the "Millau Trade Round" (Lichfield 2000). In the weeks leading up to the Tarn rally, Bové promised the festival would be a political, festive, and peaceful demonstration. The planning committee booked three popular French rock bands and constructed an open-air auditorium for an anti-free-trade rally and conference. During the weeks before the event, national and international press such as London's the *Independent* began referring to the festival as an "Alter-globalization Woodstock," linguistically linking it to the burgeoning new social movements of the U.S. Left that were associated with the 1960s (June 26, 2000).

Even weeks before the event, French media coverage was often quite negative. Because Millau was the site of both Bové's trial and the festival, journalists portrayed the town's citizens as inevitable victims of anticipated vandalism. The media repeatedly invoked the events in Seattle, predicting a similar scenario to take place in Millau. As in the United States, the French mainstream media framed Seattle protestors in a negative light. Instead of declaring U.S. armed forces guilty of turning against unarmed and vulnerable citizens, the media depicted the protestors as out of control. It was common knowledge that Seattle authorities had removed the city's mayor, determining that he had been guilty of overreacting. Yet the idea of violent protesters remains fixed in national and international consciousness to this day.

Britain's popular newspaper the *Independent* described the anticipated Seattle-sur-Tarn in the following way:

> After Seattle and Davos, the small town of Millau in the south of France fears this week that it may become the latest casualty of violent protests against the globalisation of trade. Something like 30,000 people from the various tribes of the "new left" — small farmers, ecologists, anarchists, anti-capitalists — will descend on the town on Friday to picket the trial of Jose Bove, a farmer who has become one of the living saints of the anti-globalisers. Mr Bove, a sheep farmer, producer of Roquefort cheese and veteran political activist, faces a possible jail sentence for his part in the demolition of a half-built McDonald's restaurant last summer. . . . Eight hundred policemen will be mobilised. Schools will be closed. The courthouse will be cordoned off. The McDonald's restaurant in the town will be shut and boarded up. CNN has rented rooms in flats overlooking the courthouse, in the expectation of tele-visual violence. . . . Thanks to his charisma, eloquence and trademark droopy moustache and pipe, Mr Bove has become one of the rallying points of the struggle against *malbouffe* [junk food] in France and in the wider international campaign against rules enforcing global trade. (Lichfield 2000)

Portrayals of Bové and the antiglobalization movement both reflected and shaped popular attitudes toward the emerging crusade in France and abroad. Both the Associated Press and Agence France-Presse tended to portray Bové as the "droopy mustached" or "living saint" of "tribes" of violent "anti-globalizers" (Agence Press, June 27, 2000; Associated Press, June 28, 2000).

Such descriptors sought to trivialize and depoliticize Bové and the movements that he helped foster. The media acted as a disciplining force, attempting to reduce Bové and other activists to powerless, humorous caricatures. At this time the BBC described Bové as "a peasant Robin Hood" (Pearce 2000), invoking the comparison between Bové and the French comic strip hero Asterix. The media often commented on the likeness between Bové and Asterix, the feisty Gaul who leads a ludicrous battle against the Roman Empire during ancient times. The Asterix reference was often hypocritical, reflecting the nation's ambivalence about Bové. While narratives presented Bové as a ridiculous buffoon, they also extolled him as an exemplary little guy fighting the big guy. These complex and contradictory representations played a role in establishing Bové as a symbol of "French individuality [by] refusing to be swamped by imperial forces" (Pearce 2003). Such portrayals increased Bové's popularity, but they often presented him and the union in nationalistic terms. One conversation I had with a union paysan in July 2000 summed up the union's take on the Asterix problem: "We can't win. Either we're stupid country bumpkins [ploucs] fighting a ridiculous battle, or we're reactionary nationalists that the Right adores" (personal communication, July 8, 2000).

Despite media's portrayal of Bové and the event, Seattle-sur-Tarn proved to be a nonviolent event. According to the Confédération Paysanne member Robert G., Bové's media-rich presence in Seattle had emboldened many in France who had been disenchanted by politics as usual. In particular, it spoke to those who perceived France's national party system as incapable of adequately addressing social and ecological problems associated with neo-liberalism and privatization. In 2000, it seemed a new generation was coming of age in France, a generation whose collective motto (inspired by the Zapatistas) was "Another world is possible." At Seattle-sur-Tarn, this slogan appeared on banners, T-shirts, and buttons. "Un autre monde est possible" was written in body paint across the bare backs of many young men who had traveled to Millau that day. The Zapatista phrase captured the utopian sensibility that marked this new movement. Rejecting a logic of instrumentalism that reduced peoples, lands, and water to commodities and profit margins, French youths at Seattle-sur-Tarn identified with an alternate vision. They sought a world built out of a logic of solidarity.

At the festival, activists young and old, farmer and nonfarmer, strolled through the open-air market. Each farm stand provided farm products (*pro-*

duits fermiers), foods rich in symbolic capital. Filling conference tents, attendees listened to paysans lecture on the union's vision of Paysan Agriculture. Every once in a while, Bové and other members of the Confédération Paysanne rode through the throngs on a hay wagon. They waved and smiled while the crowd cheered them on. According to several actors I talked to following the festival, Seattle-sur-Tarn was peaceful, jovial, and brought forth fond memories of the Larzac movement. Like the Larzac, Seattle-sur-Tarn brought together a broad spectrum of actors, farmers, and nonfarmers to fight for a shared cause.

From the stage, Bové addressed festival participants, reminding them of the struggles that still lay ahead. In numerous speeches, Bové tried to keep the momentum going against the WTO. He discussed the upcoming WTO meeting in Cancún, Mexico. Bové explained that organizers for the trade body vowed to never again hold its meetings in a major city such as Seattle that could be readily accessible to protestors. "Cancún, Mexico, is the site for the next meeting," Bové shouted into his microphone. "If we can't be there physically, we will protest all over the world symbolically. We must mobilize to make sure that the Cancún summit is a failure. We must put the 146 member governments under citizen's arrest so that they can't sign an agreement in Cancún!" (Agence France-Presse 2000).

In the next few years following Seattle-sur-Tarn, Bové and the Confédération Paysanne enjoyed tremendous popular support in the French agricultural world. By 2003, this support led the union to win 28 percent of the seats in the chamber of agriculture. This feat signaled that nearly one-third of all French farmers at the time shared the union's concerns and goals; the industrial model of agriculture appeared to be politically challenged on a significant level in France. With the general support of the French populace, the government had difficulties disciplining Bové for his previous anti-GMO activities. Upon returning to France after his U.S. voyage, Bové was tried in 2000 for the 1999 McDo action. As in his trial in Nérac, Bové sent a clear message to the media: he reversed the charges by asserting that fast food, GMOs, and free trade would be symbolically tried in court rather than Bové himself. Once again, Bové transformed the trial into a forum to communicate an alter-globalization message. At the trial's end, he received a disappointing fourteen-month sentence. Yet, as usual, Bové made good use of the period leading up to his incarceration. In press interviews he publicly contested the political validity of both the charges and the punishment. He framed his acts as an attempt to defend the public good from corporate harm. In September 2002, Bové was still engaged in the protracted process of actively appealing his fourteen-month sentence. But that sentence was not all that troubled him that year. At the same time, he awaited a judge's decision on another sentencing for a crop pull that took place in 2000. In this action, Bové and four hundred others destroyed a field of genetically modified canola in the southwestern town of Gaudies. For this action, Bové faced up to five years in prison and a maximum fine of nearly US$15,000 for damages. It is not uncommon for rigorous and public activists to face multiple sets of charges, appeals, and sentences at a given time. Always drawing from cultural symbolism and metaphor, Bové and eight others wore "girls' frocks" to their trial in Foix. The frocks were a cultural reference to a local conflict in the Middle Ages between peasants and tax collectors. In the Middle Ages, male peasants would protest state hunting laws that forbade them from entering the forest. By disguising themselves in white girls' frocks, they fooled state gamekeepers. They could enter the forest to hunt without being heavily taxed. The frocked peasants were known as the *demoiselles* (maidens). "Our battle against GMOs has much in common with that of the demoiselles," said Bové to a reporter. "We too are running against a French justice system opposed to common protest action and deaf to the concerns of citizens" (Agence France-Presse 2002).

In 2003, Bové received ample coverage of his impending, yet long-awaited, sentence for the McDo affair. In France, as in many countries, the pace and process of sentencing and imprisoning high-profile citizens can be politically charged as legal authorities consider the implications of sentencing practices for public opinion. In the case of Bové, many in the union explained that he was fortunate to have popular support on his side. As national secretary Jean-Pierre Testard said to me, "They take their time with Bové. They hope to wait until the public loses interest in him to put him in prison. They saw what happened when he was imprisoned the first time! What a mess that was for the government!" (personal communication, August 21, 2005).

But by June 2003, French legal authorities had grown weary of waiting and instead took abrupt unexpected action. The government orchestrated a highly dramatic sequence in which they ordered one hundred police officers to surround Bové's home in rural Millau. When Bové opened his front door, he was immediately taken into the state's custody and flown by helicopter to prison. Several weeks later, Bové was interviewed by France's national television show *Les 4 vérités* (The four truths). In this exchange, Bové reflected on the government's decision to transform his delivery to prison into sensationalist news. According to Bové, at the time of his arrest, he was merely living and working on his sheep farm near Millau. He was neither hiding his whereabouts nor presenting a threat to police. For Bové, the government's helicopter-and-police strategy was an attempt to portray him as a dangerous and fleeing criminal. "Surrounding my home with one hundred police and dragging me into a helicopter in handcuffs was clearly a political act," Bové said with contained disgust during the interview. In an interview I conducted with him, he noted, "After waiting years to take me off to jail, they thought they might as well make it a grand gesture, to justify the wait" (personal communication, September 2, 2003).

French and European media generally sided with Bové decrying the airlift as overkill. French print and television media intently focused on this event, often describing it as a "commando-style" operation. Britain's BBC ran a story on June 23 titled "French Anger at Bové 'Commando' Arrest" (BBC News 2003). Describing the event as a "strong-arm tactic," the reporter wrote, "Bové was snatched from his farm in southern France in a dawn commando-style operation that involved scores of police officers."

In addition to garnering the support of the media, Bové had many allies among the French Left. Leaders of the Green, Socialist, and Communist Parties spoke in Bové's defense at the harsh treatment of a union man. Julien Dray, leader of the Socialist Party, showed his support, saying on Canal 2, France's major network news program, "The government has chosen confrontation" (June 24, 2003). Leaders of various trade unions spoke out as well. Marc Blondel of the union Force Ouvrier (Workers' Power) said, "It was particularly shocking that a union official should be taken to prison like a dangerous outlaw" (BBC News 2003). In the Left's reaction we can see once again how Bové presented himself to the world and how the world received him. For years Bové's image had transcended the identity of "union man" defending workers' rights. He had become a postindustrial hybrid entity: part worker, part alter-globalization activist, part ecologist, and part Gandhian international humanist. Yet despite his stretching of the definition and role of a traditional French union man, his identity and message still resonated with those on the Left willing to regard him as one of their own.

France's right wing, however, saw the arrest differently. President Chirac's party supported the arrest, stating, "José Bové went into battle and he knew the risks" (my translation). By comparing Bové's symbolic attacks on a McDonald's to a warrior going to battle, Chirac's party exaggerated the dimensions of Bové's actions to justify the government's sensationalist and militaristic arrest tactics. At this time, Nicolas Sarkozy was France's interior minister. Sarkozy also defended the police tactics. According to Sarkozy, "Because it is Bové, who speaks perfect English and who the media adore, must the government refuse to apply a juridical decision? What's the problem? Where's the scandal?" (BBC News 2003; my translation). Aware that the French public was not pleased with the harsh arrest tactics, Sarkozy delivered a statement to normalize the government's actions. Instead of directly trivializing the public's reaction, Sarkozy minimized the significance of the tactics. For Sarkozy, the arrest tactics were not even fit for discussion. They were not scandalous, problematic, or unusual in any way. Sarkozy's mention of Bové's "perfect English" in several news interviews reflects his attempt to undermine Bové's cultural appeal.[1] The social capital embedded in Bové's English-speaking abilities is palpable in Sarkozy's statement. Sarkozy attempts to invalidate Bové by revealing him as a fraudulent folk hero. For Sarkozy, there exists an unbridgeable chasm between being an English-speaking and sophisticated political operator, and being a paysan. According to Sarkozy's depiction, Bové shared little in common with his non-English-speaking French supporters. During this time, many actors in powerful institutions attempted to destabilize Bové's public acceptance by destroying his folksy image. Despite the government's attempts to defile his identity as a paysan, Bové triumphed again. He received considerable coverage the day Chirac publicly agreed to reduce his sentence from fourteen months to four. One month later, on Bastille Day, Bové reaped even more attention when Chirac paroled Bové's sentence entirely. These events were largely due to political pressure from the French Left.

Outside France, Bové garnered significant media focus from 2000 to 2002 for spearheading numerous anti-GMO actions internationally. Bové began traveling to India, Brazil, Palestine, Mexico, Canada, and other countries to participate in crop pulls and rallies; he also often committed acts of civil disobedience. In each interview, Bové continued to link the problem of GMOs to questions of neoliberal trade, privatization, life patents, and the world's farmers' right of access to land, water, and indigenous seeds.

In 2001, Bové participated in a counterconference to be held simultaneously in Qatar, where the next cycle of WTO meetings took place. This
cycle of WTO meetings was part of what was called the Doha Round, begun
in Doha, Qatar, in the Persian Gulf in 2001. WTO leaders chose Doha as the
site for the first ministerial-level meeting of the Doha Development Round
for a specific reason. At the Battle of Seattle two years earlier in 1999, activists had proven capable of tarnishing the WTO's reputation and canceling
its meetings. In a post-Seattle era, WTO organizers would never hold a key
meeting in an accessible international city such as Seattle. From now on,
the WTO would take great care to hold its meetings in locations outside the
United States that would prove hard to reach for activists. Doha was financially and politically inaccessible to most protestors. Qatar is only bordered
by one country — Saudi Arabia. The rest of Qatar is surrounded by water,
the Persian Gulf. Accessing visas to enter Qatar proved impossible for thousands who would have otherwise attended the countersummit. The round
that began in Doha continued in Cancún, another location that prevented
on-the-ground preplanning for organizations such as the Direct Action Network. Even so government actors put in place security and surveillance measures weeks before the meetings, creating militaristic zones around the trade
meetings. Thousands of Mexican and international activists either were officially prohibited from attending the meetings or found themselves banned
from crossing the border to Mexico. Despite the extensive efforts taken by
the WTO to make its meetings unreachable to protestors, activist groups did
make their way to Cancún to protest the WTO by the thousands. Although
there lacked sufficient space in Cancún for protestors to plan a "Battle of
Cancún," their presence there flagged the continuity of an alter-globalization
activism still percolating internationally.

THE WORLD SOCIAL FORUM: ALTER-GLOBALIZATION BOVÉ

In 2001, building on the momentum of the growing alter-globalization
movement, an informal alliance of groups from around the world came
together to create an annual countersummit to the World Economic Forum
held each January in Davos, Switzerland. Bové was a key speaker at the first
gathering in Porte Alegre, Brazil. To express solidarity with rural peoples
oppressed by a global neoliberal system, he shared a panel with members of
the Brazilian movement of landless farmworkers. Like the Peoples' Global
Action, this movement was inspired greatly by the encuentros created by

the Zapatista movement in Chiapas, Mexico. There is a clear theme that runs through the Zapatista's encuentros, Peoples' Global Action, and the World Social Forum. Each gathering represents an attempt to provide a space where groups can articulate problems and solutions related to life in an increasingly neoliberal world.

These gatherings also share a commitment to creating an alternative to a traditional Left marked by hierarchical and labor-centric parties. Like the Encuentros and Peoples' Global Action, the World Social Forum was born out of a call for a "new internationalism" emerging in a post-Marxist world (de Sousa Santos 2006, 38). The People's Global Action and the World Social Forum emerged during a distinct historical juncture. The worker was no longer the vanguard revolutionary subject, just as the industrial factory was no longer the primary site for revolutionary activity. Instead, actors like paysans, the landless, indigenous peoples, and women's groups started to fight for the disenfranchised edged out of the industrial project. These actors seek a world based on a different logic than the one that brought industrial capitalism into place (Escobar et al. 2004).

As the World Social Forum has developed over the years, it has come to be called by many "the movement of movements." Boaventura de Sousa Santos provides insight into what makes the World Social Forum special. It proposes no single political or economic model such as communism, socialism, anarchism, or social democracy. Yet actors who identify with the World Social Forum's aims tend to identify with an antineoliberal stance, as well as a (loosely defined) commitment to nonviolent direct action. For de Sousa Santos, the World Social Forum is a "critical utopia" in that it explores what is possible, albeit in a critical way (de Sousa Santos 2006, 3).

In so doing, those who created the World Social Forum rejected taken-for-granted Western models of what a utopian society would be. The World Social Forum confronts the "sociology of absences" by creating a space in which individuals rendered absent from powerful institutions (in other words, disenfranchised by a neoliberal global economy) can have their concrete presence recognized (de Sousa Santos 2003, 4). It provides a space where the "sociology of emergences" can be explored by those alter-globalization activists seeking alternatives to the dominant order. According to de Sousa Santos: "The sociology of emergences . . . consists in undertaking a symbolic enlargement of knowledge, practices, and agents in order to identify therein the tendencies of the future (the Not Yet) upon which it is possible to intervene so as to maximize the probability of hope vis-à-vis the probability of frustration" (2003, 2).

Since 2001, the World Social Forum has been held annually in such countries as Brazil, India, and Pakistan. Each forum brings together between 60,000 and 160,000 activists from more than 130 countries. In addition to these large gatherings, the organizers have created an array of regional and national social forums, including the European Social Forum, the Asian Social Forum, the U.S. Social Forum, and the Mediterranean Social Forum. The objective of both national and international World Social Forums is to give voice to "Southern epistemologies" (de Sousa Santos 2006, 19). Such epistemologies—or ways of knowing—represent new economic, cultural, and political visions that resonate with actors such as those in the Confédération Paysanne. Many groups who participate in the forum are geographically isolated and politically disenfranchised. In this way, the World Social Forum enables actors to become aware of common problems and objectives. During the five-day event, the forum offers hundreds of workshops, lectures, plenaries, and panels that address issues of landlessness, indigeneity, sex and gender liberation, and economic and political alternatives.

In addition to providing educational and networking opportunities, the World Social Forum offers groups an occasion to demonstrate together around particular issues. At the first gathering in Porte Alegre, Bové co-led a march of thirteen hundred Brazilian farmers working on a plantation owned by Monsanto. At the plantation, the group conducted a crop pull of genetically modified corn and soy. Using a gesture perhaps borrowed from the Karnataka farmers, the Brazilian workers burned genetically modified seeds found in storerooms and destroyed documents in the company's offices. In a pamphlet called "Report on the First World Social Forum, Porto Alegre Brazil," the U.S. Green Party activist Carol Brouillet described the event as "Bové and the others taking possession of the Monsanto plantation, planting their own crops, pledging to turn the farm into a model of sustainable agriculture" (2001). During the demonstration, activists held placards featuring phrases such as "Another world is possible" and "People are not commodities." These slogans crystallize a set of meanings communicated by actors who are refusing an instrumentalizing system that is seen as caring little for the world's poor and the environment. Following the demonstration, Bové was arrested and threatened with deportation. In response, activists gathered outside the prison where he was briefly detained. His detainment was met with strong outrage by those in Brazil and internationally, making headlines in major newspapers. Surprised by the turmoil that ensued following his arrest, the Brazilian government dropped all charges against him. At the final closing of that first World Social Forum, many in the crowd held banners proclaiming, "We are all Bové!" Actors such as de Sousa Santos, Bové, and many Confédération Paysanne members seek to explore knowledge, practices, and agents excluded from determining what is indeed possible in the future. Bové has participated in nearly every World Social Forum, including regional gatherings.

At the fourth World Social Forum in Mumbai, India, in 2004, Bové was once again a significant voice, delivering the inaugural speech to a crowd of a hundred thousand activists and decrying neoliberalism and promoting a logic of solidarity. Standing beside the Nobel laureates Shirin Ebadi and Joseph Stiglitz, Bové challenged the monopoly multinationals have over water and agriculture. According to Al Jazeera, on January 17, 2005, Bové chanted to the crowd, "Nestle, Coca-Cola, leave our countries, give us our rights!" He continued, "The WTO has to get out of agriculture. Its policies are threatening our future." In the online publication *Countercurrents*, Krishna Kumar reported Bové to have coined the slogan "Globalize your struggles to globalize your hopes" (Brouillet 2001).

POSTINDUSTRIAL PRIVATIZATION: WATER WARS

In February 2004, Bové extended his focus to include the privatization question. After the World Social Forum in Mumbai, he was invited to inaugurate the World Water Conference in Kerala, India, in the region of Plachimada. Bové spoke in support of struggles against what he called water hijackers, including the Coca-Cola Company, for exploiting natural resources throughout the world (Kumar 2004). The privatization of services such as water is endemic in the postindustrial condition. As powers in the Global North exhaust the limits of industrial production, corporations search for ever-broader extraindustrial sites for capital accumulation. At such a juncture, the question of water becomes a contentious issue. Water was once considered by analysts on the Left as an externality lying outside, yet necessary to, the capitalist system. Under postindustrial capitalism, however, water became a new and powerful commodity (Shiva 2002). In other words, whereas water was once culturally understood as a public resource, it is now recast as a private service. Corporations and states are buying and selling reservoirs, rivers, groundwater, and even segments of ocean as monies change hands between rich and poor countries.

For Bové and the union, water privatization is a further instance of the commercialization (*marchandizement*) of life itself. For decades, private firms such as Coca-Cola, Vivandi, and PepsiCo have used satellite technologies to identify reservoirs and groundwater in countries such as India and Mexico (Shiva 2002). After purchasing water rights from leaders of poor countries, they render waters inaccessible to farmers and citizens for irrigation, drinking, and other subsistence uses. As local wells (and subsistence fields) dry up, local peoples are obliged to walk greater distances daily to reach sources. Privatized water is often shipped to processing plants where it is bottled and transported throughout the Global North, where middle-class consumers increasingly prefer bottled to tap. In many countries, the price of a bottle of water is significantly more expensive than a bottle of Coca-Cola or other sodas. Other sources of water in poor rural areas are sold to private firms, which subsequently divert waterways such as rivers and lakes to provide services in megacities for privileged consumers who can afford to pay for potable running water (NACLA News 2007).

At the Kerala World Water Conference in Plachimada, Bové inaugurated an event directly across from the Coca-Cola processing plant. Local conference organizers used loudspeakers so that each word of the conference would be audible to plant workers and officials (Barlow 2004). Addressing a crowd of five thousand people (largely headed up by women's associations), Bové said in his opening speech: "The struggle of Plachimada is part of the worldwide struggle against transnational companies that exploit natural resources like water. The companies have made water a priced commodity to make profit. We will take this issue across the globe as the finest example of the over-exploitation of water resources driven by Coca-Cola and Pepsi. . . . Yours is a just struggle and you have the support of France and farmers and those in other alter-globalization movements in different parts of the world" (quoted in Kumar 2004). As we have seen before, Bové functions as a hybrid entity empowered to speak to, and on the behalf of, a range of subaltern actors. As a citizen of an EU country, he has significant cultural and material privilege. Yet as a paysan, standing in solidarity with peasants in the Global South, he shares a common refusal of the instrumental logic embedded in neoliberal privatization. His promise of moral support also has material implications. For example, resource sharing, such as the transportation costs of

European actors, to attend protests (to enhance media appeal), bolsters the voice of actors whose causes are otherwise unheard in the Global South.

Bové's presence in international social movements—or movements that extend beyond national borders—is worthy of analysis (see Smith, Chatfield, and Pagunco 1997; Tarrow 1998). As a member of La Via Campesina, among other international organizations, Bové plays a key role in helping to globalize struggles related to water, land, agriculture, and indigenous rights and identity. As de Sousa Santos suggests (2003, 12), international activists can never replace on-the-ground efforts marked by rich local constituencies. Bové's presence at such forums, however, can provide a stabilizing force, supporting local groups and organizations. And as Sonia Alvarez suggests, internationalist identity solidarity can be "salutatory for local movements," enhancing the public visibility of claims made by movements in the host country, providing activists with a shared though continually resignified political language, discursive frameworks, and organizational practices (Alvarez 2000, 9). Sometimes, such internationalist actions yield impressive results. In response to the water conference, the Kerala government took action on February 18, 2004, by ordering the Coca-Cola Company to close for four months. Acknowledging the corporation's deleterious effects on the local water system, the Kerala government publicly called for a thorough investigation of damages caused.

The water-privatization question was not new for Bové. As early as the fall of 1999 Bové and the Confédération Paysanne led an anti-Vivandi action in Paris. I was present at this demonstration, so I can confirm that it embodied the union's distinct style of direct action. After more than two hundred protestors rushed the stairwells of the Vivandi headquarters, they set about the daylong occupation by creating a festive atmosphere. Armed with boxes of bread, cheese, wine, and pâté, paysans and supporters spent the day laughing and picnicking along the wall-to-wall gray carpets that lined Vivandi's expansive offices. During this action, protestors watched a TV screen provided by Vivandi that allowed picnickers to observe Bové's live interviews with major French TV channels just outside the building. During the interviews, protestors inside the building cheered as Bové drew connections between the privatization of water and the privatization of the world's seed supply through agricultural biotechnology. "What will be left?" Bové asked the reporter. "Once the world's corporations control everything, what will they privatize next, the air?"

Chapter Ten

FOOD SOVEREIGNTY DISCOURSE:
AN ALTER-GLOBALIZATION FRAMING OF FOOD

Central to the postindustrial condition is the explosion of alternative discourses on food. Discourses on food risk and quality are often employed by actors on both sides of debates on food systems, providing means to legitimize a range of claims about the value and meaning of food. Bové and his political allies have played a key role in defining and disseminating an alternative food discourse. Perhaps the most central and key discourse on food that emerges during the 1990s and early 2000s is food sovereignty. In 1996, La Via Campesina formally adopted the term *food sovereignty* at the UN-sponsored World Food Summit in Rome. The World Food Summit has served as a central site for those in the alter-globalization movement who are focused on food and agriculture. The summit is coordinated by the Food and Agriculture Organization of the United Nations. Activists in 1996 held their own countersummit to discuss global food-related crises and asserted the sovereign right that all communities should have in determining their own food supply (Desmarais et al. 2010, 21). A revealing set of keywords is embedded in the "Declaration on World Food Security and World Food Summit Plan of Action."[2] Terms such as *rights*, *nutritious*, *hunger*, and *population* appear repeatedly in the two-page document, emphasizing the food predicament of inhabitants of the Global South. The document describes the causes of hunger in southern nations:

– Constraints on access to food
– Inadequacy of household and national incomes
– Man-made disasters
– Increased population
– Conflict, terrorism, corruption, environmental degradation

There are problematic patterns of consumption and production in industrialized countries. This World Food Summit document suggests a technique of governance that runs through supranational bodies by addressing questions of food and agriculture. Exercised power is discreet and veiled, normalizing a set of hunger-inducing practices driven by industrial nations. The term *trade* is used abundantly in this two-page declaration. Yet the authors acknowledge no link between neoliberal trade practices and the lack of available food or farmable land for southern smallholders. Instead, the document's creators make vague references to problems such as "man-made disasters" or "unsustainable" consumption and production in industrialized countries that contribute to world hunger.

Such omissions are central to the study of a "sociology of absences" described by de Sousa Santos (2006, 15). De Sousa Santos explores how powerful institutions often create situations in which "what exists is in fact actively produced as non-existent" (2006, 15). The World Food Summit's omission of subaltern actors "wastes the social experiences" (2006, 18) of smallholders and indigenous peoples who hold crucial knowledges about food and agriculture. While the document "makes absent" powerless victims of neoliberal agricultural policy, it also obscures powerful institutions and policies that cause their disempowerment. Discussions of the WTO, as well as structural adjustment programs and southern debt, are conspicuously absent. The World Food Summit declaration shrinks the world of what de Sousa Santos calls "the field of credible experiences" (2006, 18). In doing so, the declaration erases local knowledges about on-the-ground mechanisms that reproduce everyday cultures of hunger and poverty in the Global South (euphemized as "food insecurity" in the declaration).

The countersummit of 1996 was called the Forum on Food Security. Actors from La Via Campesina, the Confédération Paysanne, and other organizations took language into their own hands, deciding in the future to replace the term *food security* with *food sovereignty*. It was there that food sovereignty discourse was born. As de Sousa Santos suggests, food sovereignty discourse empowers actors by transforming them from passive and invisible objects into active and agents of power. For de Sousa Santos, we need discourse that "transforms impossible into possible objects, and noncredible subjects into visible credible subjects" (2006, 15). Food sovereignty discourse grasps elusive impossible objects, such as neoliberal capitalism, that insidiously drive global food systems. By making the machinations of food scarcity visible and understandable, actors in these groups also transform themselves into "visible credible subjects" who are otherwise erased and trivialized.

The World Food Summit was clearly a site of discursive creativity and gave rise to a new and powerful narrative about food sovereignty. The summit was also a site for creative direct action. Bové and several activists sauntered into a field of genetically modified olive trees just outside the city. In true satirical style for the union, Bové covered the tips of several branches with condoms. As symbols of reproductive protection, the condoms called attention to the problem of cross-pollination between trees that were genetically modified and those that were not. This symbolic and humorous event was recorded in many websites and news stories around the world. It helped others make the link between GMOs and the increasing global threat against local and national food sovereignty.

The transition from the term *security* to *sovereignty* is an interesting cultural-linguistic discursive move worthy of examination. Food sovereignty discourse widens what de Sousa Santos calls "the field of credible experiences" (2006, 17). By drawing once again on Raymond Williams's attention to keywords, we can see how specific terms emerge at particular historical junctures, both reflecting and producing societal realities (1976). The keyword *security* functions to normalize and even erase many of the causes and effects of food scarcity. In contrast, the keyword *sovereignty* expands the horizons of what could be thought and said about the causes and effects of hunger, landlessness, and neoliberalism generally. The term *food security* is problematic and complex. In the Global North, notions of food security invoke a consumer idiom bound up in ideas of food risk or safety related to GMOs, mad cow disease, and so on. Food security discourses arise as powerful institutions pair the militaristic term *security* (associated with state power) with the term *food*. Together the terms form what Williams calls a "semantic cluster" capable of symbolizing a nation's ability to protect its population from hunger-related harm. The concept fails, however, to problematize food-production method and scale and the commodification of food in a global market. Food security discourse is central to a postindustrial agricultural condition. It promotes paternalistic and neocolonial agendas to send so-called food aid to impoverished southern nations. Yet it does so without understanding how the many farmers of southern nations came to be landless in the first place. Powerful institutions rarely state how and why such peoples became unable to feed their communities as they had for thousands of years before the colonial period. Food aid can abate starvation for many people in poor countries in the short term. But in the long term, it perpetuates a trend of postindustrial dumping of cheap subsidized industrial foodstuffs from the Global North to the Global South. Ironically, practices and discourses surrounding food aid legitimize and reproduce the model of capital-driven industrial agriculture that perpetuates the cycle of global hunger among the landless. By moving from discourses on food security to sovereignty, subaltern actors made visible their right to produce their own food rather than simply receive aid in the name of bolstering food security.

At the countersummit that ran parallel to the World Food Summit in Rome that year, activists from the Forum for Food Sovereignty presented their own statement, "The Declaration of Nyéléni."[3] I identified the topic of each paragraph and the keywords that surface in each one:

- The right to food and food sovereignty. Keywords: *rights, safe, nutritious, healthy, domestic markets* (the text's authors use the keyword *rights* five times in the six-line paragraph).
- Access to, management of, and local control of natural resources. Keywords: *Access, management, local control, natural resources, genetic resources, land, water, livelihoods, sustainable.*
- Small-scale family and community-based agroecological food production. Keywords: *agroecology, production systems, sustainable.*
- Trade and food sovereignty. Keywords: *equitable, fair-trade system, development, human rights.*

The differences between the objectives of the World Food Summit and its opponent, the Forum for Food Sovereignty, are too numerous to go into at length here. However, it is valuable to analyze some of the language that World Food Summit officials deploy when pointing to various actors in the global food arena. The World Food Summit actors invoke a particularly charged keyword, the ecumenical *we*, when referring to those in powerful northern nations who have composed their declaration. When speaking about southern actors, they deploy abstract and generic keywords such as *everyone, populations, people, men and women,* and *future generations.*

The authors of "The Declaration of Nyéléni" use language quite differently. They describe peoples around the world with keywords that suggest specific groups or communities of actors, such as *individuals, groups, peoples,* and *nations.* The Nyéléni authors also cast actors in terms of cultural identity or rural vocation by describing them as *small-scale farmers, peasants, fisherfolk, pastoralists,* and *Indigenous Peoples.* In contrast, the authors of the World Food Summit document never refer to the cultural identities or specific food systems associated with southern actors. By invoking those disenfranchised from the global food system in this generic way, World Food Summit actors contribute to a sociology of absences. They invisibilize subaltern actors by omitting them from a document crafted by a powerful institution.

For the authors of the World Food Summit document, personhood and agency rest in the hands of leaders of powerful countries and institutions. The peoples they seek to serve are presented as passive recipients of the summit's sound food policy. By invoking food sovereignty discourse, the authors of "The Declaration of Nyéléni" linguistically reclaim personal and community agency. Through choosing a particular set of terms, they identify themselves as peoples who have the ability to produce food for themselves. They suggest that problems such as hunger are the result of powerful nations who are unwilling to grant the poor access to adequate land and waterways necessary for community-based agriculture.

By discursively shifting from a language of food security to food sovereignty, actors suggest a transfer in the locus of control. The term *sovereignty* implies a kind of autonomy among subaltern actors whose presence and agency are discursively erased from the global food picture, dissolving them into faceless populations (Morton and Spivak 2007, 16). The keyword *sovereignty* suggests a meaningful shift in how subaltern actors choose to understand themselves. Yet, as with many terms, *sovereignty* has a checkered past. As Foucault points out, the term *sovereignty* dates back to the twelfth century and suggests a monarch's power over a territory and his or her ability to rule over others by enforcing codified law (1991, 97). The modern meaning of sovereignty was formalized in the Treaty of Westphalia of 1648. According to this treaty, the monarch's state, territories, and borders should enjoy supremacy over the church. Paradoxically, the notion of food sovereignty invoked by subaltern actors appropriates the idea of state sovereignty associated with authoritarian and feudal forms of centralized power. States themselves invoke the term *sovereignty* to challenge some aspects of globalization that they find problematic. According to many analysts of globalization, the rise of the WTO and other supranational bodies threaten state authority (see Barfield 2001; Slaughter 1997). *Sovereignty* as a keyword is associated with at least three sets of meanings when invoked in different cultural contexts. For some historians, the term suggests the monarchical state seeking asylum from the church. For state agents representing member countries of the WTO, sovereignty is a way to describe the state as vulnerable and worthy of defense. For subaltern actors, sovereignty entails the self-determination of local on-the-ground communities.

The WTO often regards discourses on state sovereignty as "protectionist" (Jackson 2006). States attempting to protect domestic markets from cheaper imported products today are often disciplined with sanctions by agents of the trade body. When southern countries protest dumping, actors often invoke the term *state sovereignty* as a discursive intervention aimed at safeguarding their own agricultural and rural lifeways—without having their concerns trivialized as protectionist. Although many alter-globalization activists identify as antiauthoritarian, they draw upon a term historically embedded in discourses of state power. They extend the idea of sovereignty to discourses of food and agriculture. And so it is that the keyword *sovereignty*, historically used to defend the sovereign power of monarchs or nation-states, morphs into a counterhegemonic discourse. Food sovereignty discourse tilts the discursive frame surrounding food issues. Those who invoke the term focus beyond questions of production methods associated with discourses on food's sustainability, safety, quality, or organic certification. Food sovereignty discourse transfers the "food frame" from an instrumental discourse of costs and benefits into a far less calculable and far more complex human rights discourse. It points to the human right to feed communities by using local land areas. Food sovereignty discourse establishes food as a political and economic entity that must be extricated from a system based on long-distance and free-trade-based global markets. In this way, notions of food sovereignty have much in common with discourses on "local foods" narratives that promote food production for direct-sale markets. Food sovereignty discourse links food shortages and global hunger to a sociopolitical system embedded in the neoliberal model.

Actors and organizations such as Bové, the Confédération Paysanne, and La Via Campesina have worked for years to circulate food sovereignty discourse through various national and international forums. In addition, they employ the discourse as a lobbying tool at UN institutions, especially the Food and Agriculture Organization and Human Rights Council. Since 1996, Bové has worked within La Via Campesina to promote food sovereignty discourse. In February 2007 he was a central figure with La Via Campesina when five hundred delegates from more than eighty countries adopted "The Declaration of Nyéléni." And in July 2007, Bové was invited to be a key speaker on food sovereignty by the Korean Peasant League and the Korean Woman Peasant Association at the Korean Social Forum—a branch of the World Social Forum. On the website for La Via Campesina, Korean there is ample coverage of this event.[4] In a story on the Forum on Food Sovereignty in Korea, there is a photograph of a Korean peasant and Bové standing side by side, in solidarity, in a green field. The two men wore nearly matching plaid shirts, smiling while forming peace signs with their hands. As the story on the website states, Bové and others from La Via Campesina had come to the Korean Social Forum to "establish and spread the concept of food sovereignty in Korea, to get a better understanding of the food sovereignty situation in other countries[,] . . . to create a strategy for the Korean people movements for the implementation of food sovereignty, and to create a national network to materialize food sovereignty in the farmers-consumer relations in the future." We see the way that food sovereignty discourse is clearly a form of resistance to a technique of governance in domains of food. Bové works to spread the discourse, enrolling other groups into adopting the term. By aligning a wide set of groups under the banner of food sovereignty, alter-globalization activists hope to more effectively resist the disciplining powers of the wto.

Actors like Bové teach groups to recast problems of food related to the wto into discourses of food sovereignty. In so doing, Bové enacts a counterhegemony that may be internationalized and solidified. By invoking food sovereignty discourse, Bové and others turn the discursive tables, displacing food-related language used by the wto. Simply by framing food in terms of sovereignty, subaltern actors inspire others to frame food according to a solidarity-based logic of social justice, self-determination, and cultural autonomy. According to Bové, there are trade practices as troubling as the wto. Bové and the union are concerned with Economic Partnership Agreements that represent micro-level trade agreements that focus on smaller, more malleable clusters of vulnerable countries (personal communication, July 12, 2007). Through Economic Partnership Agreements, neoliberal trade agents manipulate poorer countries in more insidious ways. Bové is concerned about these more private trade agreements that exist outside the national spotlight. Economic Partnership Agreements have been forged among Korea, Thailand, and the Philippines and between Indonesia and Japan. They have been brokered between eu states and many African countries as well. In these agreements, nations are often coerced into trading their agricultural products for services such as electricity or telecommunications. In addition, state agents trade land that peasants use for subsistence agriculture for areas to be used for industrial and other landfill waste (Stevens 2006).

On the food front, state sovereignty and food sovereignty are often at odds with supranational institutions such as the Codex Alimentarius. Since the WTO was formed in 1994, the Codex Alimentarius has served as the sole body charged with evaluating a country's claims against importing food-stuffs they consider problematic. In other words, the Codex Alimentarius is the sole body that can allow a particular state to keep a specific foodstuff from being imported into its borders. And once again the singular criterion accepted by the Codex Alimentarius for rejecting a foodstuff is risk. The UN originally established the Codex Alimentarius in 1962. Its mission was to serve as a trade commission that would regulate issues of food trade. According to many in the alter-globalization movement, the Codex has become an undemocratic body that protects the interests of corporations rather than citizens destined to eat the foodstuffs it approves. According to many farmers in the Confédération Paysanne, the Codex has been overtaken by the interests of multinationals. At numerous meetings at the union headquarters, paysans discussed frustrations with the ways in which the Codex engaged in pharmaceuticals, agro-chemicals, and biotechnology, as well as other domains. During meetings discussing the WTO and agriculture, paysans expressed frustration regarding the ways in which a powerful international body like the Codex could control what kinds of foods France would be obliged to import.

Although corporations produce the foodstuffs that are presented to the Codex Alimentarius for approval, the Codex does not hold corporations responsible for proving that foodstuffs are risk free. Instead it requires member-states to execute such research. In many cases, member-states refuse to import a foodstuff approved by the Codex Alimentarius without being able to scientifically prove that there is no significant risk. This was the case when the EU refused to import hormone-treated beef. In such cases, countries face harsh economic sanctions for failing to comply with Codex Alimentarius norms. In this way, the Codex Alimentarius is a disciplining power for coercing member-states to align themselves with the objectives of the WTO.

Testing foodstuffs for potential risks is a lengthy, expensive, and complex process. Codex Alimentarius supporters know that few states or grassroots organizations have the capacity to execute risk-based studies. A nation's science bodies are increasingly dependent on private corporations for research monies. Yet corporations producing foodstuffs associated with hormones or GMOS, for instance, need their products to be accepted by the Codex Alimentarius. Thus they are often uninterested in conducting such risk-based research.

The Codex Alimentarius is yet another instance of governmentality in the neoliberal network that upholds the WTO.[5] While promising to protect consumer safety when it comes to food, the Codex subtly compels member-states to become docile bodies that will abide by an instrumental rationality of risk. Issues of social-economic justice, solidarity, and the integrity of social fabrics are deemed irrelevant to matters of free trade. As an antidote to bodies such as the Codex, discourses on state sovereignty function as a form of governmentality. In this instance, one powerful institution attempts to exert rule over the other. In the name of state sovereignty, WTO member-states confront the Codex, invoking a state's rights to protect its populations as an indirect means to contest the power, reach, and legitimacy of supranational bodies such as the WTO (Slaughter 1997, 195). In table 2, we can see two distinct discourses about food, each with its own set of opposing rationalities. While one draws from neoliberal and industrial narratives about food, the other draws from discourses on food sovereignty.

The European Referendum, a Run for President, Parliament, and a New Social Movement

FIGHTING EUROPEAN PRIVATIZATION

From 2003 to 2004, Bové focused more closely on the European front. Concerned with the instrumental logic of privatization, Bové sought to publicize the EU's intent to establish a European constitution that contained a set of neoliberal economic mandates designed to encourage competition for services among member-states. According to the proposed constitution, European member-states would be unable to maintain autonomy in designing their own public health or education systems. Instead, private corporations would compete to "buy" and manage those services within the EU. Most public services would thus be subject to free-market competition. A range

Table 2. Neoliberal industrial discourse versus food sovereignty discourse

AGRICULTURAL ISSUE	NEOLIBERAL INDUSTRIAL DISCOURSE	FOOD SOVEREIGNTY DISCOURSE
Food rationality	Food is a fungible commodity.	Food is a human right linked to culture, identity, and self-determination.
Agricultural rationality	Production is for exports and for the agri-foods industry. Only those who can produce food industrially and efficiently should do so.	Production is for local markets everywhere. All rural peoples have the right to produce food.
Food-pricing rationality	Free market should determine food prices.	Farmers and communities must determine prices that allow for quality of life and food.
Trade rationality	Free trade and deregulation stimulate a robust agricultural economy.	Food and agriculture must be removed from all free-trade agreements.
Food-related health rationality	If the Codex Alimentarius approves a foodstuff as posing no significant threat to health, that food is acceptable and must be imported.	Local communities should be able to determine if a food is healthy (e.g., not containing hormones, GMOs, high-fructose corn syrup, toxic residues, and sugar and fat) and worthy of importation.
Hunger rationality	Hunger is caused by low productivity associated with overpopulation and ineffective industrial production.	Hunger is caused by smallholders' lack of access to land and water and by problems of social inequality.
Resource rationality	Resources such as land, water, and forests should be privatized and controlled by corporations and governments.	Local communities should control their own resources.
Seed rationality	Seeds are a patentable commodity to be genetically modified by multinationals tailoring to the industrial model. GM seeds will stop hunger, solve environmental problems, and improve health.	Seeds are integral to a biological commons and should never be patented. Farmers should always be free to improve, save, or exchange their own seeds. GM seeds interfere with these practices and are generally harmful to health and the environment.

Table 2. *Continued*

AGRICULTURAL ISSUE	NEOLIBERAL INDUSTRIAL DISCOURSE	FOOD SOVEREIGNTY DISCOURSE
Support-to-farmers rationality	Private banks, governments, and corporations should provide rural credit, loans, and subsidies (when possible).	Each country should provide support for smallholders through subsidies and fair loaning and credit practices.
Export rationality	Free trade allows northern countries to fairly and freely sell or donate their surpluses to needy, poor southern nations.	Dumping allows northern countries to destroy southern food economies by saturating them with cheap subsidized foodstuffs.
Smallholder rationality	Smallholders (who do not produce efficiently through the industrial model) should be dramatically reduced.	Smallholders are stewards of seed, lands, and water. Their local knowledges and understanding of internal markets is necessary for creating healthy agricultural systems.
Subsidy rationality	Subsidies allow large-scale northern industrial farmers to produce needed surpluses for agrifoods and export markets.	Northern subsidies lead to dumping. If used ethically, subsidies can be directed toward family farmers to support direct sale and sustainable farming.

of public services including transportation, postal, and public utilities would become privatized and directed by corporations. For Bové, the logic of this constitution represented yet another egregious example of what he calls a "world for sale" (Bové 2001). As we have seen, agriculture is privatized when multinationals attain monopolies on seed production and agrochemical inputs through biological patents. In the same way, multinational corporations work with the WTO and state bodies to allow public services to be privatized. Vandana Shiva calls the biological patent an infringement on the "biological commons" (1999), and Bové and paysans also feel strongly that public services should constitute a public commons under citizen control.

In 2005 Bové and his supporters worked with representatives of The Netherlands to form a bloc strong enough to stop the proposed constitution. On May 29, 2005, 55 percent of the French electorate voted against adopting the constitution. This vote sent shockwaves across Europe (anonymous Confédération Paysanne paysan, personal communication, May 21, 2005). Political agents who supported the constitution spoke out vigorously against the grassroots mobilization that led citizens to reject it. Many supporters framed popular critique of the constitution as a vote against the neoliberal direction that the EU is currently taking (Hainsworth 2006). As is often the case in the alter-globalization movement, members of the extreme Right in France were aligned with the far Left in rejecting the constitution. Both sides regarded the constitution as a form of political and economic centralization that would compromise state sovereignty. Strangely, most French trade unions supported the constitution. The Confédération Paysanne received significant press coverage for departing from the overall trend among French trade unions. It was openly criticized for rejecting the constitution on the basis that it purportedly supported a neoliberal system (de Boisgrollier and Gordon 2005, 17).

BOVÉ FOR PRESIDENT AND PARLIAMENT

Two years after the referendum, Bové continued to focus on neoliberalism, this time using the French electoral system as a forum for raising awareness and support for an antineoliberal movement in France. In February 2007, Bové announced that he and his "antiliberal" party (*liberal* is the French term for neoliberal) would enter the public sphere of the race for the presidency. Deciding it was time to "decree an electoral uprising against economic liberalism," Bové threw his hat into the ring, focusing his campaign on issues such as environment and globalization (*Independent* 2007). French critics of Bové compared his run for president to Ralph Nader's controversial U.S. campaign of 2000. Many feared that Bové, like Nader, would further fracture France's divided Left. They were concerned his run could increase right-wing Sarkozy's chances to win.

Undeterred, Bové continued his presidential campaign. On March 12, 2007, Bové appeared on the French television show *Les 4 vérités*. At the time of the interview, he was both preparing for his campaign and awaiting the court's decision for crop pulls conducted in 2005. Bové was well aware that he would face either house arrest (obliged to wear an electronic bracelet), a night-prison sentence, or a standard prison sentence. Bové was asked by the interviewer how he felt about the sentencing. He responded: "It's a political decision. . . . Clearly, if I'm wearing an electronic bracelet or am obliged to return to prison each night, I will be unable to circulate. I'm an activist. I'm using the electoral system as a way to communicate a clear antineoliberal message. Clearly, they are conducting their own prison campaign as a way to make my own political campaign impossible" (my translation). Bové explained during this interview that his presidential campaign created a space in which he could bring together members of the Communist and Green Parties as well as citizens to fight for a unified cause. In this interview Bové explains why he chose to run for president: "You can't change society without challenging the logic of the WTO, the European trade agreements, and the privatization of public services. We don't just want a new referendum for a different European constitution. We want a new European citizen, not a European free market. Sarkozy is a dangerous man. I will do all I can to fight the Right." Bové's position was clear. By asserting the need for more than a series of single objectives, he called for a new logic. Through his campaign, he articulated the need for a "new European citizen," one infused with a rationality built out of solidarity rather than capitalist individualism.

By March 2007, Bové secured the forty thousand signatures from citizens and five hundred signatures from elected officials necessary to enter the race. He thus became one of eleven candidates to run for the presidency. Yet on April 22 he learned that he lacked a majority vote needed to continue on to the main election. In the primaries, Bové had received 1.32 percent of the popular vote, equaling 483,000 votes. On May 6, right-wing candidate Sarkozy was elected president.

According to a key union secretary, Pascale R., from the start everyone at the union considered Bové's run symbolic. They saw his campaign as potentially opening a space in which to stimulate public debate. "You have to admit, though," said Pascale R., "close to half a million votes was something. It showed there's a voice in this country that would like to be heard" (personal communication, April 19, 2008). Bové's run for the presidency kept the union's name and vision of solidarity in the press. During this time, the union was able to further extend its visibility and potency in the French media. As in his early years of celebrity, wherever Bové traveled, so went the name of the union. And as usual, the media presented Bové as "former leader of the Confédération Paysanne" even though the nonhierarchical union has no leaders per se.

Undeterred by his symbolic, yet failed, run for president, Bové decided to run for the European Parliament in 2009. By the time parliamentary elections were held, he was the top candidate for the southwestern European constituency. He was chosen as a member of Europe Ecologie, a powerful coalition of environmentalist political parties, including the Green Party. EuroparlTV reported that on June 7, 2009, Europe Ecologie won more than 16 percent in a proportional election system. Bové sees his role as parliamentarian as a mandate to keep issues such as GMOs at the forefront of public environmental discourse. He has tremendous support in this endeavor: to date, twenty-three out of twenty-seven members of the European Parliament are against lifting the de facto moratorium on genetically modified crops. But, as usual, Bové's focus is not fused to a single issue such as GMOs. He continues to contextualize single issues within a broader economic and social system that could shape a new world where a solidarity-based logic infuses education, environment, and work. Bové said to me in an interview: "We must transcend the logic of the market. We must focus on education and environment—issues faced by everyone. As for the question of agriculture, it is clear that farmers across the world must be able to make a viable living from their work" (personal communication, February 18, 2009).

AMIES DE LA CONFÉDÉRATION PAYSANNE AND LES FAUCHEURS VOLONTAIRES: BACK ON THE LARZAC TRACK

As Bové's popularity soared in the early years after the McDo incident, the union received much media coverage, flagging the organization as a dynamic site for civic attention and activism. For months the union was inundated with calls and e-mails from French activists outside the farming world seeking to join paysans' demonstrations and other activities. In 2000, the union founded the organization Amies de la Confédération Paysanne (Friends of the Confédération Paysanne). Since its formation, the association has offered an engaging website, conferences, and other events that provide a forum where those outside the farming world may work together with paysans to fight for a shared cause. Amies de la Confédération Paysanne is an exciting example of the new social movements that are emerging across various postindustrial, post-Marxist landscapes. Here we see the rise of sectors of civil society questioning systems of food production as well as the rationality behind industrial capitalism itself. The post-Marxist nature of such endeavors speaks to the rise of movements that focus beyond questions of labor and class. Dedicated to preserving paysan identity and culture, Amies de la Confédération Paysanne also addresses problems of GMOs and antinuclear activism and provides ways for activists to join international discussions and actions related to food sovereignty and free trade.

Amies de la Confédération Paysanne has a key historical precedent, the Larzac. When that movement came to a close in 1981, a group of paysans in the south-central Avéyron region established the Larzac Foundation in 1982. Paysans created the foundation, seeking to sustain an arena in which farmers and nonfarmers could continue to support each other's political goals. After the events surrounding Bové and McDo in 1999, the foundation changed its name to Larzac-Solidarités (Larzac in Solidarity). Today, Larzac-Solidarités focuses still on paysans' rights, and it also works to promote French anti-nuclear activism and conducts Palestinian support work. Today, Amies de la Confédération Paysanne and Larzac-Solidarités represent crucial bridges between French rural and urban worlds. Such alliances are still relatively novel in a country that has traditionally located political activity within domains of political parties and unions.

The Confédération Paysanne is the first major French union to become a truly heterogeneous entity, establishing robust activist forums for actors whose identities extend beyond realms of agriculture, labor, and class. Beginning in 2004, Bové and the union launched yet another successful civil society initiative, the Faucheurs Volontaires (Voluntary Reapers). The Faucheurs Volontaires are a group of paysans and nonfarmers from across France who echo the spirit of the Larzac. The Faucheurs Volontaires' main activity is engaging in almost monthly crop pulls of genetically modified crops growing in open-air field trials throughout the country. Using the union's comical and rhetorical style, the Faucheurs Volontaires describes its crop pulls as "neutralizing GMOs" (*neutralisant*) the way one might neutralize a toxic substance or a dangerous force, rendering it harmless (personal communication with an anonymous faucheur, September 21, 2010). Whereas nonfarmers had often participated informally in Confédération Paysanne crop pulls, the formation of the Faucheurs Volontaires formalized their involvement in anti-GMO actions.

When the Faucheurs Volontaires was first founded, the group applied for, but was denied, the political and economic status awarded French nonprofit associations.[6] The Faucheurs Volontaires is a bit of a French anomaly, acting more like an autonomous grassroots organization than an official association or party. French grassroots movements that lie outside political parties, unions, or government-approved associations have limited history and political clout. The relative success of the Faucheurs Volontaires thus represents a historically intriguing coup for its members. Linked to but independent of the Confédération Paysanne, the Faucheurs Volontaires unites alter-globalization youths, ordinary citizens, and members and leaders of ecology and consumer groups. During crop pulls, Faucheurs Volontaires members tread through field tests and commercialized sites, symbolically or literally reaping plants, sometimes wearing hazard suits in the style of Greenpeace, and other times dressed in jeans and T-shirts. Building on the post-McDo sensibility that sent a message of inclusivity and expansiveness to those outside the farming world, the Faucheurs Volontaires also retains the sensibility of May 1968. Protestors often wear whimsical costumes, banging on drums and dancing in the streets during rallies and political actions.

Since their introduction to France in the early 1990s, nearly all genetically modified crops cultivated in France have gone through experimental field tests. In such field tests, a private company or public science body (or both) pays an individual farmer to plant and harvest experimental crops. The precise location of such experiments, by law, must be posted at the local prefecture or town hall of a municipality. Such public postings make field tests identifiable to anti-GMO activists intent on conducting crop pulls.

Various Faucheurs Volontaires members place their videos of particular actions on the Internet. In many of the videos, one can see Bové, other paysans, and anti-GMO activists marching through fields, breaking cornstalks in a jovial fashion. Because all of the videos are made by French activists and are in French, I'll describe one I found that is typical of the kind posted.

In March 2006, I found a video titled "Fauchage 2006." In the video an anonymous young man faces the camera, seated in a car on the way to an action. He states the date, February 2, 2006, saying, "This is my first Faucheur action. I'm kind of excited about it." He states that the Faucheurs Volontaires members that day will number three hundred and will take down fifteen hectares of genetically modified corn. In the next scene we see a group of activists composed primarily of young men and women along with a few older activists. In a sort of scattered fashion, the group makes its way to a dirt road facing a set of cornfields. Some are wearing T-shirts with the Faucheurs Volontaires logo and graphic. Several young men amble around shirtless, sporting long dreads. In the next sequence, Bové appears on the scene, holding a small megaphone and directing the crowd. In his usual rapid-fire, no-nonsense speaking style, he directs everyone to stay in line, one behind the other, as they make their way through the field. "Stay together," he warns the group. Those who have conducted crop pulls are aware of the hazards associated with the practice. In addition to getting terribly lost in the great maze of cornfields, activists are at risk of getting quietly picked away from the scene by police. As the group sets off into the fields, there is an air of celebration. Over the sound of snapping corn, the video captures the activists giggling, cheering each other on as they break cornstalks over their knees. This action is a symbolic reaping because the activists are breaking the cornstalks rather than gathering them in garbage bags to subsequently plop before a town hall.

As the scene progresses, a few police officers appear in the field, as well as some press. Bové stands among the busy Faucheurs Volontaires members, speaking into a series of microphones. He talks in serious tones about the lack of public debate on GMOs as well as their dangers and implications for the world's farmers. As this scene unfolds, the few police officers stand with crossed arms, wearing bemused expressions. Some appear to be bantering good-naturedly with activists who are still busy at work thwacking stalks of corn over their knees. At the end of this sequence, the field is determined done. Bové asks the Faucheurs Volontaires members to remain in their groups as they return from the cornfield to the road. As they file out of the field in lines, the activists chant, "J'en veux pas des OGM" (I don't want no GMOs). Back on the dirt road, Bové explains that the owner of the field is about to arrive, bringing with him more police officers. He instructs the group members to decide who among them will volunteer to be arrested. By signing their names on police officers' clipboards, the participants admit to committing an act of civil disobedience. From the video, it appears about ten Faucheurs Volontaires volunteer to be arrested along with Bové.

In the next scene an energetic rally explodes outside the police station as the Faucheurs Volontaires members who were not arrested await the arrival of their arrested comrades by police car. When the vehicles arrive, several of the free members conduct a temporary sit-in before the car, blocking its passage. Meanwhile, a dreadlocked, shirtless young man sings and plays his guitar in a reggae style, smiling and laughing before a shaky handheld camera. A helicopter eerily hovers over the small and impromptu rally. After the arrested Faucheurs Volontaires members are escorted into the police station, the rally steps up its energy as night falls. Nearly everyone in the crowd is tapping on some type of metal object. While an older woman in a wheelchair smiles, ringing a small bell, young men hammer their hands on street signs, bang on the windows of the police building, and beat on drums, cymbals, and tin can lids. All together the demonstrators chant at hypnotic speed, "Liberez nos comrades! Liberez nos comrades!" (Free our comrades!). In the final scene a man exits the police station and informs the crowd that the arrested will not be detained. Everyone cheers and more drumming ensues.

From 2003 to 2004, forty-nine individuals were arrested for destroying several Monsanto-funded field trials. In many instances, activists were tried in tribunals rather than regular courts of law. In France, tribunals are often created in small towns or villages where a formal court of law does not exist. In December 2005, after a well-publicized trial, the court of Orléans made a historic decision when it dropped charges against the forty-nine arrested. According to the judge, the Faucheurs Volontaires members acted out of necessity, asserting that the state had not provided adequate and necessary precautions and had thus failed to protect human rights to a healthy environment (José Bové, personal communication, April 18, 2006).

In July 2008, the struggle of the Faucheurs Volontaires and the Confédération Paysanne continued. The Confédération Paysanne published a press release titled "OGM: Le Principe de precaution pour preserver des paysans droit de travailler" (GMOs: The precaution principle to preserve the paysan's right to work) (Confédération Paysanne 2008b). According to the press release from July 2, 2008, five activists faced the local judge of Carcassone to address crop pulls carried out in 2006 in Trebes (in the Aude region of France). Using its signature rhetorical style, the union stated that the activists in question were participating in "citizen-based 'research' on MON810 corn," and that by arresting them, state bodies were obstructing paysans' "right to work" (my translation). According to this logic, the Faucheurs Volontaires members, as French citizens, were assisting the union in carrying out important research-based work necessary to maintaining paysans' status as farmers. In response, Monsanto representatives argued that it was in fact their company whose "freedom to work" was obstructed by the Faucheurs Volontaires. At the trial itself, twenty-four Faucheurs Volontaires members stepped forward, joining the arrested five, stating that they too had participated in the research conducted by the group that day. In response, the tribunal formally recognized the collective nature of the research and agreed to frame the event as an act of civil disobedience rather than a mere act of property damage. In French courts, only paid workers, or members of state-recognized associations, have the right to make "obstructions to work" claims. As Monsanto was neither a worker nor an association, its charges held no weight in the French legal system. Lawyers for the Confédération Paysanne argued that the state itself was responsible for having created a situation in which the Faucheurs Volontaires had become obligated to defend the precaution principle. According to this logic, Monsanto was abusing the precaution principle by planting MON810. Having conducted inadequate field trials for the product, Monsanto was accused of potentially contaminating fields in the area that was GMO free.

The Confédération Paysanne awaited its next appearance before the tribunal on September 17, 2008. The union planned to argue for the incompatibility between genetically modified crops and nonmodified crops in open-air fields. In addition, it invoked critical discourses, including the "monopolization of life" by private corporations such as multinationals. It also made a case for the collective rights of paysans and citizens to protect and maintain a future in which paysans have the right to work to unite as citizens to fight for healthy and quality food (Confédération Paysanne 2008b). Once again the Confédération Paysanne effectively stretched the discursive field beyond questions of GMO-related risk. In addition to talking about food safety, it also invoked solidarity-based notions of workers' rights, the rights of ordinary citizens to healthy and quality food, and the commoditization of life.

Two years later, Faucheurs Volontaires was still in full swing and continued to address current GMO-related issues and participate in trials that dragged on for years. In February 2010, the union issued the following press release: "OGM, Malgré la moratoire: Le procé continue, le combat continue!" (GMOs, Despite the moratorium: The trial continues, the combat continues!) According to the press release, Bové and Isabelle Ibarrondo (a paysan from the Herault region of France) faced a judge in Beziers just a few days prior. The two were summoned for participating in a symbolic crop pull of 14 square meters (150 square feet) of Monsanto's MON810 corn along with 150 other Faucheurs Volontaires members in August 2007. Taking emblematic Faucheurs Volontaires action, activists dumped a truckload of uprooted genetically modified corn before a police station, and the officers agreed that the pile was a public menace. Activists in turn demanded that police ask the French government to respect its moratorium on cultivating GMOs. Just three months earlier, out of respect to the precaution principle, the government had finally put the moratorium in place. For Bové and Ilbarrondo, the state's actions were contradictory. While recommitting itself to the precaution principle, the government accused the Faucheurs Volontaires of wrongdoing. According to the Confédération Paysanne's press release, "the state is denying a collective and deeply anchored social movement that has continually refused GMOs in France. Despite the moratorium, the GMO menace persists along with the trials against them. The combat will thus continue!" The union announced its continued support for Bové and Ilbarrondo during their trial.

Faucheurs Volontaires continued to keep both the union and the GMO issue on the French map. In addition, each arrest and trial served to use the legal system as a forum in which to conduct public debate on social issues. The GMO issue is economic, cultural, and political in nature. Single issues such as GMOs are inseparable from broader issues such as the vitality of the rural sphere and the commoditization of life in general. The union kept the nation's finger on the pulse of a wider set of questions regarding the kind of logic that should infuse agriculture or life itself. Should it be one of instrumental profit or one of solidarity?

GMOS AND FRANCE: LA LUTTE CONTINUED . . .

To understand the place and meaning of the French GMO moratorium, it is useful to look back to the mid-2000s. In February 2006, the WTO announced that Europe had violated international trade policies by restricting the cultivation of genetically modified foods for commercial use. This ruling formally ended the de facto GMO moratorium in Europe that had been in place since 1998. This moratorium, known in France as the Engagements du Grenelle (Grenelle Engagements), emerged from a series of negotiations among a broad and diverse network of actors working to prevent future commercialization of genetically modified seeds in France. While some feared for the future of small French seed companies, others were concerned about problems of irreversibility that occur when genetically modified fields cross-pollinate with other fields and contaminate them permanently. Yet others understood that furthering the model of agriculture associated with GMOs would prove ruinous to the last of French paysans. The fate of the Engagements du Grennelle remained unclear following the ruling by the WTO in

2006. The French presidential elections were only a year away. With a generally anti-GMO political climate in France, no incoming candidate wanted to take a positive stance on GMOs.

At the time, I communicated with a union representative, Alan P., who captured the general feeling at the union: "Commercialized GMOs or experimental GMOs. We don't want any of it. The WTO's ruling will not stop our cause." As the de facto moratorium came to a close, government actors braced themselves for considerable public criticism. In April 2007, France's new right-wing president, Nicolas Sarkozy, came into power. At first, Sarkozy attempted to maintain public support by skirting the issue of GMOs, deploying ambiguous discourses on food quality and environment. Desperate for popular support, Sarkozy did his best to demonstrate to the public that he had sound environmental politics and would thus protect the nation's food supply. Later that year, however, Sarkozy capitulated. He publicly stated that France would comply with the WTO's demand to lift the ban on the commercialization of GMOs on French soil. Even while complying with the trade body, Sarkozy did not want to lose support of the populace. Sarkozy and the ministry of environment publicly announced they would continue to respect the Engagements du Grennelle by maintaining a freeze on all genetically modified seeds, except one variety of Monsanto's corn, MON810. All other GMO seeds remained banned for commercial use. Bové and the Faucheurs Volontaires were not assuaged by Sarkozy's promise. According to Bové and many at the union, it would only be a matter of time before Sarkozy broke his agreement to "respect the Engagements du Grennelle" (personal communication with anonymous union national secretary, March, 19, 2007). Indeed, one month after Sarkozy stated he would respect the Engagements du Grennelle, he announced that this decision would remain in place only until the completion of a full review of GMO technologies, which would be done by February 9, 2008.

Preempting Sarkozy's February 2008 decision, Bové and the Faucheurs Volontaires launched a campaign one month before Sarkozy's verdict was due. They used a Gandhian pacifist tactic practiced by members of the new paysan movements of the 1970s: a hunger strike. On January 3, Bové and fifteen members of the Faucheurs Volontaires received significant media attention when they publicly announced a one-month hunger strike during which the fasters would ingest nothing but water. In 1990, Bové conducted a similar hunger strike, drinking only mineral water for eighteen days. At that time, he was protesting the then president Mitterrand's proposed changes to agricultural subsidies for farmers. This time, Bové and the other protesters said they would "not eat until the government imposes a year-long ban on genetically modified crops" (translation mine) (Agence France-Presse, January 1, 2008). In television coverage of the event by Canal 2's evening news on January 2, French viewers watched Bové and fifteen others drag mattresses and bedding up a flight of stairs into an empty studio occupied by press and supporters. When interviewed, Bové asserted the necessity of the strike: "At times like these, what other means of protest are left to us? Protesting in the streets? We are unwilling to passively await the decision of Sarkozy to come out in one month—a decision that might simply be then delayed for yet another month. We want a firm confirmation that Sarkozy will respect the Engagements du Grennelle."

The term *Engagements du Grennelle* is historically significant. Protestors initially coined the term *Grenelle* during negotiations following the May 1968 riots. After a month of intense political conflict, the French labor ministry drew up the Grenelle Engagements at its headquarters on the Rue de Grenelle in Paris. Since that time, the term *Grenelle* has been generally defined as an inclusive multiparty debate that brings together governmental actors as well as nongovernmental actors such as members of various political associations. As Henri M. at the union suggests, "A Grenelle is like one endless meeting that brings together a bunch of otherwise disparate groups" (personal communication, March 3, 2008). The fusion of the term *Grenelle* and the GMO issue signaled the continuation of the 1968 sensibility of autonomy that marked this period. *Grenelle* became a keyword, forming what Williams calls a "network of usage," clustered with terms such as GMO, *neoliberalism*, and *free trade* (1976). Just as 1968 brought together students, workers, university professors, and farmers, the question of GMOs also convened a heterogeneous set of actors such as farmers, consumers, ecologists, and antineoliberalists. This Grenelle articulated a cultural logic that deviated from the instrumental sensibility of capital-driven society.

As for those engaged in the hunger strike, they were able to promptly put an end to their ordeal. Seven days after the strike began, Sarkozy made an agreement to "respect the Engagements du Grennelle" (Agence France Press, January 9, 2008). The de facto moratorium on commercialized seeds (excluding MON810) remained in place. Thus, when the Faucheurs Volontaires conducted its crop pull of MON810 in 2007, it was in direct protest to a partial moratorium on just one crop perceived as contradictory, unjust, and unacceptable.

On July 14, 2010, Britain's journal the *Ecologist* made a dramatic announcement. Journalists wrote that the EU had promised to end the current model for making GMO policy on a European level. Such a move allowed individual European nations the right to determine their own GMO policies (*Ecologist* 2010). Yet according to M. Rougest, a national secretary at the Confédération Paysanne, this news was not all that it seemed to be: "Now, pro-GMO countries will have the ease of hurrying through the EU authorization process on particular GM crops" (personal communication, January 19, 2000). Stefanie Hundsdorfer echoed this sentiment in the *Ecologist*, asserting that "individual bans cannot replace a scientifically sound EU-level safety procedure as contamination (from genetically modified crops) does not stop at national borders" (*Ecologist* 2010, 27). For paysan M. Rouget, "The EU simply wants to appease pro-GMO countries. It just recently authorized the first genetically modified crop in twelve years, a starch potato. The Confédération Paysanne will continue to fight this trend to, little by little, end the moratorium" (personal communication, August 20, 2010).

THE CONFÉDÉRATION PAYSANNE AND THE WTO TODAY: FAILURES AND COLLAPSES?

Since the WTO's formation in 1994, its meetings have served as focal points for popular protest from civil society groups. While the Battle of Seattle in 1999 garnered the most international attention, the Doha Round of the WTO (that began in 2001) also provided sites for ongoing protests by groups representing disenfranchised sets of small-scale farmers, fishers, workers, indigenous peoples, women's groups, and citizens' groups. While protests take place at (or near) WTO sessions, the meetings also spawn protests in capital cities globally. Before and during each meeting, civil society actors from across the world travel to Geneva, reminding delegates of the trade body of their demands. They work continually to remind delegates of the political consequences that may ensue at home should they make damaging compromises (Wallach 2008, 1).

The Doha Round in particular has been marked by a series of seemingly irreconcilable disagreements between rich and poor countries. More often than not, these conflicts lead to meetings described as "failures" and "collapsed." Drawing from Williams (1976), I assert that *failure* and *collapse* have become keywords in discourse related to the WTO. These keywords form networks of usage with other terms such as *conflict* and *public opposition*. When using Google to search for the terms *WTO* and *failure*, 5,200,000 entries surfaced. *Collapse* summoned about half as many, 2,770,000 entries. *WTO success* brought forth only 32,900. After scrolling carefully through pages of *WTO success* entries, I noted that many references to *success* were reporters' speculative hopes for successful outcomes in the future, near successes, or hopes for relative success in a larger context of "failures." As there are fewer posts written in French on the Internet, it was intriguing to note that when I searched for the French term *OMC échec* (WTO failure), there were 383,000 entries. *OMC conflict* rang up 342,000. *OMC réussite* (success) struck 182,000.[7]

A press statement by Lori Wallach of Public Citizen is an example of the negative narratives that surround the WTO today. Wallach reflects on a collapse of the Doha Round of WTO negotiations that took place in Qatar in July 2008: "Countries' unwillingness to concede on particular themes is the proximate cause for the collapse, but government positions were based on strong public opposition in many poor and rich nations alike to expanding WTO scope and authority after more than a decade of experience of the WTO's damaging outcomes. By calling a ministerial summit to try to force agreement on a WTO expansion agenda opposed by many countries, WTO Secretary General Pascal Lamy set up the conditions for yet another direct blow to the beleaguered global commerce agency's shaky legitimacy" (Wallach 2008, 1). As the director of Public Citizen, Wallach is a major actor in the alter-globalization network. By describing the WTO as "beleaguered" and "shaky," she speaks indirectly to the role played by civil society in destabilizing the WTO. For Wallach, civil society agents are effectively preventing the organization from expanding its reach, achieving its goals, and marshaling power against poor countries. Actors such as Wallach often describe resistance to the trade body by invoking a social-justice framework. She contrasts a solidarity-based logic of civil society actors against the neoliberal and instrumental profit-seeking logic of the WTO.

At the Confédération Paysanne, a similar discussion emerged regarding the failures associated with the Doha Round. In two press releases issued in July 2008, the Confédération Paysanne comments on the ongoing failure of trade negotiations. According to the union member Dominique Marcel,

"Such failures lead many to consider the future viability and legitimacy of the organization itself" (personal communication, August 15, 2008). As Marcel suggests, trade-related conflicts between northern and southern countries will continue to prevent the organization from opening global markets for the benefit of wealthier nations. As poor countries increasingly receive the support of international progressive grassroots and nongovernmental organizations such as La Via Campesina, leaders of poor nations appear to be emboldened, refusing to accept the disciplining power of the WTO itself.

These are two excerpts taken from the press releases issued in 2008 on July 29 and July 30. Each provides a window into the Confédération Paysanne's response to the policies of the WTO:

> International governments must appreciate the urgency of establishing international rules supporting production, producers, and consumers — rather than economic speculation. India's and China's ability to maintain agricultural systems, despite importations, is a step in the right direction toward food sovereignty. We need a global organization that supports the livelihoods of family and small-scale farmers. . . . For years, proponents of free trade promised we'd soon be praising the benefits of open markets. The reality of these last months, with soaring food prices, proves that this is neither the best means for food production nor the best means for distributing food in a climate of popular need. (Confédération Paysanne 2008b; my translation)

> The Confédération Paysanne denounces the all-out marketing associated with the WTO. Most countries do not wish to see these negotiations continue. The key points of disagreement rightly concern agriculture. The desire to sell off agriculture, goods, and services for next to nothing, for the sole benefit of commercial exchange, is unacceptable. Any agreement that ends with an obligation to lower the rights to tax [imports] will essentially lead to an unsound agreement. The Confédération Paysanne reasserts that all agricultural policy must focus on the protection of borders. A true study of the effects of deregulated markets must be completed. The absence of protection of agricultural markets means an open door to speculation — a situation that will lead to dramatic consequences in domains of food, society, and ecology. . . . For the sake of food sovereignty, a right that more and more countries demand, the WTO must get out of agriculture! (Confédération Paysanne 2008a; my translation)

We see the ongoing tension played out between an instrumental logic of neoliberal capital and a rationality of solidarity. In the first release, we see the Confédération Paysanne call for international rules that would support peoples rather than speculators. There is a clash between two irreconcilable logics, one humanitarian and the other individualistic and profit-oriented, in "OMC: Un échec porteur d'espoir" (WTO: Failure brings hope). The second release, issued the day after, "OMC: Mieux vaut pas d'accord plutôt qu'une braderie" (WTO: Better forgo an agreement than gain a sell-out), contests the instrumental logic of the WTO, which reduces agriculture, food, goods, and services to mere commodities for commercial exchange. According to these statements, "dramatic consequences" for food, society, and ecology will ensue should the WTO's instrumental logic be allowed to reign unfettered. Both press releases invoke food sovereignty discourse, demonstrating how this new counterhegemonic discourse is bolstering claims against the WTO. In these releases, the Confédération Paysanne strived to solidify a logic of solidarity embedded in food sovereignty discourse that stands in contrast to market logic. The last sentence, written in a moralistic voice ("For the sake of food sovereignty"), portrays the idea of food sovereignty as an increasingly international demand. Gaining international status, the discourse amplifies and legitimizes a collective insistence by many subaltern groups to remove food items and agricultural products from WTO guidelines altogether.

THE CONFÉDÉRATION PAYSANNE'S POLITICAL STATUS TODAY

It is a precarious endeavor to determine the relative success or failure of an organization at any given time in history. Each year presents a new set of economic and political challenges and opportunities. The union reached its highest level of measurable success in 2003 by winning 28 percent of the seats in the chamber of agriculture. But by 2011, that number came back down to 20 percent. It had returned to the same percentage as in 1997, when I first encountered the Confédération Paysanne. But as this story illustrates, questions of success and failures are complex and contradictory in any social movement. While the number of seats won in the chamber of agriculture is significant, there are so many other factors at play that shape the societal effects of the Confédération Paysanne in France and internationally.

Benoir Grenart has been a key salarier at the union for more than fifteen years. According to Grenart, the union is currently trying to maintain political ground during a period when France is led by a right-wing president: "It isn't easy [*c'est pas évident*] to do this when the president has a strong neoliberal vision. This isn't good for the country and its agricultural system" (personal communication, January 19, 2011). Grenart commented on Bové's ongoing commitment to the union through his work on Roquefort producers' rights and supporting the Faucheurs Volontaires: "As Bové no longer holds a central official title in the union, he is now simply a vital and active member." According to Grenart, since Nérac there have been divergent views among union members about Bové's tactics and objectives: "While many support Bové, happy with his efforts to establish the union as a site for serious economic change, others are critical of Bové's vision." As Grenart suggests, "Many see the Conf. as a vehicle for reforming or improving agricultural systems within a social democracy—not for dramatically transforming social democracy itself." Yet, he adds, "Bové is tremendously valued at the Conf. He's given so much to strengthen it, to really see where it could go— even if there have been real limits constraining what the Conf. could ultimately do within the system."

Today, the union is still vigorous and optimistic, yet struggling. It is not alone, as many progressive organizations struggle in an era of increasing neoliberalism. "What can you do?" said Sophie T., a union paysan who has worked for decades to further the cause: "You have to be optimistic. If you're not, well, then, that's not very helpful to others, is it? My optimism is solidarity. It's in solidarity with those who have even less than we do that we continue the struggle. And things always change. Who would have thought, in 1997, that the WTO would be seen as a failure? Or that GMOs would be still banned? Or that we'd have gotten where we are now? We have a name that's respected. I would never have thought all this could happen" (personal communication, February 11, 2010).

On the union's website, an invitation went out to paysans and supporters to participate in three days of debate, "L'avenir des paysans et des aliments que nous desirons" (The future of paysans and the food we desire). From June 29 to July 1, 2011, demonstrators were asked to meet directly next to the Assemblée Nationale (French National Assembly) in Paris. Established during the French Revolution, the Assemblée Nationale constitutes one of two houses of the parliament (the other house being the Senate). The Assemblée Nationale is currently reexamining the Loi de Modernization Agricole (Law of Agricultural Modernization). According to the union, the law restructures "a model of agriculture that leads to the further disappearance of paysans."

The union's call for direct action says, "The disengagement of a state that replaces solidarity for profit-driven private insurance . . . signal[s] an end to a model of agriculture grounded in sound public policy. . . . For three days, paysans will demand an end to neoliberalism dictated by the WTO. From this day onward, let us create a project based on the right to food sovereignty" (my translation). For three days, paysans from throughout the country brought their protest to Paris. In doing so, the union hoped to show France, Europe, and the world that they will continue to pursue a logic of solidarity in domains of food and life itself.

Conclusion

The postindustrial condition gave rise to new sets of civil society actors seeking a logic to guide society. The willingness among much of the French populace to accept Bové as a national hero speaks to a societal desire for original forms and expressions of social solidarity. It also reflects a growing popular critique of a mode of capitalist production that looks at life, food, and humanity through an instrumental lens.

During the early 2000s, Bové and the union drew positive media coverage and political support, transforming arrests, trials, and sentences into arenas to further elaborate a collective alter-globalization message. In a post-Seattle era, Bové went beyond the ordinary role of activist paysan as he embraced an increasingly differentiated set of postindustrial issues. By focusing on global problems such as the privatization of water, electricity, and other services, Bové addressed issues well outside the realm of agriculture. He even countered neoliberal dimensions of the proposed European constitution. In addition to his participation in direct action, Bové's presidential run and his election to the European parliament signal his commitment to continuing the struggle by appealing to policymaking political bodies.

Bové and the union built upon the Larzac tradition to create new organizations such as the Faucheurs Volontaires and Amies de la Confédération Paysanne. As in the Larzac, these organizations brought together actors from both within and outside the farming world to use nonviolent strategies in a shared struggle for an antineoliberal cause. Bové drew upon the national media mightily, attempting to bring awareness to problems associated with neoliberal politics as they grew in prominence toward the end of the decade. A hunger strike, a run for the presidency, and becoming part of the European parliament allowed Bové to keep questions of GMOs and neoliberalism in the popular consciousness.

Since 1999, the Confédération Paysanne has successfully disrupted hegemonic postindustrial discourses on food that often normalize neoliberal industrial agricultural systems of food production. In addition to popularizing the incalculable and cultural- and quality-based term *la malbouffe*, the union has worked to promote discourses on food sovereignty. Unlike discourses on food sustainability and organics, food sovereignty discourse pushes discussions beyond critiques of production methods associated with food quality and safety. In contrast, food sovereignty discourse posits food as a political and cultural human right; food becomes something of great value that cannot be traded away through global markets.

Both the WTO and the Confédération Paysanne have taken a hit during the last few years. Yet both institutions remain standing, so the tale continues. Less powerful sets of actors impact powerful institutions, disrupting hegemonic notions of science, agriculture, and life itself. By staying the course, and articulating a consistent message of solidarity, the Confédération Paysanne has not only managed to survive for more than twenty years; it has flourished, striving to make the world and its inhabitants a little less instrumental and a little more solidaire.

11

Conclusion

*French Lessons; What's
to Be Learned?*

In considering the French case, four main sets of conclusions emerge that may prove useful to both scholars and activists interested in social movements, science controversies, or political ecology: (1) activists need to cultivate discursive reflexivity. This means developing greater self-awareness of the ways that actors construct claims for or against particular social and political issues; (2) food-related social movements need to be located within the postindustrial condition (periodizing the French case in the rubric of postindustriality allowed me to pose sets of questions that were unique to the paysans' situations); (3) the "French contradiction" arises when a nation that actively supports the WTO, globalization, and fast food also supports an alter-globalization movement critical of McDonald's; and (4) anthropologists can begin to develop an anthropology of instrumentalism—an anthropology capable of identifying and analyzing moments when social movements respond to perceived instrumentalism that reduces the world and its inhabitants to commodities.

Discursive Reflexivity

The first lesson I gleaned from studying the French controversy is the importance of discursive reflexivity. I found a consistent lack of awareness among both paysans and alter-globalization activists regarding the ways in which they frame their arguments generally. The immediacy with which actors invoked discourses related to food risk or quality, for instance, reflected limited self-consciousness regarding why (and to what effect) actors chose particular discursive frames in specific contexts. This lack of awareness is linked to a broader problem of hegemonic knowledges. There exists a realm of discussion (and its linguistic components) that remains invisible, dwelling within the realm of the hegemonic, or taken for granted. For example, many take for granted ideas such as *state* or *capitalism* because they are ubiquitous and pervasive. Without even thinking, we accept and receive these components of our society as normal, constant, and immutable. As agents for social change, it is helpful to render the invisible visible, bringing the rationale behind the words we choose to consciousness. Toward that objective, we should critically discuss the various terms we use to define problems and solutions related to particular political struggles. By identifying the keywords that we use, we may explore their deeper histories, studying how their networks of usage have changed over time. In turn, we may examine the forces that led keywords to enjoy the forms of power they muster at particular historical junctures.

In the French case, the term *la malbouffe* constituted a counterhegemonic discourse to risk from 1999 to 2003. By invoking the term, Bové was able to reconfigure the discursive terrain. He established himself and other paysans as experts with access to the food knowledge scientists and other experts lacked. He asserted paysan cultural knowledge as a valid and legitimate frame for evaluating food. He was able to do this despite the fact that powerful institutions such as the WTO and the Codex Alimentarius accepted only risk-related food claims as valid. By 2003, the union's discourse widened beyond discourse of la malbouffe to emphasize food sovereignty. Whereas discussions about la malbouffe allowed paysans to bolster claims about ambiguous notions of food quality, food sovereignty discourse goes a few steps further. It has allowed paysans and others in the alter-globalization movement to establish entirely new criteria for evaluating food practices. Foodstuffs could now be judged on measures associated with issues of social justice and power.

The improvisational nature of social movements leads most activists to establish their frames, terms, and language on a semi-intentional and trial-and-error basis. Activists rarely put their discursive cards on the table to study them critically at the beginning of a political campaign. If they did, however, they might reach their goals in a more transparent, self-conscious, and principled way. In the French case, the union's humanitarian principles of solidarity and social justice took nearly a decade to get out of the gate in the form of food sovereignty discourse that embodied a cogent alter-globalization message. Had union members invoked principles of food quality and social justice simultaneously from the beginning, they may have been better able to push public discussion in a direction that mirrored the union's underlying principles and goals.

Discursive reflexivity leads activists to identify hegemonic discourses, thoughtfully determining how and when to appropriate, contest, or counter these discourses by engendering new ones. In the French case, the discursive shift from food risk to food sovereignty was powerful, and the union expanded beyond an instrumental rationality to include an explicitly solidarity-based framework. This case shows that it often behooves groups to destabilize established hegemonic discourses, moving them from instrumental logics to logics based on social justice. Increasingly, it seems that publics are ready to accept appeals to what is right, just, and ethical rather than what drives the profit motive along.

Discursive reflexivity is crucial. Those who control language determine the terms and actors regarded as legitimate players in a debate. By taking hold of a discursive frame, activists can choose to democratize public discussion. They can widen the range of actors regarded as credible enough to speak about the world in which they live. In the French case, politicians and scientists could speak to GMO-related risk during the first phase of the controversy. From 1999 onward, a range of civil-society agents emerged who felt empowered to speak publicly on the issue. Actors ranging from paysans, consumers, and students to workers and alter-globalization activists believed they had the right to make claims not just about food but about quality of life in the broadest sense.

Locating Food-Related Social Movements
within the Postindustrial Condition

Contextualizing social movements about food and food science within the postindustrial condition allowed me to periodize a contemporary GMO-related controversy. By establishing this story in postindustrial agricultural France, I could identify the special challenges faced by actors in powerful institutions, French smallholders, and alter-globalization activists struggling to make sense of life at this historical juncture. The Confédération Paysanne is a producer-driven movement that must be situated in a postscarcity context. Postwar France gave rise to a postwar agricultural policy. In turn, this policy supported an industrial model that created postscarcity surpluses while also leading to paysans' deplorable postindustrial conditions. Postindustrial agricultural surpluses led to price drops, which edged paysans out of a once robust and diverse French agricultural economy. As subsidy-granting bodies favored extensive large-scale operations, paysans were unable to receive sufficient monies. Union members were thus obliged to devise an alternate production rationality that justified their existence on ethical rather than instrumental grounds.

The union's theme song, "Trois petites fermes, c'est mieux qu'un grand" (Three small farms is better than a big one), establishes the large-scale industrial model as a problem worthy of ethical inquiry. The assertion that smaller farms allow for more smallholders to receive subsidies endows the keyword *small* with a solidarity-based ethos. In this way, agricultural scale assumes ethical meaning against the backdrop of a large-scale industrial model. Industrial agriculture reduces postindustrial paysans to extraneous entities. Those who are lucky are able to eke out a low-income living. Those who are even luckier may receive subsidies to carry out multifunctional tasks, such as maintaining the tourist aesthetic of rural zones. It is also vital to locate the agro-foods industry, and export-agriculture, within the context of post-industriality. Doing so helps shed light on the new ways that farmers are called upon to produce foodstuffs not for direct consumption but for industrial production, export, and trade articulations. This requirement demands that farmers produce new kinds of products for historically novel destinations and systems. While industrial-scale growers provide materials destined, for example, for industry and trade, paysans are unable to compete with large-scale producers for subsidies. In a postindustrial context, paysans must reinvent themselves as morally and culturally superior entities, distinct from industrial counterparts such as FNSEA farmers.

This story also shows how postindustrial agriculture is integral to the Global South. French paysans translate the survival of the individual smallholder into a question of international humanitarianism that they extend to their southern comrades. Eschewing an individualistic logic, they appeal to a solidaire rationality. They contest the effects of both industrial and postindustrial conditions on smallholders who are disenfranchised by the agricultural market worldwide. For union paysans, agricultural dumping on smallholders in the Global South is an egregious instance of postindustrial agriculture. They feel a moral responsibility to fight dumping just as they would resist any practice that threatened smallholders struggling to survive. And then food sovereignty discourse went global after La Via Campesina invoked it to unite smallholders resisting a dehumanizing postindustrial agricultural condition. Smallholders from both the Global North and South now stand together under a common banner of agricultural humanistic solidarity.

By contextualizing food debates in a postindustrial agricultural condition, we can identify counterstrategies devised by smallholders placed in an unusual situation. By establishing themselves as more than moral agents, smallholders present themselves as possessing rural and cultural expertise that extends beyond realms of food production. Working in concert with subsidy bodies, union paysans developed discourses and practices such as multifunctionality. While many in the union see multifunctionality as problematic, others see it as a necessary evil. For others in the Global South, the idea of multifunctionality-based subsidies is appealing. Many look to this northern practice in hopes that southern governments may consider adopting the model. Multifunctionality, as a northern discourse, is indeed a postindustrial condition. It obliges European smallholders to revise their self-understandings as actors charged with serving communities by engaging in rural beautification practices outside the realm of food production.

Understanding postindustrial agriculture as both a national and global condition also enabled me to historically locate the cacophony of critical discourses surrounding food associated with the postindustrial period. Early on in my research, I noted how discourses on food-related health, risk, and quality functioned as forms of governmentality. I was thus able to note the ways in which particular food discourses muted and veiled underlying machinations of power that sought to strengthen the industrial model (Inda 2005). Early in my research I also came to appreciate how discourses of risk constituted a form of governmentality. The governmentality concept, first developed by Foucault (1991), provided a framework for understanding how actors in powerful institutions (e.g., science and state bodies) appeal to hegemonic discourses. Over time I was able to appreciate how various actors use risk discourse as a technique of postindustrial governance. When actors frame GMOs by invoking risk, they discipline paysans and other nonscientists within the societal controversy. The social-justice analysis of GMOs is rendered invisible or simply invalid. Identifying risk as a powerful discourse led me to appreciate the work it performs in normalizing practices associated with biotechnology, industrial agriculture, and agro-foods industries. Knowingly or unknowingly, actors in science and state bodies deploy risk discourse to depoliticize discussions about agricultural policy (see McCullough, Pingali, and Stamoulis 2005; Vorley 2004).

As I cultivated my own discursive reflexivity, I could identify moments when paysans reproduced dominant discourses on food risk and quality in their attempts to establish themselves as valid brokers in GMO food debates. By invoking narratives about la malbouffe, paysans granted themselves cultural authority to speak about the value of artisanal, traditional, and even organic foods. They were able to assert cultural authority about agriculture even though many paysans use chemicals and petroleum-based production methods, albeit on a small scale. The contradictions of the "chemicalized paysan," I argue, are born out of a postindustrial condition. While some union paysans do use artisanal or organic production methods, others find such practices financially or culturally inaccessible. These paysans are obligated to negotiate paths through a complex set of societal expectations that require paysans to present themselves in particular ways. They are compelled to devise creative and often contradictory strategies to establish their identities and farm practices as necessary in a system that largely establishes them as expendable (Goodman and Redclift 1991).

I was particularly struck by the ways that postindustrial agriculture calls upon both producers and consumers to make sense of changing food systems. The emerging agro-foods and fast-food industries, as well as changing subsidy policies that favor an industrial model, emerged in a relatively short period of time following World War II. The eruption of moralistic discourses on agriculture signals a moment when sectors of the French public try to maintain a sense of cultural control over their food supply within a rapidly changing system. Value-laden narratives about food's naturalness, sustainability, quality, or artisanal status represent ways that actors, powerful and disenfranchised, attempt to establish new ways of talking about food in a historically novel postindustrial landscape.

Once I viewed GMOs as a postindustrial artifact, I came to understand how agricultural biotechnology came to be used by so many farmers when there is so little data indicating that GMO seeds provide long-term benefits, such as reduced pesticide or increased production. In speaking with many officials at biotechnology companies, I became aware that a product does not have to increase production per se to be successful. The hype generated by marketing firms that promoted GMOs proved the power of advertising in a postindustrial world. Agro-chemical companies such as Monsanto and Novartis swallowed their competition, buying up small seed companies in the 1980s and 1990s. This strategy speaks to an overtly postindustrial objective. Recognizing the financial limits of industrial production associated with agro-chemicals, these companies knew they needed to go biological or get out. Monsanto's ability to transform itself into a "life science" company speaks to the marketing power associated with a postindustrial age. Pairing industrial-produced chemical inputs with genetically modified seeds is postindustrial genius. Requiring farmers to buy the chemical-seed packages was a coup par excellence for such companies. The privatizing logic embedded in seed patents is also integral to the postindustrial agricultural condition. Paysans' resistance to seed patents is essential to their struggle to oppose an increasingly spreading logic of privatization. Both the postindustrial paysan and the biotechnology firm oppose, yet are historically connected to, postindustrial entities. While the historical forces driving paysans and GMOs are clear, their respective objectives could not be more different. While the former attempts to establish a production rationality based on solidarity, the latter attempts to establish a new production rationality based on profits and monopoly.

Locating new social movements related to food in the postindustrial context proved fruitful. I was able to better comprehend the strategies and logics underlying these movements. In particular, I identified and analyzed the creative ways in which a hybrid and international set of actors (farmers, students, workers, and indigenous peoples) come together to contest an instrumental logic associated with both the industrial and postindustrial conditions.

Understanding social movements today requires periodizing them carefully. It is necessary to examine the international networks through which they emerge while tracing information flows that run through those networks. For instance, I followed the circuits through which information about the WTO and GMOs traveled. Doing so allowed me to grasp the ways that communication technologies and international antineoliberal forums helped foster sets of movements that were determined to challenge perceived negative aspects of the postindustrial condition. In particular, locating the Confédération Paysanne's struggle in a postindustrial condition allowed me to better appreciate the historically unprecedented hurdles the union must traverse in order to survive. Promoting smallholders in an era of industrial agriculture means crafting a new rationality for smallholders' collective existence. They are called upon to communicate a rationality that must be built from a different logic altogether. This logic might not increase the sale of the union's products among French consumers. Yet it weaves the union into an international alter-globalization social movement. This movement may prove capable of raising awareness among the French public, helping them to consciously choose to support a form of agriculture that enriches its historical rural zones. Unable (and often morally unwilling) to present their methods as more productive or cheaper than their industrial opponents, the Confédération Paysanne is compelled to popularize not just a different model of agriculture but a different world drawn from a solidaire logic. Mottos such as "The world is not merchandise" and "Another world is possible" speak to a humanitarian logic of solidarity that regards farming as more than a means to a profitable end. It redefines the agricultural enterprise as a way to farm while also recapturing the humanitarian dimensions of community life that diminish as lands and food are reduced to commodities.

Disentangling the French Contradiction

Understanding the postindustrial agricultural condition provides insight into what is called the "the French contradiction" (Meunier 2000). Since Bové and the Confédération Paysanne rose to prominence, there has been a wave of critical media pointing to the alleged hypocrisy of "the French people" in relation to questions of food and free trade. Both French and international media have highlighted the contradiction between a France that embraces postindustrial entities such as McDonald's and globalization while rejecting them at the same time. Since I embarked on this project, I have been confronted, sometimes aggressively, by those disturbed by this perceived contradiction. I have been challenged by disconcerted actors, both within and outside France. On two occasions, well-known anthropologists from the United States have confronted me harshly. Both times, these interactions took place during the question-and-answer period following a paper I presented at meetings held by the American Anthropological Association. "Give me a break," a high-profile scholar said before the audience. "The French love everything American. They just love to hate it too! If you don't see that, your research is ridiculous!" Many are genuinely confused by the popularity of an anti-McDo and antiglobalization sentiment in a country where the government is in favor of globalization and fast food and is supportive of the WTO. After all, the director of the powerful trade body is Pascal Lamé, a Frenchman. Sometimes, invoking a similar set of contradictions in one's own country brings clarity. The United States is the birthplace of fast food and is home to the largest number of McDonald's franchises. It is also the first country to launch the most developed anti-McDonald's movement. Across the United States, small-scale communities (and even urban neighborhoods) have led decade-long campaigns to keep McDonald's, and other franchises, out of their communities. Ironically, participants of these movements are often the same people who shop at big-box stores such as Home Depot or Walmart. When questioned about this contradiction, actors will often say, "What can I do? I can't afford to shop at the one local store that sells the same stuff for three times the price."

Anthropology is fortified with an inimitable ethnographic tool kit. Anthropologists conducting fieldwork are expected to examine the uneven and contradictory cultural terrains of any given society. They are also called upon to convey the heterogeneity among actors within specific cultures. It is the anthropologist's job to understand the cultural contradictions, for instance, that led U.S. citizens to elect George W. Bush to office, not once, but twice. It falls under the purview of the anthropologist to hold this knowledge while also understanding the impressive amounts of public ridicule and disgust directed at Bush. Just as not everyone in the United States wanted Bush for president during his years in office, not everyone in France was thrilled when Nicolas Sarkozy became president in 2007. Civil society is formed by overlapping and contradictory sets of actors. Each set is endowed with its own cluster of values and practices, however uneven these values and practices may be.

If ethnography is the study of culture, then it is also the study of cultural contradictions assumed a priori. It seeks to untangle the various cultural threads that create an otherwise intractable Gordian knot of bewildering cultural practices and beliefs. If living in the United States—host to the most robust anti-McDonald's movement—renders every citizen a hypocrite, then indeed the United States is the most hypocritical country of all. The media and political pundits often posit France and the United States in monolithic terms. After doing so, they blame the denizens of each country for being hypocritical when groups support or refuse aspects of their world, such as globalization. Perhaps it is the media, pundits, and critics who create popular frustration and confusion about the peoples and cultures associated with various countries. Being mindful of the role the media plays in portraying various publics in monolithic terms could help us to read the alleged hypocrisy as societal discord or ambivalence.

In my study of this social movement, I began with the working assumption that any movement is marked by degrees of disjuncture. I expected to see a mismatch between mainstream perspectives of civil society and marginal behaviors of social activists. The very existence of social movements suggests the heterogeneous and complex composition of civil society. Social movements are visible signs of a society internally at odds with itself. The presence of such conflict does not entail hypocrisy, but rather the meaning of societal dissidence and resistance to dominant social and political orders. Since 1999, there has been a panoply of media in and outside France addressing the French contradiction. A good example is an article written in 2000 by Sophie Meunier, research associate at the Center for International Studies and lecturer at the Woodrow Wilson School of Public and International Affairs at Princeton University. In "Just Say Non" Meunier writes: "Anti-Americanism and a stubborn Gaullist independence in foreign policy have often marked French political discourse. These traits are coming to the fore once again in France's wildly popular anti-globalization movement. Today, a complex mix of political, economic, and cultural reasons explains the French resistance to 'Anglo-Saxon global capitalism.' If sustained, France's stand could become a model for other countries seeking an alternative to the new, American-style world economy." Meunier expresses sympathy with the French cause, citing it as a potential model for other countries seeking alternatives to the "American-style world economy." She even admits that the cause of French resistance to global capitalism stems from a mix of political, economic, and cultural factors. Yet Meunier fails to differentiate between a heterogeneous set of actors who make up the French contradiction (e.g., French social movement actors, actors entirely uninvolved in food debates, and actors engaged in powerful institutions). Instead she presents a misleading monolithic depiction of France. If this represents a sympathetic response to the French contradiction, there are many more that feature a patently cynical sentiment. Several articles covering the French contradiction blame not only France but Bové himself for being disingenuous and fraudulent. In 2000, the *Times* of London ran an article that crystallized this France-as-hypocrite theme:

> Bové admits the contradiction, some might say hypocrisy, of a modern, high-tech France that worships his creed while rushing for convenience food and devouring Hollywood films. . . . As he launches his second book in a year, Bové has, of course, a few contradictions of his own. To the public, he is a humble *paysan* who spends time milking his beloved ewes on the Larzac plateau and struggling with local farmers against injustice. In reality, he has become a full-time *personnage médiatique* juggling TV appearances with near non-stop travel to citizens' summits from the Americas to East Asia. . . . With trademark pipe in hand, the moustachioed "Saint José" patiently explains that his peasants' revolt has nothing against the Americans or the British, even if hamburgers were his target and Gandhi his model for resistance against the oppressor. "Our struggle is not with the American 'Great Satan,'" says Bové. "It's with the multinationals. A lot of them happen to be American. I tell the Americans that what we did in dismantling the McDonald's restaurant was what they did in Boston when they threw the English tea into the sea." (April 1, 2000)

The *Times* of London establishes a contradiction between a high-tech and modern France and a hypocritical France that worships Bové's creed. In this statement, we see a reporter invoke a monolithic portrayal of a nation-state regarded as two-faced. Bové rejects U.S.-originated McDonald's burgers while claiming that "his revolt has nothing against the Americans and the British." Bové's attempt to explain the difference between anticorporate and anti-American activism evidently eluded the reporter. His reference to the Boston Tea Party, which he frequently invoked when accused of anti-

Americanism, was lost on the reporters as well. By bringing up the Boston Tea Party, Bové tried to emphasize the historical parallels between his own resistance against the WTO and resistance taken by U.S. Americans (albeit centuries ago) against the British colonial forces. Unable to depict the complex and hybrid nature of Bové's multiple roles and identities, the *Times* of London lampoons him as a book-writing, jet-setting TV persona. If a journalist is unfamiliar with the union's historical trajectory, he or she may be incapable of capturing the complexities associated with a famous international paysan activist. Bové was reduced to a two-dimensional humble sheep-loving paysan who fights solely for good food.

My hope is to shed light on the multiple layers that constitute identity and cultural reality. In my research, I found Bové neither saint nor Satan, neither merely a humble lover of sheep nor a cold and calculating political operator. In reality, he is as complex as the rest of us. While committed to the cause of French small-scale sheep farmers, he also fights for international causes. Just as he is anti-McDo, he is equally critical of all multinationals promoting a neoliberal agenda that he regards as harmful to peoples and natures throughout the world. His supporters and critics alike occupy the same complex and multiplicitous world. Bové is obliged each day to negotiate his way through a society that confronts each of us with contradictory and baffling sets of decisions. He is called upon to conduct himself as morally as possible in a post-industrial world dominated by an instrumental logic of profit making and private accumulation. And as many of us know, this is no easy task.

Anthropology invites us to take a closer look, exploring the uneven terrain of cultural opinion and behavior. It is no more paradoxical for a Bové to surface in a proglobalization France than it was for the Battle of Seattle to take place in the context of a proglobalization United States. Just as George W. Bush was president of the United States for eight consecutive years, the country was also home to an antiwar and an alter-globalization movement that was slowed by 9/11, but is still active and percolating—most recently, in the form of the Occupy Wall Street movements that began in New York City in September 2011. Ironies and complexity abound. While the United States is the sole nation among the G20 countries unwilling to sign the climate accords, its populace became one of the first industrialized countries in the Global North to elect a man of color as president.

While I have done my best to portray the actors I studied in a dignified and respectful way, I have also tried to convey the complexity of a postindustrial condition that leads many of them to make compromises that can be perceived as less than exemplary. Indeed, the various ways in which members of the Confédération Paysanne accommodate the system, reifying themselves as romantic wholesome petits paysans, could be regarded negatively through a calculating and cynical lens. Yet when viewed through a culturally compassionate lens of complexity, these actions are perhaps necessary moments of strategic essentialism (Morton and Spivak 2007, 126; Cheater 1999). As Gayatri Spivak once suggested (she has since revoked this assertion), marginalized identity-based groups are often called upon to emphasize group unity by invoking an essentialized and often contradictory self-understanding. Truly impressive is the creative ability of these French smallholders to take a centuries-old pejorative identity of paysans and transform it into a symbol for rural dignity, humanism, and antineoliberalism.

Toward an Anthropology of Instrumentalism

The anthropology of modernity has a vital role to play in studying cultural expressions of disenchantment associated with late capitalism. Increasingly, the actors whom anthropologists study perceive the world as being reduced to a series of objects to be bought and sold. The instrumental logic of the postindustrial era leads corporations to commodify entities previously outside the realms of capital investment. During recent decades, air has literally been for sale. Environmental agents have married their interests to those of corporations, rendering carbon emissions a tradable commodity. Water is a privatized resource, and the genetic codes embedded in seeds are available for patenting by public science bodies and multinational industries. As food production falls into the hands of megacorporations, a range of actors articulate disenchantment with agriculture systems. More and more, groups including consumers' organizations, ecology groups, farmers' unions, and indigenous associations perceive farming and its products as stripped of local meanings and practices. Anthropologists seeking to understand this cultural dissatisfaction must study the social movements in which actors speak to and resist this postindustrial condition.

As the French case demonstrates, civil society's resistance to perceived instrumental logics should not be trivialized. Such resistance is not a mere rejection of isolated cultural artifacts such as GMOs, McDonald's hamburgers, tradable carbon emissions, or privatized water. Actors' criticisms of specific issues are usually earnest. Yet their collective refusal pushes beyond concern with particular foods or trade practices. Actors are often rejecting the instrumental and profit-seeking logic that brought each problem into place. An anthropology of instrumentalism grasps the commodification of cultural and biological realms as a problem worthy of ethnographic study. It takes a humanistic look at controversies over food, science, technology, and globalization. Seeking a broader underlying logic that ties seemingly disparate issues together, anthropologists may identify keywords and discourses that express actors' holistic perceptions of the worlds in which they live.

Discourses such as la malbouffe spoke to a cultural dismay regarding homogenized food. Consequently, food sovereignty discourse constitutes a solidaire response to this disenchantment. Food sovereignty discourse is a creative way for actors to express demoralization associated with foods embedded in industrial and free-trade systems. By framing food in terms of community control over agriculture, actors add a social-justice and humanitarian sensibility to previously instrumental discussions about food. By calling for food sovereignty, actors such as Bové and those in the Confédération Paysanne and La Via Campesina open a discursive space where activists around the world can discuss food in terms of a right to a particular rural way of life. As solidaire discourses challenge criteria and practices associated with the WTO, social activists create alternative forums in which such discourses are deemed legitimate. The title of Bové and Dufour's first book says it all: *The World Is Not for Sale* (2001). In this best-selling book (and in subsequent publications by Bové), the authors do not simply compose a grocery list of random concerns. Instead they point to a logic applied to a society and nature that they find undignified. They reject a logic that regards the world and everything in it as potential commodities.

Studying social movements means that anthropologists must resist the trend to portray various publics as irrational if they rebuff, for instance, food-related technoscience innovation such as GMOs. As a study of cultural complexity, anthropology can enrich discussions of public engagements with technoscience. Anthropologists concerned with societal instrumentalism may enhance social-science forums dedicated to understanding popular behavior related to such issues as food, nature, and technoscience. These forums are often frequented by psychologists, legal agents, and bioethicists. Unfortunately, many social scientists are unaware of how an instrumental rationality informs the lives of the people they study. Anthropologists have the opportunity to amplify the concerns of actors who express displeasure with economic and political systems they perceive as dehumanizing. For instance, actors who refuse to eat GMOs but who smoke tobacco are often deemed irrational by social scientists. They are portrayed as curious subjects for those engaged in public-perception studies (Marris 2001). By determining that no individual could rationally oppose GMOs while smoking a pipe, public-perception agents deem anti-GMO smokers foolish and erratic. When social scientists view publics this way, their goal becomes to educate illogical publics about the relatively low risks associated with eating GMOs. Their objective is to help potential consumers of GMOs to get beyond their childish fears. In contrast, an anthropology of instrumentalism adopts a critical stance toward institutions that fund and shape the ways in which social scientists portray various publics. As a discipline, anthropology must become aware of the instrumentalizing discourses that migrate into social-science research practice. Social scientists and others interested in understanding the social movements surrounding technoscience would benefit from listening for signs of cultural disenchantment associated with a pervasive rationality of instrumentalism often surrounding new technoscientific artifacts.

As we've seen in the French case, there exists a visible line between the dots of GMOs, McDo, and the WTO. Actors allied with the Confédération Paysanne and Bové were not just concerned about food or free trade. They were also concerned with a logic of privatization and dehumanization embedded in practices such as seed patents and an agro-foods industry trolling the globe for cheap foodstuffs to process, distribute, and retail. Looking for an alternate world, alter-globalization activists have set their eyes on a prize: galaxies away from profit margins and so-called free-trade deals. As this story suggests, actors in these movements are often fighting for something they believe in: the challenge of making another world possible. Many depicted in this story seek to create a world that goes beyond one based on profit and the social and ecological destruction associated with capital-driven practice. Instead, they are trying to build a new world built out of a logic of social solidarity and hope for a more humane and ecological world.

Chapter One

1. By 1993 or 1994, the term *genetically modified organisms* became the predominant way to talk about micro-organisms, plants, animals, seeds, foods, and products produced by introducing new genes into the nucleus of an organism. The term GMO immediately became an acronym so popular that many people I encountered knew what GMOs are but had no idea what the acronym meant. Of note is the fact that beginning in the 1970s, scientists and industry agents originally used the terms *genetically engineered* and *genetically engineered organisms*. In the early 1990s, marketing strategists for biotechnology firms exchanged the less technical and more ambiguous-sounding term *modified* for *engineered*. Thus the GMO was born. Many activists throughout the world continue to reject the term *modified*, seeing it as an attempt by powerful institutions to use an innocuous term connoting "slight change" (modified) to mask the fact that they see the GMO as dramatically altered in potentially dangerous ways. Maintaining the acronym *GMO*, most activists still use the term *manipulated* instead of *modified* (genetically manipulated organisms). I use the generic popular term *GMOs* to refer to products and processes related to genetically modified products. I use the term *genetically modified* when referring to a specific product such as milk, seed, or corn.

2. GMOs often have sets of names that are integral to their individual and compel-

ling genealogy. In examining the "naming story" of recombinant Bovine Growth Hormone (also known as r-BGH), we see how agro-science naming practices often render visible conflicting sets of agricultural agendas, values, and commitments. Industry and government officials first named their product r-BGH to describe a genetically engineered hormone injected into cows to increase milk production. Produced solely by Monsanto, r-BGH was called by its trade name, Posilac.

However, industry officials soon decided to change the name of the product to recombinant Bovine Somatotropin (r-BST), exchanging the lesser-known term *somatotropin* for the word *hormone*. Although the terms *somatotropin* and *hormone* both refer to a particular growth hormone in cows, industry officials found that the term *hormone* raised concerns among consumers and ecology groups. Vermont dairy farmers and ecological activists rejected the term *r-BST* on the grounds that it deflected attention from the fact that the product is indeed a patented growth hormone (Tokar 1999), which, in addition to enhancing existing problems of overproduction, also causes a series of health problems for cows, leading to increased reliance on antibiotics and so on.

3. Activists tend to describe a de facto no-labeling policy because, to this day, no jurisdiction has mandated the labeling of genetically engineered foods in the United States. There is still an ongoing controversy over voluntary labeling (companies labeling their products "r-BGH-free" or "free of artificial hormones"). In 2008, several states, prodded by Monsanto, tried to prohibit "negative labeling," but were defeated. To this day, Monsanto has several lawsuits filed against companies in the United States that use labels that identify genetically modified milk, for instance, as "artificial-hormone free."

4. There are producer-led organizations in the United States and Canada that fight against GMOs. Yet these organizations have largely failed to capture national attention or appeal to sufficiently affect government policy. In the United States, producer-driven groups such as the National Family Farm Coalition have been able to provide a "farming face" for the movement. However, they have not been able to garner the kind of visibility or public support that French unions such as the Confédération Paysanne have.

5. Current regulations regarding certified organic foods require that they be free of genetically modified raw materials, irradiation, synthetic chemicals, hormones, and antibiotics. Certified organic foods may be classified as "100 percent organic," "certified organic," or "made with organic ingredients."

6. The term *alter-globalization* was coined in the late 1990s in response to the Zapatista motto, "Another world is possible." As the term for *globalization* in French is *mondialization* (translated loosely as "worldization"), French activists sought to retain the idea of *worldization*, which they saw as implying the possibility of a unified and balanced world. The prefix *alter-* suggests notions of alterity, alternatives, and change. Thus, rather than use the term *antimondialization*, French activists tend to use the term *altermondialization* to express the idea that an alternate world is pos-

sible. The English term *alter-globalization*, then, suggests a way of creating a unified world that is driven by a logic of solidarity rather than the capitalist market.

7. The term *Bt crops* refers to plants genetically engineered to contain a soil-dwelling bacterium, *Bacillus thuringiensis* (Bt), that is toxic to certain agricultural pests. Since the 1920s, Bt has been incorporated into pesticides and has been favored because it appears to present no negative effects on plant, wildlife, or beneficial insects. By 1996, biotechnology companies had genetically implanted Bt into the nucleus of corn, cotton, potatoes, and other plants. Of concern to anti-GMO activists is that, as yet, there has been no adequate study of the health impact on humans (or animals) eating Bt toxin embedded within each cell of a plant. Also of concern is the potential pest resistance that results when Bt toxin is used on an unprecedented scale within an intensive and extensive industrial model.

8. *Etic* and *emic* are anthropological terms that refer to the vocabularies of social scientists and the people and groups they study. While *emic* refers to words used by people *within* particular cultures, subcultures, or groups that are studied, *etic* refers to the terms used by outsider-experts attempting to analyze cultures of interest. My use of the terms *instrumental* or *solidarity based* are thus etic terms because they are not generally used by members of the groups with whom I engaged.

Chapter Five

1. During my fieldwork, there was much talk among French paysans, consumer groups, government bodies, private corporations, and scientific organizations regarding the source of revenues for both Écoropa and Greenpeace-France. Écoropa, for its part, was widely rumored to be financed by the right-wing brother of Britain's Teddy Goldstein (the editor of the *Ecologist*). Greenpeace-France was in turn rumored to be heavily financed by U.S. corporations conspiring to undermine France's own burgeoning biotechnology industry.

Chapter Ten

1. It is worth noting that Bové's spoken English is far from perfect. French and international media often invoked Bové's "perfect English" to discredit his identity as an unworldly French paysan. When I first met Bové in 1997, he informed me that he spoke "the English of a four-year-old," and unlike many French actors I met who were eager to practice their English with me, Bové was completely disinterested in doing so. When we traveled to the United States in 1999, Bové was encouraged by many in the French delegation to speak English. Seattle was the first time he pushed himself to speak to a wide audience in English. His English at that time was halting and often difficult to understand for U.S. audiences who nonetheless described his speaking style as "endearing and charming." In following Bové on YouTube over the years, I have noted that his English has only slightly improved. It remains strongly accented and awkwardly phrased, with a limited vocabulary. Gaining mas-

tery over the English language does not appear to be among Bové's key objectives. Nor do his English-speaking abilities render him very different from other Europeans conversant in English. Of interest here is the collective intention among some powerful actors to discredit the popular hero by pointing to his ability to speak English, usually only associated in France with elites.

2. The 1996 version of the Declaration can be found online: www.fao.org/docrep/003/w3613e/w3613e00.htm.
3. To read the Declaration of Nyéléni, go to www.nyeleni.org/spip.php?article290.
4. To find the article on the Forum on Food Sovereignty in Korea, go to the La Via Campesina website, viacampesina.org. Enter "Forum on Food Sovereignty in Korea." Reported by Federasi Serikat Petani Indonesia, Friday, August 17, 2007.
5. Dr. Rolf Grossklaus is the individual charged with managing the Codex's Committee on Nutrition and Foods for Special Dietary Uses. Interestingly, Grossklaus is also the head of the risk assessment company that provides science-based advice to the Codex on risk-related food issues. Many regard Grossklaus's role in the Codex as a conflict of interest.
6. France enacted an Association Loi de 1901 (Association Law of 1901) that grants nonprofit status to groups (containing at least two members) that claim a specific nonprofit objective. Often associations such as consumer or ecology associations can request meeting space in public buildings and political protection for freedom of speech. In 2006 there were over one million active associations in France. In a French political milieu dominated by multiple political parties and unions, the association has become a key French forum in which citizens gather to work toward common intellectual, aesthetic, leisure-related, or political goals. Few groups asking for association status are denied, because the criteria for association status are extremely broad and ambiguous. The fact that the government denied the Faucheurs Volontaires such status was both symbolic and political, constituting, according to many in the movement, an attempt to deny it even this most modest status of institutional recognition.
7. OMC is the acronym for Organization Mondiale de Commerce (the French translation for World Trade Organization).

WORKS CITED

Agence France Presse. "OGM: Vers la cause de sauvegarde, projet de loi renvoyé au printemps." January 8, 2002.

————. "José Bové en grève de la faim contre les OGM." January 2, 2008.

————. "OGM: Sarkozy promet de respecter l'Engagement du Grennelle." January 9, 2008.

Alvarez, Sonia E. 2000. "Translating the Global: Effects of Transnational Organizing on Local Feminist Discourses and Practices in Latin America." *Cadernos de Pesquisa* No. 22.

Alvarez, Sonia, and Leonard Horowitz. 2008. "Beyond the Civil Society Agenda? 'Civic Participation' and Practices of Governance, Governability and Governmentality." Paper presented at the Watson Institute for International Studies. Brown University. Wednesday, September 17.

Asad, Talal, James Fernandez, Michael Herzfeld, Andrew Lass, Susan Carol Rogers, Jane Schneider, and Katherine Verdery. 1997. "Provocations of a European Ethnography." *American Anthropologist* 99 (4): 713–30.

Atkins, Peter, and Ian Bowler. 2001. *Food in Society: Economy, Culture, Geography.* New York: Oxford University Press.

Aubenas, Florence, and Miguel Benassayag. 1999. *La fabrication de l'information: Les journalistes et l'idéologie de la communication.* Paris: La Découverte.

Aubineau, A. 1997. "De 1987 a 1997: Une autre politique agricole." *Campagnes Solidaires* (March): 13.

Barfield, Claude E. 2001. "Free Trade, Food Sovereignty, Democracy: The Future of the World Trade Organization." Heinonline. *Chicago Journal of International Law.*

Barlow, Maude. 2004. "On the Road." *Canadian Perspectives* (autumn):12.

Baron, H. 1997. "Racines: 1945–1960." *Campagnes Solidaires* (March): 5.

Basson, A. 1997. "Poule aux oeufs d'or n'existe pas." *Campagnes Solidaires* (March): 24.

Baudry, J. 1997. "Visite L'AGPB." *Campagnes Solidaires* (March): 25.

BBC News. 2003. "French Anger at Bove Commando Arrest." June 23.

Bhabha, Homi. 1994. *The Location of Culture.* New York: Routledge.

Blaikie, Piers, and Harold Brookfield, eds. 1987. *Land Degradation and Society.* New York: Methuen.

Blanc, M. 1977. *Les paysanneries françaises.* Paris: Delarge.

Bodiguel, Marivonne. 1975. *Les paysans face au progress.* Paris: Presses de la FNSP.

Boissevain, Jeremy. 1992. *Revitalizing European Rituals.* London: Routledge.

Bookchin, Murray. 1971. *Post-Scarcity Anarchism.* Edinburgh: AK Press.

Bové, José. 2001. "A Farmer's International?" *New Left Review* 12 (November–December): 89–101.

Bové, José, and François Dufour. 2001. *The World Is Not for Sale: Farmers against Junk Food.* London: Verso.

Brouillet, Carol. 2001. "Report on the First World Social Forum, Porto Alegre, Brazil 2001." www.communitycurrency.org/WSF.html.

Brouwer, Floor. 2004. *Sustaining Agriculture and the Rural Environment: Governance, Policy, and Multifunctionality.* Northampton, MA: Edward Elgar Publishing.

Bryant, Raymond L. 1998. "Power, Knowledge and Political Ecology in the Third World: A Review." *Progress in Physical Geography* 22 (1): 79–94.

Bryant, Raymond L., and Sinead Bailey. 1997. *Third World Political Ecology.* New York: Routledge.

Buttel, F. H. 2003. "The Global Politics of GEOs: The Achilles Heel of the Globalization Regime?" In *Engineering Trouble: Biotechnology and Its Discontents,* edited by R. S. Schurmann and D. D. T. Kelso. Berkeley: University of California Press.

Callon, Michel. 1986a. "The Sociology of an Actor-Network: The Case of the Electric Vehicle." In *Mapping the Dynamics of Science and Technology,* edited by Michel Callon, John Law, and Arie Rip, 19–34. London: Macmillan Press.

———. 1986b. "Some Elements of a Sociology of Translation: Domestication of the Scallops and Fisherman." In *The Science Studies Reader,* edited by Mario Biagioli, 67–84. New York: Routledge.

———. 1987. "Society in the Making: The Study of Technology as a Tool for Sociological Analysis." In *The Social Construction of Technological Systems,* edited by W. E. Bijker, T. P. Hughes, and T. P. Pinch, 85–103. Cambridge, MA: MIT Press.

———. 1997. "Actor-Network Theory: The Market Test." Presented at the Actor

Network and After Workshop, Centre for Social Theory and Technology, Keele University, UK. October 11.

Casa-Cortes, Maria Isabel, Michal Osterweil, and Dana E. Powell. 2008. "Blurring Boundaries: Recognizing Knowledge Practices in the Study of Social Movements." *Anthropological Quarterly* 81 (1): 17–42.

Chavagne, Yves. 1988. *Bernard Lambert: 30 ans de combat paysan.* Baye: Editions La Digitale.

Cheater, Angela. 1999. "Power in the Postmodern Age." In *The Anthropology of Power: Empowerment in Changing Structures,* edited by Angela Cheater. New York: Routledge.

Confédération Paysanne. 1997. "Technologies génétiques: Pour un moratoire sur la mise en culture et la commercialisation pour l'application du principe du précaution." Paris: La Confédération Paysanne.

———. 2008a. "OMC: Mieux vaut pas d'accord plutôt qu'une braderie." Press release, July 29.

———. 2008b. "OMC: Un échec porteur d'espoir." Press release, July 30.

———. 2010. "OGM: Malgré la moratoire: Le proce continue, le combat continue!" Press release, February 15.

Conway, Janet. 2004. *Identity, Place, Knowledge: Social Movements Contesting Globalization.* Halifax, Nova Scotia: Fernwood Publishing.

Copley, A. R. H. 1989. *Sexual Moralities in France, 1780–1980: New Ideas on the Family, Divorce, and Homosexuality.* New York: Routledge.

Dargie, James. 2001. "Biotechnology, GMOs, Ethics and Food Production." Presented at the Food and Agriculture Organization of the United Nations, Stockholm, June 29.

Débatisse, Michel. 1963. *La Révolution silencieuse, le combat des paysans.* Paris: Calmann-Lévy.

de Boisgrollier, N. 2005. "The European Disunion." *Survival* 47 (3): 261–80.

de Boisgrollier, Nicholas, and Philip H. Gordon. 2005. "Why the French Love Their Farmers." The Brookings Institute, November 15, http://www.brookings.edu/opinions/2005/1115france_gordon.aspx.

Debons, Claude, and Joel Le Coq. 1997. *Routiers, les raisons de la colère.* Paris: Les Editions de l'Atelier/Editions Ouvriers.

Debord, Guy. 1967. *The Society of the Spectacle.* Translated by Donald Nicholson-Smith. New York: Zone Books.

Deluchey, Guy. 1992. *Moi Tarzan.* Paris: Editions Seuil.

de Rosnay, Stella, and J. de Rosnay. 1981. *La malbouffe: Comment se nourrir pour mieux vivre.* Paris: Decouverte.

Desmarais, A. 2007. *La Vía Campesina: Globalization and the Power of Peasants.* Halifax, Nova Scotia: Fernwood Publishing.

Desmarais, Annette Aurelie, Nettie Wiebe, and Hannah Wittman, eds. 2010. *Food Sovereignty: Reconnecting Food, Nature and Community.* Halifax, Nova Scotia: Fernwood Publishing.

de Sousa Santos, Boaventura. 2003. "The World Social Forum: Toward a Counter-Hegemonic Globalisation (Part I)." Paper presented at the XXIV International Congress of the Latin American Studies Association, Dallas, March 27–29.

————. 2006. *The Rise of the Global Left: The World Social Forum and Beyond*. London: Zed Books.

————. 2007. *Another Knowledge Is Possible: Beyond Northern Epistemologies*. London: Verso.

Duby, G., and A. Wallon. 1977. *Histoire de la France rurale*. Paris: Le Seuil.

Ecologist. 2010. "EU's 'Dangerous' Move to Nationalise GM." July 14, 1.

Économie Rurale. 1988. "Un siècle d'histoire agricole française, 1880–1980." Vol. 184, 31.

Escobar, Arturo. 1992. "Culture, Practice and Politics: Anthropology and the Study of Social Movements." *Critique of Anthropology* 12 (4): 395–432.

————. 1996a. "Constructing Nature: Elements for a Post-structural Political Ecology." In *Liberation Ecologies: Environment, Development, Social Movements*, edited by Richard Peet and Michael Watts, 46–59. New York: Routledge.

————. 1996b. *Encountering Development: The Making and Unmaking of the Third World*. Princeton: Princeton University Press.

————. 1998. "Whose Knowledge, Whose Nature? Biodiversity, Conservation, and the Political Ecology of Social Movements." *Journal of Political Ecology* 5: 53–82.

————. 2002. "Worlds and Knowledges Otherwise: The Latin American Modernity/Coloniality Research Program." *Cuadernos de CELDA* 16: 31–57.

————. 2009. "Self-Organization, Complexity, and Post-Capitalist Cultures." In *World Social Forum: Challenging Empires*, edited by Jai Sen and Peter Waterman, 349–57. Montreal: Black Rose Books.

Escobar, Arturo, and Sonia E. Alvarez, eds. 1992. *The Making of Social Movements in Latin America: Identity, Strategy, and Democracy*. Boulder, CO: Westview Press.

Escobar, Arturo, Jai Sen, Anita Anand, and Peter Waterman. 2004. *The World Social Forum: Challenging Empires*. New Delhi: Viveka.

Ételin, M. 1998. "Les OGMs en question." *Rouge et Vert*. February.

Ewald, Francois. 1991. "Insurance and Risk." In *The Foucault Effect: Studies in Governmentality*, edited by Graham Burchell, Colin Gordon, and Peter Miller. Chicago: University of Chicago Press.

Fantasia, Rick. 2004. "Fast Food for a Classless Society." *Le Monde Diplomatique*, April 26: 6–7.

Featherstone, David. 2005. "Towards the Relational Construction of Militant Particularisms: Or Why the Geographies of Past Struggles Matter for Resistance to Neoliberal Globalisation." *Antipode* 37 (2): 250–71.

Foucault, Michael. 1976. *The History of Sexuality*. Vol. I. New York: Pantheon Books.

————. 1991. "Governmentality." In *The Foucault Effect: Studies in Governmentality*, edited by Graham Burchell, Colin Gordon, and Peter Miller, 87–104. Chicago: University of Chicago Press.

Ganis, Rich. 2002. "Is Industrial Scale Organic Farming Really Organic? USA: Organic Goes Industrial." Center for Informed Food Choices. November 15.

Gibson-Graham, J. K. 2006. *A Post-Capitalist Politics*. Minneapolis: University of Minnesota Press.

Giddens, Anthony. 1981. "A Contemporary Critique of Historical Materialism." *Power, Property and the State*. Vol. I. London: Macmillan.

Glipo, Arze. 2003. "An Analysis of WTO-AOA Review from the Perspectives of Rural Asian Women." Paper presented at the International Workshop in the Review of the WTO-AOA, Geneva, Switzerland, February 19–21.

Goddard, Victoria, R. Joseph, and Cris Shore. 1994. "Introduction: The Anthropology of Europe." In *The Anthropology of Europe: Identity and Boundaries in Conflict*, edited by Victoria Goddard, R. Joseph, and Cris Shore, 1–40. Oxford: Berg Publishers.

Goodman, David, and Michael Redclift. 1991. *Refashioning Nature: Food, Ecology, and Culture*. London: Routledge.

Goupillon, C. 1996. "Les risques de la dissemination des plantes transgéniques pour l'environnement." *Le Courrier de l'Environnement de l'INRA* 27: 29–34.

Graeber, David. 2002. "A Movement of Movements: The New Anarchists." *New Left Review* 13 (January–February): 61–73.

———. 2009. *Direct Action: An Ethnography*. Edinburgh: AK Press.

Gramsci, Antonio, and Quintin Hoare. 1971. *Selections from the Prison Notebooks of Antonio Gramsci*, edited by Geoffrey Nowell-Smith. New York: International Publishers.

Grantham, George W. 1980. "The Persistence of Open-Field Farming in Nineteenth-Century France." *Journal of Economic History* 40 (3): 515–31.

Gupta, Akhil. 1998. *Postcolonial Developments: Agriculture in the Making of Modern India*. Durham: Duke University Press.

Haeckel, Ernst. 1968. *The History of Creation*. Translated by E. Ray Lankester. 3rd ed., vol. 1. London: Kegan Paul, Trench & Co., 1883.

Hainsworth, Paul. 2006. "France Says No: The 29, May 2005 Referendum on the European Constitution." *Parliamentary Affairs* 66 (1): 98–117.

Haraway, Donna. 1991. *Simians, Cyborgs, and Women: The Reinvention of Nature*. New York: Routledge, 183–203.

Harvey, David. 1991. *The Conditions of Post-Modernity: An Enquiry into the Origins of Cultural Change*. Oxford: Blackwell Publishing.

Heller, Chaia. 1999. *Ecology of Everyday Life: Rethinking the Desire for Nature*. Montreal: Black Rose Books.

———. 2001a. "From Risk to Globalization: Discursive Shifts in the French Debate about GMOs." *Medical Anthropology Quarterly* 15 (1): 25–29.

———. 2001b. "McDonald's, MTV, and Monsanto: Resisting Biotechnology in the Age of Informational Capital." In *Redesigning Life: The Worldwide Challenge to Genetic Engineering*, edited by Brian Tokar, 405–20. London: Zed Books.

————. 2002. "From Scientific Risk to *Paysan* Savoir-Faire: Peasant Expertise in the French and Global Debate over GM Crops." *Science as Culture* 11 (1): 5–39.

————. 2004. "Risky Science and Savoir-Faire: Peasant Expertise in the French Debate over GM Crops." In *The Politics of Food*, edited by Marianne Elisabeth Lien and Brigitte Nerlich, 81–101. Oxford: Berg Publishers.

————. 2006. "Post-Industrial 'Quality Agricultural Discourse': Techniques of Governance and Resistance in the French Debate over GM Crops." *Social Anthropology* 14 (3): 319–34.

————. 2007. "Techné vs. Technoscience: Ambiguities of Food Quality in the French Debate over GM Crops." *American Anthropologist* 109 (4): 603–16.

Hermitte, Marie Angèle. 1995. *Le sang et le droit: Essai sur la transfution sanguine.* Paris: Éditions de Seuil.

Hervieu, B. 1993. *Des paysans qui ont osé : Histoire des mutations de l'agriculture dans une France en modernization; La révolution silencieuse des années cinquante.* Paris: La Fondation pour le Progress de l'Homme.

————. 1996a. *Au bonheur des campagnes (et des provinces).* Marseille: L'Aube.

————. 1996b. *Les agriculteurs.* Paris: Presse Universitaire de France.

Herzfeld, Michael. 1987. *Anthropology through the Looking Glass: Critical Ethnography at the Margins.* Cambridge: Cambridge University Press.

Hewison, Robert. 1987. *The Heritage Industry: Britain in a Climate of Decline.* London: Methuen.

Holt-Gimenez, Eric, and Loren Peabody. 2008. "Solving the Food Crisis: The Causes and the Solutions." *FoodFirst.org,* June 2.

Horkheimer, Mark. 1947. *Eclipse of Reason.* New York: Oxford University Press.

Inda, Johnathan Xavier, ed. 2005. *Anthropologies of Modernity: Foucault, Governmentality, and Life Politics.* Oxford: Blackwell Publishing.

Kaplan, W. 2004. "Biotechnology Patenting 101." Working Paper, Council for Responsible Genetics.

Kasaba, Resat, and Faruk Tabak. 1995. "Fatal Conjuncture: The Decline and Fall of the Modern Agrarian Order during the Bretton Woods Era." In *Food and Agrarian Orders in the World-Economy,* edited by Philip McMichael, 79–93. Westport, CT: Praeger.

Kumar, Krishna. 2004. "Resistance in Kerala." *Frontline* 21 (3), July.

Laclau, Ernesto, and Chantal Mouffe. 1985. *Hegemony and Socialist Strategy: Towards a Radical Democratic Politics.* London: Verso Books.

Latour, Bruno. 1983. "Give Me a Laboratory and I Will Raise the World." In *Science Observed: Perspectives on the Social Study of Science,* edited by Karin D. Knorr-Cetina and Michael Mulkay. London: Sage.

————. 1986. "The Powers of Association." In *Power, Action, and Belief: A New Sociology of Knowledge?,* edited by John Law, 264–80. London: Routledge and Kegan Paul.

————. 1987. *Science in Action: How to Follow Scientists and Engineers through Society.* Milton Keynes: Open University Press.

————. 1988a. *The Pasteurization of France*. Cambridge, MA: Harvard University Press.

————. 1988b. "The Prince for Machines as Well as for Machinations." In *Technology and Social Process*, edited by B. Elliott, 20–43. Edinburgh: Edinburgh University Press.

————. 1991. "Technology Is Society Made Durable." In *A Sociology of Monsters: Essays on Power, Technology and Domination*, edited by J. Law, 103–31. London: Routledge.

————. 1998. "On Actor-Network Theory: A Few Clarifications." Centre for Social Theory and Technology, Keele University, UK, January 11, http://www.nettime .org/Lists-Archives/nettime-1-9801/msg00019.html.

Launey, M. 1983. *Repertoire des archives centrals de la jeunesse ouvrière chrétienne*. Paris: Centre National de la Recherche Scientifique.

Law, John. 1987. "Technology and Heterogeneous Engineering: The Case of Portuguese Expansion." In *The Social Construction of Technological Systems: New Directions in the Sociology and History of Technology*, edited by W. E. Bijker, T. P. Hughes, and T. J. Pinch. Cambridge, MA: MIT Press.

Law, John, and John Hassard, eds. 1999. *Actor Network Theory and After*. Oxford: Blackwell and the Sociological Review.

Leff, Enrique. 1995. *Green Production: Toward Environmental Rationality*. New York: Guilford Press.

————. 1999. *Cultivating Dissent: Work, Identity, and Praxis in Rural Languedoc*. Albany: State University of New York Press.

Leontidou, Lila. 2004. "The Boundaries of Europe: Deconstructing Three Regional Narratives." *Identities: Global Studies in Power and Culture* 11 (4): 593–617.

Levidow, Les, and Susan Carr. 1997. "How Biotechnology Regulation Sets a Risk/ Ethics Boundary." *Agriculture and Human Values* 14: 29–43.

————. 2009. *GM Food on Trial: Testing European Democracy*. New York: Routledge.

Lichfield, T. 2000. "French Town to Become Seattle-Sur-Tarn as Protester's Trial Begins." *Independent*, June 26.

Lizet, B., and François Ravignant. 1987. *Comprendre un paysage: Guide practique de recherches*. Paris: INRA.

Marcus, George. 1995. "Ethnography In/Off the World System: The Emergence of Multi-Sited Ethnography." *Annual Review of Anthropology*, October 24: 95–117.

Marris, Claire. 2001. "Public Views on GMO's: Deconstructing the Myths." *EMBO Reports* 2 (7): 545–48.

Martin, Emily. 1994. *Flexible Bodies*. Boston: Beacon Press.

McCullough, Ellen B., Prabhu L. Pingali, and Kostas G. Stamoulis, eds. 2005. *The Transformation of Agri-Food Systems: Globalization, Supply Chains and Smallholder Farmers*. London: Stylus Publishing.

McMichael, Philip. 1994. *The Global Restructuring of the Agri-Foods System*. Ithaca, NY: Cornell University Press.

————. 1995. *Food and Agrarian Order in the World Economy*. Westport, CT: Green-
wood Publishing Group.

————. 2000. "Globalization: Trend or Project?" In *Global Political Economy: Contemporary Theories*, edited by Ronen Palan. London: Routledge, 149–71.

————. 2004. "Biotechnology and Food Security: Profiting on Insecurity?" In *Global
Tensions: Challenges and Opportunities in the World Economy*, edited by Lourdes
Beneria and Savitri Bisnath, 200–232. New York: Routledge.

Meadows, Donella, Dennis Meadows, Jorgen Randers, and William Behrens. 1972.
The Limits to Growth: A Report on the Predicament of Mankind. Rome: Club of
Rome.

Mendras, Henri. 1984. *La fin des paysans*. Arles: Actes Sud.

Menzel, Peter, and Faith D'Aluisio. 2006. *Hungry Planet*. Napa, CA: Material World
Books.

Meunier, Sophie. 2000. "Just Say Non." *Foreign Affairs*, July/August 14–21.

Morgan, Kevin, Terry Mardsen, and Jonathan Murdock. 2006. *Worlds of Food: Place,
Power, Provenance in the Food Chain*. Oxford: Oxford University Press.

Morris, Nigel. 2007. "Protester Bové Runs for President." *Independent* (London), February 2.

Morton, Stephen, and Gayatri Spivak. 2007. *Ethics, Subalterneity and the Critique of
Postcolonial Reason*. Malden, MA: Polity Publications.

Mosse, George. 1964. *The Crisis of German Ideology: Intellectual Origins of the Third
Reich*. New York: Grosset and Dunlap.

NACLA News. 2007. "Privatizing Waters and the Criminalization of Protest." July 24.

Nader, Laura. 1969. "Up the Anthropologist: Perspectives Gained from Studying Up."
In *Reinventing Anthropology*, edited by Dell Hyme, 284–311. New York: Pantheon.

Nash, J. 2005. *Social Movements*. Oxford: Blackwell Publishing.

Neesen, J. M. 1993. *Commoners: Common Right, Enclosure and Social Change in Eng-
land (1700–1820)*. Cambridge: Cambridge University Press.

Ong, Aihwa. 1987. *Spirits of Resistance and Capitalist Discipline: Factory Women in
Malaysia*. Albany: State University of New York Press.

Pandian, Jacob. 1985. *Anthropology and the Western Tradition: Toward an Authentic
Anthropology*. Chicago: Waveland Press.

Parodi, M. 1981. *L'économie et la société français depuis 1945*. Paris: A. Colin.

Paulson, Susan, and Lisan Gezon, eds. 2005. *Political Ecology across Spaces, Scales, and
Social Groups*. New Brunswick, NJ: Rutgers University Press.

Pearce, J. 2003. "France's Farm Crusade." *BBC News*, June 30.

Peet, Richard, and Michael Watts, eds. 1993. "Development Theory and Environment
in an Age of Market Triumph." *Economic Geography* 68 (3): 227–53.

————. 1996. *Liberation Ecologies: Environment, Development, and Social Movements*.
New York: Routledge, 1–45.

Perigord, M. 1996. *Le paysage en France*. Paris: Presse Universitaires de France.

Plant, Sadie. 1992. *The Most Radical Gesture: The Situationist International in a Postmodern Age*. London: Routledge.

Pochon, A. 1997. *Les champs du possible: Plaidoyer pour une agriculture durable*. Paris: La Découverte.

Polanyi, Karl. 1957. *The Great Transformation*. Boston: Beacon Press.

Polanyi, Karl, and Harry W. Pearson. 1977. *The Livelihood of Man: Studies in Social Discontinuity*. New York: Academic Press.

Pollan, Michael. 2006. *The Omnivore's Dilemma*. New York: Penguin.

Rabinow, Paul. 1996. *Making PCR: A Story of Biotechnology*. Chicago: University of Chicago Press.

Rapp, Rayna. 1999. *Testing Women, Testing the Fetus: The Social Impact of Amniocentesis in America*. New York: Routledge.

Robbins, Paul. 2004. *Political Ecology: A Critical Introduction*. Oxford: Blackwell Publishing.

Rocheleau, Dianne, Barbara Thomas Slayter, and Esther Wangari. 1996. "Gender and a Feminist Political Ecology Perspective." In *Feminist Political Ecology: Global Issues and Local Experience*, edited by Dianne Rocheleau, Barbara Thomas Slayter, and Esther Wangari, 27–33. New York: Routledge.

Rogers, Susan Carol. 1991. *Shaping Modern Times in Rural France*. Princeton: Princeton University Press.

———. 2001. "Anthropology in France." *Annual Review of Anthropology* 30: 481–504.

Sanoussi, Bilall, and Francesco Rampa. 2006. *Alternative to EPAs: Possible Scenarios for the Future ACP Trade Relations with the EU*. European Center for Development Policy Management. Policy Management Report No. 11. February 2006.

Sayer, Derek. 1991. *Capitalism and Modernity: An Excursus on Marx and Weber*. London: Routledge.

Schell, Orville. 1985. *Modern Meat: Antiobiotics, Hormones, and the Pharmaceutical Farm*. New York: Vintage.

Shinn, T. 1978. "State Bodies in the Industrial Sector: The Genesis of the Profession of Engineer, 1750–1920." *Revue Française de Sociologie* 19 (1): 39–71.

Shiva, Vandana. 1988. *Staying Alive: Women, Ecology, and Development*. London: Zed Books.

———. 1993. *Monocultures of the Mind: Perspectives on Biodiversity and Biotechnology*. London: Zed Books.

———. 2002. *Water Wars: Privatization, Pollution, and Profit*. Cambridge, MA: South End Press.

Singleton, Valerie, and Mike Michael. 1993. "Actor-Networks and Ambivalence: General Practitioners in the UK Cervical Screening Programme." *Social Studies of Science* 23 (2): 227–64.

Slaughter, Anne-Marie. 1997. "The Real New World Order." *Foreign Affairs* 76 (5) (September–October): 193–97.

Smith, J., Charles Chatfield, and Ron Pagunco, eds. 1997. *Transnational Social Movements and Global Politics: Solidarity beyond the State*. Syracuse, NY: Syracuse University Press.

Smith, Neil. 1996. "The Production of Nature." In *FutureNatural: Nature, Science, and*

Culture, edited by George Robertson, Melinda Mash, Lisa Tickner, Jon Bird, Barry Curtis, and Tim Putnam, 35–54. London: Routledge.

Spivak, Gayatri Chakravorty. 1996. "Can the Subaltern Speak?" In *The Spivak Reader: Selected Works of Gayatri Chakravorty Spivak*, edited by Donna Landry and Gerald MacLean, 211–31. New York: Routledge.

Star, Susan Leigh. 1991. "Power, Technologies and the Phenomenology of Conventions: On Being Allergic to Onions." In *A Sociology of Monsters: Essays on Power, Technology and Domination*, edited by John Law, 26–56. London: Routledge.

Staudenmaier, Peter. 1995. "Fascist Ideology: The 'Green Wing' of the Nazi Party and Its Historical Antecedents." In *Ecofascism: Lessons from the German Experience*, edited by Janet Biehl and Peter Staudenmaier, 5–32. San Francisco: AK Press.

Steinmetz, George. 1994. "Regulation Theory, Post-Marxism, and the New Social Movements." *Comparative Studies in Society and History* 36 (1): 176–212.

Stevens, Christopher. 2006. "The EU, Africa and Economic Partnership Agreements: Unintended Consequences of Policy Leverage." *Journal of Modern African Studies* 44: 441–58.

Strathern, Marilyn. 1980. "No Nature, No Culture: The Hagen Case." In *Nature, Culture and Gender*, edited by Carol MacCormack and Marilyn Strathern, 174–223. Cambridge: Cambridge University Press.

Tarrow. Sidney. 1998. *Power in Movement: Social Movements and Contentious Politics*. Cambridge: Cambridge University Press.

Thomas-Slayter, Barbara, and Dianne Rocheleau. 1995. *Gender, Environment, and Development in Kenya: A Grassroots Perspective*. Boulder, CO: Lynne Rienner Publishing.

Thoreau, Henry David. 2007. "Civil Disobedience." In *My Thoughts Are Murder to the State: Thoreau's Essays on Political Philosophy*, edited by David M. Gross, 42–79. New York: Create Space.

Tokar, Brian. 1999. *Earth for Sale: Reclaiming Ecology in the Age of Corporate Greenwash*. Boston: South End Press.

Touraine, Alain. 1971. *The Post-Industrial Society: Tomorrow's Social History; Classes, Conflicts and Culture in the Programmed Society*. New York: Random House.

———. 1988. *The Return of the Actor: Social Theory in Postindustrial Society*. Translated by Myrna Godzich. Minneapolis: University of Minnesota Press.

———. 2000. *Can We Live Together? Equality and Difference*. Translated by David Macey. Stanford: Stanford University Press.

Tsing, Anna L. 2005. *Friction: An Ethnography of Global Connection*. Princeton: Princeton University Press.

Van den Ban, A. W. 1999. "Agricultural Development: Opportunities and Threats for Farmers and Implications for Extension Organizations." *Journal of Agricultural Education and Extension* 6 (3): 145–56.

Vorley, Bill. 2004. "Supermarkets and Agri-Food Supply Chains in Europe: Partnership and Protest." In *Supermarkets and Agri-Food Supply Chains*, edited by D. Bruch and G. Lawrence. Queensland, Australia: Edward Elgar Publishing.

Walker, P. A. 2005. "Political Ecology: Where Is the Ecology?" *Progress in Human Geography* 29 (1): 73–82.

Wallach, Lori. 2009. "Statement of Lori Wallach, Director, Public Citizen's Global Trade Watch Division." Washington, DC: Public Citizen. July 19.

Wallerstein, Immanuel. 1984. *Historical Capitalism*. London: Verso.

———. 1991. *Geopolitics and Geoculture: Essays on the Changing World-System*. Cambridge: Cambridge University Press.

Weber, Eugene. 1976. *Peasants into Frenchmen: The Modernization of Rural France (1870–1914)*. Stanford: Stanford University Press.

Williams, Raymond. 1976. *Keywords: A Vocabulary of Culture and Society*. New York: Oxford University Press.

Wise, Timothy A. 2004. "The Paradox of Agricultural Subsidies: Measurement Issues, Agricultural Dumping, and Policy Reform." Global Development and Environment Institute, Working Paper No. 04–02.

Wolf, Eric. 1972. "Ownership and Political Ecology." *Anthropological Quarterly* 45 (3): 201–5.

———. 1982. *Europe and the People without History*. Berkeley: University of California Press.

Wynne, Brian. 1991. "Uncertainty and Environmental Learning: Reconceiving Science and Policy in the Preventative Paradigm." *Global Environmental Change* 2 (June): 111–12.

Yapa, Lakshman. 1996. "Improved Seeds and Constructed Scarcity." In *Liberation Ecologies: Environment, Development, and Social Movements*, edited by Richard Peet and Michael Watts, 69–85. New York: Routledge.

Index

CHAIA HELLER is visiting assistant professor of gender studies at Mount Holyoke College. She is the author of *Ecology of Everyday Life: Rethinking the Desire for Nature*.

Library of Congress Cataloging-in-Publication Data

Heller, Chaia.
Food, farms, and solidarity : French farmers challenge industrial agriculture and genetically modified crops / Chaia Heller.
p. cm. — (New ecologies for the twenty-first century)
Includes bibliographical references and index.
ISBN 978-0-8223-5118-4 (cloth : alk. paper)
ISBN 978-0-8223-5127-6 (pbk. : alk. paper)
1. Agriculture and state — France.
2. Farmers — Political activity — France — History — 20th century.
3. Genetically modified foods — Political aspects — France.
4. Sustainable agriculture — France.
5. Anti-globalization movement — France.
I. Title.
II. Series: New ecologies for the twenty-first century.
HD1947.H45 2013
338.1′844 — dc23
2012011642